MW00669335

THE CAMBRIDGE HANDBOOK OF CLASSICAL LIBERAL THOUGHT

Polls suggest up to 20 percent of Americans describe their beliefs as "libertarian," but libertarians are often derided as heartless Social Darwinists or naïve idealists. This illuminating handbook brings together scholars from a range of fields (from law to philosophy to politics to economics) and political perspectives (right, left, and center) to consider how classical liberal principles can help us understand and potentially address a variety of pressing social problems including immigration, climate change, the growth of the prison population, and a host of others. Anyone interested in political theory or practical law and politics will find this book an essential resource for understanding this major strand of American politics.

M. TODD HENDERSON is the Michael J. Marks Professor of Law and Mark Claster Mamolen Research Scholar at the University of Chicago Law School, where his research interests include corporations, securities regulation, and law and economics. Previously he served as clerk to the Honorable Dennis Jacobs of the US Court of Appeals for the Second Circuit, practiced appellate litigation at Kirkland & Ellis in Washington, DC, and was an engagement manager at McKinsey & Company in Boston.

The Cambridge Handbook of Classical Liberal Thought

Edited by

M. TODD HENDERSON

University of Chicago School of Law

CAMBRIDGE
UNIVERSITY PRESS

CAMBRIDGE
UNIVERSITY PRESS

University Printing House, Cambridge CB2 8BS, United Kingdom

One Liberty Plaza, 20th Floor, New York, NY 10006, USA

477 Williamstown Road, Port Melbourne, VIC 3207, Australia

314–321, 3rd Floor, Plot 3, Splendor Forum, Jasola District Centre, New Delhi – 110025, India

79 Anson Road, #06–04/06, Singapore 079906

Cambridge University Press is part of the University of Cambridge.

It furthers the University's mission by disseminating knowledge in the pursuit of
education, learning, and research at the highest international levels of excellence.

www.cambridge.org
Information on this title: www.cambridge.org/9781108416931
DOI: 10.1017/9781108242226

© Cambridge University Press 2018

This publication is in copyright. Subject to statutory exception
and to the provisions of relevant collective licensing agreements,
no reproduction of any part may take place without the written
permission of Cambridge University Press.

First published 2018

Printed in the United States of America by Sheridan Books, Inc.

A catalogue record for this publication is available from the British Library.

Library of Congress Cataloging-in-Publication Data
NAMES: Henderson, M. Todd, editor.
TITLE: The Cambridge handbook of classical liberal thought / edited by M. Todd Henderson.
DESCRIPTION: Cambridge, United Kingdom ; New York, NY : Cambridge University Press, 2018. |
Includes bibliographical references.
IDENTIFIERS: LCCN 2018010377 | ISBN 9781108416931 (hardback)
SUBJECTS: LCSH: Liberalism.
CLASSIFICATION: LCC JC574 .C355 2018 | DDC 320.51/2–dc23
LC record available at https://lccn.loc.gov/2018010377

ISBN 978-1-108-41693-1 Hardback

Cambridge University Press has no responsibility for the persistence or accuracy
of URLs for external or third-party internet websites referred to in this publication
and does not guarantee that any content on such websites is, or will remain,
accurate or appropriate.

For Richard Epstein – who else?

Contents

Contributors

Todd Henderson University of Chicago School of Law

Leonard E. Read Foundation for Economic Education

Lawrence W. Reed Foundation for Economic Education

Ralph Raico Buffalo State College

Jonathan H. Adler Case Western Reserve University School of Law

David E. Bernstein George Mason University School of Law

Jason Brennen Georgetown University

Art Carden Samford University

Richard A. Epstein New York University School of Law/University of Chicago Law School

Aziz Z. Huq University of Chicago Law School

Justin (Gus) Hurwitz Nebraska College of Law

Jacob T. Levy McGill University

Geoffrey A. Manne International Center for Law and Economics

Michael B. Rappaport University of San Diego School of Law

Mario J. Rizzo New York University

Louis Michael Seidman Georgetown University

Ilya Somin George Mason University

James Y. Stern William & Mary Law School

Fernando R. Téson Florida State University

Preface

This book arises out of a symposium on classical liberal thought at the University of Chicago Law School in 2015. The Law School aspires to two precepts in its pursuit of truth: the value of interdisciplinary inquiry and the importance of diverse voices being heard. Applying these, the Ordower Symposium (named after our distinguished alumnus and benefactor Mark Ordower) featured scholars of law, economics, and philosophy. In addition, the attendees were not all classical liberals – sympathetic voices, hostile voices, and agnostic voices were all heard during the two-day event. Those voices are represented in this volume. In the pages that follow, you will find the views of classical liberal stalwarts like Richard Epstein, progressives like Michael Seidman, and everything in between. The book also features a range of styles and modes of inquiry, from law to economics to philosophy. On behalf of the participants in the symposium and the contributors to this book, we hope you learn from this work as much as we did from engaging with each other about fundamental questions regarding the proper role and nature of government in our society.

Acknowledgments

Many minds worked together to produce this book. Although my name is on the cover, I am merely the choreographer. Here is a nonexhaustive list of those that made this book possible (for a sense of the vast number of people left off this list, see Chapter 6's description of the minds and labor that go into making a simple pencil):

- Mark and Jane Ordower provided the inspiration and the money to make the symposium from which these chapters are drawn happen.
- The staff at the University of Chicago Law School did their typical terrific work to pull the event off with style and professionalism.
- My colleagues at Chicago and elsewhere gave the symposium and this book its intellectual content.
- Three anonymous reviewers generously gave their time and imprimatur to the project.
- Matt Gallaway and his team at Cambridge University Press greenlighted the project and brought it to market.
- Finally, my wife, Tara, tolerated me staring at my computer endlessly and ranting to her about Hayek and von Mises and Friedman and Stigler and Director and Epstein and on and on for the past twenty-plus years. That, my friends, is the definition of unconditional love.

Introduction

Todd Henderson

The 2016 election featured two of the most unpopular major-party candidates in American history, leading many (or, at least, me) to believe that the Libertarian Party had a chance. In a hopeful story in the May 29, 2016, issue of the Washington Times, the author described the Libertarian ticket of two former governors – Gary Johnson (New Mexico) and William Weld (Massachusetts) – as "the strongest presidential ticket in [the Libertarian Party's] history," and claimed that the libertarians were "throwing down the gauntlet" to the two major parties. Johnson and Weld got about 3 percent of the popular vote and won no votes in the Electoral College. Faith Spotted Eagle, a member of the Yankton Sioux Nation, got more electoral votes.[1] Needless to say, the libertarian moment that many believed was at hand in 2016 passed uneventfully. Boy, was I wrong (and disappointed)!

To make matters worse, very little about America today seems consistent with the classical liberal ideal. No current member of the Supreme Court could fairly be described as a classical liberal, nor are many politicians. Moreover, political correctness and calls for government regulation of so-called hate speech are rampant on college campuses. The ever-growing power of the administrative state also belies the claim we live in classically liberal times.

Government and its role in our lives is also bigger than ever. President Trump's proposed 2018 budget requested spending of over $4 trillion. This is more than double the final budget President Clinton submitted in 2000. The federal government has doubled in size in under twenty years! This is obviously a bipartisan phenomenon. The role of government in our lives did not go down because of the Republican wave election of 1994, despite the explicit promise – in the Contract with America – that they would reduce it. Government has grown consistently larger

---

[1] Robert Satiacum Jr., a Clinton delegate from Washington, voted for Spotted Eagle as a "faithless elector."

over time, regardless of who is in charge. Those on the political Right in America are at serious risk of becoming Charlie Brown, running up to the football with hope despite repeatedly being duped by the Lucies we put in office.

Nevertheless, polls suggest about 10 to 20 percent of Americans describe their beliefs as "libertarian," and libertarian ideas have been ascendant in recent years. As of 2017, seven states and the District of Columbia legalized recreational use of marijuana, and nineteen other states permit medicinal use. This trend is consistent with the classical liberal view expressed by nineteenth-century English jurist Baron Bramwell in his broad philosophy of "live and let live." John Stuart Mill put this catch phrase in more philosophical terms, which he called the "harm principle." In his book, "On Liberty," Mill declared the harm principle as the basis for a just society:

> The object of this Essay is to assert one very simple principle, as entitled to govern absolutely the dealings of society with the individual in the way of compulsion and control, whether the means used be physical force in the form of legal penalties, or the moral coercion of public opinion. That principle is, that the sole end for which mankind are warranted, individually or collectively, in interfering with the liberty of action of any of their number, is self-protection. That the only purpose for which power can be rightfully exercised over any member of a civilized community, against his will, is to prevent harm to others. His own good, either physical or moral, is not a sufficient warrant. He cannot rightfully be compelled to do or forbear because it will be better for him to do so, because it will make him happier, because, in the opinion of others, to do so would be wise, or even right . . . The only part of the conduct of anyone, for which he is amenable to society, is that which concerns others. In the part which merely concerns himself, his independence is, of right, absolute. Over himself, over his own body and mind, the individual is sovereign.[2]

The private use of marijuana could be reasoned to cause others harm through a contorted causal chain, but there is increasing societal consensus that the primary person users may harm is themselves, and that does not justify mobilizing the violence of the state to coerce different choices.

There have been other victories. In *Joseph Abbey v. Castille*, a federal court considered a Louisiana rule requiring retailers of caskets to be licensed funeral directors. The Benedictine monks at St. Joseph Abbey challenged the constitutionality of the regulations on due process grounds – that is, that the due-process guarantee of the Constitution protects people from government action that is not justified on public (as opposed to private) interest grounds. In essence, the monks argued that the Louisiana Board of Embalmers and Funeral Directors promulgated the rules to serve the interests of funeral directors by insulating them from potential competition. The district court agreed, holding that it was "unconstitutional to

---

[2]   John Stuart Mill, On Liberty (1859).

require those persons who intend solely to manufacture and sell caskets be subject to the licensing requirements for funeral directors and funeral establishments."[3] The federal court of appeals for Texas, Louisiana, and Mississippi affirmed. While the Fifth Circuit shied away from espousing "a judicial vision of free enterprise,"[4] the willingness to put government regulation of economic affairs to scrutiny is a long-standing dream of classical liberal lawyers. In fact, the mission of the Institute for Justice, a libertarian public interest law firm, is to overturn the *Slaughterhouse Cases*, which held that the Due Process Clause did not restrict the regulatory authority of the states in this way.[5] If the *Castille* case portends a renewed judicial interest in flyspecking economic regulation, it will add a substantial classical liberal constraint on government, even in the absence of widespread political support in state houses or Congress.

Although for classical liberals this result is clearly second best, it is a reality that they will probably accept. It would be better, of course, if legislatures did not pass statutes impinging on human liberty in the absence of demonstrable social harms (that exceed social benefits). But empowering federal judges to intervene on occasion when they do, provides a check on extensions of unjustified government activity. After all, classical liberal thinkers are not opposed to government regulation per se, but rather more circumspect about the need for additional regulation. Aaron Director, a longtime professor at the University of Chicago said it best: "Laissez faire has never been more than a slogan in defense of the proposition that every extension of state activity should be examined under a presumption of error."

This view is broadly shared on the political right in America, especially in the sometimes fetishization about the structural design of our Republic. In his first dissent as an associate justice of the Supreme Court, Neil Gorsuch put it this way when urging a party to take their case to the legislature, instead of the courts:

> To be sure, the demands of bicameralism and presentment are real and the process can be protracted. But the difficulty of making new laws isn't some bug in the constitutional design; it's the point of the design, the better to preserve liberty.[6]

So, what is the future of classical-liberal thought in law and policy? What does classical liberal thought have to say about matters of pressing public concern, ranging from immigration policy to consumer welfare regulation to the growth of the prison system?

This book collects some voices on these issues in the hopes about advancing the conversation. Chapter 1 sets the stage with an historical overview by the great Ralph Raico, who died in 2016. This essay was influential in the formation of my own views of political philosophy, and it is reprinted here with permission of the Future of

---

[3] Joseph Abbey v. Castille, 835 F. Supp. 2d 149 (E.D. La. 2011), aff'd, 712 F.3d 215 (5th Cir. 2013).
[4] 712 F.3d 215 (5th Cir. 2013).
[5] 83 U.S. 36 (1873).
[6] Perry v. Merit Systems Protection Board, __ U.S. __ (2017), June 23, 2017.

Freedom Foundation. Although not a complete history, its ten-thousand-foot view articulates a compelling narrative of what made the west prosper over the past several centuries. It is unfortunately a history that is lost to most historians.

In Chapter 2, the philosopher Jason Brennan challenges the cartoon version of libertarians – that they only care about liberty, and thus are indifferent to actual human conditions of suffering. Brennan rehabilitates classical liberalism from a bad reputation it earned from the pens of Ayn Rand or Murray Rothbard, who's thick conceptions of liberty admitted a thin conception of human compassion. To make a positive case for classical liberalism, Brennan goes back to its roots, finding in Adam Smith and other early thinkers a commitment to what we call social justice. Brennan makes a welfarist case for liberty.

A central foundation of classical liberalism are well-defined property rights, premised on the right being held by the discoverer or first user. In Chapter 3, economist Art Carden defends this foundational principle against criticisms that delineating property from among communally owned things is selfish. Carden argues that it is not the first-comer who is "lucky" but the latecomer; the first in time does not *take* from the commons but *gives* to it by doing the difficult work of identifying potentially valuable property, manipulating it to become valuable, and then bringing it into the market to be exchanged. When the uncertain nature of materials and the impact of work is considered, rules that seem to be about selfishness turn out to be other regarding.

If the subject of Chapter 3 – who owns what? – is at one end of the spectrum of classical liberal ideas, law professor David Bernstein's topic in Chapter 4 – should libertarians favor antidiscrimination laws? – is at the other. Classical liberals, most prominently Richard Epstein (who we will hear from in Chapter 16), often oppose statutes, such as the Civil Rights Act of 1964, on the grounds that freedom of association is a more important social value, and that left to its own devices competitive markets will reduce discrimination to tolerable levels. The willingness to stand up for this First Amendment right has caused some critics to label libertarians as racists. Bernstein confronts this charge head on in Chapter 4. He points out the asymmetry of this argument, noting that when liberals defend the right of Nazi's to march, it does not turn them into Nazis. Principles by their nature admit uncomfortable cases. Bernstein goes on to situate the debate about speech and association in the modern context, offering insightful commentary on cases involving the tension between the constitutional rights of individuals doing business and the interests of individuals to be free from harmful discrimination. Whether you are persuaded by Bernstein's argument, at the very least this chapter should take the sting out of the cry that classical liberals are uncaring racists.

Another area in which classical liberals might appear to be vulnerable to substantive attacks is in the field of environmental policy. Pollution is the classic example of an externality that seems to compel government action as a means of addressing persistent collective action problems. In Chapter 5, law professor Jonathan Adler argues that well-defined property rights can be an effective mechanism for addressing a range of environmental issues, using examples ranging from pollution to fisheries. Although there are challenges to defining property rights in some areas, such as ocean-based fisheries, Adler demonstrates with convincing case studies that it is possible to utilize classical-liberal approaches to address environmental concerns. One of these tough cases that Adler identifies is the topic of global warming, since the earth's atmosphere represents the biggest commons we can imagine. Yet, Adler argues that libertarian principles and approaches may even be valuable here, issuing in effect a call to arms to classical-liberal scholars to take more seriously environmental issues and the potential welfare gains from attacking them using tools of classical-liberal thinking.

Chapter 6 is a reprint of Leonard Read's iconic biography of a Mongol 482 pencil assembled, fabricated, and finished by Eberhard Faber Pencil Company. It sounds silly at first, but none other than Milton Friedman called Read's essay the best illustration of Adam Smith's invisible hand and of F. A. Hayek's concept of dispersed, local knowledge. Whenever classical liberals hear claims from politicians or law professors about how a complex process or industry could be managed better by a centralized group of so-called experts, a common retort is: "No one knows how to make a pencil!" This comment doesn't make a great deal of sense until one reads and appreciates Read's essay. If something as simple as a pencil is beyond the ken of any individual or even group of highly talented and motivated individuals, the argument goes, how could anyone possibly try to plan the multi-trillion-dollar US health care system. An old (and probably apocryphal) story tells of a Soviet visitor to London who, amazed by the abundance in British supermarkets, asks to meet the person responsible for getting bread into the city. A cheeky response would have been to hand the Russian a copy of "I, Pencil."

Law professor Ilya Somin presents a summary of his forthcoming book on what he calls "foot voting" in Chapter 7. He claims that voting with your feet, whether among political jurisdictions (either within a country or across countries) or among competing firms in commerce is better at achieving political freedom than voting at the ballot box. Somin argues that exit is superior to voice (to use the terminology of Albert Hirschmann) in politics. This result obtains, he claims, across various theories of political freedom, ranging from consent to positive liberty to nondomination accounts. There are a range of historically grounded objections to relying on exit as a means of political accountability, including our experience with invidious exclusion of certain groups and the possibilities of poverty traps limiting exit. Somin does not shy away from these objections, and in doing so demonstrates that libertarian theories are not mere pie-in-the-sky fantasies of Ayn Rand, but can lead to institutional reforms that can help expand political opportunities, while mitigating potentially downsides.

In the next chapter, we move from high theory to the practical details of government administration. In Chapter 8, law professor Michael Rappaport takes

us on a grand tour of administrative law, as currently practiced by powerful administrative agencies foreign to the classical liberal tradition. While some classical
liberals, such as Richard Epstein, and conservatives, such as Philip Hamburger,
advocate getting rid of the administrative state lock, stock, and barrel, Rappaport
takes a much more practical and lawyerly approach to trying to advance the mission
of a more classically liberal state. The key ingredient in Rappaport's approach is the
doctrine of separation of powers, which, he argues, advances classical liberalism in
several ways: it limits government power, it furthers the rule of law, it increases
accountability, and it reduces the pathologies of administrative law, such as capture
or political meddling with expertise. While Rappaport admits sympathy to those in
the classical liberal tradition who would prefer a world of small government to one
with big government, the chapter takes a realistic approach, noting contingent on
having a big government (which may be unavoidable, at least in the short run),
the classical liberal should strictly prefer one with strong separation of powers to
one with weak separation of powers. Rappaport makes his case in a comprehensive
treatment of administrative law, covering the key cases, doctrines, and details of
administration in a way that is refreshingly pragmatic and in touch with the
important of foundational tenets of classical liberalism.

Political theorist Jacob Levy's contribution – in Chapter 9 – is a bucket of cold
water dumped over the head of the classical liberal thinker. Levy, who considers
himself a classical liberal, rejects the core principle of that particular faith stretching
back to Locke and Jefferson and beyond. For them, as for most of us today, classical
liberalism is antipolitical or perhaps prepolitical. Locke's harm principle and
Jefferson's social contract set forth in the Declaration of Independence assert that
the purpose of the state is to protect rights. Levy calls this limited conception of
classical liberalism "absurd" and "an end-run around politics" that he believes has
made classical liberal ideas less relevant to actual governing than ideal. Looking out
at the state of modern politics, Levy sees strands of illiberalism in society (for
example, populism, nationalism) that need to be confronted, and it is insufficient,
he argues persuasively, to retreat to the enumerated powers of the Constitution. Levy
demands classical liberals reengage with ordinary politics instead of retreating to
towers of formulaic principles.

Although, given its emphasis on a minimal state, classical liberalism is often
thought of as a species of right-wing politics in the United States, there are numerous places where libertarian policy preferences are more aligned with the left wing
of American politics. Classical liberals have historically been abolitionists, feminists,
sympathetic to gay rights, against the "war on drugs," and skeptical about mass
incarceration, especially the racial composition of prisons. These commitments are
evident throughout this book. In Chapter 10, law professor Fernando Tesón provides
another example of how far libertarians diverge from current Republican politics,
making the classical liberal case for a much more open immigration policy. Tesón
rejects claims by those hostile to immigration, grounded in national security, hoary

notions of sovereignty, or cultural nativism, as well as those supportive of immigration, grounded in the value of diversity. Instead, Tesón bases his argument on solidly bourgeois notions of economic opportunity and equal dignity. For a classical liberal like Tesón, perhaps no policy is a clearer way to increase social welfare than a liberalization of our immigration policy.

Economist Mario Rizzo provides an assessment of recent criticisms of neoclassical economics in Chapter 11. The biggest development in economics over the past few decades has been the surge in "behavioral" economics. While all economics is about behavior of humans, the Nobel-winning work of Daniel Kahneman, Richard Thaler, and others has suggested that prevailing economic models are incomplete insofar as they purport to describe people as "rational" human actors. Since much classical liberal theory and politics is premised on economic models of competitive markets, behavioralism can be thought of as an attack on classical liberals. In fact, it is probably not a coincidence that the rise of behavioralism came after a period of several decades in which neoclassical economic models completely reshaped American law, often in a more classically liberal direction. Mario Rizzo argues that the differences between these competing approaches is insufficiently clear. In a return to first principles, Rizzo attempts to reframe our understanding of economic models by considering in detail what we mean when we say "rational" and "irrational." The classical liberal, progressive, and everyone in between will be challenged to rethink their assumptions about economics.

The foundational precept of classical liberalism is private property. (Bodily autonomy is as well, but few deny its importance today.) In Chapter 12, law professor James Stern defends private property against critics, like Thomas Grey, who argue that it is a construct that merely reflects the regulatory choice of the state. Stern grounds his defense against the property relativists in a consideration of the current law of intellectual property, specifically, copyright and patent law. Stern argues that we do not merely call intellectual property "property," out of convenience or otherwise, but rather that intellectual property's structures and doctrines are consistent with and shaped by the fundamental features of property, writ large. Moreover, Stern points out, that an attempt to describe intellectual property as merely a means of achieving public ends fails to account for the law and policy in the field.

The term "classical liberal" and "libertarian" are often used synonymously, and, in fact, they are often used that way throughout this book. But in Chapter 13, law professor Gus Hurwitz and law and economics scholar Geoffrey Manne tease out an important distinction – views about technological change may create a tension between these two strands of thought. Libertarians generally embrace technology, especially modern information technology, as a means of empowering individuals. This can be seen in the fantastical claims about the potential of the Internet to create superempowered individuals free from government constraint. Of course, governments can also use technology, making this position somewhat naïve. But the schism with classical liberals is along another dimension. Starting from Locke, the classical liberal ideal depends on a strong state capable of enforcing property rights and maintaining a peaceful civil society governed by the rule of law. This includes not just ISIS and China, but muggers on the streets of Chicago and fraudsters peddling get-rich-quick schemes and bogus remedies. Hurwitz and Manne explore the proper role of the state and the ways in which technology may upset the historical alliance between classical liberals and libertarians in this thought-provoking chapter.

As the faculty sponsor of the student chapter of the Federalist Society at the University of Chicago Law School, one of my jobs is to deliver the annual "Introduction to the Federalist Society" remarks during the first week of a new school year. (That I inherited this job from Richard Epstein when he decamped to NYU for the Fall each year, is one of the great honors of my professional life.) In these remarks each year, I make a point of arguing for the cross-party nature of classical liberal ideals. To do this, I frequently cite statistics about incarceration rates in the United States, especially the racial nature of them. In Chapter 14, my progressive colleague at Chicago, Aziz Huq, elaborates on this point, urging classical liberal scholars to do more work on the issue of incarceration. After all, if the goal of a political philosophy is to actually impact policy choices, then coalitions must be built, and this in turn depends on goodwill being earned. Common ground can be found among Left and this strand of the Right in America, but it will require classical liberal thinkers to be more forceful in their rejection of the pro-prison agenda that earns Republicans electoral victories. Huq gives several persuasive arguments for why classical liberal thinkers should be against the carceral state, and why this bargain might be the right one to strike.

The final two chapters present a debate of sorts between law professors Michael Seidman and Richard Epstein. The written chapters are a summary and extension of a passionate debate witnessed by participants at the end of the conference. Seidman, a highly regarded man of the Left, had been a playful interlocutor during the event, but when he rose as the penultimate speaker, he set forth his normative views on the content of classical liberalism, as he understands it. Chapter 15 is an enumeration of seven "problems" that Seidman believes are fatal to classical liberalism as a political philosophy, let alone a recipe for guiding American policy making. In classical Seidman style, the points are sharp. In the final chapter, Epstein, the most prolific and articulate defender of classical liberalism in the legal academy today, if not anywhere, responds in kind. Epstein takes Seidman's arguments seriously, offering a robust defense of classical liberalism to each objection, using legal arguments, philosophy, and empirical judgments based on real-world policy. These two chapters taken together paint a fairly complete picture of the two rival political ideals that are competing for the attention and blessing of the American electorate and of policy makers in Washington and across America.

1

The Rise, Fall, and Renaissance of Classical Liberalism

Ralph Raico

Editor's note:

In 1992, Ralph Raico, a professor of history at Buffalo State College and former student of F. A. Hayek, penned a brief history of classical liberalism, or, as he called it, liberalism. The piece appeared in three parts and was dedicated to the memory of Roy A. Childs Jr. I read the essay for the first time when I was a senior in college studying civil engineering. I was a rather unformed conservative at the time, and my head was full of differential equations and facts about soil and seismic loads. My free time was occupied by the javelin and preparing to join the Army. I did not have time for or much interest in ruminations on the proper nature of the state. But a friend studying at the Woodrow Wilson School at Princeton recommended Raico's essay to me as a quick and heady read that would "show you a series of doors that you will not regret opening." I took the advice to read it, and over the past several decades have opened doors with labels like "Hayek" and "Mises" and "Hazlitt" and "Bastiat" as a result.

I found the essay again several years later, printed it out (on a dot-matrix printer in my apartment in Hemet, California), and stuck it under my geological core sample forms on my clipboard. During a break from the excavation of a dam, I sat in my Ford F-150 pickup, the one with the Metropolitan Water District of Southern California seal on the door, drank coffee out of a thermos just like the rest of the guys (it was all guys), and flipped back to the essay, now all covered in dust. I read it again because I was thinking of applying to law school, and I remembered its appeal as an appetizer of great ideas across a vast sweep of history. Of particular interest at the time was a single sentence toward the end: "At the University of Chicago, Milton Friedman, George Stigler, and Aaron Director led a group of classical-liberal economists whose specialty was exposing the defects of government action." I had never heard of the University of Chicago, but made a mental note to look it up. I found it referenced in the "Insiders' Guide to Law Schools" as one of the top law schools in the United States, and decided there and then that it was the place for me.

At Chicago, I studied with Richard Epstein, Frank Easterbrook, Dan Fischel, Dick Posner, Bill Landes, Merton Miller, Gary Becker, and countless other giants of the Chicago School. The impact on me was profound. When I left Princeton after four years, I knew more about tensile strength of various solids and had memorized Bernoulli's equation, but I was fundamentally the same person as when I entered. Three years at Chicago made me anew. I became a classical liberal, or, to use Professor Raico's term, liberal.

I have the great fortune to be a faculty member at Chicago, and get to play a small part in carrying on the tradition of classical liberalism here. To this end, and with the generous donation of Mark and Jane Ordower, I hosted a conference, "The Future of Classical Liberalism," at Chicago in 2015. The papers reprinted in this volume came out of the conference. In putting this volume together, I was reminded of Professor Raico's essay, and took the time to reread it. It was then I learned of his passing in December 2016. The Future of Freedom Foundation, which published the essay, granted permission to reprint it here. The essay provides a concise introduction to an intellectual tradition that is increasingly under siege in America and across the world. My hope for this book is that it will be a reminder of this tradition and a call to action for scholars interested in understanding it and pushing it forward.

I am indebted to Professor Raico for putting me on a path that has defined my working life. I never met him, so I did not have a chance to tell him in person about the influence he had on me with this essay and his other work. This tribute is my attempt to remedy that fault.

PART 1

Classical liberalism – or simply liberalism, as it was called until around the turn of the century – is the signature political philosophy of Western civilization. Hints and suggestions of the liberal idea can be found in other great cultures. But it was the distinctive society produced in Europe – and in the outposts of Europe, above all, America – that served as the seedbed of liberalism. In turn, that society was decisively shaped by the liberal movement.

Decentralization and the division of power have been the hallmarks of the history of Europe. After the fall of Rome, no empire was ever able to dominate the continent. Instead, Europe became a complex mosaic of competing nations, principalities, and city-states. The various rulers found themselves in competition with each other. If one of them indulged in predatory taxation or arbitrary confiscations of property, he might well lose his most productive citizens, who could "exit," together with their capital. The kings also found powerful rivals in ambitious barons and in religious authorities who were backed by an international Church. Parliaments emerged that limited the taxing power of the king, and free cities arose with special charters that put the merchant elite in charge.

By the Middle Ages, many parts of Europe, especially in the West, had developed a culture friendly to property rights and trade. On the philosophical level, the doctrine of natural law – deriving from the Stoic philosophers of Greece and Rome – taught that the natural order was independent of human design and that rulers were subordinate to the eternal laws of justice. Natural-law doctrine was upheld by the Church and promulgated in the great universities, from Oxford and Salamanca to Prague and Krakow.

As the modern age began, rulers started to shake free of age-old customary constraints on their power. Royal absolutism became the main tendency of the time. The kings of Europe raised a novel claim: they declared that they were appointed by God to be the fountainhead of all life and activity in society. Accordingly, they sought to direct religion, culture, politics, and, especially, the economic life of the people. To support their burgeoning bureaucracies and constant wars, the rulers required ever-increasing quantities of taxes, which they tried to squeeze out of their subjects in ways that were contrary to precedent and custom.

The first people to revolt against this system were the Dutch. After a struggle that lasted for decades, they won their independence from Spain and proceeded to set up a unique polity. The United Provinces, as the radically decentralized state was called, had no king and little power at the federal level. Making money was the passion of these busy manufacturers and traders: they had no time for hunting heretics or suppressing new ideas. Thus, de facto religious toleration and a wide-ranging freedom of the press came to prevail. Devoted to industry and trade, the Dutch established a legal system based solidly on the rule of law and the sanctity of property and contract. Taxes were low, and everyone worked. The Dutch "economic miracle" was the wonder of the age. Thoughtful observers throughout Europe noted the Dutch success with great interest.

A society in many ways similar to Holland had developed across the North Sea. In the seventeenth century, England, too, was threatened by royal absolutism, in the form of the House of Stuart. The response was revolution, civil war, the beheading of one king and the booting out of another. In the course of this tumultuous century, the first movements and thinkers appeared who can be unequivocally identified as liberal.

With the king gone, a group of middle-class radicals emerged called the Levellers. They protested that not even Parliament had any authority to usurp the natural, God-given rights of the people. Religion, they declared, was a matter of individual conscience: it should have no connection with the state. State-granted monopolies were likewise an infringement of natural liberty. A generation later, John Locke, drawing on the tradition of natural law that had been kept alive and elaborated by the Scholastic theologians, set forth a powerful liberal model of man, society, and state. Every man, he held, is innately endowed with certain natural rights. These consist in his fundamental right to what is his property – that is, his life, liberty, and "estates" (or material goods). Government is formed simply the better to preserve the right to property. When, instead of protecting the natural rights of the people, a government makes war upon them, the people may alter or abolish it. The Lockean philosophy continued to exert influence in England for generations to come. In time, its greatest impact would be in the English-speaking colonies in North America.

The society that emerged in England after the victory over absolutism began to score astonishing successes in economic and cultural life. Thinkers from the continent, especially in France, grew interested. Some, like Voltaire and Montesquieu, came to see for themselves. Just as Holland had acted as a model before, now the example of England began to influence foreign philosophers and statesmen. The decentralization that has always marked Europe allowed the English "experiment" to take place and its success to act as a spur to other nations.

In the eighteenth century, thinkers were discovering a momentous fact about social life: given a situation where men enjoyed their natural rights, society more or less runs itself. In Scotland, a succession of brilliant writers that included David Hume and Adam Smith outlined the theory of the spontaneous evolution of social institutions. They demonstrated how immensely complex and vitally useful institutions – language, morality, the common law, above all, the market – originate and develop not as the product of the designing minds of social engineers, but as the result of the interactions of all the members of society pursuing their individual goals.

In France, economists were coming to similar conclusions. The greatest of them, Turgot, set forth the rationale for the free market:

> The policy to pursue, therefore, is to follow the course of nature, without pretending to direct it For, in order to direct trade and commerce it would be necessary to be able to have knowledge of all of the variations of needs, interests, and human industry in such detail as is physically impossible to obtain even by the most able, active, and circumstantial government. And even if a government did possess such a multitude of detailed knowledge, the result would be to let things go precisely as they do of themselves, by the sole action of the interests of men prompted by free competition.

The French economists coined a term for the policy of freedom in economic life: they called it laissez-faire. Meanwhile, starting in the early seventeenth century, colonists coming mainly from England had established a new society on the eastern shores of North America. Under the influence of the ideas the colonists brought with them and the institutions they developed, a unique way of life came into being. There was no aristocracy and very little government of any kind. Instead of aspiring to political power, the colonists worked to carve out a decent existence for themselves and their families.

Fiercely independent, they were equally committed to the peaceful – and profitable – exchange of goods. A complex network of trade sprang up, and by the mid-eighteenth century, the colonists were already more affluent than any other commoners in the world. Self-help was the guiding star in the realm of spiritual values as well. Churches, colleges, lending-libraries, newspapers, lecture-institutes, and cultural societies flourished through the voluntary cooperation of the citizens.

When events led to a war for independence, the prevailing view of society was that it basically ran itself. As Tom Paine declared:

> Formal government makes but a small part of civilized life. It is to the great and fundamental principles of society and civilization – to the unceasing circulation of interest, which passing through its million channels, invigorates the whole mass of civilized man – it is to these, infinitely more than to anything which even the best instituted government can perform that the safety and prosperity of the individual and the whole depend. In fine, society performs for itself almost everything which is ascribed to government. Government is no further necessary than to supply the few cases to which society and civilization are not conveniently competent.

In time, the new society formed on the philosophy of natural rights would serve as an even more luminous exemplar of liberalism to the world than had Holland and England before it.

PART 2: TRIUMPHS AND CHALLENGES

As the nineteenth century began, classical liberalism – or just liberalism as the philosophy of freedom was then known – was the specter haunting Europe – and the world. In every advanced country the liberal movement was active.

Drawn mainly from the middle classes, it included people from widely contrasting religious and philosophical backgrounds. Christians, Jews, deists, agnostics, utilitarians, believers in natural rights, freethinkers, and traditionalists all found it possible to work toward one fundamental goal: expanding the area of the free functioning of society and diminishing the area of coercion and the state.

Emphases varied with the circumstances of different countries. Sometimes, as in Central and Eastern Europe, the liberals demanded the rollback of the absolutist state and even the residues of feudalism. Accordingly, the struggle centered around full private property rights in land, religious liberty, and the abolition of serfdom. In Western Europe, the liberals often had to fight for free trade, full freedom of the press, and the rule of law as sovereign over state functionaries.

In America, the liberal country par excellence, the chief aim was to fend off incursions of government power pushed by Alexander Hamilton and his centralizing successors, and, eventually, somehow, to deal with the great stain on American freedom – Negro slavery.

From the standpoint of liberalism, the United States was remarkably lucky from the start. Its founding document, the Declaration of Independence, was composed by Thomas Jefferson, one of the leading liberal thinkers of his time. The Declaration radiated the vision of society as consisting of individuals enjoying their natural rights and pursuing their self-determined goals. In the Constitution and the Bill of Rights, the Founders created a system where power would be divided, limited, and hemmed in by multiple constraints, while individuals went about the quest for fulfillment through work, family, friends, self-cultivation, and the dense network of voluntary associations. In this new land, government – as European travelers noted with awe – could hardly be said to exist at all. This was the America that became a model to the world.

One perpetuator of the Jeffersonian tradition in the early nineteenth century was William Leggett, a New York journalist and antislavery Jacksonian Democrat. Leggett declared:

> All governments are instituted for the protection of person and property; and the people only delegate to their rulers such powers as are indispensable to these objects. The people want no government to regulate their private concerns, or to prescribe the course and mete out the profits of their industry. Protect their persons and property, and all the rest they can do for themselves.

This laissez-faire philosophy became the bedrock creed of countless Americans of all classes. In the generations to come, it found an echo in the work of liberal writers like R. L. Godkin, Albert Jay Nock, H. L. Mencken, Frank Chodorov, and Leonard Read. To the rest of the world, this was the distinctively, characteristically American outlook.

Meanwhile, the economic advance that had been slowly gaining momentum in the Western world burst out in a great leap forward. First in Britain, then in America and Western Europe, the Industrial Revolution transformed the life of man as nothing had since the neolithic age. Now it became possible for the vast majority of mankind to escape the immemorial misery they had grown to accept as their unalterable lot. Now tens of millions who would have perished in the inefficient economy of the old order were able to survive. As the populations of Europe and America swelled to unprecedented levels, the new masses gradually achieved living standards unimaginable for working people before.

The birth of the industrial order was accompanied by economic dislocations. How could it have been otherwise? The free-market economists preached the solution: security of property and hard money to encourage capital formation, free trade to maximize efficiency in production, and a clear field for entrepreneurs eager to innovate. But conservatives, threatened in their age-old status, initiated a literary assault on the new system, giving the Industrial Revolution a bad name from which it never fully recovered. Soon the attack was gleefully taken up by groups of socialist intellectuals that began to emerge.

Still, by mid-century the liberals went from one victory to another. Constitutions with guarantees of basic rights were adopted, legal systems firmly anchoring the rule of law and property rights were put in place, and free trade was spreading, giving birth to a world economy based on the gold standard.

There were advances on the intellectual front as well. After spearheading the campaign to abolish the English Corn Laws, Richard Cobden developed the theory of nonintervention in the affairs of other countries as a foundation for peace. Frederic Bastiat put the case for free trade, nonintervention, and peace in a classic form. Liberal historians like Thomas Macaulay and Augustin Thierry uncovered the roots of freedom in the West. Later in the century, the economic theory of the free market was placed on a secure scientific footing with the rise of the Austrian School, inaugurated by Carl Menger.

The relation of liberalism and religion presented a special problem. In continental Europe and Latin America, freethinking liberals sometimes used the state power to curtail the influence of the Catholic Church, while some Catholic leaders clung to obsolete ideas of theocratic control. But liberal thinkers like Benjamin Constant, Alexis de Tocqueville, and Lord Acton saw beyond such futile disputes. They stressed the crucial role that religion, separated from government power, could play in stemming the growth of the centralized state. In this way, they prepared the ground for the reconciliation of liberty and religious faith.

Then, for reasons still unclear, the tide began to turn against the liberals. Part of the reason is surely the rise of the new class of intellectuals that proliferated everywhere. That they owed their very existence to the wealth generated by the capitalist system did not prevent most of them from incessantly gnawing away at capitalism, indicting it for every problem they could point to in modern society.

At the same time, voluntary solutions to these problems were preempted by state functionaries anxious to expand their domain. The rise of democracy may well have contributed to liberalism's decline by aggravating an age-old feature of politics: the scramble for special privilege. Businesses, labor unions, farmers, bureaucrats, and other interest groups vied for state privileges – and found intellectual demagogues to rationalize their depredations. The area of state control grew, at the expense, as William Graham Sumner pointed out, of "the forgotten man" – the quiet, productive individual who asks no favor of government and, through his work, keeps the whole system going.

By the end of the century, liberalism was being battered on all sides. Nationalists and imperialists condemned it for promoting an insipid peace instead of a virile and bracing belligerency among the nations. Socialists attacked it for upholding the "anarchical" free-market system instead of "scientific" central planning. Even church leaders disparaged liberalism for its alleged egotism and materialism. In America and Britain, social reformers around the dawn of the century conceived a particularly clever gambit. Anywhere else the supporters of state intervention and coercive labor-unionism would have been called "socialists" or "social democrats." But since the English-speaking peoples appeared for some reason to have an aversion to those labels, they hijacked the term "liberal."

Though they fought on to the end, a mood of despondency settled on the last of the great authentic liberals. When Herbert Spencer began writing in the 1840s, he had looked forward to an age of universal progress in which the coercive state apparatus would practically disappear. By 1884, Spencer could pen an essay entitled, "The Coming Slavery." In 1898, William Graham Sumner, American Spencerian, free-trader, and gold-standard advocate, looked with dismay as America started on the road to imperialism and global entanglement in the Spanish-American War: he titled his response to that war, grimly, "The Conquest of the United States by Spain."

Everywhere in Europe there was a reversion to the policies of the absolutist state, as government bureaucracies expanded. At the same time, jealous rivalries among the Great Powers led to a frenzied arms race and sharpened the threat of war. In 1914, a Serb assassin threw a spark onto the heaped-up animosity and suspicion, and the result was the most destructive war in history to that point. In 1917, an American president keen to create a New World Order led his country into the murderous conflict "War is the health of the state," warned the radical writer Randolph Bourne. And so it proved to be. By the time the butchery ended, many believed that liberalism in its classical sense was dead.

PART 3: THE TWENTIETH CENTURY

The First World War was the watershed of the twentieth century. Itself the product of antiliberal ideas and policies, such as militarism and protectionism, the Great War fostered statism in every form. In Europe and America, the trend toward state intervention accelerated, as governments conscripted, censored, inflated, ran up mountains of debts, co-opted business and labor, and seized control of the economy. Everywhere "progressive" intellectuals saw their dreams coming true. The old laissez-faire liberalism was dead, they gloated, and the future belonged to collectivism. The only question seemed to be: which kind of collectivism?

In Russia, the chaos of the war permitted a small group of Marxist revolutionaries to grab power and establish a field headquarters for world revolution. In the nineteenth century, Karl Marx had concocted a secular religion with a potent appeal. It held out the promise of the final liberation of man through replacing the complex, often baffling world of the market economy by conscious, "scientific" control. Put into practice by Lenin and Trotsky in Russia, the Marxist economic experiment resulted in catastrophe. For the next seventy years, Red rulers lurched from one patchwork expedient to another. But terror kept them firmly in charge, and the most colossal propaganda effort in history convinced intellectuals both in the West and in the emerging Third World that communism was, indeed, "the radiant future of all mankind."

The peace treaties cobbled together by President Woodrow Wilson and the other Allied leaders left Europe a seething cauldron of resentment and hate. Seduced by nationalist demagogues and terrified of the Communist threat, millions of Europeans turned to the forms of state worship called Fascism and National Socialism, or Nazism. Though riddled with economic error, these doctrines promised prosperity and national power through integral state control of society, while fomenting more and greater wars.

In the democratic countries, milder forms of statism were the rule. Most insidious of all was the form that had been invented in the 1880s, in Germany. There Otto von Bismarck, the Iron Chancellor, devised a series of old-age, disability, accident, and sickness insurance schemes, run by the state. The German liberals of the time argued that such plans were simply a reversion to the paternalism of the absolutist monarchies. Bismarck won out, and his invention – the welfare state – was eventually copied everywhere in Europe, including the totalitarian countries. With the New Deal, the welfare state came to America.

Still, private property and free exchange continued as the basic organizing principles of Western economies. Competition, the profit motive, the steady accumulation of capital (including human capital), free trade, the perfecting of markets, increased specialization – all worked to promote efficiency and technical progress and with them higher living standards for the people. So powerful and resilient did this capitalist engine of productivity prove to be that widespread state intervention, coercive labor-unionism, even government-generated depressions and wars could not check economic growth in the long run.

The 1920s and '30s represent the nadir of the classical-liberal movement in this century. Especially after government meddling with the monetary system led to the crash of 1929 and the Great Depression, dominant opinion held that history had closed the books on competitive capitalism, and with it the liberal philosophy.

If a date were to be put on the rebirth of classical liberalism, it would be 1922, the year of the publication of *Socialism*, by the Austrian economist Ludwig von Mises. One of the most remarkable thinkers of the century, Mises was also a man of unflinching courage. In *Socialism*, he threw down the gauntlet to the enemies of capitalism. In effect, he said: "You accuse the system of private property of causing all social evils, which only socialism can cure. Fine. But would you now kindly do something you have never deigned to do before: would you explain how a complex economic system will be able to operate in the absence of markets, and hence prices, for capital goods?" Mises demonstrated that economic calculation without private property was impossible, and exposed socialism for the passionate illusion it was.

Mises's challenge to the prevailing orthodoxy opened the minds of thinkers in Europe and America. F. A. Hayek, Wilhelm Roepke, and Lionel Robbins were among those whom Mises converted to the free market. And, throughout his very long career, Mises elaborated and reformed his economic theory and social philosophy, becoming the acknowledged premier classical-liberal thinker of the twentieth century.

In Europe and particularly in the United States, scattered individuals and groups kept something of the old liberalism alive. At the London School of Economics and the University of Chicago, academics could be found, even in the 1930s and '40s, who defended at least the basic validity of the free-enterprise idea. In America, an embattled brigade of brilliant writers, mainly journalists, survived. Now known as the "Old Right," they included Albert Jay Nock, Frank Chodorov, H. L. Mencken, Felix Morley, and John T. Flynn. Spurred to action by the totalitarian implications of Franklin Roosevelt's New Deal, these writers reiterated the traditional American creed of individual freedom and scornful distrust of government. They were equally opposed to Roosevelt's policy of global meddling as subversive of the American Republic. Supported by a few courageous publishers and businessmen, the "Old Right" nursed the flame of Jeffersonian ideals through the darkest days of the New Deal and the Second World War.

With the end of that war, what can be called a movement came into being. Small at first, it was fed by multiplying streams. Hayek's *Road to Serfdom*, published in 1944, alerted many thousands to the reality that, in pursuing socialist policies, the West was risking the loss of its traditional free civilization. In 1946, Leonard Read established The Foundation for Economic Education, in Irvington, New York, publishing the works of Henry Hazlitt and other champions of the free market. Mises and Hayek, now both in the United States, continued their work. Hayek led in founding the Mont Pelerin Society, a group of classical-liberal scholars, activists, and businessmen from all over the world. Mises, unsurpassed as a teacher, set up a seminar at New York University, attracting such students as Murray Rothbard and Israel Kirzner. Rothbard went on to wed the insights of Austrian economics to the teachings of natural law to produce a powerful synthesis that appealed to many of the young. At the University of Chicago, Milton Friedman, George Stigler, and Aaron Director led a group of classical-liberal economists whose specialty was exposing the defects of government action. The gifted novelist Ayn Rand incorporated emphatically libertarian themes in her well-crafted best-sellers, and even founded a school of philosophy.

The reaction to the renewal of authentic liberalism on the part of the left – "liberal" – more accurately, social-democrat-establishment was predictable, and ferocious. In 1954, for instance, Hayek edited a volume entitled *Capitalism and the Historians*, a collection of essays by distinguished scholars arguing against the prevailing socialist interpretation of the Industrial Revolution. A scholarly journal permitted Arthur Schlesinger Jr., Harvard professor and New Deal hack, to savage the book in these terms: "Americans have enough trouble with home-grown McCarthys without importing Viennese professors to add academic luster to the process." Other works the establishment tried to kill by silence. As late as 1962, not a single prominent magazine or newspaper chose to review Friedman's *Capitalism and Freedom*. Still, the writers and activists who led the revival of classical liberalism found a growing resonance among the public. Millions of Americans in all walks of life had all along quietly cherished the values of the free market, and private property.

The growing presence of a solid corps of intellectual leaders now gave many of these citizens the heart to stand up for the ideas they had held dear for so long.

In the 1970s and '80s, with the evident failure of socialist planning and interventionist programs, classical liberalism became a worldwide movement. In Western countries, and then, incredibly, in the nations of the former Warsaw Pact, political leaders even declared themselves disciples of Hayek and Friedman. As the end of the century approached, the old, authentic liberalism was alive and well, stronger than it had been for a hundred years.

And yet, in Western countries, the state keeps on relentlessly expanding, colonizing one area of social life after the other. In America, the Republic is fast becoming a fading memory, as federal bureaucrats and global planners divert more and more power to the center. So the struggle continues, as it must. Two centuries ago, when liberalism was young, Jefferson had already informed us of the price of liberty.

2

Back the Future

New Classical Liberalism and Old Social Justice

Jason Brennan

According to the critics, libertarians and classical liberals are impractical extremists. Classical liberals believe we ought to respect liberty though the sky falls. They prioritize formal, negative liberty at the expense of positive liberty. They are unconcerned with social justice or poverty. They are more concerned to protect a millionaire's fifth car from excise taxes than to see a starving child eat or a sick person heal. And, of course, they are completely unaware of the problem of market failures.

Left-leaning economist Jeffrey Sachs says that for libertarians, "compassion, justice, civic responsibility, honesty, decency, humility, and even survival of the poor, weak, and vulnerable – are all to take a back seat" to liberty.[1] Leftist philosopher Brian Barry complains that the libertarian philosopher Robert Nozick is

> proposing to starve or humiliate ten percent or so of his fellow citizens (if he recognizes the word) by eliminating all transfer payments through the state, leaving the sick, the old, the disabled, the mothers with young children and no breadwinner, and so on, to the tender mercies of private charity, given at the whim and pleasure of the donors and on any terms that they choose to impose.[2]

Now, even other left-liberal philosophers think Barry is unfair to Nozick.[3] Still, we can understand Barry's irritation. He sees Nozick arguing that justice requires strict observance of negative private property rights without concern for the distributional consequences. At the same time, Barry sees the less reputable but more famous libertarian thinker Ayn Rand proclaiming that morality leaves no room for altruism. The classical liberal and Nobel laureate economist F. A. Hayek asserts that social justice is a mirage. According to Hayek, talking about social justice is

---

[1] www.huffingtonpost.com/jeffrey-sachs/libertarian-illusions_b_1207878.html.

[2] Brian Barry, "Review of Robert Nozick, *Anarchy, State, and Utopia*," in 3 POLITICAL THEORY 331–332 (1975).

[3] See, for example, Jeremy Waldron, "What Plato Would Allow,"37 NOMOS 138 (1995).

not more coherent than asking what color the number four is. Many of the left interpret him as saying that liberty is all that matters, regardless of how well it makes people's lives go.

Thus, mid-twentieth-century libertarianism and classical liberalism began to appear antihumanitarian. No political philosophy can survive being antihumanitarian. In the end, most of us regard it as a test of a theory of justice that when the theory's vision of justice obtains, that is a cause for celebration rather than something to bemoan. If achieving justice, as some theory conceives it, would cause us generally to be miserable and poor, then justice would be a curse rather than a blessing.

Mid-twentieth-century classical liberal and libertarian thought indeed seemed vulnerable to this kind of criticism. But that is surprising, given their intellectual roots.

In 1776, a revolution began. Of course, I speak here not of American colonials replacing their constitutional monarchy with an otherwise similar constitutional regime. Rather, in 1776, Adam Smith published *The Wealth of Nations*.

Smith revolutionized economics and philosophy by arguing that we should judge the wealth of nations not by the size of the king's treasury or the strength of his fleet, but by the fullness of the common man's stomach and the opportunities available to his children. The European monarchs vied, Yertle the Turtle–style, for the largest empires. But Smith's careful calculations proved that forming and maintaining such empires cost more in taxes than the value of the raw materials the colonies generated.[4] These empires enriched kings and gun makers but hurt almost everyone else. Smith was writing at the beginning of a dramatic increase in living standards. He was witnessing firsthand something we had never seen before: a society-wide escape from extreme poverty. Smith argued that the way to make the poor rich is to instantiate a stable system of property rights, the rule of law, and open trade. Smith saw justice as a positive-sum game: just institutions tend to make everyone a winner. Just institutions make it so that other people's talents and other countries' development are a boon rather than a threat. For Smith, justice was not so much about taxing Peter to feed Paul, but about putting Peter and Paul in a position where they would not need government or private charity.

Contemporary classical liberal thought is in the midst of a renaissance. Just as renaissance artists had to relearn from the Romans what their dark age fathers forgot, so contemporary classical liberals are relearning from Smith what their twentieth-century forebears forgot. Contemporary classical liberals can and usually do say that they care about many of the same things modern egalitarian liberals care about. They can agree that one test of a flourishing society is the end or minimizing of domination, poverty, and medical want, and the spread of knowledge, opportunity, peace, prosperity, culture, and full political autonomy. They care that people are

---

[4] See LANCE DAVIS and ROBERT HUTTENBACK, MAMMON AND THE PURSUIT OF EMPIRE (1987).

actually able to do the things they value and make good use of their rights, not just that people are protected from interference.

The difference between the best forms of classical liberalism and egalitarian liberalism is not entirely about values, but instead often about *empirical* claims about what it takes to achieve these values in the real world. New classical liberals are not so much synthesizing left-liberalism and classical liberalism as they are instead clarifying the basic concerns that have driven the mainline classical liberal thought all along.[5] Classical liberals have always been animated by a concern for social justice, even if they did not call it that.

This chapter paints, using broad strokes, a picture of contemporary classical liberal thought. I explain how new classical liberals have responded to the twentieth-century criticisms, and how they have integrated the best ideas from the Left. In particular, I respond to each of these critiques:

1. Classical liberals advocate "merely formal" liberty instead of substantively good results.
2. Classical liberals dumb down their theories of justice to accommodate ignoble human motivations.
3. Classical liberals fail to advocate institutions which guarantee good outcomes.
4. Classical liberals ignore the importance of positive liberty.
5. Classical liberals do not care about social justice.

As we will see, classical liberals have good responses to each of these criticisms. I am not here trying to prove classical liberalism's responses are always correct – that takes more work than one can do in a short chapter. The point is to help critics realize that classical liberalism is not the cartoon they make it out to be.

THE TWENTIETH-CENTURY SPLIT

The terms "libertarianism" and "classical liberalism" refer to a body of related views about politics, philosophy, and economics. As a body of related ideas, classical liberalism has the unity of a neighborhood more than a house. Asking what distinguishes classical liberalism from other political views is more like asking what distinguishes Midtown from Chelsea than like asking how the Empire State Building fits together.

That said, here is a workable characterization of classical liberalism. Classical liberals generally believe that, as a matter of justice, each individual should be imbued with a wide sphere of autonomy. Each individual should be granted a wide sphere of personal and economic freedom to decide for herself how she will live.

---

[5] JOHN TOMASI, FREE MARKET FAIRNESS (2008) (characterizing contemporary classical liberalism as a synthesis of Rawlsian and Hayekian ideas).

Classical liberals advocate free and open societies based on cooperation, tolerance, and mutual respect. They believe that individuals should not be sacrificed to achieve greater social stability, economic efficiency, or desirable cultural ends.

In general, classical liberals also argue that granting everyone a wide scope of personal and economic liberty generates good consequences, whereas restrictions on liberty produce bad consequences. Classical liberals are not starry-eyed about freedom. They accept that granting people the freedom to choose means that people can and often will choose poorly. Nevertheless, they argue, free societies are generally more prosperous and tend to produce greater scientific knowledge and artistic advances. Classical liberals accept that markets and civil society can fail, but they argue government agents generally lack both the competence and the motivation to intervene in ways that fix rather than exacerbate the problems.[6] The power we grant government to save our children will often be used to control them instead.

On their face, these are two very different sets of arguments. The first set argues liberty is an end in itself, or something we owe to people because they are ends in themselves. The second set says that liberty is good as an instrument for generating other valuable outcomes. Philosophers would call the first set *deontological* and the second set *consequentialist*.

Early classical liberals such as Adam Smith, David Hume, or John Locke were not quite aware of the deontology/consequentialism distinction. They tended to jump between both sets of arguments without any apparent worries that they were crossing intellectual boundaries.

In the twentieth century, philosophers tended to think these two sets of arguments were in conflict. We were supposed to pick a side: deontology or consequentialism, not both. Around this time, we saw a split in libertarian and classical liberal thought. Classical liberal economists such as Milton Friedman tended to argue for free markets and free societies on almost purely consequentialist grounds. Libertarian philosophers tended to defend freedom entirely on rights-based arguments. Some were willing to bite big bullets: For instance, Murray Rothbard (in his philosophical work) argued our property rights are so strong that one cannot step onto a person's property to rescue an infant left starving on the lawn.[7]

Contemporary libertarian or classical liberal thought has far more in common with Adam Smith's way of thinking than what we see in Murray Rothbard or Robert Nozick. Adam Smith, David Hume, and other early classical liberals saw themselves as philosophers studying the humane sciences, which encompassed and integrated the fields we would now call philosophy, economics, political science, and sociology. Interestingly, contemporary libertarian and classical liberal scholars tend to do the same.

---

[6] For an overview, see DENNIS MUELLER, PUBLIC CHOICE III (2003).

[7] MURRAY ROTHBARD, THE ETHICS OF LIBERTY 100 (1998).

"MERELY FORMAL LIBERTY" AND THE VALUE OF INSTITUTIONS

Suppose the US government amends the Constitution. It adds a new right. This right, unlike the others, cannot be amended, changed, or infringed. The Constitution declares that no state interest can outweigh it. The text of the amendment reads: "The right of citizens to fly at one billion miles per hour shall not be violated."

Ceteris paribus, a world in which governments respect this right is freer than a world in which they do not. Yet – at least as of now, when we have not invented *Star Trek*–style warp drives – this kind of freedom has little value. How much would you be willing to pay for such a right? The right has some novelty value, but it is not the type of right that people would fight and die to protect. So far as contemporary physics is concerned, it is physically impossible to fly at one billion miles per hour. Thus, this right has little worth.

Even the most ardent defender of rights needs to admit that at the extreme, some liberties or rights have no worth. They do not make a difference to the quality of one's life. Any sensible person would, if she could, trade away the right to fly a billion miles per hour for something else. As Karl Marx might say, this right is *merely formal* and lacks any *substance.*

Marx and other thinkers on the left often downplay the worth of rights against interference. Marx argued that there was a problem with classical liberalism. Classical liberals wanted to guarantee everyone, rich and poor, certain rights against arbitrary interference from government or others. However, Marx said, poverty can make those rights *worthless.* Marx might say, to the average person, the right to own a yacht is worthless because she lacks the material means to acquire a yacht. Take a young woman growing up in an abusive household, in grinding poverty, in a drug- and gang-infested part of town. Telling her that she has the right to become a CEO and a billionaire is like telling her she has the right to fly a billion miles per hour.

Later Marxists often say that what the poor need is a *substantive* right to property, that is, a guarantee that they would actually acquire property. Formal rights alone do not matter. The poor do not need them. From the armchair, that sounds right. Could it be wrong?

Philosophers often treat Marx's question – *are merely formal liberties valuable?* – as a conceptual question. They seem to think they can answer it with thought experiments. But what if instead we treat Marx's question as open to empirical investigation? When we do, we find Marx's complaints miss the point.

Almost all people everywhere throughout human history lived under what we now would refer to as "extreme poverty." Macroeconomist Brad Delong estimates that in 5000 BC, per capita world product – the total amount of yearly economic production worldwide per person – was only about $130 (in 2002 USD), and barely doubled by 1800 to $250.[8] Economist Angus Maddison, whose historical data

---

[8] BRAD DELONG, MACROECONOMICS 120 (2002).

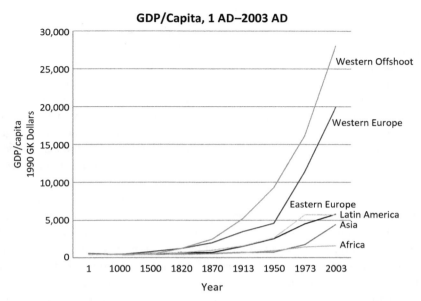

GDP/Capita, 1 AD–2003 AD

FIGURE 2.1.[9]

is widely used, offers higher numbers: $457 (1990 dollars) in 1 AD, rising to $712 in 1820.[10] There were occasional dark and golden ages, but no long prolonged, society-wide escape from extreme poverty.

But then something changed and the stagnation stopped (see Figure 2.1). In the past two hundred years, per capita world product has increased by a factor of at least thirty.[11] Almost everyone got richer. Notice that even the poorest regions enjoyed *some* growth. It is not that the rich countries got rich as the poor countries got poorer, which would suggest a zero-sum process by which the rich got rich at the poor's expense. Rather, wealth has been *created*.

Why did this happen? The dominant explanation in development economics today has returned more or less to the explanation Adam Smith defended in *The Wealth of Nations*. It holds that sustained economic growth resulted not from empire, from conquest, from good geography, or from an abundance of natural resources, but instead from having good economic and political institutions.[12] As economist Gérard Roland summarizes, the institutional theory of growth, especially

[9]   Chart made using data from Maddison, supra note 9 at 70.
[10] ANGUS MADDISON, CONTOURS OF THE WORLD ECONOMY, 1–2030 AD: ESSAYS IN MACRO-ECONOMIC HISTORY 70 (2007).
[11] World per capita income as of 2014 is approximately $16,100 in 2014 US dollars, up from under $500 in 1800. https://www.cia.gov/library/publications/the-world-factbook/fields/2004.html
[12] James A. Robinson, Daron Acemoglu, and Simon Johnson, "Institutions as a Fundamental Cause of Long-Run Growth," in HANDBOOK OF ECONOMIC GROWTH 1A 386–472 (2005).

the work by economists Daron Acemoglu and James Robinson, "has quickly become the dominant view on explaining growth."[13] No one in the economics literature thinks that institutions are *all* that matters, but, as economist Dani Rodrik summarizes, "the quality of institutions trumps everything else."[14]

Countries with robust systems of private property, protected by the rule of law, and governed by strong, inclusive states, offer much better prospects for significant and sustained development than those that lack such protections. Marx might say that these merely formal rights do not guarantee that the poor do well. He is right, though as I will argue later, guarantees are beside the point. Still, the *real* freedom Marx desires is found in commercial societies with robust protections of "merely formal freedom," and nowhere else.

There is nothing particularly *libertarian* or *classical liberal* about this argument. This view – that the institutions of robust private property rights, open markets, and the rule of law are vital to development – is shared by economists left and right, libertarian and not. It is also widely ignored by political philosophers. The reason is not so much that philosophers have powerful critiques of mainstream development economics – they do not – but rather that most political philosophers have a method of theorizing about institutions that biases them toward making certain basic mistakes. Contemporary classical liberals, whatever their faults, at least lack this bias.

CRUDE GOVERNMENTALISM

Most political philosophers, classical liberals excluded, tend to suffer from a bias I will pejoratively call *crude governmentalism*. Crude governmentalism is the fallacy that occurs in the following kind of argument:

1. Some goal G is an important goal of justice; it is one of the standards by which we judge institutions good or bad.
2. If something is a goal, of justice, then the government ought to guarantee it occurs.
3. Therefore, we ought to have our government issue a set of laws and create a legal bureaucracy, which guarantee that G occurs.

The first premise in an argument like this offers some test of what makes institutions good or bad. To take a definition from Nobel Laureate economist Douglas North, "Institutions are the rules of the game in a society or, more formally, are the humanly devised constraints that shape human interaction."[15] G could stand in for

---

[13] Gérard Roland, Development Economics 108 (2014).

[14] Dani Rodrik, Arvind Subramanian, and Francesco Trebbi, "Institutions Rule: The Primacy of Institutions Over Geography and Integration in Economic Development," 9 J. Econ. Growth 131, 135 (2004).

[15] Douglas North, Institutions, Institutional Change, and Economic Performance 3 (1990).

any number of goals: good education, sufficient medical care, good health, general prosperity, the welfare of the least advantaged working class citizens, equality, happiness, art, the development of human capabilities, positive freedom, or whatnot.

Premise 2 is where the trouble usually starts. Premise 2 says that once we have identified some goal we want our institutions to achieve, then this somehow tells us as matter of logic that we need a particular set of institutions to achieve those goals. If G is the test of a good institution, then, surely, it follows that we need to *make sure* G happens. So therefore, we want a *guarantee* that G will happen. So therefore, we need the government to issue a legal guarantee. As soon as you say, "I think good societies have flourishing arts communities," you are thereby committed to a robust central government and something like the NEH. As soon as you say, "Good institutions help us escape poverty," you are committed to mass redistribution, a welfare state, and other government-backed guarantees. Or so hidden reasoning behind premise 2 goes.

But, again, what if we treat premise 2 not as an armchair conceptual point, as philosophers are inclined to do, but as an empirical claim? An economist might note that there is a significant gap between the claim "We ought to judge institutions by how well they achieve some goal G," and the claim that government ought to create a bureaucracy that guarantees G.

To know whether government should do requires knowing at least (A) what government is likely to do well, and (B) what the institutional alternatives are. We cannot move straightforwardly from principles of justice to any particular view of institutional design without knowing a fair bit of political economy.

Illustrate, consider the following argument:

1. Government ought to promote human welfare and is licensed to do whatever it takes to do so.
2. If government ought to promote human welfare and is licensed to do whatever it takes to do so, then we should have a welfare state that guarantees through legal means that no one falls below a particular standard of welfare.
3. Therefore, we should have a welfare state that guarantees through legal means that no one falls below a particular standard of welfare.[16]

Suppose for the sake of argument that premise 1 is correct. Even with that charitable assumption, premise 2 is questionable. We would need to check whether welfare states actually improve welfare best, in the long run, compared to the other institutional arrangements. If we care about welfare, we would not take that for granted.

A legal guarantee that the government will achieve some goal is merely one of many ways we might try to accomplish that goal. Whether the legal guarantee works is always an empirical question. There is a difference between guaranteeing in the

[16] JOHN RAWLS, JUSTICE AS FAIRNESS: A RESTATEMENT 135–9 (2001).

sense of rendering inevitable – as when Acemoglu and Robinson say that extractive economic regimes guarantee widespread poverty – and guaranteeing in these that the government expresses a firm commitment to achieve some goal through its laws and bureaucracies – as when the second Bush administration guaranteed no child would be left behind in school.

A guarantee in the second sense need not be a guarantee in the first. Indeed, not only is it possible for a legal guarantee to fail to achieve its goal, but such a guarantee could even *cause* the failure itself. Imagine a government said it would guarantee everyone would be a millionaire by offering an unconditional basic income of $1 million in current US dollars. That arrangement would undermine itself. Hardly anyone would choose to work, and so there would not be enough taxes to pay for the basic income.

More subtly, even if you think government ought to help promote some goal, note that it has two ways of promoting the value: directly and indirectly. For example, suppose you think the government ought to ensure the economy grows. It could attempt to do this directly, by subsidizing new corporations, offering grants to businesses, or spending money for the purpose of stimulus. Or it could try to do it indirectly, by maintaining a basic institutional framework (such as the rule of law, constitutional representative democracy, courts, and property rights) under which people will be incentivized to act in ways that spontaneously lead to growth. It is an empirical, social scientific question as to what mix of direct and indirect methods works best to achieve this goal. The crude governmentalist mistakenly assumes direct methods work better than indirect. But, in this case, economics tends to find that indirect methods work better overall.

Crude governmentalism glosses over the hard questions. Worse, crude governmentalism also causes us to see each other as moral enemies, even when our disagreements are about empirical matters. For a crude governmentalist, to care about something just is to want the government to fix it. Thus, suppose I reject minimum wage legislation on the grounds that I think it does not work.[17] I argue the only way to enrich the poor is to increase productivity. A crude governmentalist would conclude that I just do not care about the poor. Crude governmentalism makes arguing over *means* impossible.

AGAINST IDEAL THEORY

Political philosophers sometimes claim their job is to do what they call "ideal theory."[18] An ideal theory of justice asks what institutions would be best if people had a perfect sense of justice and were always willing to comply with just institutions

---

[17] David Neumark and William Wascher, Minimum Wages (2010).

[18] For example, see G. A. Cohen, Rescuing Justice and Equality (2008); G. A. Cohen, Why Not Socialism? (2009); David Estlund, Democratic Authority 258–76 (2008).

and what morality requires. A "nonideal theory" of just institutions asks what institutions would be best in light of the fact that people are as they actually are – at times morally flawed, not always willing to do what justice requires, and responsive to the incentives they face.

As the Marxist philosopher G. A. Cohen might say, in a perfectly just society, by hypothesis, all citizens are themselves perfectly good and just. Accordingly, the kinds of institutions that would be useful, necessary, or workable in ideal circumstances might be entirely different from the institutions we would want in nonideal, realistic circumstances. To take an obvious example, we might say that in a perfectly just society, there would be no need for criminal courts or police.

Cohen further claims that ideal theory is where the action is in political philosophy. The point of political philosophy is to identify what makes a society just. According to Cohen, John Rawls, Robert Nozick, and most other market-friendly political philosophers dumb down their theories of justice to accommodate real human beings' defective moral motivations.

Ideal theory makes institutional questions much easier. In the real world, if we create positions of great power, we have to worry that people will use that power for their own selfish ends. If we create government regulatory agencies, we have to worry that corporations and unions will lobby these agencies to pass rules that benefit the few at the expense of the many. If we hold property in common, we have to worry that people will overuse it. We have to worry people will free ride on others' efforts or take advantage of their generosity.

Some classical liberal philosophers think ideal theory is incoherent.[19] Other classical liberals think there is nothing wrong with working on ideal theory, but we must be careful not to jump back-and-forth between ideal and nonideal theory in when arguing about institutions.[20]

Cohen makes this very mistake. In *Why Not Socialism?*, Cohen first describes how socialism would work if only people were angels. He then describes some of the bad behavior we see in real-life capitalism with realistic, flawed people. He then asks us which system seems better. Almost everyone agrees that socialism with angels is better than capitalism with realistic, flawed people. He concludes, "A ha! Deep down you all agree that socialism is better than capitalism!"

But Cohen has not compared apples to apples and oranges to oranges. Even if we agree that socialism with angels is a more just system than capitalism with realistic, flawed people, it might not be the *socialism* that is doing the work. Rather, it is Cohen asking to imagine socialism with *morally perfect people*. What Cohen needs to do, but never does, is consider whether capitalism with angels would be better or

---

[19] For example, David Schmidtz, "After Solipsism," Oxford Studies in Normative Ethics 6 (2017); Gerald Gaus, The Tyranny of the Ideal (2016); Jacob Levy, "There Is No Such Thing as Ideal Theory," 33 Soc. Philos. Policy 312 (2016).

[20] Jason Brennan, Why Not Capitalism? (2014).

worse than socialism with angels. (Cohen more or less admits that capitalism with realistic people is better than socialism with realistic people.) Cohen's *Why Not Socialism?* is not an argument for socialism so much as an argument that life would be better if only people were morally flawless.

In response, a similar mistake from Marx, John Rawls says, "We must be careful here not to compare the ideal of one conception with the actuality of the other, but rather to compare actuality with actuality, and in our particular historical circumstances."[21] This is excellent advice, but Rawls himself fails to heed it. Instead, his argument for his preferred economic regime relies on the very mistake Cohen and Marx make, and the mistake he advised us to avoid.

When Rawls discusses his favored political-economic regimes, he imagines that people have perfectly just motivations, and he explicitly imagines away many of the problems those regimes would face in the real world. However, when Rawls argues against his disfavored regimes, he invokes the kinds of problems that would only occur if people had imperfect motivations.

For instance, Rawls knows that in the real world, the social insurance, redistributive, and regulatory institutions he favors would lead to significant moral hazard and rent seeking.[22] However, when Rawls theorizes about which set of institutions best realizes his theory of justice, he simply dismisses these concerns. He says he is doing ideal theory. We imagine that people have a perfect sense of justice, and we thus imagine a world in which people are immune to moral hazard and would never dare engage in rent seeking.[23]

Yet, Rawls also claims that the regimes he dislikes are unjust because they might permit wealthy people to use their wealth to buy government power for their own ends. But, by Rawls's stipulated ground rules, we are supposed to be doing ideal theory, and imagining that people have a perfect sense of justice.[24] If people had a

---

[21] RAWLS, supra note 16 at 178.

[22] A policy is said to cause "moral hazard" when it induces people to take more risks or make dumb choices, because the policy allows these people to externalize the costs of their decisions onto others. So, for instance, welfare state policies encourage at least some people not to save enough, to have children out of wedlock, and be unemployed instead of taking a job. "Rent seeking" refers to when corporations, unions, or special interest groups lobby the government to manipulate the legal or regulatory environment in their favor.

[23] For example, id at 137 ("Much conservative thought has focused on the last three questions mentioned above, criticizing the ineffectiveness of the welfare state and its tendencies toward waste and corruption. But here we focus largely on the first question, leaving the others aside. We ask: what kind of regime and basic structure would be right and just, could it be effectively and workably maintained?").

[24] Id at 136, says there are four basic questions we can ask about a regime:

   A. Are the regime's institutions right and just?
   B. Could a regime's institutions be effectively designed to realize its declared goals?
   C. Would citizens comply with the regime's institutions and with whatever rules apply to them?
   D. Would citizens be competent to play whatever role they hold?

perfect sense of justice, they would not buy government power for their own selfish ends, since by hypothesis this is unjust.

Rawls says it is useful to put aside questions of political economy. He says we should instead just imagine that institutions always accomplish their intended ends.[25] But that is probably the last thing we would want to do, regardless of whether we are doing ideal or nonideal theory.

THE END OF IDEOLOGICAL BATTLES OVER "LIBERTY"

The classical liberal philosopher Isaiah Berlin introduced a distinction between *negative* and *positive* conceptions of liberty.[26] Berlin thought that he had not merely identified two different ways natural language uses the word. Rather, he thought he had identified an ideological fault line. We have to choose one side or the other. But, as we will see, that was probably a mistake.

In the abstract, negative liberty connotes the absence of certain constraints, impediments, or obstacles. Positive liberty connotes the presence of certain powers, capacities, or abilities.[27] For instance, one might say that a person enjoys negative liberty to the extent she is free from interference from others. One might say that a person enjoys positive liberty to the extent she has the power to achieve her ends.

Berlin seemed to think that different conceptions of liberty entailed different views of government. He thought advocates of a purely negative view of liberty – liberty as noninterference – would want sharply limited governments, to prevent government from interfering with liberty. He thought advocates of a positive view of liberty – liberty as self-mastery or as the capacity to do as one pleases – would want an expansive government that would try to guarantee positive liberty through grants, welfare programs, and the like. For a long time in the twentieth century, philosophers seemed to agree. The left would accuse classical liberals of having an impoverished negative conception of liberty. Classical liberals in turn would complain that "positive liberty" is not liberty at all, or was an idea introduced by Marxists to corrupt our thinking.

But, upon reflection, this debate seems to presuppose crude governmentalism. Even Berlin has fallen into the trap. Figuring out what the word "liberty" means does not automatically imply that liberty so defined is valuable or something we are owed by right. Further, even if we determine that liberty so defined is valuable or something we have a right to, this leaves open what, if anything, government ought to do. To show government should have some role in protecting and

He tells us (at 137) that we should put aside questions B–D and just focus on question A, asking what kind of regime would be just if it could be workably maintained.
[25] Id at 137–8.
[26] ISAIAH BERLIN, FOUR ESSAYS ON LIBERTY (1969).
[27] Berlin had in mind the capacity of self-mastery in particular, but other philosophers with positive conceptions of liberty think of freedom as the capacity to achieve one's ends or goals.

promoting a given kind of liberty requires, at least, showing that government is likely to be successful if it takes that role.

Once again, even if we determine that government ought to promote or protect a given kind of liberty, it can do so directly or indirectly. For instance, Marxists often view possessing wealth as a kind of positive liberty. The government might attempt to provide this to citizens directly through welfare programs, redistribution, subsidies, and grants. Alternatively, it might attempt to do it indirectly, by providing a basic institutional framework (such as the rule of law, a well-defined property rights regime, and courts) under which citizens can be expected to act in ways likely to generate significant wealth for all.

New classical liberals can and do concur with Marx that citizens should have the effective means to exercise their wills, to do as they please (provided they do not violate other citizens' rights), and to lead their conceptions of the good life. But, they say, this does not tell us that negative liberty does not matter. On the contrary, negative liberty matters in part because, historically, protecting negative liberties is the most important and effective way of promoting positive liberty.[28] In the real world, we do not have to choose between promoting positive liberty or respect negative liberty, as Berlin worried. Instead, in real world, we can promote positive liberty by respecting negative liberty. The typical citizen of a Western nation today enjoys far more positive liberty than a medieval king. This occurred because Western countries adopted functional background institutions, institutions that, over time, gave citizens the incentives and means to promote positive liberty through their commercial, literary, scientific, and cultural activities.[29]

MAKING SOCIAL JUSTICE SAFE FOR LIBERTARIANS

Thirty years ago, most philosophers would have claimed that the big difference between classical and left-liberals concerned their views of social justice and economic freedom.[30] According to the received view, we are forced to choose: social justice or extensive economic freedom, but not both. Classical liberals

---

[28] For example, DAVID SCHMIDTZ and JASON BRENNAN, A BRIEF HISTORY OF LIBERTY (2010).

[29] Economists such as Nathan Rosenberg, Douglas North, and Robert Thomas claim that the West grew rich because it got its formal legal institutions right. NATHAN ROSENBERG and L. E. BIRDZELL JR., HOW THE WEST GREW RICH (1986); DOUGLAS NORTH and ROBERT PAUL THOMAS, THE RISE OF THE WESTERN WORLD: A NEW ECONOMIC HISTORY (1976). See also RONDO CAMERON and LARRY NEAL, A CONCISE ECONOMIC HISTORY OF THE WORLD (2003); ANGUS MADDISON, CONTOURS OF THE WORLD ECONOMY, 1–2030 AD: ESSAYS IN MACRO-ECONOMIC HISTORY (2007).

[30] Principles of distributive justice are meant to explain what the proper "distribution" of wealth, income, or other basic goods should be. Principles of "social justice," are a subset of principles of distributive justice. Advocates of social justice believe that distributive justice requires some sort of special emphasis on the poor. So, for example, a meritocrat believes that people should have income in proportion to their desert or merit. The meritocrat would thus accept a principle of distributive justice but not a principle of social justice.

supposedly choose economic freedom at the expense of social justice, while their more humane brethren across the aisle choose social justice at the expense of economic freedom.

Of course, mid-twentieth-century classical liberals advertised their opposition to social justice. Hayek argues that "justice" applies only to the products of deliberate human will; as such the pattern of holdings in a free market is neither just nor unjust, fair nor unfair. Nozick concurs: "There is no more a distributing or distribution of shares than there is a distributing of mates in a society in which persons choose whom they shall marry."[31] For Nozick, in a free society, asking whether it is fair that I make more money than my neighbor is no more sensible than asking whether it is fair my neighbor has more friends than I do.

However, while early classical liberals did not proclaim any explicit commitment to social justice – after all, the concept had not been developed yet – we find the *ingredients* of a commitment to social justice within the views of many classical liberals. Adam Smith's critique of mercantilism is founded upon a concern for the working poor. Smith measures the wealth of a nation not in terms of aggregate product but in terms of the substantive opportunities for success enjoyed by all.[32]

Even Hayek's attitude toward social justice is more ambiguous than he lets on. Hayek says there exists "a genuine problem of justice in connection with the deliberate design of political institutions." Although he rejects using the term "social justice" to refer to that genuine problem, Hayek also says that he has no basic disagreement with Rawls's idea that justice could serve as a (process-independent) standard of evaluation of a society's basic social institutions.[33]

Contemporary classical liberals often now have an explicit commitment to social justice. Many now embrace social justice, seeing it as a standard that enables them to capture and clarify the moral ideals that have long undergirded classical liberalism. But rather than saying economic liberty must come at the expense of social justice, as left-liberals often claim, they say (as Adam Smith did, in his own way) that economic liberty is in part a means for generating socially just outcomes.

WHEN SOCIAL JUSTICE AND ECONOMIC LIBERTY COME TOGETHER:
IMMIGRATION RIGHTS

I will demonstrate this point with a particular example. Many on the left, such as Thomas Pogge or Peter Singer, complain that the West is rich while the third world remains poor. They argue that this calls for massive redistribution from the first world to the third world. Whether such redistribution would work is itself a

---

[31] Robert Nozick, Anarchy, State and Utopia 149–50 (1974).
[32] For example, see *ED*, 567; see also *LJ*, 83, 343; *WN* I.viii.27, 91.
[33] F. A. Hayek, Law, Legislation and Liberty, Volume 2: The Mirage of Social Justice 100 (1976).

complicated empirical question; many economists think it cannot succeed in lifting the undeveloped world out of poverty.[34]

But while left-liberal philosophers have generally focused on defending global redistribution, classical liberal philosophers have focused on defending immigration rights, a form of economic freedom that has far greater potential to liberate the world's poor.

Right now, it is easy for capital to move across borders. But unskilled laborers are forbidden to move to countries where there is higher demand for their labor. They are thus left sitting ducks for economic exploitation.

From an economic standpoint, immigration restrictions are in the first instance a kind of import quota on foreign labor, akin to import restrictions on cars or clothing. Normally, such restrictions lead to inefficiencies and deadweight losses, as they prevent mutually beneficial trades from occurring, and force people to buy from less productive providers.

Many economists have tried to estimate the deadweight losses from immigration restriction. Their estimates are staggering. In a recent meta-analysis, Michael Clemens reviews various peer-reviewed published estimates and finds that the estimated *gains* from open borders amount to 50–150 percent of current world product, with the mean estimate being about 100 percent of world product.[35] In other words, by closing borders we forgo approximately $100 trillion in production.

Some of the higher estimates assume that nearly every worker will move in search of better paying jobs. That's not true – people care not only about money but also about living in cultures where they feel at home. Still, Clemens says, even if we more conservatively assume that only a small fraction would move if given the freedom to do so, the gains would still amount to $20–60 *trillion* to the world economy, year after year, with compounding growth on top of that. Much of this would go to the poorest workers, and much would go to everyone else.

No other policy comes even close to having the same potential to address world poverty. Even allowing poor foreigners short-term work in rich societies vastly outperforms aid in terms of development potential. A recent study compared the economic effects of short-term work by farmers from Haiti in the United States, where no US workers are available. Comparing these to the effects of more traditional assistance, the study found that the policy raised workers' earnings on average by a staggering fifteen times.[36]

---

[34] For example, ANGUS DEATON, THE GREAT ESCAPE 268–74 (2013); CHRISTOPHER COYNE, DOING BAD BY DOING GOOD (2013); Hristos Doucouliagos and Martin Paldam, "The Aid Effectiveness Literature: The Sad Results of 40 Years of Research," 23 J. ECON. SURV. 433 (2009).

[35] Michael Clemens, "Economics and Immigration: Trillion Dollar Bills on the Sidewalk," 25 J. ECON. PERSPECTIVES 83 (2011).

[36] See Michael Clemens and Hannah Postel, "Shared Harvest: Temporary Work Visas as US-Haiti Development Cooperation," *Center for Global Development Briefs* (1/23/17), available at www.cgdev.org/shared-harvest-temporary-work-visas-us-haiti-development-cooperation.

Notice the difference between how classical liberals and left-liberals approach this problem. Some on the Left see the third world is stuck in poverty, and advocate a zero-sum transfer of wealth. On their view, justice makes the first world a loser and the third world a winner. Some on the Left deny this; they say the first world is permitted to focus entirely on internal redistribution and is not obligated to redistribute to the third world.[37] Still, this view also presumes that helping the third world must come at the first world's expense. But the classical liberal defense of open borders is positive-sum: immigration helps both people in the third world and those in the first world.

Classical liberals do not simply claim that open borders would lead to tremendous economic growth. They also claim that we owe each other the right to immigrate as a matter of respect. Consider this thought experiment, from Michael Huemer:

Starvin' Marvin

Starvin' Marvin heads to the market looking for food. Marvin has little to trade. However, suppose there are people at the market willing to trade food for whatever Marvin has. Imagine that unless someone stops him, Marvin will successfully get to the market, make the trade, and eat. However, now imagine that you forcibly prevent Marvin from getting to the market. You post guards to keep him out. The guards continually capture Marvin and turn him away. Marvin can't barter for food. He starves and dies.[38]

In this situation, Huemer contends, Marvin's blood is on your hands. You do not simply *fail to help* Marvin. Instead, you *actively hurt* Marvin by using violence to prevent him from making a trade with a willing partner.

Huemer contends that immigration restrictions are analogous to the Starvin' Marvin case. Such restrictions impose poverty, suffering, and death on some of the most vulnerable people in the world. Some people in rich countries want to hire poor foreigners. The foreigners want the jobs. These jobs can sometimes make the difference between life and death. But the United States and other countries post armed sentries around their markets.

Of course, there are a large number of objections to opening borders. Some of these objections are empirical: opponents claim open borders will lead to crime or strain public goods. Others are philosophical: opponents claim that countries have a special right to refuse immigrants.

I will not try to refute these objections here.[39] Still, I provide a general formula for a response. If someone claims that open borders would produce some bad outcome,

---

[37] For example, DAVID MILLER, ON NATIONALITY (1995). Miller has long argued that egalitarian redistribution is justified inside single countries but not between countries.

[38] This paraphrases Michael Huemer, "Is There a Right to Immigrate?" 36 SOC.THEORY PRACT. 429 (2010).

[39] For a lengthy response, see BAS VAN DER VOSSEN AND JASON BRENNAN, GLOBAL JUSTICE AS GLOBAL FREEDOM chapters 2–4 (Forthcoming).

they first need to provide us with real evidence that it would indeed cause that outcome. Speculation is not enough. Second, they need a good argument about why it would be the government's job to try to cause that outcome. For instance, even if we admit that open borders might, say, eliminate France's distinctive music scene, that would not obviously be sufficient to justify immigration restrictions. At the very least, the benefits outweigh the costs. Third, we need to know why the argument for closing borders between countries does not also imply we should close borders within countries. For instance, if "stopping crime" were a good reason to forbid Mexicans from immigrating to the United States, would it also not be a good reason for Vermont to forbid white people from West Virginia or black people from Washington, DC from immigrating? Fourth, we need to know why the argument does not also suggest giving the government a host of other illiberal powers. For instance, Paul Collier worries that immigrants from illiberal countries bring their dysfunctional cultures with them, and for that reason should be forbidden from immigrating to liberal countries.[40] But, if he is willing to override a presumptive freedom of movement to protect liberal culture, then this suggests he would be willing to override, say, freedom of speech for illiberal groups, if doing so is necessary to protect liberal culture.

CONCLUSION

Classical liberalism began as a humanitarian philosophy. Perhaps it was lost in the wilderness in the twentieth century. But, no matter, to humanitarianism it has returned.

One upshot of all this is that, at least within the broad liberal camp, the interesting debates are now mostly questions of political economy (about how institutions work) rather than basic moral philosophy. The debate is not so much about matters but what mix of institutions will be best deliver shared liberal goals.

The classical liberal lesson is that we have to work with the crooked timber of human nature. We should look to design institutions that create positive-sum interactions, that incentivize largely selfish people to work to help rather than prey upon each other. When we think about what we want our institutions to do, we have to evaluate them based on how they are likely to work, not based on the nobleness of our intentions. We have to take seriously the idea that the very tools we create to achieve our goals might instead undermine them. In short, the debate now is more about identifying and weighing market and government failures and market and government successes.

---

[40] PAUL COLLIER, EXODUS: HOW MIGRATION IS CHANGING OUR WORLD 68 (2013).

3

More and Better

Resources Defined through Property and Exchange

Art Carden

INTRODUCTION

John Locke's famous principle of property acquisition by first-user appropriation came with a proviso specifying what had to be left for others. Some of Locke's critics have suggested that the proviso – that one can withdraw an object from the commons as long as one leaves "enough, and as good" for others – is self-contradictory because to remove an object from the commons necessarily leaves less for others to appropriate. Appropriation and the ensuing social process creates abundance that does not impede another's ability to obtain property.

Furthermore, private property rights help us determine through experiment and exchange which objects are actually goods. Finally, rental income to land and natural resources is very small as a percentage of national income, so if there was an injustice in appropriation of rights by first users it is reflected in a very small share in national income today.

First-user appropriation does not merely leave "enough, and as good." It contributes to a positive-sum process that generates "more, and better."[1] First-user appropriation does more than this, though. By bringing objects into the realm of property and exchange, first-user appropriation contributes to a process by which we can determine whether or not an object is a *resource* in that we can identify ways to use it to satisfy wants. More important than the mixture of labor with objects withdrawn from the commons is the mixture of knowledge with those objects. Institutions encouraging voluntary cooperation and market exchange – classical liberal institutions – comprise a set of mechanisms that allow us to harness knowledge we ourselves do not

---

[1] David Schmidtz, "The Institution of Private Property," in DAVID SCHIMDTZ AND ELIZABETH WILLOW, ENVIRONMENTAL ETHICS: WHAT REALLY MATTERS, WHAT REALLY WORKS (2011). Reprinted in JONATHAN ANOMALY, GEOFFREY BRENNAN, MICHAEL C. MUNGER, AND GEOFFREY SAYRE-MCCORD, EDS. PHILOSOPHY, POLITICS, AND ECONOMICS: AN ANTHOLOGY 147–59 (2015).

have, stored in minds that are not ours, and acquired for purposes we do not ourselves know. The knowledge-harnessing capability of these institutions is rooted in private property. By drawing objects into the processes that make this possible, first-user appropriation specifically and property rights more generally fulfill Locke's proviso that we must leave "enough, and as good."

ORIGINAL APPROPRIATION LEADS TO MORE AND BETTER

Vernon Smith defines "property" as "that over which an individual human, or association of humans, exercises some priority of action with respect to other humans."[2] There is a large and well-documented literature on how private property rights are essential for prosperity; indeed, Smith (2008:18) writes as much, noting that property rights are necessary for "self-sustaining economic development and the reduction of poverty."[3] Smith's "priority of action" is similar to North's statement that "(t)he essence of property rights is the right to exclude."[4] Property rights are an essential element of economic freedom, and the literature on the salutary effects of economic freedom is summarized by Hall and Lawson.[5]

The study of property rights and how they develop is central the problem of explaining economic change over time. North put it this way:

> For the economic historian, the key problems are to explain the kind of property rights that come to be specified and enforced by the state and to explain the effectiveness of enforcement; the most interesting challenge is to account for changes in the structure and enforcement of property rights over time.[6]

I am attempting nothing so ambitious as a complete accounting for the emergence and development of property rights. Rather, I am exploring how one theory of property and how it is established, specifically, Locke's notion of original appropriation, is defensible because it kickstarts the processes by which goods emerge and by which we achieve Smith's "self-sustaining economic development and the reduction of poverty."

Locke begins with the assumption that everything is owned in common, but survival requires that people withdraw objects from the commons and deploying them for their own purposes, the most rudimentary of which will be food and protection from the elements. John Locke defended appropriation of objects out the commons and transformation of those objects into *property*:

---

[2]   VERNON SMITH, RATIONALITY IN ECONOMICS: CONSTRUCTIVIST AND ECOLOGICAL FORMS 17 (2008).
[3]   Id at 2018.
[4]   DOUGLASS C. NORTH, STRUCTURE AND CHANGE IN ECONOMIC HISTORY 21 (1981).
[5]   Joshua C. Hall and Robert A. Lawson, "Economic Freedom of the World: An Accounting of the Literature," 32 CONTEMPORARY ECONOMIC POLICY 1 (2014).
[6]   DOUGLASS C. NORTH, STRUCTURE AND CHANGE IN ECONOMIC HISTORY 21 (1981).

Though the earth, and all inferiour creatures, be common to all men, yet every man has a property in his own person: this nobody has any right to but himself. The labour of the body, and the work of his hands, we may say, are properly his. Whatsoever then he removes out of the state that nature hath provided, and left it in, he hath mixed his labour with, and joined to it something that is his own, and thereby makes it his property.[7]

There is a (possible) catch, what came to known as the "Lockean proviso":

... this labour being the unquestionable property of the laborer, no man but he can have a right to what that is once joined to, at least where there is *enough, and as good*, left in common for others.[8]

At first glance, the proviso seems like a contradiction. The universe contains a finite number of objects, and to remove an object from the commons means fewer objects are available for others. Schmidtz summarizes several claims that the Lockean proviso makes property appropriation logically impossible.[9] As he explains, it seems obvious to many critics of the Lockean proviso that those who come first are the truly lucky ones, and their good luck comes at the expense of those who no longer have access to the resources-cum-property. "If we take something out of the cookie jar, we *must* be leaving less for others. This appears self-evident. It has to be right." Schmidtz continues: "But it's not right."

Why not? Schmidtz makes the important point that private property turns zero-sum or negative-sum tragedies of the commons into positive-sum opportunities for exchange. Appropriation does more than leave "as much and as good." It makes *more and better* possible by establishing clear rights to *exclude* others from the use of an object and, therefore, the need to persuade others through deliberation or exchange to use an object in a certain way.

One might object that as a matter of justice the first appropriator is luckier than the one who comes after. This isn't obvious, however. There is certainly a degree of luck to the initial allocations of property in land and other objects found in nature, but the first appropriator is now "lucky" enough to be responsible with turning a (superficially) disordered and chaotic plot of ground into something conducive to want satisfaction. Those who get the property *first* are not necessarily the lucky ones. Property is not autonomously productive. To use the simplest example, land is a stubborn servant that must be carefully tended if it is to be kept clear of the briars, thorns, and weeds that get in the way of nutritious foodstuffs. Plants growing on land that has been cleared, fertilized, and tended still require careful attention lest they be devoured by pests.

---

[7] John Locke, Two Treatises of Government 145–46 (1824) [1690]

[8] Id at 146, emphasis added.

[9] Schmidtz, *supra* note 45.

Property is necessary for economic growth because of the incentives it creates.[10] A property owner has the right to exclude others from its use and, therefore, the right to exclude others from what that property can be used to produce. He has, in short, the right to exclude others from all future output accruing to a piece of land or other asset and, therefore, incorporates into her decisions the actions she takes that might compromise the fertility of the property. He has a right to the net present value of what the property can produce and therefore has an incentive to augment rather than consume the property's productive capacity to the greatest extent possible. Secure property rights convert the commons with its attendant tragedies into resources people have strong incentives to use wisely.

GOODS DEFINED IN THE PROCESS OF THEIR EMERGENCE

A turn toward liberty and a widespread embrace of free markets, private property, and voluntary exchange have created a cornucopia in the world's richest countries, and the diffusion of these institutions globally has led to a large-scale global exodus out of extreme poverty, with the share of the world's population living on less than $2 per day falling from year to year.[11] Property is not only important in that it has contributed to the cornucopia. It is also important in that it has helped us define the cornucopia's contents. Appropriation more than satisfies Locke's "enough, and as good" proviso because it allows us to define which objects are, in fact, actually *goods*.

The concepts of "enough" and "as good" require reference points. Enough – of what? As good – as what? "Enough" and "as good" have meaning with reference to individual wants, and it is by experience with objects withdrawn from the commons that we are able to ascertain the relationship between the objects' attributes and our wants.

For the Lockean proviso to be logically impossible, something would already have to be identifiable as a resource before it is removed from the commons. An object is a resource if someone can use it to satisfy a want, but whether something is a resource or not is a function of human ingenuity, not the innate characteristics of the object.[12] We take objects out of the commons on the expectation that they will be resources, and then trial and error shows us which objects are resources and which objects are not. Appropriation is not a barrier to "enough, and as good" for others. It initiates the process by which objects are defined as resources and goods – and the process by which we can learn what "enough" and "as good" mean.

---

[10] McCloskey (2010) notes that while property rights are necessary for economic growth, they are not sufficient. DEIRDRE N. MCCLOSKEY, BOURGEOIS DIGNITY: WHY ECONOMICS CAN'T EXPLAIN THE MODERN WORLD (2010).

[11] Xavier Sala-i-Martin, "The World Distribution of Income: Falling Poverty and ... Convergence, Period," 121 QUARTERLY JOURNAL OF ECONOMICS 351 (2006).

[12] JULIAN SIMON, THE ULTIMATE RESOURCE 2 (1996).

A good, to adapt and combine definitions from Menger (1871) and Debreu (1954), is an object with physical, temporal, and spatial characteristics suitable for the satisfaction of a want and available in sufficient quantity as to satisfy the want.[13] In an abstract sense, objects in the commons can be defined in terms of their physical, temporal, and spatial characteristics – the what, when, and where of an object where the "what" is a description of its chemical structure and objectively measurable properties. For example, what we call "dirt" could be an amalgam of atoms and molecules of a given weight and taking up a specified amount of space with a location defined by a vector linking it to some stellar reference point. In the abstract, this is conceivable.

If we were armed with sufficient knowledge of chemistry and physics we could describe these properties of all objects in the universe. They would not, however, tell us anything useful about the relationship between the objects' attributes and their suitability for satisfying wants. An object can only be a resource or a good if we have a reasonable expectation that it can be used to satisfy wants and if we are willing to consume time and treasure to obtain it. The relationship between an object's attributes and want satisfaction is learned through experience, and by that experience the object comes to be defined as a good with reference to that experience. The appropriator learns from the experience and mixes this knowledge with the properties of the object in order to define it as a good with reference to his wants. Importantly, he need not know the physical, temporal, and spatial attributes of the good or the physical and chemical mechanisms by which it produces a particular effect when acted upon in a given way. He only has to believe that a good satisfies a want and be in a position to learn whether that belief is accurate, but that learning is crucial to defining an object withdrawn from the commons as a resource or a good.

Trial and error generates knowledge about the relationship between goods and want satisfaction. In our rudest states, we want for food and protection from the elements, and hence we experiment by removing objects from the commons and asking "can I eat this?" and "will that protect me from the wind, the sun, and the rain?" Experience – sometimes very harsh experience – shows us which objects satisfy wants and which do not.

The idea that we know independent of experience and exchange the goods-character of objects in the commons is implicit in the objections to Locke's notion of original appropriation discussed by Schmidtz (2011).[14] As Buchanan (1982) wrote of order, the "good" is defined in the process of its emergence: appropriation, experiment, and exchange together form a mechanism by which people ascertain an object's capacity to satisfy wants.[15] In this light, "enough" and "as good" are

---

[13] Gerard DeBreu, Theory of Value (1954); Carl Menger, Principles of Economics (2007) [1871].
[14] Schmidtz, supra note 42.
[15] James M. Buchanan, "Order Defined in the Process of Its Emergence" (1982), in James M. Buchanan, David Gordon, Israel Kirzner, et al., "Readers' Forum, Comments on 'The

concepts embedded in social context. They are identified and given meaning as people appraise the objects they confront in the process of appropriation, experiment, and exchange.

As societies become more complex and as division of labor proceeds, we are able to refine our wants and move past our most basic needs for food and shelter. We cooperate with others, and as the division of labor proceeds and more transactions come to be mediated by market prices, our social experiments take the form of buying and selling while in principle revolving around the same question: "will this satisfy a want?" The wants are not as extreme – "will this cup of coffee provide me with more satisfaction than anything else I could get for $2 at the moment?" is not as urgent as "will eating the berries on that bush keep me from starving?" – but the principles and processes surrounding their satisfaction are the same. We learn by trial and error.

Appropriation is a convenient mechanism for learning about and acting upon objects' properties with minimal conflict. People enter the world with different skills that they can use to satisfy their preferences subject to scarcity.[16] Scarcity means that our ideas about what is to be done will almost inevitably come into conflict with one another as it is exceedingly unlikely that we will reach conclusions about what is to be done with each object we encounter.

In addition to material and temporal constraints – there are only so many objects, and decisions and deliberation consume valuable time – we are bound by moral and cognitive constraints. "The qualities of the mind," according to Hume (1896), "are *selfishness* and *limited generosity*."[17] Hume's friend Adam Smith (1776) and, almost two centuries later, F. A. Hayek (1948) would emphasize the cognitive constraints.[18] These unhappy imperfections are remedied by the fact that we can participate in society:

> In man alone, this unnatural conjunction of infirmity, and of necessity, may be observed in its greatest perfection. Not only the food, which is required for his sustenance, flies his search and approach, or at least requires his labour to be produc'd, but he must be possess'd of cloaths and lodging, to defend himself against the injuries of the weather; tho' to consider him only in himself, he is provided neither with arms, nor force, nor other natural abilities, which are in any degree answerable to so many necessities.
>
> 'Tis by society alone he is able to supply his defects, and raise himself up to an equality with his fellow-creatures, and even acquire a superiority above them.

Tradition of Spontaneous Order'" by Norman Barry. Library of Economics and Liberty. Online: http://econlib.org/library/Essays/LtrLbrty/bryRF1.html.

[16] Cf. David Hume, A Treatise of Human Nature 514 (1896) [1739].

[17] Id at 494.

[18] Adam Smith, An Inquiry into the Nature and Causes of the Wealth of Nations (1904) [1776], Edwin Cannan, ed. Library of Economics and Liberty. Online: www.econlib.org/library/Smith/smWN.html; F. A. Hayek, Individualism and Economic Order (1948).

By society all his infirmities are compensated; and tho' in that situation his wants multiply every moment upon him, yet his abilities are still more augmented, and leave him in every respect more satisfied and happy, than 'tis possible for him, in his savage and solitary condition, ever to become.[19]

Property and exchange are the stuff of a commercial society in which people are competing with one another for the privilege of using goods in the ways they see fit. As Smith emphasized at the beginning of *The Wealth of Nations*, the particular attribute of the kind of society in which, in Hume's words, "all his infirmities are compensated" and "his abilities are still more augmented" is the division of labor. Mises (1920) and Hayek (1945, 1948) would later show that a complex division of labor requires prices for – and therefore private ownership of – the means of production.[20] Hayek (2002) argues that "Which goods are scarce, however, or which things are goods, or how scarce or valuable they are, is precisely one of the conditions that competition should discover."[21]

Prices emerge as substitutes for direct apprehension and experience as the division of labor deepens and grows more complex. People have different talents, tastes, expectations, and capacities for mental, physical, and moral effort. Economic *rivalry*, which Lavoie (1985) defines as "the clash of human purposes," can be resolved in a system of private property rights as it helps us reconcile our different talents and tastes and negotiate our way to coordination of otherwise mutually-incompatible plans.[22] It "is a necessary component of the entrepreneurial market process [that] leads to a beneficial coordinating process that makes complex capitalist production in a monetary system possible".[23] Competitive bids and offers for labor, consumption goods, capital goods, and natural resources capture people's ever-evolving beliefs and expectations about the wants that can be satisfied by using and combining objects that have been revealed as resources.

Smith (2008) identifies an important problem with respect to how we theorize about social systems: "The personal knowledge that underlies specialization and exchange at any time is dispersed, private, and therefore asymmetric in all social systems."[24] The problem applies to how we theorize about property. Appropriation and exchange are processes whereby we identify heretofore undiscovered attributes of objects previously in the commons, but those attributes are context-dependent, emerging from their interaction with the "artifactual structure" they confront when

---

[19] DAVID HUME, A TREATISE OF HUMAN NATURE 485 (1896) [1739].

[20] LUDWIG VON MISES, ECONOMIC CALCULATION IN THE SOCIALIST COMMONWEALTH (1920), S. Adler, trans. available at: www.mises.org; F. A. HAYEK, INDIVIDUALISM AND ECONOMIC ORDER (1948).

[21] F. A. Hayek, "Competition as a Discovery Procedure," 5 QUARTERLY JOURNAL OF AUSTRIAN ECONOMICS 9, 13 (2002).

[22] DON LAVOIE, RIVALRY AND CENTRAL PLANNING: THE SOCIALIST CALCULATION DEBATE RECONSIDERED 22 (1985).

[23] Id at 22.

[24] Smith, supra note 43 at 7.

removed from the commons.[25] The attributes conducive to want satisfaction are revealed in experiment and exchange, and they are in this sense inseparable from the social process. Appropriation and exchange allow us to care for one another without necessarily caring about one another in more than an abstract sense. By economizing on knowledge and transmitting it through the price mechanism, property and exchange help us transcend our moral and cognitive limitations.

APPROPRIATION SATISFIES EGALITARIAN CRITERIA

Is appropriation objectionable on the grounds that it reduces the range of potentially-appropriable objects available to others? I don't think it is for several reasons. First, by bringing objects into the realm of exchange, appropriation leads to more and better; it doesn't simply leave "enough, and as good."[26] Second, appropriation brings objects into a private property system that makes use of everyone's social knowledge without privileging the knowledge of a surrogate who arrives late on the scene. Third, we identify the relationships between objects' attributes and our wants via appropriation, experiment, and exchange. Continuing on, appropriation is defensible in other ways, as well.

Fourth, as Schmidtz (2011) points out, the appropriator is not the lucky one.[27] The latecomer is. Eroding property rights erodes others' rights – the latecomers in particular – to benefit from one's use of property.[28]

It is unclear what crime the first appropriator has committed against someone who shows up later and who was not "fortunate" enough to arrive on the scene before our ancestor's experience helped define the objects before him. The latecomer may not be able to appropriate his own land – hardly likely in our ancient past, however – but he benefits from the first appropriator's acquisition and use of property because he now has at his disposal all of our ancestor's knowledge embodied in the plants he is cultivating and the animals he is pasturing. He can harness this through exchange, which allows him to deploy our ancestor's knowledge – knowledge which the latecomer does not have – for his own purposes.

The latecomer has an opportunity to participate in a more extensive division of labor, and he had access to knowledge embodied in objects that was not available to the first appropriator and that, in fact, had to be created by that first appropriator and his trading partners. Someone who strikes oil while digging a backyard garden is fortunate because we now know the properties of oil conducive to want satisfaction. Someone who strikes oil while scratching the ground five hundred or a thousand or ten thousand years ago is not fortunate in the same way because, at the time, we had

---

[25] The term "artefactual structure" is from North (2005).
[26] Cf. Schmidtz, *supra* note 42.
[27] Id.
[28] Smith, *supra* note 43 at 17.

not yet discovered the characteristics of oil that make it valuable today. The first appropriator could make use of objects with at-the-time undiscovered properties. His descendants can make use of objects that embody the knowledge of the ages and that have become *goods*. If anyone is fortunate, it is the latecomer. He can deploy the wisdom of the ages. His ancestors had to create it.

Fifth, the initial distribution of land and natural resources does not, as such, matter that much as a determinant of national income. Moller (2017) points out that the vast majority of income in the United States accrues to labor income, with rental income to land making up less than 5 percent of national income.[29] Income accruing to ownership of natural resources *as such* is insufficient as a source of modern inequality. Moreover, the gains from industrialization went primarily to unskilled workers, not the owners of land and capital.[30]

CONCLUSION

Locke's proviso that the property appropriator needs to leave "enough, and as good" is not the contradiction it seems. For reasons explored by David Schmidtz, appropriation converts a negative-sum war of all against all in the commons into a positive-sum game of cooperation and exchange. Second, it isn't at all clear what "enough, and as good" mean apart from the experiments that emerge due to private property and exchange.

Property rights become especially important the more complex a society becomes and as the division of labor grows finer. When the size and scope of the market increase, the number of voices that have to be considered increases, as well, and it becomes even more difficult to identify the valuable attributes of goods and services without reference to prices formed in competitive markets.

That something is a "resource" is usually assumed by participants in debates over property rights, but for an object to be a resource we need to be able to identify ways in which it can be employed to satisfy wants. This can only happen when an object is removed from the commons and then subjected to trial-and-error processes of experiment and exchange. In short, property rights are prerequisites for the emergence of the knowledge required before we are to know whether something is or is not a resource.

Finally, appropriation is robust to egalitarian objections. The latecomer can take advantage of the knowledge obtained by the first appropriator and by all those who came before, and in a wealthier society in which the vast majority of national

---

[29] Dan Moller, "Property and the Creation of Value," 33 Economics and Philosophy, 1–23 (2017); See the series "Rental Income of Persons" (without Capital Consumption Adjustment), available at https://fred.stlouisfed.org/series/B049RC1A027NBEA. Last accessed Thursday, February 16, 2017.

[30] Gregory Clark, A Farewell to Alms: A Brief Economic History of the World 230–58 (2007).

income comes from services, original appropriation does not appear to be an insurmountable barrier to those who wish to own land or other natural resources.

The future of classical liberalism as an intellectual program should explore the knowledge-generating properties of alternative property rights arrangements. As a political program, classical liberals should pursue reforms that bring more and more objects into the realm of private property and exchange so that they can be deployed in a process that makes maximal use of social knowledge. Private property is useful as a process characteristic when we consider the development of a Great Society, to borrow the language of Adam Smith. While individual situations might give us pause as to the degree to which we should have faith in others to use liberty and property wisely, the downstream consequences of interfering with individual choices – even bad ones – are difficult if not impossible to foresee.

4

The Boundaries of Antidiscrimination Laws

David E. Bernstein

Perhaps nothing is more harmful to the libertarian "brand" than skepticism of antidiscrimination laws that apply to private parties. When he was running for Senate in 2010, Senator Rand Paul, a Republican with libertarian leanings, expressed his doubts about the provision of the 1964 Civil Rights Act that bans discrimination in restaurants, hotels, and other businesses. Bloggers and editorialists responded with a deluge of negative, and often unfair or inaccurate, commentary about the libertarian position on antidiscrimination laws.

The most serious charge has been that libertarian skepticism of antidiscrimination laws that apply to private entities reflects, at best, insensitivity to race discrimination. One blogger, reflecting a significant swath of progressive sentiment, argued that no matter how committed to racial egalitarianism any individual libertarian claims to be, "Libertarianism is a racist philosophy. Libertarians are racists."

This is a rather odd criticism. For both philosophical and utilitarian reasons, libertarians are presumptively strongly opposed to any government regulation of the private sector. It naturally follows that libertarians, while strongly opposed to racial discrimination by the government, presumptively oppose restrictions on private sector discrimination. It's hardly an indication of racial animus, or even insensitivity, for libertarians to enunciate the exact same position on antidiscrimination laws that they take in all other contexts.

The progressive libel of libertarians as racial troglodytes for their consistent defense of private-sector autonomy is ironic, given that similar illogic has so frequently been used against modern liberals. When liberals defended communists' free speech and employment rights in the 1950s, their critics accused them of being communist sympathizers, if not outright communists. More recently, progressives have been accused of being American-hating jihadist sympathizers when they stood up for the rights of terrorism suspects. Critics have also charged liberal civil libertarians with abetting racism for opposing hate speech laws.

The hate speech example is particularly telling. Some progressives argue that if libertarians were more sensitive to the concerns of minorities, they would sacrifice their anti-statist principles to the goddess of antidiscrimination. If so, progressives should similarly sacrifice their support for freedom of speech. In fact, some have. But as yet, the American Civil Liberties Union (ACLU), the bellweather of liberal civil libertarian sentiment, has maintained its strict opposition to government punishment of hate speech.

Confronted with the hate speech analogy, progressives of a civil libertarian bent will typically reply that supporting freedom of speech is completely different from supporting the right to engage in discriminatory action. After all, speech is just speech – sticks and stones, and whatnot – while discriminatory actions cause real distress to the victims. And besides, they argue, the marketplace of ideas can be trusted to ensure that egalitarian views will emerge victorious.

This argument does not stand up to close scrutiny. Hate speech can harm members of minority by directly causing psychological distress or inciting violence. And indirect harms from hate speech can be catastrophic if advocates of racist views are able to win control of the government. While minorities can generally find productive economic niches in even highly prejudiced but market-oriented societies, there is no safe haven for minorities if racist ideas dominate politics and lead to harsh discriminatory legislation.

Also, a free economic market protects minorities from discrimination to some degree because businesspeople have an economic incentive to hire the most productive workers and to obtain the most customers. By contrast, individual voters and political activists have no corresponding incentive to overlook or overcome their personal prejudices. Concern for the financial bottom line mitigates the temptation of economic entrepreneurs to discriminate; concern for the electoral bottom line, meanwhile, often leads politicians to stir up resentment against minorities. If anything, then, if one is concerned with the rights of minorities and has faith in the regulatory capacities of government, speech should be a more fruitful target for regulation than the economic marketplace.

As suggested earlier, supporters of antidiscrimination laws typically focus on laws banning racial discrimination. They do so because opposition to race discrimination has great historical and emotional resonance in a nation that had institutionalized racial oppression, including chattel slavery, for hundreds of years. However, federal antidiscrimination laws also apply to discrimination based on religion, sex, age, disability (including one's status as a recovering drug or alcohol addict), pregnancy, marital status, veteran status, and more. State and local antidiscrimination laws cover everything from sexual orientation to political ideology to weight to appearance to membership in a motorcycle gang.

The proliferation of antidiscrimination laws explains why even libertarians who are especially sensitive to America's history of racism are loath to concede the principle that the government may ban private sector discrimination. There is no natural limit to the scope of antidiscrimination laws, because the concept of anti-discrimination is almost infinitely malleable. Almost any economic behavior, and much other behavior, can be defined as discrimination. Whom people employ, befriend, marry, and love are all products of one sort of discrimination or another, including discrimination based on education level, discrimination based on family connection, discrimination based on looks, and discrimination based on personality.

The obvious retort is that antidiscrimination laws should be limited to "real" discrimination. But there is no consensus as to what constitutes "real" discrimin-ation, nor, not surprisingly, does there appear to be any principled definition that legislatures have followed.

One can, for example, define discrimination as treating the alike unequally, but antidiscrimination law does not always follow this definition. Federal antidiscrimi-nation law, for example, requires employers not simply to treat disabled and non-disabled alike, but to make costly "reasonable accommodations" for the disabled. Employers have the same legal obligation to their religious employees.

In short, to concede the general power of government to redress private discrimin-ation through legislation would be to concede virtually unlimited power to the government. Libertarians, however, are often willing to make certain exceptions to their opposition to antidiscrimination laws, so long as they can identify an appropri-ate limiting principle.

Consistent with long-standing classical liberal suspicion of monopolies, many libertarians would allow the government to ban discrimination by such entities. Even more libertarians would endorse antidiscrimination laws applied to monop-olies that were created or sustained by government edict, including labor monop-olies. For example, once the Wagner Act of 1935 granted American labor unions the exclusive power to represent workers, it was not "unlibertarian" for civil rights groups to try to file lawsuits seeking to guarantee that those unions represent all employees without discrimination.[1] The Anglo-American common law, much beloved by liber-tarian legal scholars, required at least some public accommodations – particularly those granted exclusive government charters or otherwise exercising monopoly prerogatives – to serve all comers.

This brings us back to the issue that got Rand Paul into hot water: Title II of the 1964 Civil Rights Act, which prohibited discrimination in public accommodations. One prominent commentator, Bruce Bartlett, has suggested that libertarian oppos-ition to Title II should serve as a reminder that the existence and persistence of Jim Crow in the South reflected libertarian sensibilities.[2]

---

[1] See David E. Bernstein, "Civil Rights and the Right to Work," Reason.com, Feb. 2016, http://reason.com/archives/2016/01/17/civil-rights-and-the-right-to.

[2] David E. Bernstein, Bruce Bartlett's Attack on Libertarianism, Volokh.com, May 20, 2010, http://volokh.com/2010/05/20/bruce-bartletts-attack-on-libertarians.

Bartlett's position is incoherent philosophically, and counterfactual historically. From a philosophical perspective, libertarianism and Jim Crow laws are completely at odds. Consistent with their classical liberal heritage, libertarians believe that the government must treat all its citizens as individuals with equal rights, and therefore may not discriminate on arbitrary grounds, like race. The government must also apply its laws fairly and impartially, including by protecting members of unpopular minority groups from private violence. A penumbra of this opposition to government discrimination is that the right to vote must not be denied for arbitrary reasons. Finally, the government may not require private parties to discriminate.

Historically, many of the leading advocates of civil rights for African Americans in the late nineteenth and early twentieth century – for example, Moorfield Storey, the first president of the National Association for the Advancement of Colored People (NAACP) – were, if not hardcore libertarians, at least classical liberal fellow travelers. In more modern times, the few prominent libertarian commentators of the early 1960s, such as Ayn Rand and Milton Friedman, supported the provisions of the 1964 Civil Rights Act that banned discrimination by state and local government officials. Conservatives, by contrast, typically bought into the notion of "States' Rights."

Rand, Friedman, and other libertarians, however, opposed on principle the application of antidiscrimination laws to private parties. Many libertarians today, however, think our predecessors were wrong in their blanket opposition to such laws, in part because they neglected some of the legal and historical context.

First, the absence of formal discriminatory legislation did not mean that libertarian principle was being respected. I've already noted that the common law barred discrimination in places of public accommodation. After the Civil War, courts, both north and south, manipulated, changed, or ignored their preexisting common law to deprive African Americans the benefit of that rule. Similarly, courts that consistently invalidated minor contractual restraints on the alienation of private property nevertheless upheld ethnically restrictive covenants that at times barred most of the residents of a given city from purchasing encumbered properties. The refusal to apply a general legal rule because the beneficiaries would be African Americans was a violation of their right to equal protection of the law.

Second, to say the least, segregation and exclusion of African Americans in public places in the South wasn't entirely a voluntary choice of business owners. Jim Crow segregation involved the equivalent of a white supremacist cartel[3] The cartel was enforced not just by overt government regulation like segregation laws, but also by the implicit threat of private violence and extralegal harassment of anyone who challenged the racist status quo. This violence and extra-legal harassment was often undertaken with the approval of local officials; the latter, in fact, were often the perpetrators.

[3]   See Damon Root, The Party of Jefferson, Reason.com, http://reason.com/archives/2007/11/27/the-party-of-jefferson.

To break the southern Jim Crow cartel there were three plausible options: (1) non-violent protest by civil rights activists; (2) a federal law invalidating Jim Crow laws, along with a massive federal takeover of local government to prevent violence and threats against, and extralegal harassment of, those who chose to integrate; or (3) a federal law banning discrimination by private parties, so that threats of violence and harassment would generally be met with an appeal to the potential victim's obligation to obey federal law.

Non-violent protest achieved some successes, such as desegregating lunch counters at chain stores in the South. These successes, however, were not necessarily scalable. Around the same time, non-violent "freedom riders" were being severely beaten and abused in small towns across the South, with the connivance or participation of local officials, for daring to try to desegregate interstate buses.[4] What happened to the freedom riders was likely more indicative of the challenges faced by activists than were the successes achieved by the sit-ins. After all, only about twenty percent of white southerners supported desegregation in 1964, and a century of evidence suggests that a majority of white Southerners were willing to use violence and intimidation to maintain Jim Crow.

In any event, libertarians need not be committed to pure political pacifism. If state and local governments are participating in and nurturing a racist cartel, it seems perfectly "libertarian" to resort to the next level of government, in this case the federal government, to resolve the problem. Admittedly, lodging authority with the federal government potentially creates its own problems. It's even more problematic, however, to expect social activists to risk life and limb to overturn an unjust system.

This brings us to option 2, a federal takeover of local government, has some appeal from a libertarian perspective, as it could have ensured that local political power was no longer put in the service of maintaining segregation. Such a takeover, however, would have been completely impractical, and, even if somehow accomplished would have destroyed what's left of American federalism, to the great detriment of liberty.

This leaves us with option 3, a federal law banning discrimination against private parties. This is what the federal government in fact did in 1964. At the time, most observers thought that the law would be ineffective, and that, for example, it would take decades of federal efforts to desegregate public accommodations such as restaurants. In fact, with the Jim Crow cartel broken, desegregation efforts were almost immediately, widely successful.[5] Not surprisingly, many prominent libertarians who have commented on the issue recently have stated that they would have voted for the 1964 Civil Rights Act, including its public accommodations provisions, to break the Jim Crow cartel that had used a combination of legislation, public and

---

[4] See RAYMOND ARSENAULT, FREEDOM RIDERS: 1961 AND THE STRUGGLE FOR RACIAL JUSTICE (2006).
[5] See, for example, CLAY RISEN, THE BILL OF THE CENTURY (2014).

private violence, and unequal protection of the laws, to enforce the discriminatory preferences of the white majority.

Nevertheless, critics of the libertarian position on antidiscrimination laws argue that to avoid being deemed reactionary or irrelevant, libertarians must more generally abandon their opposition to private sector antidiscrimination laws. Indeed, Governor Gary Johnson, the Libertarian Party candidate for president in 2012 and 2016, seemed to take this advice to heart in his attempt to run a "mainstream" campaign. At one point, Johnson went so far as to agree that a Jewish bakery owner should be required to bake a cake with Nazi symbols requested by a customer.[6]

Besides the political ramifications of opposing popular civil rights legislation, many critics of adopting a laissez-faire posture toward discrimination in the private sector seem to believe that antidiscrimination laws somehow magically transform members of despised minority groups into full equal citizens in the eyes of the majority. Even a generally sober commentator like George Will believes that Title II of the 1964 Civil Rights Act "not only got African-Americans into public accommodations, [but] changed the thinking of the white portion of the country as well."[7]

Antidiscrimination laws can plausibly accelerate trends toward greater tolerance of minorities. These laws can also force a local majority, such as southern whites in the 1960s, to heed the values of a national majority, such as non-southern whites, who by 1964 had turned strongly against racial segregation.

Antidiscrimination laws are unlikely, however, to provide much protection to a minority group when the majority of the voting population is hostile to that group. America's landmark civil rights legislation was enacted and implemented in the 1960s, when racial attitudes of whites had already liberalized substantially, especially in the North but to some extent in the South. By contrast, in the 1930s, when white public opinion was solidly hostile to African-Americans, liberal President Franklin Roosevelt refused to support even the anti-lynching legislation his Republican predecessors had supported. Roosevelt eventually supporting a weak federal fair employment law only because he was afraid that African American protests about employment exclusion might impede the nascent war effort.

Antidiscrimination laws, in other words, typically follow, rather than cause, the liberalization of attitudes toward minority groups. Contrary to conventional wisdom, the effect of antidiscrimination laws on public attitudes is rarely dramatic. Even the 1964 Civil Rights Act did not noticeably accelerate the pace of liberalization of whites' racial attitudes. The Act was surely not a panacea to racism. As late as 1995, only 48 percent of Americans approved of marriages between blacks and whites (compared to over 90 percent as of this writing).

---

[6]   Should a Jewish Baker Be Forced to Bake a Nazi Cake?, www.youtube.com/watch?v=
      COItiKtHWyg.
[7]   George Will, "Rand Paul Is 'Frivolous'," ABCNEWS.COM, May 23, 2010, http://blogs.abcnews
      .com/politicalpunch/2010/05/george-will-rand-paul-is-frivolous.html.

Given their strong anti-statist presumptions, libertarians will generally remain presumptively opposed to the panoply of modern private sector antidiscrimination laws. (This includes, by the way, libertarian opposition to conservative attempts to ban private sector affirmative action preferences.) Many libertarians, however, would likely support antidiscrimination laws if they evolved into default rules that parties could contract around if desired. For example, an antidiscrimination law could replace the common law "at will" employment with a default rule that no employer may discriminate based on a variety of criteria. If an employer nevertheless wished to retain the right to discriminate on one of the prohibited bases, it would have to acknowledge that desire to potential employees, and, therefore, inevitably to the public at large. The subject of default rules, however, requires significantly more attention than this chapter can give it.

Beyond that, the basic federal laws banning discrimination in employment, housing, and public accommodations, as originally conceived in 1964 – before the courts and civil rights bureaucracies devised problematic doctrines like "disparate impact" liability – were relatively benign. If everyone from farmers to military contractors to environmental groups is able to successfully lobby the government to protect their interests, it's not especially troubling that members of minority groups, who have more legitimate grievances than most legislative supplicants, also use legislation to protect their interests.

That doesn't mean that libertarians have some obligation to support basic private sector antidiscrimination legislation; rather, I think that from both a moral and tactical perspective, opposition to such legislation should be rather low on the libertarian priority list. Indeed, it would be troubling if there was a sudden popular move to repeal antidiscrimination legislation, if it were unaccompanied by broader libertarian political trends, because it would suggest that opposition to such laws came arose from hostility to minority groups, not from opposition to Big Government.

Libertarians can and should insist, however, that a line be drawn at the point where such laws infringe on the constitutional rights to freedom of speech, freedom of religion, expressive association, and other civil liberties. The drafters of the 1964 Civil Rights Act were reasonably sensitive to such concerns, and limited the scope of the Act accordingly. For example, religious organizations, small businesses, and private clubs were exempted from provisions of the Act. In the decades since, though, civil liberties have increasingly come to be seen by antidiscrimination activists as inconvenient and unnecessary obstacles to a discrimination-free world.

The result has been, for example, attempts to force private Christian schools to hire unmarried pregnant teachers, to suppress campus speech that allegedly creates a "hostile" (or more recently "unsafe") environment, to punish individuals who decline to accept gay roommates, and to prosecute neighborhood associations for objecting to the placement of halfway houses in their neighborhoods. (These and many more examples are documented in my 2003 book, *You Can't Say That! The Growing Threat to Civil Liberties from Antidiscrimination Laws.*)

The growing infringement of antidiscrimination laws on freedom of conscience has been primarily a product of overzealous administrative agencies and courts, rather than new legislation. Perhaps most notably, courts have held that laws prohibiting discrimination in "places of public accommodation" apply to parties, such as private membership organizations, that are not places, are not public, and are not accommodations, at least as these words are normally used in English.

Courts and administrative agencies have also been broadening the definition of what constitutes illegal "discrimination." Courts have held, for example that declining to bake a cake for a same-sex wedding constitutes illegal "discrimination" against customers based on sexual orientation. Assuming that a commercial bakery does not otherwise discriminate, this is wrong. The bakery is discriminating against participating in activities its owner considers immoral, but not because of his customers' sexual orientation. If a heterosexual customer had asked the bakery to prepare a cake for a same-sex wedding, the owner would have still declined. But if a gay couple had asked the bakery to bake a cake for an impending law school graduation, the owner would have agreed to do so. For that matter, if a same-sex couple that was heterosexual but was marrying to share a platonic relationship and the economic benefits of marriage (such as employer-based health insurance), the bakery would have still declined to bake the cake.

Meanwhile, the owner also would also, presumably, decline to cater other ceremonies he found immoral, such as a devil-worshiping ceremony, a polygamous heterosexual marriage, or a Buddhist offering to idols. Having a blanket policy against catering events contrary to the owner's religious or other worldview cannot reasonably be construed as discrimination based on sexual orientation.

The rationale for nevertheless holding the bakery owner liable for discriminating based on sexual orientation is that same-sex weddings are so intrinsically connected to sexual orientation that to discriminate against such weddings is in effect to discriminate against gays. This once again seems wrong. Imagine a photographer, who instead of being a conservative Christian, is a whole-earth hippie type. He tries to run his business consistent with his moral views. Among those views is his belief that circumcision is a violation of a child's human rights. He has Jewish clients, but when one of them asked him to photograph his son's brit milah (circumcision) ceremony, the photographer declined, stating that he refuses to photograph circumcision celebrations because he does not want to feel morally complicit.

Assume the photographer lives in a jurisdiction that bars discrimination based on religion. Infant circumcision combined with a public celebration is inextricably tied to the Jewish religion, given that the Torah not only commands it, but states that any uncircumcised male "shall be cut off from his people." Would it make any sense in this context to argue that the photographer is guilty of discrimination against Jews, because "when a law prohibits discrimination on the basis of religion, that law similarly protects conduct that is inextricably tied to religion?"

Public opinion as reflected in legislation might not ultimately reach what I think are the sensible solutions to these matters. But it bears repeating that the massive expansion of laws banning discrimination in public accommodations law to matters that don't properly fit into that category has been accomplished by administrative agencies and courts, not because legislatures have seen fit to so after public debate.

Given the courts' role in this and other extralegal expansions of antidiscrimination laws, it's not surprising Americans can't rely on the courts to protect them from antidiscrimination laws that infringe on constitutional rights. Even the Supreme Court has been uneven. In the 1980s, a series of Supreme Court rulings suggested that the government's purported "compelling interest" in "eradicating" even trivial forms of discrimination justified running roughshod over the First Amendment. The Supreme Court seems to have backed away from this position, but the prevailing sentiment among the younger generation of legal scholars is that the Court's earlier stance was correct. Few law professors, for example, were willing to defend the Boy Scouts' right to establish its own membership policies when the Scouts defended that right before the Supreme Court in *Boy Scouts of America v. Dale.*

More recently, and shockingly, the Obama Justice Department, stocked with a younger generation of liberal lawyers, argued to the Supreme Court that the "ministerial exception," a constitutional doctrine that protects religious institutions from being sued for discrimination and other illegal acts, should be entirely abandoned. Fortunately, the Supreme Court disagreed 9–0, but it makes one wonder what a future liberal Supreme Court dominated by the rising generation of liberals might bring.

Marc Stern of the American Jewish Congress, frustrated with the refusal of his liberal colleagues to accept religious exemptions to civil rights laws, noted that antidiscrimination principle "is taking on a quasi-religious status. Maybe for some people questioning civil rights [legislation] is like questioning God." If so, it's not surprising that the libertarian position on antidiscrimination laws attracts such fierce criticism.

The laudable goal of the ever-broadening antidiscrimination edifice is to achieve a fairer, more just society. Laudable goals, however, don't justify giving the government excessive authority, or disguising the implications of doing so.

5

Environmental Protection

Final Frontier or Achilles Heel?

Jonathan H. Adler

Environmental protection presents a tremendous challenge to classical liberalism. The environmental consequences of contemporary civilization are awesome and profound. In some formulations, the need to address environmental risks and redress environmental harms challenges the very notion of limited government.[1] "Everything is connected to everything else," after all.[2] Environmental concerns are persistent and pervasive, and all productive activity generates some form of environmental "externality." Thus, if externalities are a justification for governmental action, then there is no end to their potential reach.[3]

---

[1] See, for example, David Orr, "The Constitution of Nature," 17 CONSERVATION BIOLOGY 1478, 1481 (2003) ("Nature is a unified mosaic of ecosystems, functions, and processes. Government, on the other hand, was conceived by the founders as a limited and fractured enterprise."). Orr argues that there is a fundamental "mismatch between the way nature works in highly connected and interactive systems and the fragmentation of powers built into the Constitution." Id.

[2] See BARRY COMMONER, THE CLOSING CIRCLE: NATURE, MAN, AND TECHNOLOGY 23 (1972) ("[E]verything ... is connected to everything else.").

[3] It is worth noting that Nobel laureate economist Ronald H. Coase, author of the immensely influential essay "The Problem of Social Cost," took a different view. As Coase explained,

> the existence of "externalities" does not imply that there is a prima facie case for government intervention, if by this statement is meant that, when we find "externalities," there is a presumption that governmental intervention (taxation or regulation) is called for rather than the other courses of action which could be taken (including inaction, the abandonment of earlier governmental action, or the facilitating of market transactions) ...
>
> The fact that governmental intervention also has its costs makes it very likely that most "externalities" should be allowed to continue if the value of production is to be maximized. ... The ubiquitous nature of "externalities" suggests to me that there is a prima facie case against intervention.

R. H. COASE, THE FIRM, THE MARKET, AND THE LAW 24, 26 (1988). See also James M. Buchanan & William Craig Stubblebine, "Externality," 29 ECONOMICA 371 (1962) (noting that externalities are only relevant in a limited set of circumstances).

Despite the challenge presented by environmental problems, classical liberal and libertarian thinkers have, by and large, devoted relatively little attention to how their principles apply in an environmental context, and even less time extending their analysis beyond abstract principle and coarse generalizations.[4] Some insist (or at least pretend) that environmental challenges are not particularly serious; nothing human ingenuity and technological progress will fail to solve (at least in the long run) – and certainly nothing that could justify government action. Others acknowledge the existence of environmental problems, but fail to think deeply about how such problems can be addressed within a classical liberal framework.

The relative failure of classical liberal thinkers to engage environmental concerns more seriously is curious and unfortunate. Curious because there are some environmental matters that are readily and competently addressed by the application of classical liberal principles; unfortunate because so many environmental concerns remain unaddressed, and many such concerns, if allowed to fester, become justifications for ever greater governmental intervention in private economic life.

The aim of this chapter is relatively modest. It seeks to identify the opportunities for and obstacles to application of classical liberalism to environmental concerns. This focus is important because environmental protection remains one of the most important policy areas in the Twenty-First century. At the same time, it is a policy area in which classical liberal work to date is hopelessly incomplete. Thinking seriously about how to address environmental concerns consistent with classical liberal ideals is essential, and failure to do so risks the classical liberal enterprise.

REVISITING THE TRAGEDY OF THE COMMONS

Many contemporary environmental problems are variations of the "Tragedy of the Commons," the concept popularized by Garrett Hardin's influential 1968 essay of the same name.[5] Hardin described the fate of a common pasture, unowned and open to all. Without limitations on access to the pasture, it would be in each herder's own interest to maximize his or her use of the commons, even at the expense of exceeding the pasture's carrying capacity. Each herder can capture all of

---

[4] There are some obvious and notable exceptions. *See, for example*, TERRY L. ANDERSON & DONALD R. LEAL, FREE MARKET ENVIRONMENTALISM (Rev. ed. 2001); ECOLOGY, LIBERTY & PROPERTY: A FREE MARKET ENVIRONMENTAL READER (Jonathan H. Adler ed., 2000); Fred L. Smith Jr., "Markets and the Environment: A Critical Reappraisal," 13 CONTEMP. ECON. POL'Y 62 (1995); TAKING THE ENVIRONMENT SERIOUSLY (Roger E. Meiners & Bruce Yandle eds., 1993); Fred L. Smith Jr., "A Free-Market Environmental Program," 11 CATO J. 457 (1992). For some of this author's efforts in this vein, see Jonathan H. Adler, "Conservative Principles for Environmental Reform," 23 DUKE ENVIRONMENTAL LAW & POLICY FORUM 253 (2013); Jonathan H. Adler, "Free and Green: A New Approach to Environmental Protection," 24 HARVARD JOURNAL OF LAW & PUBLIC POLICY 653 (2001).

[5] *See* Garrett Hardin, "The Tragedy of the Commons," 162 SCIENCE 1243 (1968).

the benefit from adding one more animal to the pasture, whereas the costs of overgrazing are spread among all of the users as a whole.

The tragedy does not follow merely from the concentrated benefits and dispersed costs of consumption of the underlying resource. It is compounded by the fact that no user of the resource has any incentive to exercise self-restraint. The user with foresight, who anticipates that the pasture will become barren in the future, gains nothing from forbearance. To the contrary, because refusing to add another animal to one's own herd does not change the incentive of other herders to do so, the foresighted herder will be aware of the need to capture gains in the present that otherwise would be lost. The herder who exercises restraint, perhaps in the hope that consuming less today will leave more for tomorrow, bears the present cost of foregone consumption without any assurance of corresponding future gains.

In a world without scarcity, open-access might not be a problem. Yet that is not the world we inhabit. Grazing pastures, like all ecological resources, have their limits. At some point, use can exceed the carrying capacity of the underlying resource. Thus, as the herders respond rationally to the incentives they face, the pasture is eventually overgrazed. "Each man is locked into a system that compels him to increase his herd without limit – in a world that is limited," Hardin wrote. The pursuit of self-interest in an open-access commons results in a tragedy; "Freedom in a commons brings ruin to all."[6]

Hardin's essay brought the "tragedy of the commons" into the popular lexicon. Yet Hardin did not originate the concept. Over a decade before Hardin published his influential essay, fishery economists documented the same underlying dynamic in the oceans.[7] Indeed, for a long time, ocean fisheries provided the textbook example of how an open-access commons would be plagued by overuse. After all, fisheries are more difficult to fence and police than pastures, and many fisheries became hopelessly overfished in the Twentieth Century.

Commons problems are readily observed in the case of unowned or open-access resources. Many pollution problems may be described in much the same way.[8] Just as a herdsman may overutilize a common pasture to graze her livestock, a factory may overutilize a river or an airshed to dispose of emissions or wastes. As with the

---

[6] Id., at 1244. Although the notion of the "tragedy of the commons" is generally associated with Hardin, he was hardly the first to identify the underlying dynamic. Indeed, the basic insight can be found at least as far back as Aristotle. *See* ARISTOTLE, ARISTOTLE'S POLITICS 57 (Benjamin Jowett trans., 1943) ("[T]hat which is common to the greatest number has the least care bestowed upon it.")

[7] *See, for example*, H. Scott Gordon, "The Economic Theory of a Common Property Resource: The Fishery," 62 JOURNAL OF POLITICAL ECONOMY 124, 135 (1954); Anthony Scott, "The Fishery: The Objectives of Sole Ownership," 63 JOURNAL OF POLITICAL ECONOMY 116 (1955).

[8] Hardin also noted that his analysis could be applied to pollution. *See* Hardin, *supra* note 5, at 1245.

herder, there is no incentive to exercise restraint. Just as the herder captures the benefits of grazing an additional animal while dispersing the costs of over-grazing on all users of the common resource, the factory owner captures the value of additional production while dispersing the pollution costs on all those who use the common watershed or airshed. And if multiple users act in the same way, the carrying capacity of the underlying resource is exceeded, and the tragedy results.[9] Indeed, in the pollution context one might expect the problem to be even more severe as the harms from "overconsumption" of the resource as a waste sink will often be borne by other users long before they impact the industrial user. The child with asthma, for example, will experience harm from increased air pollution long before pollution is severe enough to impact the polluting factory's productivity.

The tragedy of the commons is not inevitable. If access to the commons can be controlled, and use restrained, the commons can be sustained. Given the need for restraints on resource use, Hardin's analysis provides a standard rationale for government regulation – "mutual coercion, mutually agreed upon"[10] – as a means of conserving the commons. If users of the common resource lack the incentive to utilize the resource in a sustainable manner, external constraints can limit use to sustainable levels, whether by limiting the pasture's use for grazing or a local airshed's use as a waste sink. For relatively small and homogenous groups, such constraints may come in the form of community norms.[11] For larger and more diverse societies, however, such "mutual coercion" inevitably comes in the form of government regulation.

The problems of centralized prescriptive regulation are well-documented, and beyond the scope of this chapter.[12] The relevant point here is that prescriptive regulation imposed by a government agency is not the only possible solution to the tragedy of the commons. There are other ways to prevent the tragedy more consistent with classical liberal principles, at least in theory. Hardin, though not a classical liberal himself, noted a more liberal alternative to prescriptive government regulation: stewardship grounded in property. "The tragedy of the commons ... is averted by private property, or something formally like it,"

---

9   While all, or perhaps nearly all, environmental problems can be analyzed as variants of the "commons" problem, it is often useful to draw finer analytical distinctions among different types of environmental concerns, ranging from pollution spillovers to the provision of public goods, among others. R. H. Coase, for instance, offers another useful framing, conceiving of many environmental problems as conflicts between competing uses of resources. *See generally* R. H. Coase, "The Problem of Social Cost," 3 JOURNAL OF LAW & ECONOMICS 1 (1960).

10   Hardin, *supra* note 5, at 1247.

11   *See generally* ELINOR OSTROM, GOVERNING THE COMMONS: THE EVOLUTION OF INSTITUTIONS FOR COLLECTIVE ACTION (1990).

12   For a discussion, see Adler, *Free*, *supra* note 4, at 657–67; *see also* Richard B. Stewart, "United States Environmental Regulation: A Failing Paradigm," 15 JOURNAL OF LAW & COMMERCE 585 (1996).

Hardin explained.[13] In this he found the same potential solution identified by his predecessors, and one that fits neatly into the classical liberal tradition.[14]

THE PROMISE OF PROPERTY

As a general rule, where resources are owned, there is less concern about their overuse. Property owners have both the ability to protect the owned resource, and a substantial incentive to ensure that the value of their property – both to themselves and to others – is maintained.[15] Both the costs of excessive consumption and benefits of sustainable stewardship are experienced by the owner. This encourages more sustainable utilization of the resource over time, and incentivizes the discovery of better management techniques. Conversely, the lack of property rights in the underlying resource leaves users with little incentive to engage in conservation efforts, as any such efforts are likely to be wasted.[16]

Owners care about the value of what they own, both now and in the future. As Harold Demsetz explained, "If a single person owns land, he will attempt to maximize its present value by taking into account alternative future time streams of benefits and costs and selecting that one which he believes will maximize the present value of his privately-owned land rights."[17] Importantly, the claim is not that *every* private landowner will prove to be a far-sighted and effective steward, but that the incentives derived from ownership will encourage owners to behave in a particular way, to the best of their ability. And as abilities vary, so too will the sustainable management of any particular owner. Importantly, those property owners which do the best job of estimating likely future income streams are likely to be rewarded with the greatest returns, reinforcing the underlying incentive structure.

---

[13] Hardin, *supra* note 5, at 1245.

[14] Gordon, *supra* note 7, at 134 ("Environmental conditions make necessary some vehicle which will prevent the resources of the community at large from being destroyed by excessive exploitation. Private or group land tenure accomplishes this end in an easily understandable fashion.").

[15] *See* Robert J. Smith, "Resolving the Tragedy of the Commons by Creating Private Property Rights in Wildlife," 1 CATO JOURNAL 439, 456 (1981) ("Wherever we have exclusive private ownership, whether it is organized around a profit-seeking or nonprofit undertaking, there are incentives for the private owners to preserve the resource."). *See also* David Schmidtz, "The Institution of Property," *in* THE COMMON LAW AND THE ENVIRONMENT 109, 110 (Roger E. Meiners & Andrew P. Morriss eds. 2000) (explaining how "property institutions convert negative-sum or zero-sum games into positive-sum games.").

[16] As Anthony Scott observes, "No one will take the trouble to husband and maintain a resource unless he has a reasonable certainty of receiving some portion of the product of his management; that is, unless he has some property right in the yield." Scott, *supra* note 7, at 116.

[17] Harold Demsetz, "Toward a Theory of Property Rights," 57 AMERICAN ECONOMIC REVIEW 347, 355 (1967); id. at 356 ("The development of private rights permits the owner to economize on the use of those resources from which he has the right to exclude others.").

It bears emphasis that the claim here is not that property rights ensure some ecological nirvana. No set of institutional arrangements can eliminate all negative environmental consequences. Nevertheless, the institution of private property, and the incentives it creates, are more conducive to sustainable utilization of resources than available alternatives.[18,19]

Empirical analyses comparing privately owned and managed resources with their politically managed (or unmanaged) alternatives tends to confirm the hypothesis. Consider oysters. Oyster beds in Maryland are managed by the state. In neighboring Virginia, the beds are leased to private parties. Across the country in Washington State, oyster beds are privately owned in fee simple. As the theory would predict, privately managed oyster beds tend to be healthier and more productive than those under state protection.[20] Comparisons between privately leased and publicly managed oyster beds in Louisiana and Mississippi, respectively, have yielded similar results.[21]

Oysters are not an isolated example. Privately owned forests exhibit higher rates of forest growth than those managed by the government or left in the public domain.[22] The United States, like many market-oriented developed nations, has experienced substantial forest regrowth over the past century, driven by net forest growth on private lands. In the second-half of the twentieth century, tree planting efforts increased nearly seven-fold, almost exclusively due to replanting on private lands.[23] In addition, dramatic increases in timber productivity on the small fraction of forest represented by tree plantations, has relieved pressure on other forest lands, leaving more land for conservation and other uses.[24] Market-driven improvements in the efficiency with which timber products are used have further relieved pressures on forests.

---

[18] Comparative institutional analysis avoids the "nirvana" problem in which an obviously imperfect institutional arrangement is compared with a hypothesized ideal norm. As Harold Demsetz explains, this approach attempts "to assess which alternative *real* institutional arrangement seems best able to cope with the economic problem."

[19] Harold Demsetz, "Information and Efficiency: Another Viewpoint," 12 JOURNAL OF LAW & ECONOMICS 1, 1 (1969) (emphasis added).

[20] Michael DeAlessi, "Fishing for Solutions: The State of the World's Fisheries," *in* EARTH REPORT 2000 at 94–95 (Ronald Bailey ed., 2000). *See also*, Richard J. Agnello & Lawrence P. Donnelly, "Property Rights and Efficiency in the Oyster Industry," 18 JOURNAL OF LAW & ECONOMICS 521 (1975) (comparing the productivity of Maryland and Virginia oyster fisheries).

[21] *See, for example*, Richard J. Agnello & Lawrence P. Donnelly, "Prices and Property Rights in the Fisheries," 42 SOUTHERN ECONOMIC JOURNAL 253 (1975).

[22] Jonathan H. Adler, "Poplar Front: The Rebirth of America's Forests," *in* ECOLOGY, LIBERTY & PROPERTY: A FREE MARKET ENVIRONMENTAL READER (Jonathan H. Adler ed. 2000); *see also* Roger J. Sedjo, "Forests: Conflicting Signals," *in* THE TRUE STATE OF THE PLANET 177 (Ronald Bailey ed. 1995).

[23] *See* Roger A. Sedjo & Douglas MacCleery, "Sustainable Forests in America?," *in* PERSPECTIVES ON SUSTAINABLE RESOURCES IN AMERICA 44 (Roger A. Sedjo ed. 2008).

[24] Adler, *Poplar*, *supra* note 21; Sedjo & MacCleery, *supra* note 22, at 43–45.

More broadly, liberal, market-oriented societies in which property rights are protected appear to experience more positive environmental outcomes.[25] As economist Seth Norton has documented, "environmental quality and economic growth rates are greater in regimes where property rights are well defined than in regimes where property rights are poorly defined."[26] Some of this is likely due to wealth effects – and the so-called Environmental Kuznets Curve – as market-oriented societies produce the wealth and technology necessary for environmental protection. Some of it is also likely due to institutional factors. Property-based systems and market institutions, for all their imperfections, tend to encourage more sustainable and efficient resource use and protection than the available alternatives.

The claim, again, is not that there are no problems with privately held ecological resources, nor is it that the resulting markets do not produce or encourage environmental problems. Rather it is that there is a general tendency toward more efficient and sustainable management of those resources that are incorporated into markets through the institution of property. Put another way, those resources that are more fully integrated into property institutions tend to be managed more sustainably than their unowned or politically managed counterparts.[27] Liberal institutions have ecological value. Where such institutions can be implemented, they tend to represent an environmentally superior – or, at the very least, a less environmentally inferior – management approach.[28]

It is important to recognize that reference to private property rights does not necessarily entail individuated ownership by profit-seeking individuals. Property rights may be held and controlled in many forms. Lands owned by the Nature Conservancy, a local land trust, or a homeowners' association are just as much private property as those owned by Ted Turner, the Disney Company, or International Paper. Many regimes characterized as "common property" are really forms of collective private ownership, a less-formal variant of a cooperative or condominium.[29] Private ownership comes in many forms, but it is distinct from a lack of ownership and either *de jure* or *de facto* ownership by the state.

---

[25] *See* RICHARD L. STROUP, ECO-NOMICS: WHAT EVERYONE SHOULD KNOW ABOUT ECONOMICS AND THE ENVIRONMENT 74–75 (2003) (summarizing research showing relationship between the protection of property rights and environmental performance).

[26] Seth W. Norton, "Property Rights, the Environment, and Economic Well-Being," *in* WHO OWNS THE ENVIRONMENT? 37, 51 (Peter J. Hill & Roger E. Meiners eds., 1998).

[27] *See, for example,* Fred L. Smith Jr., "Reappraising Humanity's Challenges, Humanity's Opportunities," *in* THE TRUE STATE OF THE PLANET, *supra* note 21, at 379.

[28] As Andrew Morriss notes, "Markets are far from perfect, of course. But, critiques of markets in general, and critiques of water markets in particular, often conflate dissatisfactions with human nature or other features of society with problems in the market." Andrew P. Morriss, "Real People, Real Resources, and Real Choices: The Case for Market Valuation of Water," 38 TEXAS TECH LAW REVIEW 973, 975 (2006).

[29] *See* Margaret McKean & Elinor Ostrom, "Common Property Regimes in the Forest: Just a Relic from the Past?," 46 UNASYLVA 3, 6 (1995) (observing that what is often referred to as "common property" can be understood as "shared private property").

The security of property rights encourages owners to pursue the enhancement of their own subjective value preferences, including both commercial and non-commercial values, as well as to take into account the subjective value preferences of others.[30] As libertarian conservationist R. J. Smith explains:

> Wherever we have exclusive private ownership, whether it is organized around a profit-seeking or nonprofit undertaking, there are incentives for the private owners to preserve the resource. . . . [P]rivate ownership allows the owner to capture the full capital value of the resource, and self-interest and economic incentive drive the owner to maintain its long-term capital value.[31]

Thus, maintaining long-term value necessarily requires considering environmental value, particularly in a time and place in which environmental values are widely held.

To be effective, property rights must protect popular and unpopular values alike, and be safeguarded against both private and public harm and expropriation.[32] Only then can private property facilitate the protection of resources that the political process might undervalue or ignore.[33] Indeed, over the course of American history, farsighted conservationists have used property rights to protect ecological resources that were underappreciated by political institutions and the public at large. For example, early conservation organizations, such as the National Audubon Society, were beginning to purchase and protect wetlands for use as bird habitat in the early 1900s – a time when wetlands were generally regarded as nuisances and the US government actively subsidized their destruction.[34] What experts viewed as dismal swamps, early conservationists recognized as ecologically valuable habitat. Had the government retained a monopoly on land management, less habitat would have been conserved. In the late nineteenth century, a handful of ranchers and private organizations saved the American bison from extinction through acquiring,

---

[30] *See* Louis De Alessi, "Gains from Private Property: The Empirical Evidence," *in* PROPERTY RIGHTS: COOPERATION, CONFLICT, AND LAW 90, 108 (Terry L. Anderson & Fred S. McChesney eds. 2003).

[31] Smith, *supra* note 15, at 456–457

[32] For instance, the excessive use of the eminent domain power could come at the expense of environmental conservation. Ilya Somin & Jonathan H. Adler, "The Green Costs of Kelo: Economic Development Takings and Environmental Protection," 84 WASHINGTON UNIVERSITY LAW REVIEW 623 (2006).

[33] It's worth noting that the political process may itself may produce a "tragedy of the commons" in which it is in the self-interest of each interest group to pursue policies that produce concentrated benefits and dispersed costs, and it is in no interest group's interest to pursue policies that maximize welfare across-the-board.

[34] On the early activities of the National Audubon Society, and its precursor, the National Committee of Audubon Societies, see FRANK GRAHAM JR., THE AUDUBON ARK: A HISTORY OF THE NATIONAL AUDUBON SOCIETY (1990). On early 20th century views of wetlands, and governmental efforts to make more "productive use" of such lands, see Jonathan H. Adler, "Wetlands, Waterfowl, and the Menace of Mr. Wilson: Commerce Clause Jurisprudence and the Limits of Federal Wetland Regulation," 29 ENVIRONMENTAL LAW 1, 19–20 (1999).

breeding and protecting them while the US government was subsidizing their slaughter.[35] As conservationist Valerius Geist observed, "Bison were initially saved by six individuals who either saw business opportunities in the existence of bison or simply wanted to save a vanishing species."[36]

Private property has enabled far-sighted conservationists to act even when the government or public at large was overtly hostile to their efforts. In the 1930s, for instance, Rosalie Edge purchased "Hawk Mountain" in Pennsylvania, and posted it against trespassing, so as to protect migratory raptor populations. Her efforts were exceedingly unpopular, for she was protecting a species disliked by farmers while simultaneously denying young boys the opportunity for target practice. Today, Hawk Mountain is an important site for raptor research.[37] Were property rights subject to less robust legal protection, such environmental resources could have been sacrificed to the demands of unsympathetic political majorities.

The transferability of private rights provides the foundation for markets and generates additional environmental benefits. If rights in resources can be transferred, then owners have an incentive to be concerned about the value that others place on the resource in question. Marketability also enhances the incentive to use resources more efficiently. As Professor Robert Glennon observes:

> An ability to transfer ownership creates an incentive to use property more productively. This is the core idea of markets. Owners of property assess the value of it to them and part with it if they will realize a profit. Buyers seek to change the use of property and capture the value added by the new use. In this process, both buyers and sellers make profits, and society benefits from increased efficiency.[38]

Water markets provide a useful example of these dynamics.[39] Transferable rights in water enable "the movement of water from low-value activities to higher-value ones" and more efficient water use. In practice, the gradual recognition of property rights and water has produced the effects one would expect. Over time, the volume of water trades, leases and purchases has been increasing.[40] Further, as various jurisdictions have begun to recognize rights in water for non-consumptive uses – such as instream flows used for conservation purposes – conservation organizations have been able to enter the market to purchase or lease water rights for the benefit of

---

[35] *See generally* ANDREW C. ISENBERG, THE DESTRUCTION OF THE BISON 164–92 (2000).

[36] Ike C. Sugg, "Where the Buffalo Roam, and Why," EXOTIC WILDLIFE, Jan./Feb. 1999.

[37] U.S. Council on Environmental Quality, "Special Report: The Public Benefits of Private Conservation," *in* ENVIRONMENTAL QUALITY 1984, 387–94 (1984).

[38] Robert Glennon, "Water Scarcity, Marketing, and Privatization," 83 TEXAS LAW REVIEW 1873, 1887 (2005).

[39] Terry L. Anderson & Peter J. Hill, "Introduction: Taking the Plunge," *in* WATER MARKETING – THE NEXT GENERATION xi (Terry L. Anderson & Peter J. Hill eds., 1997) ("the efficacy of markets for averting resource shortages is no better demonstrated than with water.").

[40] Jedidiah Brewer et al., "Transferring Water in the American West: 1987–2005," 40 UNIVERSITY OF MICHIGAN JOURNAL OF LAW REFORM 1021, 1042 (2007).

threatened fish populations.[41] The recognition of property rights in water gives farmers a potentially marketable asset, and the demand for instream rights from conservationists, recreationists, and others creates a financial incentive to "use" water in ways that benefit species and local ecosystems.[42] As a consequence, where robust water rights are recognized, voluntary, cooperative transactions to reallocate water have begun to replace lobbying and political maneuvering. Rather than seek the imposition of additional regulatory controls which may trigger conflict and litigation, conservation organizations can negotiate with farmers and ranchers to purchase, lease, or otherwise transfer water rights. Unfortunately, marketable water rights are the exception rather than the rule, and tremendous inefficiencies in water utilization remain.

Markets in ecological resources can also facilitate adaptation to changing ecological conditions, as might occur due to climate change.[43] Indeed, the primary virtue of markets is not the generation of static efficiency, but the constant pressure to allocate resources to their highest valued uses, even as the value of competing uses changes over time. Markets are an immensely powerful means of discovering and aggregating time and place specific information, including subjective value preferences, and markets are constantly adapting as such information, or the conditions upon which it is based, evolves. In the case of water, for instance, market prices communicate information about the relative supply and demand for particular uses in particular places. Price changes encourage resource owners to consider voluntary transactions to transfer resources to higher valued uses. Even the United Nations' Intergovernmental Panel on Climate Change has noted that "improving the functioning of water markets could help create the kind of flexibility needed to respond to uncertain changes in future water availability" caused by climate change.[44]

PROPERTY AT SEA

A challenge for classical liberalism is that it is not always easy to extend property and other foundational market institutions to ecological resources. The costs of defining and defending property rights in ecological resources are often quite substantial,

---

[41] *See* TERRY L. ANDERSON & PAMELA SNYDER, WATER MARKETS: PRIMING THE INVISIBLE PUMP 120 (1997).

[42] TERRY L. ANDERSON & DONALD R LEAL, ENVIRO-CAPITALISTS: DOING GOOD WHILE DOING WELL 94–95 (1997).

[43] *See generally* Jonathan H. Adler, "Water Rights, Markets, and Changing Ecological Conditions," 42 ENVIRONMENTAL LAW 93 (2012).

[44] *See* K. Duncan et al., *North America, in* CLIMATE CHANGE 2001: IMPACTS, ADAPTATION, AND VULNERABILITY: CONTRIBUTION OF WORKING GROUP II TO THE THIRD ASSESSMENT REPORT OF THE INTERGOVERNMENTAL PANEL ON CLIMATE CHANGE 735, 748 (James J. McCarthy et al. eds., 2001).

potentially exceeding any potential economic or ecological benefit.[45] The development and recognition of such rights may also take time. In addition, there may be political, cultural, or social conditions impeding a robust property rights regime.[46] Yet these obstacles are not always as great as it may at first seem. Where tried, creative efforts to extend property rights to ecological resources have often proved ecologically valuable.

Consider marine fisheries. As noted above, the world's ocean fisheries provided the classic example Hardin's "tragedy of the commons."[47] Not only are fisheries often open-access, fish that are in the waters today, of course, may not be there tomorrow. This uncertainty creates the additional short-term incentive to catch as many fish today as possible, because every fish left in the ocean for tomorrow is one that got away.[48] The incentive for fishermen is clear, "an additional fish caught is money in the individual's pocket, but the cost of one less fish available to breed or to be caught another day is spread among all fishermen."[49]

Hardin's theoretical "tragedy" has played out across the waters as many of the world's largest fisheries have drastically declined and others ultimately collapsed, despite substantial regulatory efforts. Private property might encourage stewardship on land, but fencing a pasture is quite different than fencing the open sea. Accordingly, it was simply assumed that property-based solutions were inapplicable to fisheries. The mobility and migration of fish, and the difficulty in monitoring property interests across the expanses of the open sea made talk of private ownership fanciful.[50] Yet private property need not entail individuated ownership. It is possible to privatize resources without dividing it into individualized parcels. At the same time, property rights in resources also need not be defined in spatial terms. Property law has long recognized interests that do not correspond with the physical metes and bounds of individual land holdings.

---

[45] *See* Terry L. Anderson & Peter J. Hill, "Privatizing the Commons: An Improvement?," 50 SOUTHERN ECONOMIC JOURNAL 438, 438 (1985).

[46] *See, for example*, Barton H. Thompson Jr., "Tragically Difficult: The Obstacles to Governing the Commons," 30 ENVIRONMENTAL LAW 241, 255–65 (2000) (noting some of the obstacles to the creation of property rights in fisheries).

[47] *See* Martin D. Smith, "The New Fisheries Economics: Incentives Across Many Margins," 4 ANNUAL REVIEW OF RESOURCE ECONOMICS 379, 380 (2012) ("The story of fisheries economics could be distilled into diagnosing the commons problem and offering a solution to it.").

[48] Gordon, *supra* note 7, at 135 ("The fish in the sea are valueless to the fishermen, because there is no assurance that they will be there for him tomorrow if they are left behind today.").

[49] *See* Donald Leal, "Saving Fisheries with Free Markets," MILKEN INSTITUTE REVIEW, 1st Quarter 2006.

[50] *See, for example*, James E. Wilen et al., "The Economics of Territorial Use Rights Fisheries, or TURFs," 6 REVIEW OF ENVIRONMENTAL ECONOMICS & POLICY 237, 240 (2012) (noting it has "generally been viewed as more problematic" to apply property rights management approaches "in nearshore and offshore marine environments because of the long-standing common belief that 'we can't fence the ocean'").

In some fisheries, the fishers themselves sought to establish *de facto* property rights in the resource through contractual arrangements, such as agreements that would limit the amount of fish caught and when fishing occurred.[51] Such reliance upon private ordering to solve a commons problem showed promise, but nonetheless ran afoul of antitrust law.[52] Contractual arrangements to limit resource exploitation may have been effective, but they also constituted a horizontal restraint of trade, leaving government management as the only viable means of conservation.

Fishery economists who recognized the nature of the marine commons problem set about thinking how to apply property rights principles to mobile ocean resources.[53] One idea that seemed promising was the notion of allocating shares of a season's catch – a quota – in order to give fishery participants property rights in the resource they sought to exploit.[54] This quota, what is often referred to as an ITQ (individual transferable quota) or "catch share," is typically a right to an assigned percentage or proportion of the total allowed annual or seasonal catch in a given fishery.[55] So, for instance, the owner of a 2.5 percent quota in a fishery with a Total Allowable Catch of 100 tons would own the right to catch 2.5 tons, but would be able to catch 5 tons if the TAC were set at 200 tons. In most such systems, shares or quota are initially allocated based on some sort of formula, such as the average volume caught over a set of prior years, or by an auction, but then continue from year to year. Insofar as the ITQ right continues into the future, ownership of a catch share provides the fisher with an incentive to ensure the fishery's sustainability over time, particularly if the quota is freely transferable.

ITQ programs have been implemented in several countries with substantial success at increasing fishing efficiency, reducing over-capitalization, and lessening the ecological impact of fishing operations.[56] A 2008 review of such programs around the world found that implementing catch-share programs "halts, and even reverses, the global trend toward widespread [fisheries] collapse."[57] Such programs cover only two percent or so of fish stocks around the world, but as of 2010 accounted

---

[51] *See* GARY D. LIBECAP, CONTRACTING FOR PROPERTY RIGHTS 73–74 (1989).

[52] *See* Jonathan H. Adler, "Legal Obstacles to Private Ordering in Marine Fisheries," 8 ROGER WILLIAMS UNIVERSITY LAW REVIEW 9 (2002); Jonathan H. Adler, "Conservation through Collusion: Antitrust as an Obstacle to Marine Resource Conservation," 61 WASH. & LEE LAW REVIEW 3 (2004).

[53] This history is summarized in Ragnar Arnason, "Property Rights in Fisheries: How Much Can Individual Transferable Quotas Accomplish?," 6 REVIEW OF ENVIRONMENTAL ECONOMICS & POLICY 217 (2012).

[54] *See* Francis T. Christy, FISHERMEN QUOTAS: A TENTATIVE SUGGESTION FOR DOMESTIC MANAGEMENT (1973).

[55] *See* Arnason, *supra* note 53, at 222.

[56] The relevant literature is summarized in Jonathan H. Adler & Nathaniel Stewart, "Learning How to Fish: Catch Shares and the Future of Fishery Conservation," 31 UCLA JOURNAL OF ENVIRONMENTAL LAW & POLICY 150 (2013).

[57] *See* Christopher Costello et al., *Can Catch Shares Prevent Fisheries Collapse?*, 321 SCIENCE 1678, 1678 (2008).

for approximately twenty-five percent of the volume of fish caught annually world-wide.[58] Another study, surveying over 200 peer-reviewed papers on the environmental effects of ITQ programs found that the creation of property rights in ocean fisheries encourages greater stewardship among fishery participants, including efforts to maintain and enforce sustainable limits on the total catch.[59] Fishery participants under ITQs often exhibit greater concern for ensuring total catch levels remain sustainable and that applicable limits are enforced than the government officials charged with such obligations. "It's the first group of fishers I've ever encountered who turned down the chance to take more fish," noted Philip Major of New Zealand's Ministry of Agriculture after the implementation of ITQs.[60]

The experience with fisheries suggests the value of learning how property rights may be extended to threatened ecological resources, particularly those we wish to simultaneously exploit and conserve. The experience also suggests how challenging such efforts can be. Only decades after fishery economists began to identify potential mechanisms for the extension of property rights to fisheries did such reforms begin to get adopted, and only recently – in the past decade or so – has conclusive empirical evidence on the value of these approaches emerged. Following this model for other resources will take no less effort and the vindication of classical liberal ideas about how to protect other resources is by no means assured.

THE PROBLEM OF POLLUTION

The application of classical liberal principles to natural resource conservation is comparatively easy compared to other environmental concerns. Pollution problems, in particular, present a serious challenge to classical liberal notions of the proper role of government. At one level, pollution would seem to present an obvious tort, readily addressed by principles of trespass and nuisance.[61] Property rights, to be meaningful must be protected against private harm, and no individual property owner has the right to use his or her property in a fashion that harms or interferes with the ability of his or her neighbor to do the same. When A's use of her property interferes with B's ability to make use of his property, we have the sort of conflict that may be solved by judicial enforcement of rights or some form of Coasean bargaining.

From a classical liberal, property-rights perspective, preventing pollution means preventing the forcible imposition of a waste or emission by one person onto the

---

[58] *See* Christopher Costello et al., *Economic Incentives and Global Fisheries Sustainability*, 2 ANNUAL REVIEW OF RESOURCE ECONOMICS 299, 302 (2010).

[59] Trevor A. Branch, *How Do Individual Transferable Quotas Affect Marine Ecosystems?*, 10 FISH AND FISHERIES 39 (2009).

[60] Quoted in DeAlessi, *supra* note 19, at 99.

[61] *See* Roger Meiners & Bruce Yandle, *Common Law Environmentalism*, 94 PUBLIC CHOICE 99 (1998).

person or property of another. Where the deposit of waste or residuals onto private property is consented to by the owner, and the physical effects of such disposal is contained on the property, there may be ecological harm, but no pollution. As explained by Terry Anderson and Donald Leal, "The free market environmental approach to pollution is to establish property rights to the pollution disposal medium and allow owners of those rights to bargain over how the resource will be used."[62] So long as such exchanges are consensual, and external harms prevented, there is no property rights violation. With no harm to property rights, there is no foul. Waste itself is not pollution. Rather, pollution is waste out of place.

Traditional common law principles embody this idea by prohibiting the forcible imposition of pollution or other harms onto the persons or property of others, even if such a forced exchange of rights would be net beneficial. For example, in one famous case from New York, the state's highest court upheld an injunction shutting down a $1 million pulp mill employing several hundred workers in order to protect the riparian rights of a single farmer.[63] "Although the damage to the plaintiff may be slight compared with the defendant's expense of abating the condition," the court held, "that is not a good reason for refusing the injunction." Such a ruling, the court explained, "would deprive the poor litigant of his little property by giving it to those already rich."[64]

A key aspect of the common-law approach to pollution control is that it serves to clarify property rights and thereby facilitate bargaining among property owners over how land will be used. (Such bargaining over the allocation of property rights is often referred to as "Coasean bargaining," after the economist Ronald H. Coase, who argued that, in the absence of transaction costs, property rights will be transferred to their highest and best use through voluntary transactions among property owners.)[65] For example, if the law clearly establishes that riparian owners have rights in a stream, and that a factory cannot dump effluent into a nearby river without their consent, the factory owner will either negotiate a settlement with the riparian owners or locate elsewhere. Such bargains were facilitated by the strong protection the common law afforded property rights.[66]

When property rights are violated by environmental pollution, landowners should have recourse in court. Legal victory is not automatic, however, as prospective plaintiffs must be able to demonstrate that they have suffered harm to a legally protected interest and that such harm is due to the conduct of another. As environmental economist

---

[62] ANDERSON & LEAL, *supra* note 4, at 132.

[63] *Whalen v. Union Bag & Paper Co.*, 101 N.E. 805 (N.Y. 1913).

[64] *Id.* at 806.

[65] *See* Coase, *supra* note 9.

[66] For examples of such negotiation in the context of stream pollution, see Roger Bate, "Protecting English and Welsh Rivers: The Role of the Anglers' Conservation Association," *in* THE COMMON LAW AND THE ENVIRONMENT: RETHINKING THE STATUTORY BASIS FOR MODERN ENVIRONMENTAL LAW (Roger E. Meiners & Andrew P. Morris eds., 2000).

Bruce Yandle explains, "Loose assertions about environmental quality and the need to protect it will not do the job. Ownership of damaged property or loss of recognized rights must be shown."[67] If a factory is belching smoke or refuse streams from an uncontrolled pipe, it may be easy to show who is responsible for the pollution and to quantify the resulting harm. Yet if the pollution in question is barely perceptible, comes in the form of trace amounts of difficult to measure but particularly harmful contaminants, or only manifests harm over time, the burdens of proof in legal proceedings may prevent any meaningful redress. The same can be said if the ultimate source of the pollution is some distance away.

Assuming a property rights violation can be shown, the traditional remedy for a trespass or nuisance was injunctive relief and the payment of damages for harm caused. This was strong medicine for industrial firms and other would-be polluters. Perhaps as a consequence, some courts eventually adopted a balancing approach whereby they compared the costs imposed upon the polluted landowner with the value of the activity to be enjoined. In such cases, courts became reluctant to award injunctive relief to private landowners, even though such an award could be effectively overturned by subsequent negotiation among the parties. In other cases, legislatures preempted common-law causes of action or declared certain levels of pollution to be permissible as a matter of law if permitted by government authorities.[68]

The complexity of many pollution problems further confounds any effort to control pollution through the assertion and enforcement of property rights in land. The problem is that many, if not most, of the pollution problems of concern today are not so simple and straightforward. The demand for environmental regulation does not arise from bilateral disputes between landowners in which one is causing an emission or waste stream to intrude upon the person or property of another. Rather, regulations are developed to address instances in which there are many alleged polluters affecting many parcels of land, when the degree and nature of causation is difficult to monitor and observe, and when the risks posed by allegedly polluting actions may be latent or uncertain.

In all but the simplest scenarios, neither legal enforcement of property rights against pollution nor low transaction costs can be assumed. Moreover, property rights in many environmental media, most notably water and air, are incomplete and undefined. These realities complicate the development of Coasean contractual solutions to pollution problems. Traditional dispute resolution systems, such as common law adjudication, may work tolerably well for relatively simple, bilateral pollution disputes where the relevant rights are well-defined and the transaction

---

[67] Bruce Yandle, "Coase, Pigou, and Environmental Rights," *in* WHO OWNS THE ENVIRONMENT? 119, 138 (Peter J. Hill and Roger E. Meiners eds., 1997).

[68] *See* ELIZABETH BRUBAKER. PROPERTY RIGHTS IN THE DEFENCE OF NATURE 127–70 (1995); Julian Morris, "Climbing Out of the Hole: Sunsets, Subjective Value, the Environment, and the English Common Law," 14 FORDHAM ENVIRONMENTAL LAW JOURNAL 343 (2003).

costs are relatively low, but may falter when the pollution at issue is generated by many sources or affects many properties. In those cases in which there many polluters, many victims, or both, transaction costs escalate rapidly and traditional property rights solutions falter.[69]

Even if transaction costs can be overcome, additional problems remain, such as how to identify when a waste stream or emission constitutes actionable pollution. It is easy to make out the nuisance case against a neighboring factory belching thick acrid smoke and sooty deposition. Yet what of harder-to-detect emissions of substances that pose uncertain risks? Some libertarian thinkers have proposed a zero-tolerance approach to any identifiable or measurable deposit of any physical substance.[70] While potentially appealing on philosophical grounds, such a philosophy is a recipe for shutting down much of modern civilization.[71] In such formulations, the reliance upon common law actions to protect the environment by protecting property rights is not a too weak remedy, but a too strong one.[72]

As difficult as many conventional pollution problems may be for classical liberal principles, the challenge posed by climate change is even greater.[73] The global atmosphere is, in many respects, the mother of all commons problems, and there is no clear way to apply classical liberal principles. Failure to do so, however, presents its own threat to classical liberal values, as conventional climate change policies are themselves a threat to principles of individual liberty and limited government. The leading greenhouse gas, carbon dioxide, is a ubiquitous by-product of modern civilization. Thus, measures to control it necessarily implicate energy use through-out the economy.

While scientists may debate the precise degree to which human activity is contributing to a gradual warming of the atmosphere, there is little dispute that human activity has contributed to such warming and will continue to do so in the future. Even warming "skeptics" admit there is an anthropogenic contribution to warming and that such warming will contribute to phenomena, such as sea-level rise, that present serious concerns. Yet there is no clear way to assign property rights in the atmosphere, no mechanism to facilitate meaningful Coasean bargaining – even nation-to-nation – nor even an institutional framework through which to

---

[69] This argument is laid out in further detail in Jonathan H. Adler, "Is the Common Law the Free Market Solution to Pollution?," 24 CRITICAL REVIEW 61(2012).

[70] *See, for example*, Murray N., Rothbard, "Law, Property Rights, and Air Pollution," 2 CATO JOURNAL 55 (Spring 1982).

[71] *See, for example*, Mark Sagoff, *Free-Market versus Libertarian Environmentalism*, 6 CRITICAL REVIEW 211, 220–21 (1992).

[72] *See* Matt Zwolinski, "Libertarianism and Pollution," *in* THE ROUTLEDGE COMPANION TO ENVIRONMENTAL ETHICS (Benjamin Hale & Andrew Light eds. 2015).

[73] For one attempt to do so, see Jonathan H. Adler, "Taking Property Rights Seriously: The Case of Climate Change," 26 SOCIAL PHILOSOPHY & POLICY 296 (2009); *see also* Dan Shahar, "Justice and Climate Change: Toward a Libertarian Analysis," 14 THE INDEPENDENT REVIEW 219 (2009); Edwin G. Dolan, *Science*, "Public Policy, and Global Warming: Rethinking the Market-Liberal Position," 26 CATO JOURNAL 445 (2006).

pursue redress for subsidiary climate-related claims, such as actions for redress of sea-level rise or other warming-induced harms.

These problems do not mean that centralized environmental regulation is an effective means of addressing environmental concerns, but they do complicate the case for a classical liberal or "free market" approach to environmental protection. Just as the creative application of property rights principles to fisheries has facilitated the sustainable management of marine fisheries, it is possible that the creative application of similar principles to pollution problems could yield more effective and equitable solutions, but this case has yet to be made. Further, the extent to which other institutional steps, such as the creative devolution of some environmental management responsibilities to more local authorities or even non-governmental institutions, has not been explored sufficiently.

CONCLUSION

There are ample reasons to be dissatisfied with conventional approaches to environmental protection. Candor, however, requires equal dissatisfaction with efforts to craft classical liberal alternatives to the modern environmental regulatory state. This is a problem, for so much is at stake. Environmental protection is an essential component of any system that seeks to protect people and their property. It is also a powerful pretext for expansive government intervention into private economic life. Protecting liberty and ecology simultaneously requires greater attention to environmental matters than classical liberals have given these questions to date. This must change if the future is to be both free and green.

6

I, Pencil

Leonard E. Read

Editor's note:

Perhaps the most important economic essay of the past century is a two-thousand-word essay written from the perspective of a wooden pencil, specifically, a Mongol 482. The genius of the essay is how it illustrates extraordinarily complex ideas – including those espoused by Adam Smith, F. A. Hayek, and others – in a way that is accessible and intuitive to everyone. It should be required reading in all American schools, where the tendency is to fetishize planning and expertise as the solution to social problems. Leonard Reed's essay uses the simplest object, taken for granted by us all, to reveal the hidden complexity in our world and how only disperse, market-driven processes enable cooperation in ways that increase human flourishing.

The essay is reprinted with permission of the Foundation for Economic Education (www.fee.org), and includes an introduction by FEE president Lawrence Reed and an afterword by Milton Friedman.

* * *

INTRODUCTION BY LAWRENCE W. REED

Eloquent. Extraordinary. Timeless. Paradigm-shifting. Classic. Six decades after it first appeared, Leonard Read's "I, Pencil" evokes such adjectives of praise. Rightfully so, for this little essay opens eyes and minds among people of all ages. Many first-time readers never see the world quite the same again.

Ideas are most powerful when they're wrapped in a compelling story. Leonard's main point – economies can hardly be "planned" when not one soul possesses all the know-how and skills to produce a simple pencil – unfolds in the enchanting words of a pencil itself. Leonard could have written "I, Car" or "I, Airplane," but choosing those more complex items would have muted the message. No one person – repeat, no one, no matter how smart or how many degrees follow his name – could create from scratch a small, everyday pencil, let alone a car or an airplane.

This is a message that humbles the high and mighty. It pricks the inflated egos of those who think they know how to mind everybody else's business. It explains in plain language why central planning is an exercise in arrogance and futility, or what Nobel laureate and Austrian economist F. A. Hayek aptly termed "the pretence of knowledge."

Indeed, a major influence on Read's thinking in this regard was Hayek's famous 1945 article, "The Use of Knowledge in Society." In demolishing the spurious claims of the socialists of the day, Hayek wrote, "This is not a dispute about whether planning is to be done or not. It is a dispute as to whether planning is to be done centrally, by one authority for the whole economic system, or is to be divided among many individuals."

Maximilien Robespierre is said to have blessed the horrific French Revolution with this chilling declaration: "On ne saurait pas faire une omelette sans casser des oeufs." Translation: "One can't expect to make an omelet without breaking eggs." A consummate statist who worked tirelessly to plan the lives of others, he would become the architect of the Revolution's bloodiest phase – the Reign of Terror of 1793–1794.

Robespierre and his guillotine broke eggs by the thousands in a vain effort to impose a utopian society with government planners at the top and everybody else at the bottom. That French experience is but one example in a disturbingly familiar pattern. Call them what you will – socialists, interventionists, collectivists, statists – history is littered with their presumptuous plans for rearranging society to fit their vision of the common good, plans that always fail as they kill or impoverish other people in the process. If socialism ever earns a final epitaph, it will be this: Here lies a contrivance engineered by know-it-alls who broke eggs with abandon but never, ever created an omelet.

None of the Robespierres of the world knew how to make a pencil, yet they wanted to remake entire societies. How utterly preposterous, and mournfully tragic! But we will miss a large implication of Leonard Read's message if we assume it aims only at the tyrants whose names we all know. The lesson of "I, Pencil" is not that error begins when the planners plan big. It begins the moment one tosses humility aside, assumes he knows the unknowable, and employs the force of the State against peaceful individuals. That's not just a national disease. It can be very local indeed.

In our midst are people who think that if only they had government power on their side, they could pick tomorrow's winners and losers in the marketplace, set prices or rents where they ought to be, decide which forms of energy should power our homes and cars, and choose which industries should survive and which should die. They should stop for a few moments and learn a little humility from a lowly writing implement.

While "I, Pencil" shoots down the baseless expectations for central planning, it provides a supremely uplifting perspective of the individual. Guided by Adam Smith's "invisible hand" of prices, property, profits, and incentives, free people accomplish economic miracles of which socialist theoreticians can only dream. As the interests of countless individuals from around the world converge to produce pencils without a single "master mind," so do they also come together in free markets to feed, clothe, house, educate, and entertain hundreds of millions of people at ever higher levels. With great pride, FEE publishes this new edition of "I, Pencil." Someday there will be a centennial edition, maybe even a millennial one. This essay is truly one for the ages.

– Lawrence W. Reed, President Foundation for Economic Education

* * *

I, PENCIL

Leonard E. Read

I am a lead pencil – the ordinary wooden pencil familiar to all boys and girls and adults who can read and write.

Writing is both my vocation and my avocation; that's all I do.

You may wonder why I should write a genealogy. Well, to begin with, my story is interesting. And, next, I am a mystery – more so than a tree or a sunset or even a flash of lightning. But, sadly, I am taken for granted by those who use me, as if I were a mere incident and without background. This supercilious attitude relegates me to the level of the commonplace. This is a species of the grievous error in which mankind cannot too long persist without peril. For, the wise G. K. Chesterton observed, "We are perishing for want of wonder, not for want of wonders."

I, Pencil, simple though I appear to be, merit your wonder and awe, a claim I shall attempt to prove. In fact, if you can understand me – no, that's too much to ask of anyone – if you can become aware of the miraculousness which I symbolize, you can help save the freedom mankind is so unhappily losing. I have a profound lesson to teach. And I can teach this lesson better than can an automobile or an airplane or a mechanical dishwasher because – well, because I am seemingly so simple.

Simple? Yet, not a single person on the face of this earth knows how to make me. This sounds fantastic, doesn't it? Especially when it is realized that there are about one and one-half billion of my kind produced in the U.S.A. each year.

Pick me up and look me over. What do you see? Not much meets the eye – there's some wood, lacquer, the printed labeling, graphite lead, a bit of metal, and an eraser.

INNUMERABLE ANTECEDENTS

Just as you cannot trace your family tree back very far, so is it impossible for me to name and explain all my antecedents. But I would like to suggest enough of them to impress upon you the richness and complexity of my background.

My family tree begins with what in fact is a tree, a cedar of straight grain that grows in Northern California and Oregon. Now contemplate all the saws and trucks and rope and the countless other gear used in harvesting and carting the cedar logs to the railroad siding. Think of all the persons and the numberless skills that went into their fabrication: the mining of ore, the making of steel and its refinement into saws, axes, motors; the growing of hemp and bringing it through all the stages to heavy and strong rope; the logging camps with their beds and mess halls, the cookery and the raising of all the foods. Why, untold thousands of persons had a hand in every cup of coffee the loggers drink!

The logs are shipped to a mill in San Leandro, California. Can you imagine the individuals who make flat cars and rails and railroad engines and who construct and install the communication systems incidental thereto? These legions are among my antecedents.

Consider the millwork in San Leandro. The cedar logs are cut into small, pencil-length slats less than one-fourth of an inch in thickness. These are kiln dried and then tinted for the same reason women put rouge on their faces. People prefer that I look pretty, not a pallid white. The slats are waxed and kiln dried again. How many skills went into the making of the tint and the kilns, into supplying the heat, the light and power, the belts, motors, and all the other things a mill requires? Sweepers in the mill among my ancestors? Yes, and included are the men who poured the concrete for the dam of a Pacific Gas & Electric Company hydroplant which supplies the mill's power!

Don't overlook the ancestors present and distant who have a hand in transporting sixty carloads of slats across the nation.

Once in the pencil factory – $4,000,000 in machinery and building, all capital accumulated by thrifty and saving parents of mine – each slat is given eight grooves by a complex machine, after which another machine lays leads in every other slat, applies glue, and places another slat atop – a lead sandwich, so to speak. Seven brothers and I are mechanically carved from this "wood-clinched" sandwich.

My "lead" itself – it contains no lead at all – is complex. The graphite is mined in Ceylon [Sri Lanka]. Consider these miners and those who make their many tools and the makers of the paper sacks in which the graphite is shipped and those who make the string that ties the sacks and those who put them aboard ships and those who make the ships. Even the lighthouse keepers along the way assisted in my birth – and the harbor pilots.

The graphite is mixed with clay from Mississippi in which ammonium hydroxide is used in the refining process. Then wetting agents are added such as sulfonated tallow – animal fats chemically reacted with sulfuric acid. After passing through numerous machines, the mixture finally appears as endless extrusions – as from a sausage grinder – cut to size, dried, and baked for several hours at 1,850 degrees Fahrenheit. To increase their strength and smoothness the leads are then treated with a hot mixture which includes candelilla wax from Mexico, paraffin wax, and hydrogenated natural fats.

My cedar receives six coats of lacquer. Do you know all the ingredients of lacquer? Who would think that the growers of castor beans and the refiners of castor oil are a part of it? They are. Why, even the processes by which the lacquer is made a beautiful yellow involve the skills of more persons than one can enumerate!

Observe the labeling. That's a film formed by applying heat to carbon black mixed with resins. How do you make resins and what, pray, is carbon black?

My bit of metal – the ferrule – is brass. Think of all the persons who mine zinc and copper and those who have the skills to make shiny sheet brass from these products of nature. Those black rings on my ferrule are black nickel. What is black nickel and how is it applied? The complete story of why the center of my ferrule has no black nickel on it would take pages to explain.

Then there's my crowning glory, inelegantly referred to in the trade as "the plug," the part man uses to erase the errors he makes with me. An ingredient called "factice" is what does the erasing. It is a rubber-like product made by reacting rapeseed oil from the Dutch East Indies [Indonesia] with sulfur chloride. Rubber, contrary to the common notion, is only for binding purposes. Then, too, there are numerous vulcanizing and accelerating agents. The pumice comes from Italy; and the pigment which gives "the plug" its color is cadmium sulfide.

NO ONE KNOWS

Does anyone wish to challenge my earlier assertion that no single person on the face of this earth knows how to make me?

Actually, millions of human beings have had a hand in my creation, no one of whom even knows more than a very few of the others. Now, you may say that I go too far in relating the picker of a coffee berry in far-off Brazil and food growers elsewhere to my creation; that this is an extreme position. I shall stand by my claim. There isn't a single person in all these millions, including the president of the pencil company, who contributes more than a tiny, infinitesimal bit of know-how. From the standpoint of know-how the only difference between the miner of graphite in Ceylon and the logger in Oregon is in the type of know-how. Neither the miner nor the logger can be dispensed with, any more than can the chemist at the factory or the worker in the oil field – paraffin being a by-product of petroleum.

Here is an astounding fact: Neither the worker in the oil field nor the chemist nor the digger of graphite or clay nor any who mans or makes the ships or trains or trucks nor the one who runs the machine that does the knurling on my bit of metal nor the president of the company performs his singular task because he wants me. Each one wants me less, perhaps, than does a child in the first grade. Indeed, there are some among this vast multitude who never saw a pencil nor would they know how to use one. Their motivation is other than me. Perhaps it is something like this: Each of these millions sees that he can thus exchange his tiny know-how for the goods and services he needs or wants. I may or may not be among these items.

NO MASTER MIND

There is a fact still more astounding: The absence of a master mind, of anyone dictating or forcibly directing these countless actions which bring me into being. No trace of such a person can be found. Instead, we find the Invisible Hand at work. This is the mystery to which I earlier referred.

It has been said that "only God can make a tree." Why do we agree with this? Isn't it because we realize that we ourselves could not make one? Indeed, can we even describe a tree? We cannot, except in superficial terms. We can say, for instance, that a certain molecular configuration manifests itself as a tree. But what mind is there among men that could even record, let alone direct, the constant changes in molecules that transpire in the life span of a tree? Such a feat is utterly unthinkable!

I, Pencil, am a complex combination of miracles: a tree, zinc, copper, graphite, and so on. But to these miracles which manifest themselves in Nature an even more extraordinary miracle has been added: the configuration of creative human energies – millions of tiny know-hows configurating naturally and spontaneously in response to human necessity and desire and in the absence of any human masterminding! Since only God can make a tree, I insist that only God could make me. Man can no more direct these millions of know-hows to bring me into being than he can put molecules together to create a tree.

The above is what I meant when writing, "If you can become aware of the miraculousness which I symbolize, you can help save the freedom mankind is so unhappily losing." For, if one is aware that these know-hows will naturally, yes, automatically, arrange themselves into creative and productive patterns in response to human necessity and demand – that is, in the absence of governmental or any other coercive master-minding – then one will possess an absolutely essential ingredient for freedom: a faith in free people. Freedom is impossible without this faith.

Once government has had a monopoly of a creative activity such, for instance, as the delivery of the mails, most individuals will believe that the mails could not be efficiently delivered by men acting freely. And here is the reason: Each one acknowledges that he himself doesn't know how to do all the things incident to mail delivery. He also recognizes that no other individual could do it. These assumptions are correct. No individual possesses enough know-how to perform a nation's mail delivery any more than any individual possesses enough know-how to make a pencil.

Now, in the absence of faith in free people – in the unawareness that millions of tiny know-hows would naturally and miraculously form and cooperate to satisfy this necessity – the individual cannot help but reach the erroneous conclusion that mail can be delivered only by governmental "masterminding."

TESTIMONY GALORE

If I, Pencil, were the only item that could offer testimony on what men and women can accomplish when free to try, then those with little faith would have a fair case. However, there is testimony galore; it's all about us and on every hand. Mail delivery is exceedingly simple when compared, for instance, to the making of an automobile or a calculating machine or a grain combine or a milling machine or to tens of thousands of other things. Delivery? Why, in this area where men have been left free to try, they deliver the human voice around the world in less than one second; they deliver an event visually and in motion to any person's home when it is happening; they deliver 150 passengers from Seattle to Baltimore in less than 4 hours; they deliver gas from Texas to one's range or furnace in New York at unbelievably low rates and without subsidy; they deliver each 4 pounds of oil from the Persian Gulf to our Eastern Seaboard – halfway around the world – for less money than the government charges for delivering a one-ounce letter across the street!

The lesson I have to teach is this: Leave all creative energies uninhibited. Merely organize society to act in harmony with this lesson. Let society's legal apparatus remove all obstacles the best it can. Permit these creative know-hows freely to flow. Have faith that free men and women will respond to the Invisible Hand. This faith will be confirmed. I, Pencil, seemingly simple though I am, offer the miracle of my creation as testimony that this is a practical faith, as practical as the sun, the rain, a cedar tree, the good earth.

* * *

AFTERWORD

Milton Friedman, Nobel Laureate, 1976

Leonard Read's delightful story, "I, Pencil," has become a classic, and deservedly so. I know of no other piece of literature that so succinctly, persuasively, and effectively illustrates the meaning of both Adam Smith's invisible hand – the possibility of cooperation without coercion – and Friedrich Hayek's emphasis on the importance of dispersed knowledge and the role of the price system in communicating information that "will make the individuals do the desirable things without anyone having to tell them what to do."

We used Leonard's story in our television show, "Free to Choose," and in the accompanying book of the same title to illustrate "the power of the market" (the title of both the first segment of the TV show and of chapter one of the book). We summarized the story and then went on to say:

> None of the thousands of persons involved in producing the pencil performed his task because he wanted a pencil. Some among them never saw a pencil and would not know what it is for. Each saw his work as a way to get the goods and services he wanted – goods and services we produced in order to get the pencil we wanted. Every time we go to the store and buy a pencil, we are exchanging a little bit of our services for the infinitesimal amount of services that each of the thousands contributed toward producing the pencil.
>
> It is even more astounding that the pencil was ever produced. No one sitting in a central office gave orders to these thousands of people. No military police enforced the orders that were not given. These people live in many lands, speak different languages, practice different religions, may even hate one another – yet none of these differences prevented them from cooperating to produce a pencil. How did it happen? Adam Smith gave us the answer two hundred years ago.

"I, Pencil" is a typical Leonard Read product: imaginative, simple yet subtle, breathing the love of freedom that imbued everything Leonard wrote or did. As in the rest of his work, he was not trying to tell people what to do or how to conduct themselves. He was simply trying to enhance individuals' understanding of themselves and of the system they live in.

That was his basic credo and one that he stuck to consistently during his long period of service to the public – not public service in the sense of government service. Whatever the pressure, he stuck to his guns, refusing to compromise his principles. That was why he was so effective in keeping alive, in the early days, and then spreading the basic idea that human freedom required private property, free competition, and severely limited government.

7

Foot Voting and the Future of Liberty

Ilya Somin

INTRODUCTION

How can we best realize the ideal of liberty in the modern world? Libertarians have made some important progress over the last seventy years, since the nadir of classical liberal ideology during the Great Depression and World War II. But we are still a long way from realizing our goals. In recent years, libertarians have suffered setbacks thanks to the resurgence of both socialism on the left and nationalism on the right.

No one idea is likely to reinvigorate libertarianism all on its own. However, libertarians and others would do well to consider the potential benefits of expanding opportunities to "vote with your feet."

One of the main goals of libertarianism – and, perhaps, liberalism generally – is expanding political freedom: the opportunity to exercise meaningful choice over the government policies we live under. The main mechanism of political choice in modern liberal democracies is ballot box voting. Voting has significant virtues. It is likely one of the reasons why democracies outperform dictatorships on many measures of economic performance, and protection for individual rights.[1]

But as a mechanism for exercising political freedom, ballot box voting has serious flaws. The average citizen has almost no chance of affecting the outcome of an electoral process. In part as a result, he or she also has strong incentives to make ill-informed and illogical decisions. Foot voting can do better on both fronts. It is, thereby, also often a superior way to enhance political freedom. Expanded foot voting can also greatly enhance human freedom and well-being in other ways.

Part I of this chapter briefly outlines three types of foot voting: voting with your feet between jurisdictions in a federal system, foot voting in the private sector, and international migration. All three involve meaningful exercises of political choice.

---

[1] See generally MORTON H. HALPERIN, JOSEPH SIEGLE, AND MICHAEL M. WEINSTEIN, THE DEMOCRACY ADVANTAGE, (2010).

In Part II, I explain how foot voting is superior to ballot box voting as a mechanism of political freedom.[2] It allows for more meaningful and better-informed choice. It is also superior from the standpoint of several leading accounts of political freedom: Consent, negative liberty, positive liberty, and nondomination.

Part III considers objections to foot voting based on theories of self-determination, under which current residents of a given territory have a right to exclude newcomers in order to protect the political freedom of the former. Such theories come in both group-oriented and individualistic variants. Group theories posit that certain groups have a right to exclude newcomers based on their ethnic, racial, or religious characteristics. Individualistic theories claim that current residents can exclude newcomers for much the same reasons that private property owners or members of a private club have a right to exclude outsiders. I argue that both have severe flaws.

Part IV discusses some institutional reforms that can help expand foot voting opportunities, while mitigating potential downsides. Finally, the Conclusion tentatively suggests some ways in which expanded foot voting can help brighten future prospects for promoting libertarian values.

I THREE MODES OF FOOT VOTING

There are three important types of foot voting in modern society.[3] First, people can vote with their feet by deciding what jurisdiction to live in within a federal system, such as a state or local government. In the United States alone there are fifty states and thousands of local governments that foot voters can choose between. Both historically and today, millions of people move from one jurisdiction to another at least in part because of preferences over public policy.[4] Some 43 percent of native-born Americans have made at least one interstate move in their lifetimes, and almost two-thirds have at least moved from one locality to another.[5]

A second mechanism for foot voting is international migration, where migrants choose what type of government they wish to live under by moving from one nation to another. Such nations as the United States, Australia, Argentina, Canada, and New Zealand were largely populated by immigrants who chose to vote with their

---

[2]   The terms "foot voting" and "ballot box voting" used here are similar to Albert Hirschman's well-known distinction between "exit" and "voice." See ALBERT HIRSCHMAN, EXIT, VOICE, AND LOYALTY: RESPONSES TO DECLINE IN FIRMS, ORGANIZATIONS, AND STATES (1970). However, ballot box voting is just one type of "voice" mechanism by which people can exercise influence over government policy, albeit the only one readily available to the vast majority of ordinary citizens.

[3]   For a previous overview of the three types on which this one is modeled, see Ilya Somin, "Foot Voting, Federalism, and Political Freedom," NOMOS: FEDERALISM AND SUBSIDIARITY, EDS. JAMES FLEMING AND JACOB LEVY (2014).

[4]   See ILYA SOMIN, DEMOCRACY AND POLITICAL IGNORANCE: WHY SMALLER GOVERNMENT IS SMARTER chapter 5 (2016).

[5]   Ibid., 166.

feet in hopes of finding greater freedom and opportunity due in large part to superior government policies in the destination country.[6]

Foot voting across international boundaries expands choice even more than domestic foot voting, because of the vast differences between national governments. The differences in policy and quality of institutions between, say, Mexico and the United States are vastly greater than those between any two American states or any two Mexican ones.

Finally, foot voting also occurs in the private sector, when we decide what goods and services wish to purchase in the market or what civil society organizations we wish to join. Such private-sector foot voting is particularly evident in the case of private planned communities and other organizations that carry out functions traditionally associated with local or regional governments, such as security, environmental amenities, and waste disposal.[7] In the United States alone, some 62 million people live in private communities such as condominium associations, and others.[8] Private planned communities have increasingly taken on a wide range of functions historically performed by government.[9] Similar institutions have become common in many other countries around the world, both advanced liberal democracies, and in developing nations.[10]

In many cases, foot voting can be undertaken even without physically moving from one place to another. In the private sector, for example, one can change schools, join a new civil society organization, or purchase a new product or service without ever changing one's place of residence.

In some situations, it is even possible to choose different governmental institutions without physical movement, as for example when people sign contracts with "choice of law" clauses that utilize the laws of a jurisdiction other than the one where they are located. Some economists and legal scholars argue for expanding the use of such mechanisms, breaking the link between territory and governance.[11]

The key attribute of foot voting that differentiates it from conventional ballot box voting is not movement, as such, but rather the ability to make an individually

---

[6] For a wide-ranging overview of the relevant history, see MASSIMO LIVI-BACCI, A SHORT HISTORY OF MIGRATION, chapters 5–6 (2012).

[7] For an overview of private planned communities, see ROBERT NELSON, PRIVATE NEIGHBORHOODS AND THE TRANSFORMATION OF LOCAL GOVERNMENT (2005).

[8] Edward Peter Stringham, *Private Governance: Creating Order in Economic and Social Life*, (New York: Oxford University Press, 2015), 131

[9] Ibid, and NELSON, PRIVATE NEIGHBORHOODS.

[10] SOMIN, DEMOCRACY AND POLITICAL IGNORANCE, 159.

[11] See, for example, ERIN O'HARA AND LARRY RIBSTEIN, THE LAW MARKET, (2009); BRUNO S. FREY AND REINER EICHENBERGER, THE NEW DEMOCRATIC FEDERALISM FOR EUROPE: FUNCTIONAL, OVERLAPPING, AND COMPETING JURISDICTIONS (2004); BRUNO S. FREY, HAPPINESS: A NEW REVOLUTION IN ECONOMICS 190–98 (2008); See Bruno Frey, "A Utopia? Government without Territorial Monopoly," 6 INDEPENDENT REVIEW 99 (2001); Abraham Bell and Gideon Parchomovsky, "Of Property and Federalism," 115 YALE LAW JOURNAL 72–115, 101–13 (2005).

decisive choice. Unlike the ballot box voter, whose vote is just one of many thousands or millions and usually has only a tiny chance of affecting the outcome, the foot voter can make decisions that have a high probability of making a difference.

Foot voting need not always be purely individualistic. Families and businesses, for example, make foot voting decisions that require the assent of more than one person. But in most such cases, there are individuals who can either make the choice all on their own or at least exercise a high degree of influence.

The exact point at which an individual's leverage becomes too small for the decision to be considered a case of foot voting rather than ballot box voting may be hard to identify. The distinction between the two is, in close cases, more a matter of degree than kind. But the difficulty of drawing a precise line between the two does not obviate important difference between them, Most important real-word cases clearly fall on one side of the divide or the other.

II HOW FOOT VOTING OUTPERFORMS BALLOT BOX VOTING

Ballot box voting is usually seen as the essence of political freedom. But it has two serious shortcomings: individual voters have almost no chance of actually affecting the outcome of most elections, and they usually have little or no incentive to make an informed choice. Foot voting is superior on both counts.

Meaningful, Informed Choice

It is difficult to claim a person has meaningful freedom if they have only a 1-in-1-million or 1-in-100-million chance of making a decision that changes the outcome.[12] For example, a person does not have meaningful religious freedom if she has only a 1-in-1-million chance being able to determine which religion she wishes to practice. Similarly, a person with only a 1-in-1-million chance of deciding what views she is allowed to express surely does not have meaningful freedom of speech. What is true of freedom of speech and freedom of religion is also true of political freedom. A person with only an infinitesimal chance of affecting what kind of government policies he or she is subjected to has little, if any, genuine political freedom.

The individual voter's infinitesimally small odds of affecting electoral outcomes also undermine political freedom in a second way: it ensures that most will not make well-informed decisions. On many normative views of freedom, its effective exercise requires at least a reasonably informed choice, at least when it comes to important issues.

---

[12] Some parts of this section are adapted from Ilya Somin, "Foot Voting, Decentralization, and Development," Minnesota Law Review (forthcoming).

Widely accepted standards of medical ethics, for example, require physicians to secure the patient's informed consent before performing an operation. As the American Medical Association (AMA) Code of Medical Ethics puts it, "[t]he patient's right of self-decision can be effectively exercised only if the patient possesses enough information to enable an informed choice."[3] Like many medical decisions, political choices also are often literally matters of life and death. For millions of people, the outcome of an election might make the difference between war and peace, wealth and poverty, or sickness and health.

Unfortunately, few electoral decisions meet the AMA's standards. Ballot box voters have strong incentives to be "rationally ignorant," because there is so little chance that their votes will matter. Survey data shows that they often lack even very basic knowledge about the candidates and policy questions at issue in any given election.[14] They also often have little incentive to analyze the information they do learn in a logical, unbiased way. To the contrary, voters have incentives to fall prey to "rational irrationality": when there are few or no negative consequences to error, it is rational to make almost no effort to control one's biases.[15] For example, voters routinely overvalue any evidence that supports their preexisting views, while downplaying or ignoring anything that cuts the other way.[16]

Decades of survey data indicate that voter knowledge levels are low, and have experienced little or no increase despite rising educational attainment, and the development of the internet and other modern technology that makes information easier to access.[17] Often, the majority of the public does not know even basic information, such as which party controls Congress, what major policies have been enacted, or which elected officials are responsible for which issues.[18] Just before the 2014 election, in which the main stake at issue was control of Congress, only 38 percent of voters knew which party controlled the House of Representatives, and a similar percentage knew which controlled the Senate.[19] Another 2014 survey found that only 36 percent of Americans can even name the three branches of the federal government: the executive, the legislative, and the judiciary.[20]

---

[13] AMA Code of Medical Ethics, Opinion 8.08 (2012), available at http://journalofethics.ama-assn.org/2012/07/coet1–1207.html.

[14] This part of the chapter builds on my book DEMOCRACY AND POLITICAL IGNORANCE: WHY SMALLER GOVERNMENT IS SMARTER, (2016), which analyzes rational ignorance and its consequences in great detail (see esp. chs. 1–4).

[15] See ibid., ch. 3, and Bryan Caplan, THE MYTH OF THE RATIONAL VOTER (2007).

[16] For a review of the evidence, see Somin, DEMOCRACY AND POLITICAL IGNORANCE, 92–97.

[17] For recent overviews of the evidence, see, for example, SOMIN, DEMOCRACY AND POLITICAL IGNORANCE, ch. 1; JASON BRENNAN, AGAINST DEMOCRACY (2016); CHRISTOPHER ACHEN AND LARRY BARTELS, DEMOCRACY FOR REALISTS: WHY ELECTIONS DO NOT PRODUCE RESPONSIVE GOVERNMENT, (2016); RICK SHENKMAN, JUST HOW STUPID ARE WE? FACING THE TRUTH ABOUT THE AMERICAN VOTER (2008).

[18] For numerous examples, see SOMIN, DEMOCRACY AND POLITICAL IGNORANCE, ch. 1.

[19] Ibid., 1.

[20] Ibid., 20.

Foot voting is superior to ballot box voting on both of these counts. It enables the individual decision maker to make a meaningful choice. And precisely because the decision actually matters, it gives him or her strong incentives to acquire relevant information and use it wisely. The person deciding where to live or what choices to make in the marketplace and civil society knows that her decisions have real consequences, and generally makes more effort to acquire information. Much empirical evidence backs these theoretical predictions.[21]

The informational advantages of foot voting loom even larger if we believe, as some political theorists do, that voters should engage in "deliberative democracy" in which they carefully consider opposing arguments and moral values, and not just merely cast ballots based on their preferences.[22] Deliberative democracy demands a higher level of knowledge and analytical sophistication than more modest versions of democratic theory do. Rationally ignorant voters are even less likely to meet those standards, than the less severe requirements imposed by merely "aggregative" views of democratic participation.[23]

In previous work, I have explained why deliberative democracy is unlikely to be made workable by incentivizing voters to participate in deliberative experiments, or by using jury-like mechanisms.[24] Foot voting will not meet all the requirements of deliberative democracy either. But it is at least likely to result in better-informed and more thoughtful decision-making than ballot box voting.[25]

Foot Voting and the Theory of Political Freedom

In addition to its general advantages as a mechanism for free, informed choice, foot voting also trumps ballot box voting under four leading standard accounts of political freedom: consent, negative freedom, positive freedom, and nondomination.

---

[21] Ibid., ch. 5.
[22] For defense of deliberative democracy, see, for example, ROBERT GOODIN, REFLECTIVE DEMOCRACY (2005); ETHAN R. LIEB, DELIBERATIVE DEMOCRACY IN AMERICA: A PROPOSAL FOR A DELIBERATIVE BRANCH OF GOVERNMENT (2004); JAMES BOHMAN, PUBLIC DELIBER- ATION: PLURALISM, COMPLEXITY, AND DEMOCRACY (1996); JOHN S. DRYZEK, DELIBERATIVE DEMOCRACY AND BEYOND: LIBERALS, CRITICS, CONTESTATIONS (2002); AMY GUTMANN AND DENNIS THOMPSON, WHY DELIBERATIVE DEMOCRACY? (2004); AMY GUTMANN AND DENNIS THOMPSON, DEMOCRACY AND DISAGREEMENT (1996); and James S. Fishkin, "Deliberative Democracy and Constitutions," 28 SOCIAL PHILOSOPHY AND POLICY 242 (2011).
[23] For detailed discussions of this point, see Ilya Somin, "Deliberative Democracy and Political Ignorance," 22 CRITICAL REVIEW 253 (2010), and SOMIN, DEMOCRACY AND POLITICAL IGNOR- ANCE, 58–62.
[24] SOMIN, DEMOCRACY AND POLITICAL IGNORANCE, 204–11.
[25] For more extensive discussion, see ibid., ch. 5.

At least since John Locke and Thomas Hobbes in the seventeenth century, many political theorists have argued that the authority of the state is legitimized by consent.[26] Ballot box voting is often seen as an indicator of such consent.

But, as critics have pointed out, it does not truly signify meaningful consent because, among other things, those who choose not to vote are not thereby exempt from the state's authority.[27] Foot voting is better, in this respect, because those who move out of a jurisdiction really can escape all (or at least most) of its laws.

The degree of consensuality is reduced by possible moving costs. But greater decentralization can mitigate that, at least to a substantial degree. Foot voting is less costly when moving intranationally than internationally, and less costly still when choosing between localities or between private sector alternatives. While expanded foot voting probably will not make political power fully consensual, it comes closer than ballot box voting.

Foot voting may be the only possible avenue to make government more consensual for the large percentage of the world's population that lives under nondemocratic regimes. Freedom House estimates that some 36 percent of the world's people live in "not free" undemocratic nations, and another 24 percent in ones that are only "partly free" (i.e., only partly democratic).[28] In such regimes, most residents have even less leverage over government policy than individual voters in a Western liberal democracy do. Many of these governments are unlikely to liberalize in the near future. Unless and until they do, emigration may be the only mechanism by which most of their subjects can refuse consent to their rule.

Another possible approach to political freedom links it to "negative" freedom more generally: people have greater political freedom to the extent that they can minimize unwanted government interference with their choices.[29] Here too, foot voting offers greater protection than ballot box voting: the ability to completely, or at least largely, avoid unwanted interference creates greater negative freedom that the ability to cast a vote that has only an infinitesimal chance of having an impact.

It is also important to remember that restrictions on freedom of movement are themselves a major imposition on negative freedom. When governments block would-be migrants from entering or leaving, they prevent millions of people from freely contracting with willing residents who wish to employ them, rent property to them, and otherwise interact with them.[30] They forcibly confine large numbers of

---

[26] See JOHN LOCKE, SECOND TREATISE ON GOVERNMENT, Peter Laslett, ed. (1963); THOMAS HOBBES, LEVIATHAN, Richard Tuck, ed. (1991).

[27] See, for example, MICHAEL HUEMER, THE PROBLEM OF POLITICAL AUTHORITY, chapter 4 (2013); A. JOHN SIMMONS, MORAL PRINCIPLES AND POLITICAL OBLIGATION 136–39 (1979).

[28] Freedom House, *Freedom in the World 2016*, available at https://freedomhouse.org/report/freedom-world/freedom-world-2016.

[29] For a leading modern work in this vein, See ROBERT NOZICK, ANARCHY, THE STATE AND UTOPIA (1974).

[30] On the ways in which migration restrictions violate negative freedom, see Michael Huemer, "Is There a Right to Immigrate?" SOCIAL THEORY AND PRACTICE 36 (2010): 429–61.

people to a lifetime of poverty and oppression in poor and often repressive societies. Few government interventions in the market and civil society restrict the freedom of so many people so severely.

Many modern political thinkers argue for a more "positive" approach to freedom that focuses on "capabilities." On this view, freedom is not just non-interference, but the actual ability to exercise autonomy, pursue your preferred projects, and enhance your capacities.[31] Here too foot voting offers greater prospects than ballot box voting.

A foot voter can potentially choose between a wide variety of governmental and private alternatives that might help him or her develop capabilities and pursue a range of possible projects. By contrast, most ballot box voters have almost no control over options available to them. Moreover, foot voters are more likely to make well-informed and unbiased choices than ballot box voters.[32] Some poor and disadvantaged people may need redistributive programs to develop their capabilities. Historically, however, expansive foot voting opportunities have been of special value to the poor and oppressed and tend to benefit them even more than the relatively well off.[33]

International migration offers a particularly powerful mechanism for enhancing positive freedom. Economists estimate that allowing free migration throughout the world would likely double world GDP.[34] Much of that benefit would go to migrants from poor nations, where their opportunities to enhance their capacities would otherwise be severely limited at best. As in the case of negative freedom, the effects are enormous. It is difficult to think of any other policy change that would enhance positive freedom for so many people so quickly.

For both positive and negative freedom, the benefits of foot voting go far beyond the narrowly "economic." Expanded foot voting opportunities can also massively enhance migrants' freedom and well-being more generally. Consider, for example, women fleeing patriarchal societies, religious minorities fleeing oppression, and people fleeing repressive tyrannical regimes of various kinds.

From the standpoint of enhancing positive freedom by expanding human capabilities,[35] the noneconomic benefits of foot voting may be just as important as the enhancement of productivity, conceived in narrow "economic" terms. In many cases, escaping from noneconomic oppression enables migrants to enormously enhance their capacities in a variety of ways.

---

[31] See, for example, AMARTYA K. SEN, DEVELOPMENT AS FREEDOM (1999).

[32] See the discussion of this issue earlier in this chapter, and also in SOMIN, DEMOCRACY AND POLITICAL IGNORANCE.

[33] For examples, see Somin, "Foot Voting, Federalism, and Political Freedom," and SOMIN, DEMOCRACY AND POLITICAL IGNORANCE, ch. 5.

[34] Michael Clemens, "Economics and Emigration: Trillion Dollar Bills Left on the Sidewalk?" 25 JOURNAL OF ECONOMIC PERSPECTIVES 83 (2011).

[35] See, for example, SEN, DEVELOPMENT AS FREEDOM.

Finally, some argue that the true essence of political freedom is "nondomination:" the state of being free from the arbitrarily imposed will of others.[36] By this standard, too, foot voting trumps ballot box voting.[37] In most cases, the individual ballot box voter finds herself under the complete domination of whichever political forces prevail in electoral competition – at least with respect to whatever issues come within the control of democratic government. And she generally has only an infinitesimal chance of changing any of their policies. If a dictator controls important aspects of your life, but gives you a 1-in-100 million chance of changing his decisions, it is pretty obvious that you are dominated by him. The same is true if a democratic majority controls your life in the same way.

In most cases, domination by a democratic majority is likely be more benevolent and less onerous than domination by a dictator. But relatively benevolent domination is domination nonetheless. A benevolent dictator who genuinely seeks to improve the lot of his subjects still exercises domination over them. The same is true of a democratic majority that similarly strives for benevolence.

If extensive opportunities for foot voting are institutionalized, by contrast, the foot voter can often use exit rights to escape unwanted impositions. That ability greatly reduces conditions of domination, even if does not completely eliminate them.

Some political theorists do not assign any intrinsic value to political freedom, and instead assess its merits on purely consequentialist grounds – for example by the extent to which it promotes happiness or utility. The informational advantages of foot voting help explain why it generally scores well on consequentialist criteria as well as intrinsic ones. Making better-informed decisions increases the likelihood of getting a beneficial result. And the welfare benefits of expanding foot voting are, in many cases, truly enormous. For international migration, they often make the difference between a life spent in dire poverty and oppression, and one spent in relative affluence and freedom. For internal foot voters, very large gains are also possible.[38] A recent study by the National Bureau of Economic Research estimates that reducing restrictive zoning rules that impede foot voting, to the levels that prevail in the median American city, could increase US GDP by 9.5 percent.[39]

---

[36] See, for example, Philip Pettit, *Republicanism: A Theory of Freedom and Government*, (1997); JAMES L. FISHKIN, TYRANNY AND LEGITIMACY: A CRITIQUE OF POLITICAL THEORIES (1979).

[37] For a somewhat similar critique of democracy from the standpoint of nondomination theory, see JASON BRENNAN, AGAINST DEMOCRACY 94–99 (2016).

[38] For recent overviews, see Somin, "Foot Voting, Decentralization, and Development," and David Schleicher, "Stuck! The Law and the Economics of Residential Stability," 127 YALE LAW JOURNAL 78 (2017), available at https://papers.ssrn.com/sol3/cf_dev/AbsByAuth.cfm?per_id= 469670.

[39] See Chang Tai-Hsieh & Enrico Moretti, "Housing Constraints and Spatial Misallocation", NBER Working Paper No. 21154 (2015), available at www.nber.org/papers/w21154. For an overview of the evidence, see Edward Glaeser, "Reforming Land Use Regulations," Brookings Institution, April 24, 2017, available at www.brookings.edu/research/reforming-land-use-regula tions/amp/.

III SELF-DETERMINATION OBJECTIONS TO FOOT VOTING

Perhaps the most obvious objection to free migration across international (and perhaps regional) boundaries is that the existing population within those jurisdictions has a right of self-determination that entitles it to keep out migrants who might change the character of the state in some way. In other words, the political freedom of foot-voting migrants may be at odds with that of ballot-box voting natives.

Some theorists argue that the authority to exclude is arises from the common ethnicity, culture, or sense of community of the current residents, who have a right to keep out those who are different.[40] Others claim that this power arises from the inhabitants' individual rights to freedom of association or property rights,[41] in much the same way as members of a club can exclude new applicants for membership or property owners can exclude those who wish to trespass on their land.[42] Both types of self-determination arguments against migration have serious flaws.

Group Rights Claims

Claims based on group membership founder on the flaws inherent in claims that there is a right to live in a polity that privileges one's particular culture or ethnic group. Among other flaws, such a right would imply the power to coerce even currently existing residents to keep them from changing their cultural practices. After all, a culture can be transformed through internal change no less than through immigration. Older generations often complain about the cultural changes created by the choices of the young. Over time, the latter often end up radically changing the manners, morals, and social norms they inherited. Yet few argue that their elders have a right to use force to prevent it, much less to the point of expelling anyone who fails to conform to the previously dominant cultural patterns.

Moreover, only a small fraction of the world's ethnic or cultural groups have a state of their own. There are currently some 200 nations in the world, but thousands of ethnic, religious, and cultural groups who lack a nation of their own, or even a province within a larger nation where they are the majority. Few would argue that the principle of self-determination entitles each such group to sovereignty over a territory from which they can exclude others. If this is true of currently stateless groups, it is difficult see why it is not equally true of those

---

[40] See, for example, MICHAEL WALZER, SPHERES OF JUSTICE, ch. 2 (1983); DAVID MILLER, STRANGERS IN OUR MIDST: THE POLITICAL PHILOSOPHY OF IMMIGRATION (2016).

[41] See, for example, ANDREW ALTMAN AND CHRISTOPHER HEATH WELLMAN, A MORAL THEORY OF INTERNATIONAL JUSTICE, ch. 7 (2011).

[42] Both analogies are advanced in Christopher Heath Wellman, "Freedom of Movement and the Right to Enter and Exit," in SARAH FINE AND LEAH YPI, EDS., MIGRATION IN POLITICAL THEORY: THE ETHICS OF MOVEMENT AND MEMBERSHIP, 83–87 (2016).

who – in most cases through conquest or historical accident – happen to have a majority in an existing nation-state.

Group-based claims for a right to exclude are particularly problematic for liberal democrats committed to principles of non-discrimination on the basis of race and ethnicity. The standard defense of racial and ethnic non-discrimination is that race and ethnicity are morally irrelevant characteristics that people have no control over.[43]

Whether you are black, white, Asian, or Hispanic says nothing about your moral worth, or what rights you should have. Most liberal democrats recoil at the idea that we should restrict people's liberty because they chose the wrong parents.

What is true of race and ethnicity is equally true of place of birth. Whether a person was born in the United States, Mexico, or China is also a morally arbitrary characteristic that she has no control over, and which should not determine how much freedom she is entitled to. Place of birth is no more indicative of the content of your character than race of birth.

Legal and political theorists who argue for racial and ethnic preferences generally do so on a strictly limited basis, usually in order to compensate for large-scale historic discrimination through, for example, race-based affirmative action programs.[44] Whatever the merits of such arguments, they clearly cannot justify systematic discrimination against migrants based on place of birth – discrimination that often targets groups who are themselves the victims of massive injustices at the hands of the rulers of the nations they seek to leave.

Obviously, place of birth might sometimes correlate with morally relevant characteristics, even though it does not cause them. People born in one nation may, among other things, be more likely to become criminals or terrorists than those born in another.

But the same is true of different racial and ethnic groups. In the United States, African Americans, on average, have higher crime rates than members of many other ethnic groups.[45] White males are disproportionately likely to become domestic terrorists.[46] It does not follow, however, that we would be justified in imposing severe restrictions on the freedom of blacks or whites as a group.

In both cases, it would be deeply unjust to restrict people's freedom merely because they happen to be members of the same racial or ethnic group as others who have committed various crimes and misdeeds. The same point applies to

[43] See, for example, Robert K. Fullwinder, "Achieving Equal Opportunity," in ROBERT K. FULLWINDER AND CLAUDIA MILLS, ED., MORAL FOUNDATIONS OF CIVIL RIGHTS (1986).

[44] For a recent example, see, e.g., RANDALL KENNEDY, FOR DISCRIMINATION: RACE, AFFIRMATIVE ACTION, AND THE LAW (2013).

[45] See, for example, Matthew Cella and Alan Neuhauser, "Race and Homicide in America: By the Numbers," *US News and World Report*, Sept. 29, 2016, available at www.usnews.com/news/articles/2016-09-29/race-and-homicide-in-america-by-the-numbers.

[46] See New America Foundation, *Terrorism in America after 9/11*, (2015), available at www.newamerica.org/in-depth/terrorism-in-america/.

potential immigrant groups singled out for exclusion merely because others born in
the same region have a disproportionate propensity to commit various wrongs.

Perhaps the ideal of self-determination allows current residents to impose racial
and ethnic restrictions on immigrants that would not be permissible in the case of
natives. But this argument is circular. It assumes the validity of the very point that
must be proven: that natives have a special right to exclude potential immigrants that
does not apply to other natives. The ethnic, racial or cultural characteristics of the
latter cannot justify uniquely negative treatment for immigrants because many
natives also have similar characteristics; yet it is not considered permissible to impose
discriminatory treatment on the latter.

Individual Rights Claims

More individualistic versions of the right to exclude migrants also suffer from serious
flaws. The most significant is that real-world states are not voluntary organizations,
but coercive ones. Unlike club members, residents of nation states are born into
their polities and not allowed to choose freely whether to live under the authority
of the government.

Political philosopher A. John Simmons argues that a state may be justified in
restricting immigration if it consists of "a substantial group of persons who willingly
create (or join) a group committed to persisting as a viable, governed territorial
polity."[47] In that event, the resulting government would have the right to "fence,
control, and exclude in the same ways that an individual landowner is."[48] But, as
Simmons seems to recognize, virtually no actually existing government meets these
criteria. None rule over only persons who "willingly" created or joined the polity
in question. To the contrary, every actual government in the world was created at
least in part through violence and coercion, and exercises power over anyone who
enters or is born within its claimed domain, regardless of whether those individuals
voluntarily agree to its authority or not.

Because of their coercive nature, governments (or the local majorities who elect
them) also cannot be properly analogized to private property owners, who have a
presumptive right to exclude others from "their" land. If states really were properly
analogous to clubs or property owners, many highly illiberal consequences would
follow. For example, they would be justified in forbidding speech that criticizes the
state's leaders, just as a property owner can usually forbid speech she disapproves
of on her land.

A truly club-like state would also be justified in expelling people with religious
or moral beliefs that the state's leaders disapprove of – just as clubs can restrict

---

[47] SIMMONS, BOUNDARIES OF AUTHORITY, 239.
[48] Ibid., 241.

membership in similar ways. Private clubs can and sometimes do limit their membership to people who practice a particular religion, or espouse a particular secular philosophy. A political club can require all members to also be members of the Democratic Party, a religious one can grant membership exclusively to Catholics, and so on.

A truly voluntary private club may well be entitled to broad rights to exclude newcomers. The same may well be true of other fully voluntary private organizations. But states – at least those that currently exist in the real world – are fundamentally different from private clubs, and should not be allowed the same kind of powers.

Addressing Political Externalities without Restricting Migration

Some critics of immigration who do not necessarily endorse strong theories of exclusionary self-determination, nevertheless worry that free migration might undermine the freedom of natives, or otherwise lead to harmful public policies. For example, migrants from an illiberal culture might vote in a government that oppresses the natives or persecutes vulnerable minorities. Such potential effects are known as "political externalities" of immigration.

In some cases, such concerns are legitimate. But, fortunately, there are often ways to deal with them short of forbidding migration itself. The most obvious is to deny the franchise to migrants until they become sufficiently assimilated and conversant in liberal values that they no longer pose a threat to the natives. In the United States, for example, immigrants cannot become citizens unless they have lived in the country for five years, demonstrate knowledge of the English language, and pass a civics test that many native-born citizens would fail.[49] When and if necessary, such standards could potentially be made more stringent; tests could become tougher, naturalization periods can be extended, and so on.

Long-term exclusion from citizenship or the franchise may be unfair or unjust to immigrants. But it is a lesser injustice than excluding them from living in the country entirely, which would force many into a lifetime of poverty and oppression in underdeveloped nations (many of them ones where the would-be migrant has little or no influence over public policy either). Exclusion from the franchise is also a lesser infringement on political freedom than exclusion from migration, and a less severe case of discrimination on the basis of place of birth.

In addition, the risk of political externalities is often overblown. Studies repeatedly show that recent immigrants actually have relatively little political influence, compared to longtime residents: even those who do have the franchise vote at lower rates, and their political influence in other respects trails that of natives even more (for example – campaign contributions, activism in parties and interest

---

[49] SOMIN, DEMOCRACY AND POLITICAL IGNORANCE, 212.

groups, etc.).[50] Data from the United States suggests that immigrants' and natives' political views strongly converge over time, especially in the second and third generations.[51]

Political externalities are also sometimes raised as an objection to internal foot voting within federal systems. Here, the problem is likely to be even less severe than in the case of international migration. Like international foot voters, domestic ones tend to have only a modest impact on the political balance of their new homes, in part because they participate in politics at a lower rate.[52]

Furthermore, migrants would have to be both very numerous relative to the preexisting population and highly skewed in their political leanings to have a major impact.[53] Let us assume, for example, that recent migrants make up 10 percent of the population of a given area, and that they vote at the same rate as other residents. If the newcomers lean 60–40 to the Democratic Party, as opposed to the Republican Party, that would still give the Democrats only a net addition of 2 percent of the total vote. In a more realistic scenario, the migrant vote is unlikely to be so lopsided, and newcomers are unlikely to vote at the same rate as previous residents.

There are rare cases where migration restrictions may indeed be the only way to prevent dire political consequences. This may be true in a scenario where would-be migrants greatly outnumber the natives, have far more illiberal views than natives, and it is politically infeasible to exclude recent arrivals from the franchise, but *is* (for whatever reason), possible to bar entry. The small nation of Estonia – faced with potential massive immigration from its very illiberal neighbor Russia – may be an example of such a case.[54]

In such a tragic situation, unrestricted migration might lead to the destruction of the very freedoms that make the destination nation attractive in the first place, killing the proverbial goose that lays the golden eggs. Fortunately, this combination of circumstances is likely to be rare.

---

[50] See SOMIN, DEMOCRACY AND POLITICAL IGNORANCE, 175–76; Bryan Caplan, "Why Should We Restrict Immigration?," 32 CATO JOURNAL 5 (2012).

[51] For an extensive overview, see Sam Wilson and Alex Nowrasteh, "The Political Assimilation of Immigrants and their Descendants," Economic Development Bulletin No. 23, Cato Institute, Feb. 24, 2015, available at www.cato.org/publications/economic-development-bulletin/political-assimilation-immigrants-their-descendants.

[52] For a more detailed discussion of these points, see SOMIN, DEMOCRACY AND POLITICAL IGNORANCE, 172–76.

[53] Ibid.

[54] Russia's population is some one hundred times larger than Estonia's, and the average Russian has very illiberal views on a wide range of issues. Due in part to Russia's power, Estonia might not be able to deny the franchise to Russian migrants for long, yet might find it feasible to continue to bar most of them. On Estonia's dilemmas with respect to its Russian minority, see Agnia Grigas, *The Politics of Energy and Memory Between Russia and the Baltic States*, (New Haven: Yale University Press, 2016), ch. 2; and Grigas, "Compatriot Games: Russian-Speaking Minorities in the Baltic States," *World Politics Review*, Oct. 21, 2014, available at www.worldpoliticsreview.com/articles/14240/compatriot-games-russian-speaking-minorities-in-the-baltic-states.

At least in the vast majority of situations, we can protect the legitimate political freedom of natives without denying it to foot-voting immigrants. Unconstrained foot voting rights may not be feasible in all cases. But it should be possible to expand them far beyond their current level without endangering legitimate rights of self-determination or creating dangerous political externalities.

IV EXPANDING OPPORTUNITIES FOR FOOT VOTING[55]

Expanding domestic and international foot voting can greatly enhance political freedom, economic welfare, and liberty more generally. But there are substantial political and institutional obstacles to it. Fortunately, there is much that can be done to expand opportunities for foot voting, while mitigating potential downsides.

Expanding Domestic Foot Voting

Promoting foot voting has a number of implications for domestic constitutional structures. The most obvious and widely accepted is the idea that citizens should be able to move freely between subnational jurisdictions, and that regional governments should not be allowed to prevent them from doing so.

In the United States and other advanced democracies, such freedom of movement is largely taken for granted. As early as 1867, the US Supreme Court struck down a state law imposing an exit tax on people seeking to migrate elsewhere.[56] Before the Civil War, however, state-imposed restrictions on internal migration were common, with many states excluding free African-Americans and persons considered likely to become public charges.[57]

Internal restrictions on migration are far more prevalent in developing nations. China's *hukou* system is a particularly well known and important example, because it affects so many people in the world's most populous nation.[58] But regional governments in some other developing nations also attempt to restrict migration in various ways. For example, some Indian states seek to keep out migrants from ethnic groups different from that of the regional majority.[59] Some ethnonationalist

---

[55] Some elements of this section are adapted from Ilya Somin, "Foot Voting, Decentralization, and Development," MINNESOTA LAW REVIEW (forthcoming).

[56] Crandall v. Nevada, 73 U.S. 35 (1867).

[57] See MARILYN P. BAESELER, ASYLUM FOR MANKIND: AMERICA 1607–1800 chs. 6–7 (1998); Gerald F. Neuman, "The Lost Century of American Immigration Law," 1776–1875, COLUMBIA LAW REVIEW 93 (1993): 833–911.

[58] See Shannon Tiezzi, "China's Plan for 'Orderly' Hukou Reform," THE DIPLOMAT, Feb. 3, 2016, available at http://thediplomat.com/2016/02/chinas-plan-for-orderly-hukou-reform/.

[59] For a recent overview, see Rameez Abbas and Divya Varma, "Internal Labor Migration in India Raises Integration Challenges for Migrants," Migration Policy Institute, Mar. 3, 2014, available at www.migrationpolicy.org/article/internal-labor-migration-india-raises-integration-challenges-migrants.

political leaders even promote violence against migrants in order to expel them and deter others from coming.[60]

Even in advanced liberal democracies, regional and local governments some-times impose severe indirect constraints on foot voting. Unlike in developing nations, such restrictions almost always take the form of indirect constraints, rather than open restrictions on freedom of movement. Their effects are, nonetheless, often severe.

In the United States, the poor and lower middle class are often impeded from moving towards job opportunities by restrictive zoning laws that artificially increase the price of housing, and occupational licensing regimes that exclude newcomers from numerous professions.[61]

Well-designed constitutional systems can do much to enhance opportunities for foot voting, while minimizing their potential downsides.[62] At a bare minimum, effective foot voting requires preventing regional governments from either forcibly excluding migrants or preventing their own people from leaving. It also requires suppression of anti-migrant violence. Sadly, the latter may be difficult to achieve in areas where legal institutions are weak or corrupt, and ethnic or religious hostilities between migrants and natives are severe.

Foot voting can also be enhanced if constitutional restrictions curtail zoning and occupational licensing laws that artificially block migration. Such laws could be blocked by stronger judicial enforcement of property rights and individual liberties, or by legislative reform at the regional or national level.

Internal foot voting can be further facilitated by enforcement of relatively tight limits on the scope of central government power, thereby devolving more issues to the regional or local level.[63] That can ensure that more issues are subject to foot voting, with lower moving costs. In many situations, moving costs can be further reduced by devolving authority to the local level, rather than to regional authorities. It is generally much easier and cheaper to move from one nearby city or town to another, than to move to a different region.

The optimal distribution of power between different levels of government cannot be determined by reference to foot-voting alone. A variety of other considerations must also be weighed. But, other things equal, enhancing opportunities for foot voting is a major consideration in favor of greater decentralization.

---

[60] Ibid; see also Sikata Banerjee, Warriors in Politics: Hindu Nationalism, Violence, and the Shiv Sena in India (1999).

[61] See David Schleicher, "Getting People Where the Jobs Are," *Democracy* (Fall 2016), available at http://democracyjournal.org/magazine/42/getting-people-where-the-jobs-are/. See also Schleicher, "Stuck!," and Ilya Somin, "Moving Vans More Powerful than Ballot Boxes," *USA Today*, Oct. 18, 2016, available at www.usatoday.com/story/opinion/2016/10/18/mobility-zoning-licensing-voting-minorities-column/91990486/.

[62] This section builds on ideas I first developed in Ilya Somin, "Foot Voting, Political Ignorance, and Constitutional Design," Social Philosophy and Policy 28 (2011): 202–26.

[63] For a fuller elaboration, see Somin, "Foot Voting, Federalism, and Political Freedom."

Foot voting can also be enhanced by political institutions that promote "competitive" rather than "cooperative" federalism. If regional and local governments are required to raise all or most of their own funds by taxing their own residents, they will have stronger incentives to adopt policies that offer attractive options to potential migrants, in order to increase revenue.[64]

As Charles Tiebout explained in his classic 1956 article, foot voting can potentially provide a wide range of options to potential movers even if jurisdictions make no special effort to compete.[65] Many options can arise simply because local and regional governments try to meet the diverse preferences of their preexisting residents, without necessarily seeking to attract migrants. But competition provides incentives for jurisdictions to offer still better options, that meet the needs of foot voters more fully.

In some situations, there is a danger that competition will result in a "race to the bottom" in which jurisdictions try to attract business investment in ways that harm ordinary citizens by, for example, damaging the environment.[66] However, "race to the bottom" concerns are greatly overstated on both theoretical and empirical grounds. Theoretically, there is no good reason to suppose that subnational governments will overvalue the needs of business interests relative to those of other foot voters, or that preferences of the former will be uniformly harmful to the latter.[67] Workers and families also vote with their feet, as do businesses that benefit from a healthy environment. Localities have incentives to cater to their needs, as well as those of business interests that may prefer laxer pollution controls. Historical evidence suggests that subnational governments have often pioneered various forms of environmental protection, and have not simply catered to the needs of mobile businesses at the expense of the general public.[68]

---

[64] See, for example, Barry Weingast, "The Economic Role of Political Institutions: Market-Preserving Federalism and Economic Development," 11 JOURNAL OF LAW, ECONOMICS & ORGANIZATION 1 (1995); and SOMIN, DEMOCRACY AND POLITICAL IGNORANCE, ch. 5.

[65] Charles Tiebout, "A Pure Theory of Local Expenditures," 64 JOURNAL OF POLITICAL ECONOMY 516 (1956).

[66] For a summary and defense of the race to the bottom theory, see Kirsten H. Engel, "State Environmental Standard-Setting: Is There a "Race" and Is It "to the Bottom?," 48 HASTINGS LAW JOURNAL 274 (1997). For other modern defenses, see, for example, Kirsten Engel and Scott R. Saleska, "Facts Are Stubborn Things: An Empirical Reality Check in the Theoretical Debate Over State Environmental Rate-Setting," 8 CORNELL JOURNAL OF LAW AND PUBLIC POLICY 55 (1998); and Joshua D. Sarnoff, "The Continuing Imperative (But Only from a National Perspective) for Federal Environmental Protection," 7 DUKE ENVIRONMENTAL LAW AND POLICY FORUM 225 (1997).

[67] For the classic theoretical critiques, see Richard Revesz, "Rehabilitating Interstate Competition: Rethinking the "Race to the Bottom" Rationale for Federal Environmental Regulation," 67 NYU LAW REVIEW 1210 (1992); and Revesz, "The Race to the Bottom and Federal Environmental Regulation: A Response To Critics," 82 MINNESOTA LAW REVIEW 535 (1997).

[68] For a more extensive discussion of the evidence, See SOMIN, DEMOCRACY AND POLITICAL IGNORANCE, 168–69.

This is not to suggest that subnational governments are immune from "capture" by business interests that might lobby for excessive pollution or other policies that enable them to benefit at the expense of the interests of the general public. Far from it.[69] But there is no inherent reason why such capture is more of a danger at the local and regional level than with central governments. The possibility of foot voting also puts constraints on such activity, as jurisdictions especially prone to it are likely to lose investors and taxpayers over time.

Foot voting may have less to offer minority groups in the many federal systems where they are actually the majority in a few regions, but widely despised elsewhere. Many federal systems were established for the specific purpose of giving regionally concentrated national minorities a jurisdiction of their own, thereby ensuring peace.[70] In such situations, it might be difficult or even impossible for individuals to move to a region dominated by another ethnic group.

For example, an Iraqi Kurd moving into a majority Arab province might reasonably fear violence or at least discrimination. Even in the absence of overt hostility, such minority groups might face painful cultural and linguistic adjustments if they move out of their home areas. A French Canadian who moves from Quebec to Alberta is unlikely to face ethnic violence or even much in the way of discrimination. But moving to a majority Anglophone province might still be a difficult transition, with substantial psychological and other costs.

But foot-voting is still potentially useful in such conditions. The federal system in question can and often should include multiple majority-minority districts.[71] For example, the French-speaking minority in Switzerland can choose between multiple majority-French cantons. Similarly, Iraq has three majority-Kurdish provinces, albeit partially unified under the Kurdistan Regional Government.[72] French Canadians would enjoy a broader array of foot voting options if Quebec consisted of multiple smaller provinces rather than one big one.

I do not suggest that any particular majority-minority jurisdiction must necessarily be broken up in order to facilitate foot-voting. Other considerations would have to be weighed before reaching that conclusion in any given case. But the foot-voting benefits of such partitions should not be neglected.

Opportunities for foot voting can also be expanded by creating more scope for foot voting in the private sector. By limiting government power and making it easier to

---

[69] For some examples of such "capture" caused in part by misinformation, see, for example, DAVID SCHULTZ, AMERICAN POLITICS IN THE AGE OF IGNORANCE: WHY LAWMAKERS CHOOSE BELIEF OVER RESEARCH (2012).

[70] See, for example, DAWN BRANCATI, PEACE BY DESIGN: MANAGING INTRASTATE CONFLICT BY DECENTRALIZATION (2009) (discussing many such examples).

[71] For other potential advantages of such a system, see Donald L. Horowitz, "The Many Uses of Federalism, "55 DRAKE LAW REVIEW 953 (2007).

[72] For a discussion of Kurdish government, see STEPHEN MANSFIELD, THE MIRACLE OF THE KURDS (2014).

form private planned communities, we can expand foot voting even further than is possible through choice in a federal system.

Private-sector foot voting has many of the same advantages as foot voting within a federal system. In some respects, it is actually superior. Private organizations are often more consensual than local or regional governments are. Membership in the former is usually more fully voluntary than in the latter. Moreover, moving costs between different private organizations are usually lower than between government jurisdictions.

It is usually possible to have a larger number of private planned communities and other similar organizations than governments within a given territory. This gives private foot-voting the edge with respect to consent, negative freedom, and at least some types of positive freedom. Easier exit also reduces the risk of domination.

Some critics argue that private governance is only feasible for the relatively affluent, or at least disproportionately advantages them.[73] But empirical evidence – including evidence from poor nations - shows that it can often be effectively used by the middle class and the poor, no less than the wealthy.[74] Even if private sector foot voting is not effective for everyone, it can greatly enhance the political freedom of a large proportion of the population. Moreover, much can be done to enhance opportunities for the poor and disadvantaged to take advantage of private governance. For example, they can be given stronger, legally protected property rights,[75] which in turn can be used to set up private communities of their own.

Expanding International Migration

Some of the greatest potential gains from expanding foot voting are those to be had from freeing up international migration.[76] From the standpoint of both economic development and a variety of noneconomic interests, the difference between living in a poor nation and a more developed one vastly outweighs that between the worst possible jurisdiction within an advanced nation and the best. But it is also fair to say that international foot voting faces stronger, more widespread, and vociferous opposition than internal foot voting. In both the United States and many European nations, strong nationalist movements have arisen that not only oppose expanding immigration but advocate greatly reducing it from existing levels.

This opposition will not be easily overcome. But the vast gains to be had from expanded migration rights make it imperative to try. Even incremental increases in

---

[73] See, for example, EVAN MCKENZIE, PRIVATOPIA: HOMEOWNERS ASSOCIATIONS AND THE RISE OF RESIDENTIAL PRIVATE GOVERNMENT (1996).

[74] For examples, see, NELSON, PRIVATE NEIGHBORHOODS, and STRINGHAM, PRIVATE GOVERNANCE.

[75] This is the theme of a large literature on development. See, for example, HERNANDO DE SOTO, THE MYSTERY OF CAPITAL, (2000).

[76] See the summary in Part I, *infra*.

international foot voting opportunities can save millions of people from what would otherwise be a lifetime of poverty and oppression.

Many objections have been offered to the idea of greatly expanding international migration rights.[77] These include fears that it will increase crime and terrorism, reduce the wages of natives,[78] overburden the welfare state, cause the enactment of destructive policies supported by immigrant voters, and lead to the spread of harmful cultural values.[79] I cannot review and assess these objections in detail here. But it is possible to sketch out a general framework for addressing them.

First, many of the standard objections to free international migration are significantly overblown. For example, the available evidence indicates that increased immigration does not lead to increases in welfare spending.[80] At least in the United States, immigrants actually have a much lower crime rate than native-born citizens do.[81] Similarly, the risk that an American will be killed by a immigrant terrorist is so infinitesimal that it is actually several times lower than the risk that he will be killed by a lightning strike.[82]

Where immigration creates genuine problems and negative side-effects, it is often possible to deal with the issue by means of "keyhole solutions" that minimize the risk without barring large numbers of immigrants.[83] If immigration does impose excessive burdens on the welfare state, receiving nations could abolish or reduce welfare payments to migrants.[84] Excluding immigrants from welfare benefits might

---

[77] I plan to discuss them in far greater detail in ILYA SOMIN, FREE TO MOVE: FOOT VOTING AND POLITICAL FREEDOM (Oxford University Press, forthcoming).

[78] See, for example, PHILIP CAFARO, HOW MANY IS TOO MANY? THE PROGRESSIVE ARGUMENT FOR REDUCING IMMIGRATION INTO THE UNITED STATES (2014); GEORGE BORJAS, IMMIGRATION ECONOMICS, chapters 4–7 (2014).

[79] See, for example, SAMUEL P. HUNTINGTON, WHO ARE WE? THE CHALLENGES TO AMERICA'S CULTURAL IDENTITY (2005).

[80] See, for example, Alex Nowrasteh and Zac Gochenour, "The Political Externalities of Immigration: Evidence from the United States," Cato Institute Working Paper, Jan. 2014, available at http://object.cato.org/sites/cato.org/files/pubs/pdf/working-paper-14-3.pdf (evidence from American states); ALBERTO ALESINA AND EDWARD L. GLAESER, FIGHTING POVERTY IN THE US AND EUROPE. A WORLD OF DIFFERENCE (2004) (evidence indicating that European nations with greater immigration actually have lower welfare spending than those with more).

[81] For a review of the relevant studies and evidence, see MARY WATERS AND MARISA GERSTEIN PINEAU, THE INTEGRATION OF IMMIGRANTS INTO AMERICAN SOCIETY (2015), 326–32.

[82] According to the National Weather Service, an average of 31 Americans were killed by lightning each year, from 2006 to 2015. National Weather Service, "How Dangerous is Lightning?" available at http://origin-www.nws.noaa.gov/om/lightning/odds.shtml. By contrast, the annual incidence of death by immigrant terrorists is far lower. See Alex Nowrasteh, "Terrorism and Immigration: A Risk Analysis, Cato Institute Policy Analysis No. 758 (Dec. 13, 2016), available at www.cato.org/publications/policy-analysis/terrorism-immigration-risk-analysis.

[83] For examples of such proposals see Bryan Caplan, "Why Should We Restrict Immigration?," CATO JOURNAL 32 (2012): 5–21. I present others in SOMIN, FREE TO MOVE (forthcoming).

[84] Cf. MARTIN RUHS, THE COST OF RIGHTS: REGULATING INTERNATIONAL LABOR MIGRATION (2014) (arguing that limiting the welfare rights of labor migrants can enable increased migration).

be unjust. But it is surely less so than forcing them to endure the far greater material deprivation of being condemned to Third World poverty for the rest of their lives.

Finally, where immigration does create negative side effects that cannot be dealt with by keyhole solutions, receiving governments can address them by tapping some of the vast wealth created by immigration itself. For example, if immigration reduces the wages of some subset of natives and this is considered a wrong requiring mitigation, the government can impose a tax on the wages of migrants (or on the profits of employers who hire them) and redistribute the proceeds to whatever subset of natives are believed to be entitled compensation.[85]

The native workers would be no worse off than before, and the immigrants would still be far better off than in their former countries, even with a higher tax rate. Such discriminatory taxation may be unjust to immigrants; I do not claim that it is necessarily the optimal policy. But it is far *less* unjust than excluding the migrants in question from the nation entirely, thus consigning most to lives of poverty and oppression in their countries of origin.

In sum, most objections to expanded migration should be addressed by a combination of assessing whether the objection is overblown, implementing keyhole solutions, and – where necessary – tapping the wealth created by immigration to mitigate negative side effects and compensate adversely affected natives.

Implications for International Law and Global Governance

As amended by a 1967 protocol, the 1951 Convention Relating to the Status of Refugees defines a refugee that governments have an obligation to accept as "A person who owing to a well-founded fear of being persecuted for reasons of race, religion, nationality, membership of a particular social group or political opinion, is outside the country of his nationality and is unable or, owing to such fear, is unwilling to avail himself of the protection of that country."[86] US domestic law has a similar definition.[87]

The argument of this chapter suggests that refugee status should be extended to a much wider range of potential migrants. People who live under repressive regimes suffer serious human rights violations even if they are not targeted for special persecution on the basis of the categories currently specified in refugee law. Moreover, those

---

[85] For this idea, see Caplan, "Why Should We Restrict Immigration?"

[86] Convention Relating to the Status of Refugees, Article 1 (1951, as amended in 1967).

[87] See 8 U.S.C. § 1101(a)(42) (Defining refugee as "any person who is outside any country of such person's nationality or, in the case of a person having no nationality, is outside any country in which such person last habitually resided, and who is unable or unwilling to return to, and is unable or unwilling to avail himself or herself of the protection of, that country because of persecution or a well-founded fear of persecution on account of race, religion, nationality, membership in a particular social group, or political opinion.").

unable to leave nations ruled by undemocratic regimes often have no chance at political freedom of any kind, except through emigration to a freer society.

Thus, at the very least, presumptive refugee status should be extended to migrants fleeing authoritarian regimes, and governments that impose severe restrictions on a variety of human rights, whether or not the migrants in question have been specifically targeted on the basis of race, religion, nationality, and other similar criteria.

Destination countries need not be required to provide welfare rights to such migrants. But they should at least not be allowed to expel or deport them, absent dire exigencies, such as a serious threat to public health.

In the short run, expansion of eligibility for refugee status might be incremental. Political feasibility almost certainly precludes it from swiftly going as far as described above. A variety of gradualistic approaches are possible. For example, initially refugee status could be expanded only to include all residents of a few of the most oppressive dictatorships, such as North Korea or those engaged in mass murder, such as (at the time of this writing) Syria. Citizens of other oppressive regimes would still have to prove that they are being targeted under the categories laid out in current refugee law. But the long-run objective should be a strong presumptive (though not absolute) right to immigrate, similar to the current strong presumptive right of emigration.

Some advocates of expanded migration rights also tend to be sympathetic to proposals for world government, or at least "global governance." But, in reality, defenders of the former should be wary of the latter. Effective political freedom through foot voting requires opportunities to escape the policies of any one government by moving out of its jurisdiction. By definition, a world government would have jurisdiction over the entire world. And at least until we have colonies in space, there will be no escaping its reach.

A government from which there is no possible exit is the ultimate obstacle to foot voting, and a potentially grave menace to political freedom generally. If it becomes oppressive or – in the worst case scenario – a totalitarian state, the result might be the near-total destruction of political freedom in the form of both foot voting *and* ballot box voting.[88]

Initially the powers of any world government are likely to be fairly limited, thereby reducing the risk it poses. It is unlikely that national governments would agree to its establishment otherwise. But even if a world government at first has only a very small chance of becoming oppressive, the risk might cumulate over time, as its powers grow. Global governance may be less risky in this respect than a full-blown world government. But the former could potentially develop into the latter over time.

The enormous size and complexity of world government would also exacerbate the problem of political ignorance. In a democratic world government, public

---

[88] For a good discussion of this danger, see Bryan Caplan, "The Totalitarian Menace," in NICK BOSTROM AND MILAN M. CIRKOVIC, EDS., GLOBAL CATASTROPHIC RISKS 512–16 (2008).

ignorance is likely to be an even more serious menace than it is now. It is even harder for rationally ignorant voters to understand government policy for the entire world than to grasp what is happening in their own country. How well are American voters likely to understand the problems of the Chinese, and vice versa?

There is a potential tension between the two themes of this section: it could be that only a world government can establish and enforce strong international migration rights. But there are ways to make progress towards the latter goal without risking the former. For example, states can expand refugee rights by making new agreements that build on and strengthen the 1951 Refugee Convention.

Both world government and strong "global governance" that falls short of a unified state have gained support from scholars and others in recent years.[89] This chapter cannot comprehensively assess the case for and against such institutions.

I certainly do not claim that their establishment can never be justified. For example, it might be foolish to reject world government if it is the only way to prevent environmental catastrophe, global nuclear war, or some other comparable worldwide calamity. But the threat world government and strong global governance pose to foot voting is an important strike against them, even if it would not always override competing considerations. At the very least, it should lead us to devote more effort to pursuing solutions to global problems that do not require worldwide centralization of government power.[90]

CONCLUSION

Expanded foot voting is not a panacea for all the problems of modern society. Neither is it a complete solution for all the difficulties facing libertarianism. But can nonetheless do much to extend freedom and increase human welfare.

Foot voting can help expand political freedom in ways that ballot box voting cannot. For many around the world, it is probably the only feasible mechanism of political choice. Moreover, state-enforced restrictions on migration are themselves major infringements on human freedom, among the most severe imposed by governments, particularly liberal democratic states that otherwise protect liberty better than repressive dictatorships. Ironically, by blocking immigration, liberal democratic states leave more people at the mercy of their authoritarian rivals. Excluding people from relatively more libertarian states similarly leaves more people under the control of more statist ones.

---

[89] For an overview of recent arguments for world government, see, for example, Craig Campbell, "The Resurgent Idea of World Government," *Ethics and International Affairs*, (2008), available at www.cceia.org/resources/journal/22_2/essay/001.html. On global governance, see, for example, ANNE-MARIE SLAUGHTER, A NEW WORLD ORDER, (2004); and THOMAS G. WEISS AND RORDEN WILKINSON, EDS., INTERNATIONAL ORGANIZATION AND GLOBAL GOVERNANCE (2013).

[90] For some examples of such approaches, see John O. McGinnis and Ilya Somin, "Should International Law Be Part of Our Law?" 59 STANFORD LAW REVIEW 1175 (2007).

Expanded foot voting can also do much to enhance the freedom and well-being welfare of people that libertarians are often accused of neglecting: the poor and oppressed of the world. Within the United States and other Western nations, breaking down barriers to mobility can help expand opportunities for the poor and disadvantaged, as was the case in previous periods in American history.[91] Increased opportunities international migration can help many who suffer in poverty and oppression in underdeveloped nations and repressive dictatorships.

Admittedly, foot-voting will not by itself lead to a fully libertarian society, conceived as one with a minimal state or otherwise severely restricted government. Many migrants will prefer jurisdictions with governments that take on more functions than most libertarians would like. But empirical evidence does suggest that foot voters tend to seek out jurisdictions that are relatively freer on both social and economic dimensions.[92]

Overall, libertarians have much to gain from expanding freedom of movement. More importantly, so do the millions of people around the world desperately in need of greater freedom and opportunity.

---

[91] For an overview of the relevant history, see Somin, "Foot Voting, Federalism, and Political Freedom."

[92] For relevant citations, see SOMIN, DEMOCRACY AND POLITICAL IGNORANCE, 166–67.

8

Classical Liberal Administrative Law in a Progressive World

Michael B. Rappaport

INTRODUCTION

Would a classical liberal administrative law be possible and desirable in the modern world of progressive government? A classical liberal administrative law would impose significantly greater checks on government than our present administrative law does. In a classical liberal world, where the government engaged in limited functions, one could easily believe that it would be possible to have much stricter limits on government agencies. But could such limits be desirably placed on administrative agencies in a world where the government undertakes the significant functions that it does in the administrative and welfare state? Or would these limits hamstring the government and prevent it from performing its essential functions in this progressive regime?

This chapter explores this question by examining whether it would be feasible and desirable to use a stricter separation of powers to establish an administrative law that placed more constraining limits on government. While the complexities of the modern world do present some challenges, I argue that, with some institutional reforms, one could apply the separation of powers more strictly to administrative agencies to promote a more classical liberal administrative law.

Classical liberalism can be defined broadly as the view that the primary political value in a society should be individual freedom and that the role of government is to protect such freedom and to promote a limited view of the public good.[1] Classical liberalism values individual freedom not merely for its own sake, but also as an essential ingredient of other systems that would lead to the public good, such as the economic market, the system of freedom of expression, and the order of religious liberty. Under a classical liberal regime, the government performs the limited duties

[1] *See, for example,* FRIEDRICH HAYEK, THE CONSTITUTION OF LIBERTY (1960); J. G. MERQUIOR, LIBERALISM: OLD AND NEW (1991).

of enforcing the rules of the market and of these other systems as well as engaging in restrained regulation and the provision of limited services, such as public goods, that these systems do not provide. Under classical liberalism, it is important that the government both perform its function well and remain limited.

Classical liberalism employed significant checks on the government to ensure that it did its job beneficially and did not exceeds its functions. Classical liberalism stood for the ideas that government should regulate through general and prospective rules, that coercion of the public be minimized, that government have only limited discretion, and that checks and balances be employed.[2] But an essential ingredient of the classical liberal limits on government was the separation of powers.[3] The traditional conception of the separation of powers both limited the government's ability to harm the polity and improved the government's incentive to perform its functions. For example, the separation of powers limited the harm that the government could impose by requiring that all three branches agree – by passing a law, prosecuting an alleged violation, and finding a person liable – before taking action against an individual. For another example, the separation of powers improved the incentives of the three branches by preventing an agency from both prosecuting and adjudicating a matter – that is, being a judge in its own case.

While the traditional law that governed federal executive branch agencies largely followed a strict conception of the separation of powers, in the twentieth century administrative law departed from this separation to allow for big government. The administrative state undertakes many functions that the government did not in the nineteenth century and would not under classical liberalism, such as extensively providing goods and services, significantly regulating private activities, and expending large amounts of funds. The traditional forms of government were thought to be too constraining for the government to be able to perform these functions. Consequently, modern administrative law modified or abandoned these constraints to allow the government greater ability to perform these functions.[4]

Under modern administrative law, administrative agencies have been given not only executive powers, but also some of Congress's legislative powers and the federal courts' judicial powers. Two principal reasons were thought to justify these changes. First, it was thought that Congress and the courts do not have the expertise to pass the rules and to adjudicate the issues that the administrative state requires. Neither Congress nor the generalist judges that make up the federal judiciary possessed the

---

[2] *See* HAYEK, *supra* note 1.

[3] It should, of course, be acknowledged that the separation of powers operated differently in different countries. But in places where it existed, it operated to limit the government. On the separation of powers in different countries, *see generally* M. J. C. VILE, CONSTITUTIONALISM AND THE SEPARATION OF POWERS (2d ed. 1998).

[4] JOSEPH POSTELL, BUREAUCRACY IN AMERICA: THE ADMINISTRATIVE STATE'S CHALLENGE TO CONSTITUTIONAL GOVERNMENT 174–77 (2017).

scientific, medical, and economic expertise necessary for these tasks. Instead, these functions were placed in a single agency that would have the necessary expertise.[5]

Second, it was thought that Congress and the courts do not have the time or capacity to, in a timely manner, legislate the large volume of rules and adjudicate the large number of cases that the administrative state requires. Consequently, it is necessary to allow administrative agencies to legislate and to adjudicate under procedures that are less demanding than those followed by Congress and the courts.[6]

But were these departures from the separation of powers really necessary for the functioning of the modern administrative state? While progressives tend to believe they were, I argue that a more classical liberal administrative law – one that imposes a much stricter separation of powers – would have been both feasible and desirable. It is true that it would be very difficult for the current administrative state to operate if one relied on Congress to pass all rules and on the current federal courts to adjudicate all claims under federal law. But that is not the only way to introduce a stricter separation of powers.

There are two basic institutional reforms that would allow Congress and the courts to retain much of their legislative and judicial authority, while still accommodating the requirements of the modern administrative state. The first reform would be the establishment of independent administrative courts. These courts ideally should be Article III courts (but they could also be Article I courts as an alternative). In either case, these courts would be assigned the formal adjudicative responsibilities of the administrative agencies. Under current arrangements, administrative law judges generally adjudicate cases, but then the agency retains the authority to reverse their decisions and therefore the agency exercises judicial power. With this reform, however, the agencies would be forced to adjudicate before independent courts and would be denied the authority to reverse these courts' decisions.

While these courts would be independent, they could be adapted to address both the expertise and time concerns. The courts should be staffed by people who have expertise not only in law, but in other important areas, such as medicine, science, or economics. In contrast to the existing administrative law judges, these independent administrative judges would not hear cases solely from a single agency, but from multiple agencies so long as the case involved their area of expertise. For example, one court might be filled with people who have both law degrees and expertise in economics, and who would hear cases from all of the agencies that involve economic matters. To allow for expeditious resolution of cases, the courts would follow the more streamlined procedures that presently govern administrative adjudications before agencies.

---

[5] *See, for example,* JAMES M. LANDIS, THE ADMINISTRATIVE PROCESS (1938).

[6] *See* LANDIS, *supra* note 5; POSTELL, *supra* note 4 at 176–77.

While these independent administrative courts would largey be trial courts, another type of independent administrative court that might or might not be desirable would be appellate administrative courts that would hear challenges to legislative regulations. These courts would also be staffed with judges who are experts in both law and another field. These courts would hear the initial challenge to a legislative regulation, which could then be appealed to a circuit court. These courts are not as clearly desirable as the trial courts, because they have the disadvantage of adding an additional level of appellate review. But these courts do have the significant benefit of allowing independent judges to contribute their expertise to the review of legislative regulations.

The second reform would involve congressional review of proposed legislative rules. Under this procedure – which is similar to but superior to the one in the various Regulations from the Executive in Need of Scrutiny Act (REINS Act) proposals – Congress would vote upon major regulations that agencies propose to implement.[7] In this way, Congress would exercise the legislative power as to whether the most consequential regulations should be enacted. But the procedure would still employ the time and expertise of the administrative agencies to draft the regulations. By restricting Congress's role to making the ultimate decision on these rules and limiting its time to debate, this procedure would allow Congress the time to make the decision, while still making use of the agencies' expertise.

To function effectively, however, the REINS Act congressional review procedure for major rules would require some reforms. One problem with the REINS Act is that agencies would have an incentive to apply the definition of major rules in a way that would allow many regulations to avoid congressional review. I therefore propose reforms that would establish more elaborate definitions and institute procedures, including judicial review by the new administrative courts, to ensure that the definitions are applied impartially. Another problem with the REINS Act is that it would allow administrative agencies to place Congress in a situation in which it must either accept or reject a proposed regulation. By allowing the agencies to formally specify problems with the proposed regulation, the reformed procedure would permit Congress to reject a regulation for specified reasons without being mistakenly perceived as opposing it overall.

With these types of changes, it would be possible to bring administrative law more in line with the separation of powers. Under these reforms, the laws that govern the nation would, as to their most important rules, be approved by Congress. Similarly, adjudications would often be conducted by genuinely independent judges.

These two reforms should be combined with a third one, which would also help restore the separation of powers – eliminating or reducing the deference that courts

---

7   On the REINS Act, *see* Jonathan H. Adler, *Placing "Reins" on Regulations: Assessing the Proposed Reins Act*, 16 NEW YORK UNIVERSITY JOURNAL OF LEGISLATION AND PUBLIC POLICY 1 (2013).

grant to administrative agencies. One of the principal ways that agencies exercise judicial and legislative power is that they receive deference from the courts on judicial review. Especially with the two aforementioned reforms, it would be possible to reduce or eliminate such deference. One type of deference involves deference to findings of law – to legal interpretations by the administrative agencies. Such deference is conferred principally through the three related doctrines of *Chevron, Auer,* and *Skidmore* deference. I argue that it would be desirable to eliminate all three types of deference for agency findings of law.

There are two other basic types of deference, however, that are harder to eliminate: deference as to findings of fact and as to determinations of policy. Still, one could reduce such deference to a limited extent. The details of these matters, which are discussed later, turn on the precise type of finding and the type of action the agency is taking. Deference as to findings of fact can be significantly reduced in what are now treated as formal agency adjudications, but less so in what are now treated as legislative rulemakings. Similarly, policy findings could be significantly reduced in adjudications, but much less so in legislative rulemakings.

Overall, then, a stricter separation of powers could be employed to make the law governing administrative agencies more in accord with the significant limitations on government contemplated by classical liberalism. While that law would help to constrain government agencies and to increase the likelihood that they take desirable actions, it would still allow the agencies to implement the large government that currently exists.

It is important to be clear about the argument that I am making. Some people maintain that the separation of powers cannot be employed in a progressive regime with large government programs. Under this view, one could have the separation of powers only if state responsibilities were limited to those consistent with classical liberalism. It is my argument that this claim is mistaken. It is true that if the separation of powers were re-established by requiring both that Congress draft all legislative regulations and that the ordinary federal courts adjudicate all administrative cases, the large government programs of the administrative state would no longer function. The government could not handle the large numbers of cases that need to be heard and of rules that need to be enacted. Nor could the government make these decisions with the requisite expertise.

But under the reforms that I propose, big government could be feasibly and desirably implemented under a much stricter separation of powers. These reformed institutions would allow many decisions to be made by people with expertise. To be sure, a stricter separation of powers would impose additional limits that would moderately slow decision making and would check decision making by agency experts. Most significantly, the congressional approval procedure would both slow down rulemaking to a small extent and have expert agency decisions reviewed by electorally accountable representatives. But these checks would hardly prevent the programs from operating. And from a classical liberal perspective, these checks would represent a significant improvement by imposing stricter limits and yielding better incentives. While a classical liberal would, of course, prefer a world with both small government and separation of powers to one with big government and separation of powers, he would prefer the latter to the present world of big government and weak separation of powers.

The reader should heed two warnings about this chapter. First, the chapter covers a lot of ground and therefore cannot confront the issues with any level of depth. The point of the chapter is to argue that the separation of powers can be used to govern existing administrative agencies, but not to make the case in detail or to address all of the counterarguments. Second, I do not mean to claim that this reform is politically feasible in the sense that it might be enacted now or in the near future. Many forces would strongly oppose the reform. My only point is that this reform, *if enacted*, could feasibly operate to implement the existing laws and programs of the administrative state.

This chapter proceeds in four parts. Part I discusses the benefits of the separation of powers both from a traditional perspective and from a more modern public choice-oriented approach. Part II then examines how Congress's delegation of rulemaking authority to the agencies might be constrained by employing a congressional approval procedure, reducing deference to agencies, and possibly employing appellate administrative courts. Part III then moves to the other major departure from the separation of powers – the delegation of adjudication authority to agencies – and argues that such authority could again be addressed by employing Article III administrative judges and reducing deference to the agencies. Part IV then briefly discusses the area of informal adjudication, explaining how guidances could be reformed and how large programs, such as Social Security Disability, could be handled.

I THE BENEFITS OF THE SEPARATION OF POWERS

The separation of powers promotes classical liberalism in several ways. It limits government authority and furthers the rule of law. It also increases the chances that the government will perform its functions in a desirable manner. And it checks agencies from pursuing, at the expenses of the public good, various problematic goals, such as promoting an extreme ideological position, a political party's interest, the agency's bureaucratic interest, or the goals of special interests.

In this Part, I explain in two sections how the separation of powers produces these benefits. First, I rely on the more traditional analysis of the separation of powers. Then, I use an analysis influenced by the more modern theories of public choice and positive political theory.

The basic separation of powers point, however, seems clear. Assigning government powers to a single entity to act as it sees fit is unlikely to be beneficial. Classical liberalism always sought to impose significant checks on government action, because it assumed that government actors, due to bad motives or lack of knowledge, would take harmful actions if left unconstrained. Under modern administrative law, agencies are given significant authority, within an ample sphere, to take discretionary actions. The separation of powers would transfer that power to three different entities and thereby limit agency discretion and improve government incentives.

A A More Traditional Analysis

1 Limits on Government Entities

The separation of powers limits government authority by requiring the action of three entities with distinct purposes and influences, rather than one entity, before an individual can be found to be in violation of the law. The legislature must enact a law, the executive must decide to bring an action against an individual, and the judiciary must determine that the individual violated the law. By contrast, if an agency exercises all three government powers, then only it need decide that a legislative rule should be enacted, that it should be enforced against an individual, and that the individual violated the rule.

The separation of powers established by the US Constitution strengthens these limits on government authority. It establishes a structure in which all three of the entities have different perspectives, making it even harder to reach agreement. The Congress is politically accountable. The judiciary is insulated from politics. And the agencies are indirectly political – with executive branch agencies enjoying significant authority, but subject to presidential control, and independent agencies enjoying significant independence for a limited term.

Another aspect of the American system is that it establishes a restricted lawmaking process, imposing what is in essence a tricameral system that ordinarily requires all three lawmaking branches (House, Senate, and President) to agree to enact a law. That those branches are each elected by different constituencies and at different times makes it even harder to enact a law.

2 The Rule of Law

The separation of powers also promotes the rule of law. The rule of law, under one common conception, refers to a situation in which the law is knowable by the public and in which it significantly constrains the actions of the executive branch.[8] Departures from the separation of powers unfortunately allow the executive to avoid the restrictions of the rule of law.

---

[8] FRIEDRICH A. HAYEK, THE CONSTITUTION OF LIBERTY Ch. 14 (1960), Richard H. Fallon, Jr., *"The Rule of Law" as a Concept in Constitutional Discourse*, 97 COLUM. L. REV. 1, 14–17 (1997).

Under an arrangement where the agency exercises combined executive and judicial powers, a single entity will have the authority to enforce the law without significant constraints. The agency can enforce a statute or rule, but then exercise significant authority as to the meaning of the provision. For example, an agency might bring an enforcement action for violation of a legislative regulation and then have significant discretion under the *Auer* doctrine to determine the meaning of that regulation.[9] Similarly, an agency can bring an enforcement action in a formal adjudication against an individual based on a statute. It will then be given significant discretion under the *Chevron* doctrine to determine the meaning of the statute.[10] Also, the agency will be given substantial discretion to find facts and set policy in such formal adjudications.

An agency that has the power to issue legislative regulations and that knows it will be given deference as to their interpretation will also have an incentive to issue vague regulations.[11] By issuing vague regulations, the agency avoids the scrutiny from notice and comment that would come from proposing clearer regulations. But then the agency can give that specific content to the regulations through its interpretation of those regulations, which would receive substantial deference under the *Auer* doctrine.

These various rules allow the government substantial authority to determine the meaning of the applicable laws in particular disputes. The agency's possession of significant discretion to determine the meaning of the law means both that the public may not know that meaning in advance and that the agency may not be constrained by it. Similarly, the deference enjoyed by the executive to make factual findings and policy determinations will give it further ability to avoid the restrictions of the law and make decisions as it pleases.

3 Improving the Incentives of the Branches

The separation of powers does not merely place limits on the government. It also helps to improve the incentives of each of the branches to reach desirable results. By contrast, combining the powers distorts these incentives. First, when the executive and judicial powers are combined, it is more difficult for the judicial power to be exercised impartially. Once the agency decides to bring an action, it has already determined that the defendant has violated the law. Psychologically, it is very difficult for an agency that is putting effort into convicting an individual to impartially adjudicate his behavior. An agency's control over the adjudication also affects how it exercises its executive power. An agency might decide to bring a questionable prosecution, because it knows that it can decide the adjudication in its own favor.

---

[9] Auer v. Robbins, 519 U.S. 452 (1997).
[10] Chevron, U.S.A., Inc. v. NRDC, Inc., 467 U.S. 837 (1984).
[11] John F. Manning, *Constitutional Structure and Judicial Deference to Agency Interpretations of Agency Rules*, 96 COLUMBIA LAW REVIEW 612 (1996).

Second, combining executive and legislative power is also problematic. When the executive and legislative powers are separated, the legislature has an incentive to pass reasonable laws, because those laws might be enforced against the legislature and its allies. By contrast, when the legislative and executive powers are combined in an agency, the agency can enact harsh regulations, knowing it will enforce them only against its opponents.[12] Similarly, when the executive and legislative powers are separated, the legislature has reason to pass relatively clear laws, so that it and its allies can have notice of what the law is. But when these powers are combined, the agency can pass unclear laws, knowing that it can choose who to enforce them against.

Third, combining legislative with judicial power has effects similar to those of combining legislative and executive power. When these powers are combined, the agency has much less incentive to pass only reasonable and clear rules, because it can use its adjudicative power to protect its friends and allies from enforcement of unreasonable or unclear rules. In addition, if the judicial power is combined with the legislative power, it may be harder for the adjudicator to impartially interpret the laws. In its role as a legislator, the agency will need to focus on deciding what is good policy. But that may make it difficult for the agency to determine what policy the agency actually enacted in its legislative rules. An agency that is adjudicating will need to ignore its current policy objectives in favor of the objectives it actually placed in the legislative regulation. But ignoring policy is more difficult if the agency's job is also to develop policy.

It is true that modern administrative law does not entirely dispense with the separation of powers or confer unlimited authority on agencies. The agencies are often required to follow certain procedures before taking actions, especially informal rulemaking and formal adjudication. But those procedures normally do not prevent the agency from ultimately adopting the policies it desires. Congress can also overturn agency actions by changing the law, but this is normally very difficult. The President has ultimate authority over executive branch agencies and significant influence over independent agencies. Thus, the President will often support actions taken by the agencies and will therefore veto laws that attempt to overturn them.

The most significant check on agencies comes from judicial review, but once again this check is limited. Judicial review of agency decisions generally involves substantial deference, so that the agency will be reversed only if the court concludes it was unreasonable or failed to explain a basic aspect of its decision. This deference applies to fact questions, to policy questions, and to legal questions, including interpretations of statutes and legislative regulations. While judicial review places limits on agencies, they are nonetheless free, within a significant area, to take whatever actions they desire.

---

[12] JOHN LOCKE, THE SECOND TREATISE OF GOVERNMENT §143, at 137 (J.W. Gough ed., Basil Blackwell 3d. ed. 1976 (1690); MONTESQUIEU, THE SPIRIT OF THE LAWS 157 (Anne M. Cohler et al. trans. and eds., Cambridge Univ. Press 1989 (1748).

4 Objections

These arguments for the separation of powers might be questioned on various grounds. Here I address two possible objections.

Advocates of judicial deference often defend it on the ground that deference reduces the extent to which judges can substitute their own values when making findings of law (or facts or policy). Such inappropriate findings are certainly a problem. And the fact that judges have the final say in specific cases makes this an even more serious concern.

But the allocation of this responsibility to judges is nonetheless probably the best – or the least-bad – solution to the problem. First, judges are less likely to be biased as to their findings of law (or facts or policy) than agencies. Judges are purposively insulated from politics or administration. They are given no other responsibilities than deciding cases and their decisions are not subject to review except by other insulated judges. By contrast, agencies are not only deciding cases, but also bringing enforcement actions, implementing a program, and developing policy. Moreover, agency officials are either supervised by or subject to the influence of the president and can often be lobbied by private parties. Thus, judges avoid many of the sources of agency biases (discussed earlier) that are created by adjudicating, enforcing, and legislating at the same time. Avoiding these biases increases the chances that judges will reach the correct decision. Unless judges are strongly deficient in expertise – something I argue later is not true in such areas as legal interpretation, where I recommend no deference – judges are more likely than agencies to reach the correct decision.

Second, someone has to have the final say, and there are strong reasons why it is better that it be judges rather than agencies. Both judges and agencies can be reversed through legislation, but it will generally be easier to reverse judicial decisions than agency decisions. Agency decisions are usually supported by the President, who can veto the legislation, whereas the President may not support judicial decisions. Moreover, as noted earlier, judges are more likely to reach the correct decision than agencies that are subject to much greater bias. Thus, a movement toward no deference – at least in the areas where expertise and time constraints do not present a serious problem for the judiciary – would be beneficial.

One can illustrate this point by considering what is sometimes thought, perhaps mistakenly, to be the reason why the D.C. Circuit embraced *Chevron* in the first place.[13] According to this view, the D.C. Circuit during the 1970s was dominated by what many people viewed as liberal activist judges who were willing to issue extraordinary decisions to promote their preferred policies. In response, the D.C.

---

[13] Perhaps the explanation in the text can account for many of the Republican judge's support for Chevron. For an alternative account of Chevron's reception in the D.C. Circuit, *see* Gary Lawson & Stephen Kam, *Making Law Out of Nothing at All: The Origins of the Chevron Doctrine*, 65 ADMIN. L. REV. 1, 39–59 (2013).

Circuit conservatives developed the *Chevron* approach as a means of constraining these liberal judges. Part of the justification for *Chevron* was that the D.C. Circuit liberals were so biased that the agencies would be better.

But even assuming that this portrayal of the Circuit's liberal judges was accurate, *Chevron* was a shortsighted response to aberrational circumstances. In any system of separated powers, there are likely to be situations, due to accidental forces, when one branch has extreme or unusual views for a time. But the design of institutions should focus on the long run, systematic effects of those institutions, not the occasional aberrational situation. In a few short years, the conservatives would take control the D.C. Circuit from the liberal judges. But *Chevron* has lived on for more than three decades, allowing agencies that combine legislative, executive, and judicial power significant opportunity to take biased actions.

Another objection to the separation of powers relates to the tricameral lawmaking system in the United States. It might be argued that this lawmaking system is undesirable because it makes it too difficult to pass regulatory legislation. Under this view, a single legislative house (or even a bicameral legislature) would make the decision better than the three entities that the US Constitution requires.

But it is very doubtful that a single house would make better decisions than the tricameral process. If a single entity were too inclined to pass regulatory laws – and therefore often passed undesirable laws – then a tricameral process would improve upon it by blocking some of these harmful statutes. Classical liberals have generally assumed that the government, in both democratic and undemocratic polities, will produce, unless significantly checked, too many undesirable regulatory laws. Classical liberals have also generally viewed the traditional bicameral legislature favorably.[14] Thus, the view that a tricameral process would be superior to a unicameral legislature fits comfortably within classical liberalism.

But even if one concluded that a unicameral (or a bicameral) legislature would be better than the tricameral process, that would not decide the question addressed here, which is whether the tricameral legislature is superior to having an agency make the principal policy decisions. Classical liberalism was quite skeptical that relatively unchecked government decision making, of the type enjoyed by administrative agencies, leads to desirable outcomes. Thus, even if one thought tricameralism was more difficult than would be optimal, one might still conclude that it was superior to agency decision making under existing practices.

A more serious problem for classical liberalism is that tricameralism might be an obstacle to deregulation. In a world with a large number of regulatory statutes, deregulatory laws are important, but tricameralism might unduly impede such laws.

---

[14] *See, for example,* ANNELIEN DE DIJN, FRENCH POLITICAL THOUGHT FROM MONTESQUIEU TO TOCQUEVILLE 68–72 (2008) (discussing support for bicameralism among French classical liberals, including Constant); JAMES M. BUCHANAN & GORDON TULLOCK, THE CALCULUS OF CONSENT (1962).

Imposing a stricter separation of powers might thus present a serious problem for deregulation.[15] One way of avoiding this difficulty would be to establish a system in which tricameral approval was required only for regulations, but not for deregulations. For example, one might allow delegations of legislative power to deregulate, but not to regulate.[16] This arrangement would establish an exception based on the value of deregulation. While I believe this exception is justified, some commentators might question whether such a value judgment is appropriate. An alternative that would involve a less controversial judgment would delegate to agencies the power only to repeal regulations that were enacted prior to the establishment of the stricter separation of powers regime I propose here. In that way, the establishment of a stricter separation of powers would not operate to protect regulations that were enacted under a more lenient system.[17]

B A More Modern Analysis

These traditional aspects of the separation of powers are important. But one can look at the desirability of the separation of powers from a more modern perspective based on public choice and positive political theory.[18] Under these approaches, the agencies are not assumed to be pursuing an uncontroversial conception of the public interest. Instead, it is often assumed that they are pursuing either private interests or controversial conceptions of the public good. Here I examine four plausible motivations of administrative agencies that can lead to bad results but can be constrained by the separation of powers: extreme ideologies, political party interests, bureaucratic interests, and special interests.

1 Extreme Ideologies

One motivation that agencies can have involves ideology. People who seek and work at jobs in a government agency are likely to have goals that they perceive as promoting the public interest. They are devoting their lives to an agency that is supposed to be promoting the public good. One can thus assume that they are

---

[15] *See* John O. McGinnis & Michael B. Rappaport, *Majority and Supermajority Rule: Three Views of the Capitol*, 85 TEX. L. REV. 1115, 1137–140 (2007) (discussing this issue in the related context of supermajority rules).

[16] I have argued in favor of a reform that would establish an administrative agency with the authority to issue rules that deregulated. *See* Michael B. Rappaport, *Using Delegation to Promote Deregulation*, 38 REGULATION 26 (2015–2016).

[17] Even if these exceptions for deregulation were not employed, one would still have to balance the disadvantages of applying the tricameral process to deregulations with the advantages of applying it to regulations. One might still conclude that the advantages of applying tricameralism to regulations outweigh the disadvantages.

[18] For an extended overview of public choice theory, see DENNIS C. MUELLER, PUBIC CHOICE III (2003).

concerned with such matters. People who work at the Environmental Protection Agency (EPA), for example, are likely to care about the environment.

That agency personnel believe they are promoting the public good, however, does not mean that they actually are. There are good reasons to doubt that the values that agency personnel hold are necessarily the correct ones. Often those values are extreme ones as compared to those held by the general population. One reason is that people who choose to work in a field often have a stronger belief in its importance simply based on circumstances. People working in the environmental field are both likely to care more about the environment than the average person and to be led, by the fact that they spend their days working on the environment, to be more focused on this area.[19]

Another reason to doubt the values of government personnel is that people who choose to work in a field often disproportionately hold certain political views. People who work in administrative agencies tend to have strongly politically liberal positions.[20] It is not entirely clear why this is the case, although one possibility is that people who choose to work in government tend to favor bigger government. Thus, the fact that government personnel happen to hold certain values or ideologies does not mean that they are the correct ones. Instead, those values may reflect biases or distortions of the institutional process.[21]

While agencies have a significant opportunity to pursue extreme or biased ideological preferences under the current system, the separation of powers would significantly check the agencies. Under the separation of powers, Congress would

---

[19] STEPHEN BREYER, BREAKING THE VICIOUS CIRCLE: TOWARD EFFECTIVE RISK REGULATION 11–19 (1993).

[20] *See, for example,* JOEL D. ABERBACH & BERT A. ROCKMAN, IN THE WEB OF POLITICS: THREE DECADES OF THE U.S. FEDERAL EXECUTIVE 168 (2000) (federal civil servants are generally to the left of political appointees of both major parties); Ralph R. Smith, *Which Party Receives the Most in Political Contributions from Federal Employees?* (May 19, 2016), www.fedsmith.com/2016/05/19/which-party-receives-the-most-in-political-contributions-from-federal-employees/ (last visited 7/24/2017).

[21] It might be objected that the values of government employees are derived from their expertise and therefore should be respected, but there are strong reasons to question this conclusion. First, the values of government employees might not derive from their learning or understanding of the facts, but might simply be subjective (or at least highly contested) values. Under this very common approach to thinking about values, that government employees with some expertise hold certain values does not suggest that they are correct. Second, if government employee values diverge from those of the general public, then this will be a problem in a democracy. It is true that classical liberalism does not usually place overriding value on democracy, usually treating it as a limited or instrumental value. But the fact that values that are influencing the law are not held by most people suggests that those values will impose additional costs, since people will generally dislike living under rules with which they disagree. Third, even if government employee ideology does derive in part from their greater knowledge – if, for example, the ideology involved a mix of factual and value beliefs – that would not necessarily mean that this ideology should be followed. The greater understanding of the facts would have to be balanced against the subjective and unrepresentative character of the values that the employees hold.

have to approve the laws, and Congress would be far less prone to ideological extremeness for various reasons. First, Congress is politically accountable to the voters overall who are less likely to have extreme values. Second, lawmaking by Congress ordinarily requires the approval of the three lawmaking branches. If even one of those branches is controlled by the opposite party, it will be difficult to enact laws that are not widely supported. Third, Congress is concerned with a wide variety of matters and therefore is unlikely to have the tunnel vision that agencies often exhibit.

To be sure the president's supervision of the agencies will place some limits on their extreme ideology. After all, the president is elected by all of the people. But this check on the extreme ideology of agencies is limited by several factors. First, the president does not have power over independent agencies. While he can influence these agencies, he cannot give them orders or remove their principal officers. Second, even as to executive agencies, the president's strong legal authority is limited by practical matters. The agencies enjoy significant authority to develop proposals and the White House does not have the time or ability to carefully supervise all of them.

Third, even though the president is elected by all of the people, that does not necessarily mean he will avoid extreme ideologies. If we assume that the president represents the median voter of his party, then he will favor policies that are a significant distance from the median voter of the country. The failure of the president to check the extremeness of agency ideology will occur most significantly when the president favors the strong regulations that agency personnel often support.

Under the separation of powers, the courts would also exercise some of the authority currently possessed by the agencies, and the courts would be less prone to extreme ideologies than the agencies. While generalist judges may adopt extreme ideologies, they would be less likely to possess these ideologies than agency personnel, because they would not be self-selecting to join a particular agency and would not spend their time deciding cases in only one area. It is true that the institutional reform I recommend would reduce the generalist character of judges – limiting their assignments to areas such as health, science, or economics. But each of these areas would encompass the work of many agencies and therefore the judges would have a much broader perspective than the agencies.[22]

---

[22] Another reason why judges might not act on extreme ideologies is that judges who serve for a long period are likely to develop a role mentality, in which they desire to follow the rules governing their role, such as rules governing legal interpretation and factual findings. This judicial role will act as a bit of a counterweight to their ideological commitments (and to the other interests discussed in this section – political party interest, bureaucratic interest, and special interests). The strength of this role mentality, however, should not be overemphasized. It is likely that it is relatively weak and might be outweighed by strong ideological commitments.

2 Political Party Interests

A second motivation that administrative agencies may exhibit is furthering the interests of the party that controls the agency. Political parties – one of which is typically led by the president – often have interests that can be furthered or hindered by administrative agencies. Those interests might involve the interests of members of the party coalition, concerns of people within the party, the party's narrow interests in winning elections, and matters of significant reputational interest of the party. For example, an agency might be able to take actions that increase the popularity of a major law passed by the party, such as the Affordable Care Act. The political party interest, then, might lead the agency to exercise its powers to further a party's interests rather than to follow the law, to find facts faithfully, or to pursue reasonable policy.

Once again, the separation of powers addresses this political party interest. Congress is much less likely to pursue a single party's interest because one of the three lawmaking branches is often controlled by the opposite party (and the majority party in the Senate may not be able to overcome a filibuster). The participation of the federal courts should also reduce party interests. First, federal judges serve for long periods and therefore may over time have less of an allegiance to the party which appointed them. Second, even if the judge exhibits an equally strong party interest but is a member of a different party than controls the agency, this will put a check on the agency's ability to further its party interest. The judge may check the agency just as divided government checks party interests as to the passage of laws.

3 Bureaucratic Interests

A third motivation that administrative agencies often exhibit is to further their own bureaucratic interests. Agencies often have interests in growing larger, in exercising more power, and in having more responsibilities, all of which expand the money and power available to the agency.[23] Agencies can do this in various ways. An agency might interpret a statute to give itself more responsibility or power. Or an agency might seek to enact a regulation that allows it more responsibility or power and therefore find facts and assert policy views to support the regulation.

> One might wonder whether agency personnel develop a role mentality that serves to lead them to behave properly. In my judgement, if agency personnel develop such a mentality at all, it is likely to have an extremely weak effect. There are important areas where there is a strong consensus as to how judges are to behave (even though there are other areas of strong disagreement). In the case of agencies, the conception of an agency role is likely to operate as a much weaker check. For example, agencies are allowed to pursue ideology as to policy, legal interpretation, and factual findings in a way that judges are not.

[23] William A. Niskanen, *The Peculiar Economics of Bureaucracy*, 58 AMERICAN ECONOMIC REVIEW 293 (1968).

The separation of powers, however, will constrain the agency's power in this context. As compared to the agencies, Congress will not have a strong preference for bureaucratic authority. Congress has a natural incentive not to empower its institutional rival, the executive branch. To be sure, Congress often favors the delegation of decisions to the executive, to avoid responsibility, but Congress's preferences here are no worse than those of the agencies. But in other respects, such as the degree of power given to the agency, Congress will often favor giving less authority to the agency. Nor would judges have an incentive to pursue the bureaucratic interest.[24]

4 Special Interests

A fourth motivation that administrative agencies often exhibit is to benefit special interests. Special interests are concentrated groups, allowing them to raise and expend funds to pursue their interests. Since special interests do not thereby suffer from rational ignorance, they can undertake to monitor the actions of administrative agencies. They also use their resources in various ways to influence the behavior of agencies, such as lobbying agency officials, submitting briefs and comments to the agency, and seeking judicial review of agency action.

While the separation of powers may not eliminate special interests, separated government would probably function better than agencies with combined powers. To be sure, Congress is unlikely to be less subject to special interests than are administrative agencies. But it is harder for special interests to enact laws through Congress, because these laws must go through the tricameral process, which is often governed by people of both parties.[25] Thus, special interests are unlikely to be able to easily enact laws.

Special interests also would be likely to have more influence over agencies than over independent courts. Courts are generally insulated from politics. Special

---

[24] While courts might not further bureaucratic interests, perhaps they would promote judicial interests. The courts might seek to interpret statutes based not on text or intent, but instead on more flexible criteria that allow them to pursue their own favored policies. This is definitely a risk of judicial interpretation, but it is less of a problem than that created by *Chevron*. The ultimate decision about what the statutory interpretation rules are is made by the Supreme Court (in the absence of congressional statute). The Court does not have a strong incentive to confer discretion on lower courts, because that discretion can be used in ways that the Supreme Court dislikes. Thus, the Court has an incentive to adopt relatively constrained interpretive methods for the lower courts. While the Supreme Court does have an incentive not to adopt those methods for itself, the Court is limited because the methods it employs for itself automatically apply to the lower courts. Moreover, even if the Supreme Court does employ different methods for itself, this is far less damaging than allowing agencies to act, since the Supreme Court decides a limited number of administrative law cases each year, whereas the agencies issue a far greater number of rules and decisions.

[25] While the tricameral process might hinder special interests from enacting laws, it might also aid them in blocking laws. On the problem of special interests blocking laws under the tricameral process, *see* my discussion *supra* p. 12.

interests cannot lobby the judges nor do judges generally receive significant job offers from private sector firms. It is true that special interests are likely to have better lawyers than do other groups. But this is their main advantage before courts, whereas they enjoy both that advantage and others before agencies.

* * *

In sum, the separation of powers will both limit agencies and increase the chances that the government beneficially performs its functions. Of course, progressives and other supporters of big government may believe that these limits will prevent the agencies from taking some desirable actions. If you have strong faith in government, then you want fewer restraints on it. But that has not been the classical liberal position.

While the separation of powers may lead to a more desirable government in general, a distinct question is whether the separation of powers would work well in our existing world of large government. One might believe that the separation of powers is too restrictive to allow the government to undertake the tasks needed to maintain the large governmental institutions of the administrative state. Although it is often thought that the separation of powers would prevent the government from having the time and expertise to successfully perform these tasks, I now argue that institutional reforms could overcome both of these challenges.

II DELEGATION OF RULEMAKING AUTHORITY

Under existing administrative law, most administrative agencies enjoy significant authority to promulgate binding legislative rules. Such legislative rules are an extremely important part of federal law. It is often said that administrative agencies pass more rules that govern the public than Congress does.[26]

Eliminating agency rulemaking is often believed to be impractical. There are two main problems with Congress passing the rules rather than the agencies. First, Congress is often thought to lack the expertise to draft these rules and to determine whether to pass them.[27] In particular, the questions involve technical and special-ized knowledge that most members of Congress do not possess. Second, Congress

---

[26] *See, for example,* Jonathan Turley, *The Rise of the Fourth Branch of Government,* WASH. POST (May 24, 2013) ("the vast majority of 'laws' governing the United States are not passed by Congress but are issued as regulations, crafted largely by thousands of unnamed, unreachable bureaucrats. One study found that in 2007, Congress enacted 138 public laws, while federal agencies finalized 2,926 rules, including 61 major regulations."), www.washingtonpost.com/opinions/the-rise-of-the-fourth-branch-of-government/2013/05/24/c7faaad0-c2ed-11e2-9fe2-6ee52doeb7c1_story.html?utm_term=.aafocf2b2eod, last visited on 6/30/2017.

[27] *See* Mistretta v. United States, 488 U.S. 361, 372 (1989) (noting that "in our increasingly complex society, ... Congress simply cannot do its job absent an ability to delegate power under broad general directives").

lacks the time to draft these rules and to reach agreement on them. The agencies are open for business throughout the year and each of the numerous agencies can work on several regulations at the same time. By contrast, Congress often is in recess and can work upon only a limited number of pieces of significant legislation at the same time. Moreover, securing agreement within a house and working out agreement among the different lawmaking branches can be extremely time-consuming.[28]

In addition to having time and expertise, administrative agencies also enjoy significant authority to enact these rules. It is true that the agencies are typically obligated to follow certain procedures, which require that they inform the public of the basis of their rules and respond to comments.[29] But these procedures do not normally prevent the agencies from ultimately enacting the regulations that they desire.

In formulating the rules, the agencies are also often required to make findings of policy, law, and facts, that are subject to review by the courts. But in each of these cases, the agencies are typically given substantial deference. Many statutes provide an agency with significant policymaking authority to decide what policy to adopt. While the agency must explain its reasoning process, it can choose the policy it desires within significant limits.[30] Statutes place legal limits on the agencies, but agencies typically enjoy *Chevron* deference as to their legal interpretations when they issue legislative regulations. When they do not receive *Chevron* deference, they still generally receive *Skidmore* deference. Finally, agencies are often required to find facts to support their rulemakings, but once again they typically enjoy significant deference as to their findings, which are reviewed under either a substantial evidence or arbitrary and capricious standard.

Given the importance and number of legislative regulations in the modern world, all such agency regulations probably cannot fully be subjected to the separation of powers. But it would be possible to significantly reduce the discretion that agencies currently enjoy. There are two basic ways of accomplishing this task. First, one can require that Congress approve the most consequential regulations. Instead of having Congress draft the regulations and reach agreement on a compromise, the agencies would draft the regulations, as they do now. The most important regulations, however, would then be sent to Congress to be approved on an up or down vote by each house (followed by presentment to the President). The rules of the legislative houses would forbid amendments to and limit debate on these proposed regulations. This congressional approval procedure would allow Congress to avoid the problems of time and expertise.

---

[28] Christopher DeMuth, *The Regulatory State*, NATIONAL AFFAIRS, Summer 2012, at 72.

[29] *See, for example,* 5 U.S.C. § 553 (2017) (APA rulemaking); 42 U.S.C. § 7607(d) ()2017) (statutory hybrid rulemaking).

[30] Motor Veh. Mfrs. Ass'n v. State Farm Ins., 463 U.S. 29 (1983).

While this approach to limiting the delegation of rulemaking authority to agencies is a familiar one from the proposed REINS Act, various problems of that proposal would need to be addressed. One issue involves determining what are the major or most consequential regulations. Although the REINS Act assumes that the statutory definition will be enforced, that assumption is not prudent. I propose various alternative ways of addressing this issue.

Another issue is the position in which the REINS Act would place the houses of Congress. Once the agency proposes a regulation, Congress would be forced to take it or leave it. This situation would be problematic because it might force Congress to accept regulations that it should disapprove. A reform of the process, however, might allow Congress a method to avoid this situation. A third issue concerns the possibility that the agency would propose regulations based in part on its prediction whether Congress would approve or reject the proposed regulation. A reform is needed to allow the agency to do so.

The second way to constrain agency authority to promulgate legislative regulations involves the scope of judicial review of the agency findings as to regulations. Under existing law, agencies enjoy deference as to their findings of policy, law, and facts. Agency authority to enact legislative regulations would be constrained if that deference were diminished. I argue that it would be feasible to eliminate deference as to the law and to reduce agency discretion as to policy and facts.

A *Requiring Congressional Approval*

1 The REINS Act

For many years, it was thought that the greater expertise and capacity of administrative agencies required that they, rather than Congress, enact most rules. But now many people argue that an institutional reform would make it possible for Congress to approve a substantial number of legislative regulations.[31]

Under this institutional reform, which has been formulated into a variety of proposed REINS Acts, major rules promulgated by an agency need congressional approval.[32] Each house of Congress is required to vote upon the regulation, subject to sharp limits on debate and amendment. If both houses of Congress approve of the regulation and it is signed by the President, then the agency may

---

[31] *See, for example,* Jonathan H. Adler, Placing 'REINS' on Regulations: Assessing the Proposed REINS Act, 16 *New York University Journal of Legislation and Public Policy* 1 (2013).

[32] There is no single REINS Act. The proposed law has been introduced in various Congresses in similar versions. For simplicity, I will focus on the versions introduced in the House in the 114th Congress. *See* Regulations from the Executive in Need of Scrutiny Act, H.R. 427, 114th Cong (2015). *See also* Regulations from the Executive in Need of Scrutiny Act, S. 226, 114th Cong. (2015) (Senate version).

promulgate it, although it is subject to the ordinary challenges for judicial review.[33] If one or both houses of Congress disapprove of the regulation, then the regulation cannot be promulgated.

Under this arrangement, Congress could largely avoid both the capacity and the expertise problems. There are a limited number of major rules (approximately 50 to 100) promulgated each year.[34] Thus, during the period in which Congress is in session, it would only have to review approximately two or three rules per week. This burden would certainly be manageable, given the limitations on debate under the REINS Act.

Congress would also have adequate expertise to undertake this role. It is true that Congress will likely have less knowledge about the regulation than does the agency. But the most important tasks for which the expertise is needed – drafting a sensible regulation and justifying it on legal, factual, and policy grounds – will be undertaken by the agency. Congress will just have to evaluate whether that regulation is desirable, which Congress could do based in part on the information that the agency will provide in its statement of basis and purpose accompanying the regulation. Significantly, Congress will have other advantages in evaluating the regulation. Its value judgments will better reflect those of the public, and the often divided government among the lawmaking branches will mean that regulations that the people generally do not support will not be enacted. Overall, Congress should have adequate expertise to perform its role in the process.

Yet, it would not hurt to provide Congress with additional information about regulations and the regulatory process. Some commentators have persuasively argued that Congress would greatly benefit from a Congressional Regulation Office that is modelled on the Congressional Budget Office.[35] Just as the Congressional Budget Office provides Congress with additional information so it is not at the mercy of the executive branch for budgeting, similarly a Congressional Regulation Office could provide Congress with information about the regulations that the agencies propose and their effect on the nation.

2 Changes to the Congressional Approval Procedure

But while Congress should be able to perform its responsibilities under a congressional approval procedure, other challenges would exist under such an arrangement. The existing REINS Act proposals have not addressed these problems, but they would need to be resolved for a successful reform.

---

[33] Regulations from the Executive in Need of Scrutiny Act, H.R. 427, 114th Cong. § 805 (2015).

[34] *See* Adler, *supra* note 18, at 23 ("From 1998 to 2010 . . . federal agencies promulgated between fifty and one hundred major rules per year").

[35] Philip Wallach & Kevin R. Kosar, *The Case for a Congressional Regulation Office*, 29 NATIONAL AFFAIRS (Fall 2016), www.nationalaffairs.com/publications/detail/the-case-for-a-con gressional-regulation-office.

A DETERMINING THE COSTS IMPOSED BY A RULE One problem involves the determination of what is a major rule.[36] At present, a similar problem exists under the Cost Benefit Executive Order and the Congressional Review Act, which apply their restrictions only to the most significant regulations – to "significant regulatory actions" and to "major rules" respectively. In both cases, the Office of Management and Budget makes the determination whether the restrictions apply to a regulation.[37] Under existing institutions, this arrangement generally can be trusted. Under the executive order, OMB has an incentive to read the definition broadly since doing so allows it to apply a cost benefit test to more regulations. In the case of the Congressional Review Act, it is true that the entire executive branch has an incentive to implement the Act narrowly to avoid congressional review. But until very recently, the Act was unimportant and OMB also had some incentive to interpret the definition broadly to the extent it overlaps with the executive order's major rule definition.

But under a congressional approval procedure, the incentives would change. Agencies and the executive branch generally would lose an enormous amount of power due to the requirement that they submit regulations to Congress for approval. Consequently, OMB itself would have much less incentive to interpret the definition of a major rule broadly or to determine that particular regulations are major rules. And the President, who supervises OMB, would have a strong incentive to require that these aspects of the major rule requirement be implemented narrowly to avoid congressional approval. Consequently, a big risk exists that OMB would implement the major rule requirement too narrowly.

To guard against such narrow implementation, Congress should adopt, with proposals from OMB and the other agencies, a methodology for determining the costs of rules.[38] That methodology should be implemented in two stages. First, the agency, subject to binding review by OMB, should make a determination whether the regulation satisfies the definition of a major rule. If OMB concludes that the regulation is a major rule, then the agency must submit the regulation to Congress.

---

[36] The REINS Act defines a major rule as one that is likely to result in "(i) an annual effect on the economy of $100 million or more; (ii) a major increase in costs or prices for consumers, individual industries, Federal, State, or local government agencies, or geographic regions; (iii) significant adverse effects on competition, employment, investment, productivity, innovation, or on the ability of United States-based enterprises to compete with foreign-based enterprises in domestic and export markets; or is made under the Patient Protection and Affordable Care Act."

Regulations from the Executive in Need of Scrutiny Act, H.R. 427, 114th Cong. § 804(2) (2015). This definition is similar to the definition of a major rule in the Congressional Review Act, 5 U.S.C. §804(2) and to the definition of a significant regulatory action in the Cost Benefit Executive Order. Exec. Order No. 12866, 58 Fed. Reg. 190 (Sept. 30, 1993) § 3(f).

[37] Exec. Order No. 12866, 58 Fed. Reg. 190 (Sept. 30, 1993) §6(a)(3)(A); 5 U.S.C. §804(2).

[38] While the REINS Act defines major rules also to include other criteria than costs, *see supra* note 36, I here focus on the cost criterion as the one that is probably the best way of identifying the most consequential rules.

If OMB concludes that the regulation is not a major rule, then the agency can promulgate the regulation. But private parties will then be able to challenge the regulation in court on the ground that it was in fact a major rule.[39] Because the issue involves technical questions, the decision should be made by an independent administrative court that has expertise in economics, without any deference for the agency or OMB's determination.[40] In this way, the agencies could be prevented from undercounting the costs of regulations, while at the same time having the decision made by someone with expertise.

B DETERMINING WHAT IS A SINGLE RULE A second problem would arise not from the undercounting of a single regulation, but from an agency dividing a single regulation into two separate regulations. Suppose, for example, an agency has a regulation that imposes costs of $140 million per year. To avoid congressional review, the agency might split the regulation into two regulations, each costing $70 million. This is a harder issue to solve than the possibility of undercounting.

To prevent such divisions, the main strategy would be to combine a definition of a single regulation with a temporal limitation. First, one could define a single regulation as a set of rules that are addressed to a single subject. Thus, if one set of rules involving a single subject were divided into two, they would still constitute a single regulation. The problem with this definition is that it difficult to define a single subject with precision. Although many state constitutions impose a requirement that legislation or referenda be limited to a single subject, the courts have struggled to establish a clear definition of that requirement.[41]

Specifying what a single subject is would also be a challenge in the area of regulations, but Congress could address the problem by providing additional guidance. Congress could specify for each statute that certain regulations constituted one or more regulations. For example, the Clean Air Act might state that each of the periodic updates for Air Quality Standards for a pollutant count as a separate regulation.[42] Where Congress addresses the specific situation, its definition should answer the question with reasonable clarity.[43] In cases where it does not address the

---

[39] Under the REINS Act proposals, it is not entirely clear whether there is judicial review of these matters. It would seem that judicial review is precluded by the provisions stating that "(a) No determination, finding, action, or omission under this chapter shall be subject to judicial review." Regulations from the Executive in Need of Scrutiny Act, H.R. 427, 114th Cong. § 805 (a) (2015). But the next section provides, "Notwithstanding subsection (a), a court may determine whether a Federal agency has completed the necessary requirements under this chapter for a rule to take effect. 114th Cong. § 805(b).

[40] For a discussion of the independent administrative courts, *see infra* at 33–6.

[41] *See, for example*, Michael B. Rappaport, *The President's Veto and the Constitution*, 87 NORTH-WESTERN UNIVERSITY LAW REVIEW 735 (1993).

[42] *See* 42 U.S.C. §7408 (2017).

[43] In focusing on the definition of a single regulation, Congress could adjust the minimum amount for it to be considered a major rule. For example, if a regulation under a specific

specific situation, more uncertainty is likely, although courts might receive guidance in these cases from how Congress answered the specific situations it did address.[44]

While this definition would still leave uncertainty, this uncertainty could be addressed by considering the timing of the rules. One should be more likely to treat two rules issued the same year as one regulation than the same two rules issued several years apart. That is not because the latter two rules are more related to one another, since both sets of rules are identical in my example. Rather, it is because it is easier for the agency to circumvent the congressional review procedure if the two rules are issued more closely in time. If the rules are issued at the same time, the agency pays no price for separating them. By contrast, if the agency is forced to issue them five years apart, then the agency pays a significant price – a five-year delay – in dividing the regulation. Consequently, one might want to adopt a presumption that two rules constituted a single regulation if issued within three years of one another. If the rules were issued between three and five years of one another, one might adopt no presumption. And if the rules were issued more than five years apart, then one might conclusively presume that they were separate regulations.

The presumption during the first three years that the rules were a single regulation would not operate to treat all rules as a single regulation. It would merely require that the agency prove that these rules addressed different subjects. Another way to describe the presumption is to say that it would treat unclear cases as involving a single regulation. Thus, unless it was clear that they were different regulations, one would treat them as a single regulation.

A separate question is which entity would have the final decision as to whether a set of rules constituted one or more regulations. I recommend employing the same procedure I proposed for determining the costs of a regulation: a decision by OMB subject to review in the independent administrative courts. If an agency decides not to submit two rules to Congress on the ground that they constitute two separate regulations, OMB should be given the authority to review that decision. Thus, the final decision within the executive branch should be made by OMB.[45] But even if OMB concludes that there are two rules, the decision should be subject to challenge in the independent administrative courts by a private party. Those courts would have both expertise and experience with these matters. In this way, the decision would be made not by an interested party – the executive branch – but instead by an independent entity.

Ultimately, the problem of determining whether two separately issued rules should be counted as one regulation would be difficult, but could be addressed

---

provision is defined as a separate regulation, but it is a smaller matter than other regulations, Congress could lower the minimum amount for treating this regulation as a major rule.

[44] The courts might also consider other matters, such as whether the two regulations involve the interpretation of a specific statutory provision.

[45] OMB should be given this authority even as to independent agencies.

through the definition of a regulation and a temporal limitation. While some regulations might avoid review, this method is likely to prevent the great majority of evasions.

C AVOIDING THE PROBLEMS OF TAKE IT OR LEAVE IT REGULATORY PROPOSALS A third issue for the congressional approval procedure is that it allows agencies to place each house of Congress in a take it or leave it situation. The agency can formulate a proposed regulation and then each house must vote on that regulation. Under the procedure in the REINS Act, Congress cannot amend the regulation and no formal procedure exists for a house even to explain why it voted against the regulation.[46]

This take it or leave it arrangement may limit Congress's ability to improve the regulation. While Congress will have the authority to block regulations proposed by an agency, the agency can game the system to make it more difficult for Congress to do so. It could combine a popular regulatory provision with an undesirable one. Congress then might be reluctant to vote against the popular provision, even though it should do so to prevent the undesirable provision from being enacted.

To guard against this problem, the congressional approval procedure should be modified to permit Congress more responses to the proposed regulation. Instead of simply being allowed to vote for or against the regulation, a house could vote against the regulation with an explanation. The resolution disapproving the regulation might detail the specific defects that the house believes plague the regulation. If the agency addressed the alleged defects by submitting a modified version of the regulation, then Congress would be forced to vote up or down on the regulation without the option of disapproving it again based on a specific defect. If the agency failed to address the defect, then Congress would not be required to vote on the regulation again.

This arrangement would provide the agency and Congress with better incentives. First, the agency could not force Congress to vote on a proposed regulation without Congress being able to formally explain its action, thereby reducing the agency's ability to lead Congress to approve a regulation that it thought undesirable. And if Congress did disapprove of the regulation for a specific reason, the agency would have an incentive to improve the law so that Congress would approve it. Moreover, if the agency addressed the defect, Congress could not avoid responsibility for disapproving the regulation by formally arguing it was still defective.

Enforcement of this rule would operate a little differently than with the previous two modifications of the congressional approval procedure. If an agency sought to resubmit a proposed regulation that Congress had disapproved for a specific defect,

---

[46] *See* Regulations from the Executive in Need of Scrutiny Act, H.R. 427, 114th Cong. §802(a)(1) (C) (providing that the joint resolution approving the bill can include only the statement "That Congress approves the [specified] rule").

then OMB should be required to review the determination and conclude that the regulation in fact addressed the defect. But OMB's determination should not be sufficient. Once received by Congress, the decision that the regulation addressed the defect should be reviewed by a congressional official, such as the legislative house's parliamentarian. In that way, the houses would not be bound by the executive branch's determination.

D LIMITS ON AN AGENCY'S POWER TO RESUBMIT REGULATIONS TO CONGRESS A fourth issue involves the agency's power to resubmit regulations to Congress after they have been disapproved. Under the REINS Act, no limits are placed on an agency's ability to resend regulations to the next Congress.[47] Presumably, the agency could resubmit regulations each year if it thought it advisable. But this should not be allowed, because it would waste Congress's time and impose needless political pressure on Congress. Instead, there should be a prohibition on the agency resubmitting to Congress a disapproved regulation, or a substantially similar regulation, for a significant period, such as five years.[48] The agency should also be prohibited from enacting these provisions as part of a non-major rule during the same period.

The enforcement procedure for this rule should be similar to those I recommend for the other reforms of the congressional approval procedure. If an agency proposes to submit a major rule to Congress, OMB should be required to find that the agency is not submitting substantially the same regulation as was previously submitted within the relevant time period. If OMB makes that finding and the regulation is submitted to Congress, then a congressional official, such as a house's parliamentarian, should also make an independent determination whether the regulation is substantially the same as one previously submitted during the relevant period.

A different procedure should be employed to ensure that an agency does not enact substantially the same regulation as part of a non-major rule. OMB should once again be required to find that the agency did not submit substantially the same rule to Congress. If OMB makes that finding and the agency promulgates the regulation, then the regulation should be subject to challenge in an administrative court on the ground that it is substantially similar to a regulation previously submitted to Congress during the relevant period.

---

[47] Regulations from the Executive in Need of Scrutiny Act, H.R. 427, 114th Cong. § 801(a)(5) (2015) (providing that if "a joint resolution of approval relating to a major rule is not enacted within the [required] period, then a joint resolution of approval relating to the same rule may not be considered under this chapter *in the same Congress* by either the House of Representatives or the Senate) (emphasis added).

[48] An alternative arrangement would not prohibit resubmission of the regulation to Congress, but instead allow resubmission if some percentage of each house of Congress, such as 25 percent, voted to permit it earlier than the five-year time period.

E AN AGENCY'S POWER TO ANTICIPATE CONGRESSIONAL POSITIONS WHEN DEVELOPING RULES A fifth issue involves whether the agency may anticipate Congress's response when proposing a regulation. Under existing law, an agency's decision about the content of a proposed regulation is often treated as a policy issue. In making such policy decisions, agencies are required to consider only legitimate matters, such as those consistent with the underlying statute. Under this system, it might be problematic for an agency to draft a regulation in a form so as to avoid the opposition of a congressional committee. Similarly, it might be problematic for an agency to draft a regulation to avoid congressional disapproval of the regulation. Should an agency be allowed to take account Congress's likely decision to approve or disapprove a proposed regulation when deciding its content?

There are three possible answers here. One might forbid the agency from taking Congress's expected reaction into account; one might allow the agency to do so; or one might allow the agency to do so only if Congress had formally announced its objection in a prior disapproval of the regulation. In my view, the agency should be permitted to consider Congress's expected reactions. After all, this would promote the important purpose of having the agency take into account the public's views, which would have been likely to influence Congress. In addition, it would be hard to enforce the contrary rule, since the agency could always claim to be pursuing its own policy views even though it was conforming to Congress's perceived views.

B *Reducing Deference to the Agency*

While the congressional approval procedure significantly limits agency rulemaking, judicial review of agency regulations will still be important. Even though major rules must be approved by Congress, such rules are still subject to challenge on judicial review.[49] Nonmajor rules, of course, are also subject to judicial review. Thus, the law governing judicial review of legislative regulations remains important.

Under the existing rules for judicial review, administrative agencies receive significant deference for their findings of law, fact and policy. Such deference involves the transference of some portion of legislative and judicial power to the agencies. Thus, reducing or eliminating that deference would further the separation of powers, and reforms that accomplish this should be adopted to the extent feasible and desirable.

This section discusses the issue of deference. I initially assume that agency decisions are reviewed by ordinary federal courts. I then discuss the possibility of employing independent appellate administrative courts and the influence that would have on these deference questions.

---

[49] Regulations from the Executive in Need of Scrutiny Act, H.R. 427, 114th Cong. § 805(c) (2015).

1 Interpretive Authority

One area where agencies enjoy significant deference involves legal interpretation. Two types of interpretive deference are related to the enactment of legislative regulations.[50] First, *Chevron* deference generally applies to an agency's interpretation of statutes that it administers under informal rulemaking and formal adjudication. Second, *Skidmore* deference involves deference provided to an agency's interpretation based on the perceived expertise of the agency.[51] While there are significant limits on what can be done to restrain discretion in other areas, such as factfinding and policymaking, I argue that one can eliminate all deference as to legal interpretation.

A CHEVRON Under the *Chevron* doctrine, the Supreme Court defers to an agency's interpretation of the statutes that it administers under certain circumstances.[52] Consequently, judicial review of agency interpretation of statutes imposes less stringent limits on agency power.

Chevron deference interferes with the separation of powers. The interpretation of statutes that agencies apply against the public is not executive power, but judicial power. When agencies are given authority to determine the meaning of a statute, the judiciary is deprived of its traditional authority. While agencies need to interpret statutes to perform their executive duties, the *final* determination of their meaning in particular cases, going back to *Marbury v. Madison* and before, involves judicial power, not executive power.[53]

Under the *Chevron* doctrine, the Supreme Court assumes that Congress intended that the agency enjoy deference as to its interpretation of statutes that it administers under certain circumstances. This assumption is unsupported.[54] Rather than relying

---

[50] Another type of interpretive deference is *Auer* deference, which generally applies to an agency's interpretation of its own legislative regulations. Since that deference does not involve the enactment of legislative regulations, I postpone discussion of that deference to the delegation of adjudicative authority section.

[51] Skidmore v. Swift & Co., 323 U.S. 134 (1944).

[52] United States v. Mead Corp., 533 U.S. 218 (2001).

[53] Philip Hamburger, *Chevron Bias*, 84 GEORGE WASHINGTON LAW REVIEW 1187, 1197–200 (2016) (discussing the related arguments that *Chevron* usurps judicial power and that *Chevron* deference requires judges to depart from their traditional duty to decide cases according to their independent judgment). To be clear, my claim that the judicial power should be understood to include the power of courts to make the final decision about the meaning of the law in cases brought before them is not a claim about the Constitution's original meaning. The originalist question is a complicated one that turns on conflicting evidence. Compare Hamburger, *supra* note 53, with Aditya Bamzai, *Justice Scalia and the Evolution of Chevron Deference*, 21 Texas *Review of Law and Policy* 295, 297–98 (2017).

[54] *See Mead*, 533 U.S. at 229 (it can "be apparent from the agency's generally conferred authority and other statutory circumstances that Congress would expect the agency to be able to speak with the force of law when it addresses ambiguity in the statute or fills a space in the enacted law"). Notably, the *Chevron* decision itself did not assume that Congress intended to delegate

on evidence of congressional intent, the Supreme Court simply assumes that the existence of an agency exercising informal rulemaking or formal adjudication would have led Congress to confer deference. The Supreme Court makes this assumption even though the pre-*Chevron* doctrine did not regularly do so and the Administrative Procedure Act is best read as not authorizing such deference.[55]

Yet, even if Congress had delegated deference to the agency, such deference should not be allowed. If the judicial power includes the power to say what the law is, then *Chevron* is inconsistent with the separation of powers. Congress should no more have authority to delegate this deference than any other type of judicial power.

In this chapter, I do recommend other types of deference, for findings of fact and policy, because it would be too difficult or undesirable to eliminate them in a progressive world. But in the case of legal interpretation, these considerations do not hold. The courts have the ability to exercise the entire authority to interpret federal statutes without the need for agency deference. Since this authority is judicial power, no problem exists with fully conferring it on the courts.

There is also no problem in distinguishing between this judicial power and impermissible policymaking authority. To be sure, some people have sought to justify *Chevron* deference on the ground that the interpretation of statutes that are not clearly resolved by Congress (step two questions under *Chevron*) is a policy issue.[56] But this argument is not well taken from a traditional separation of powers perspective. While a distinction certainly exists between cases under step one and step two of *Chevron*, that distinction should be understood not as that between judicial interpretation and policymaking, but as that between clear legal questions and close legal questions. Cases under step two are close questions in which different judges might disagree in good faith about the correct answer.[57] But that

---

this question. *See* Chevron v. NRDC, 467 U.S. 837, 865 (1984) (noting that deference should be conferred whether or not Congress "consciously desired the Administrator" to make the decision).

[55] *See* Aditya Bamzai, *The Origins of Judicial Deference to Executive Interpretation*, 126 YALE LAW JOURNAL 908, 965–85 (2017) (discussing various approaches to judicial review of agency findings of law prior to the APA);Thomas W. Merrill, *Judicial Deference to Executive Precedent*, 101 YALE LAW JOURNAL 969 (1992).

[56] Richard J. Pierce Jr., *Chevron and Its Aftermath: Judicial Review of Agency Interpretations of Statutory Provisions*, 41 VANDERBILT LAW REVIEW 301 (1988). Under *Chevron*, step one cases involve matters where Congress has "directly spoken to the precise question at issue." Step two cases involve matters when "the statute is silent or ambiguous with respect to the specific issue." *Chevron, supra* at 842–43.

[57] There is also a clear distinction between policy questions and legal questions. If the Congress confers policymaking discretion on an agency, the law will determine the scope of that policy discretion. For example, the legal question might ask what is the scope of the public interest standard that the statute imposes – that is, how much discretion is conferred on the agency? Once one has decided how much discretion there is, the agency can exercise it. Thus, de novo review is consistent with policymaking discretion.

does not turn such close questions into policy questions. These close legal questions should be decided by judges using traditional legal methods of interpretation.[58]

One of the arguments offered to justify *Chevron* deference is that agencies are better at interpreting their own statutes than are generalist courts. Yet, there are strong reasons to doubt this claim. First, appellate courts are particularly good at interpreting statutes. To put the point differently, if appellate courts are not good at interpreting statutes, then what are they good at? Much of federal judicial practice involves statutory interpretation. It is true that agencies may have more experience with their own statutes, but agencies are also more biased about their own authority. If agencies do have more expertise, they can use that expertise to make more persuasive arguments that should allow them to win in court without the need for deference.

If one does believe that expertise is an important ingredient of statutory interpretation, this concern could be addressed by the optional reform discussed later of employing appellate administrative judges who possess expertise. Since such judges would have expertise but would also be independent, they would be better than agencies at interpreting statutes.

Another way to address a perceived lack of expertise on the part of ordinary circuit court judges would be to eliminate deference for pure questions of law, but to allow deference for mixed questions of law and fact. This was one of the standards of review employed prior to the emergence of *Chevron* deference.[59] Much can be said for this standard. One advantage is that it would allow the courts to make the major decisions on the meaning of the law, while permitting agencies deference as to the typically smaller cases involving the application of law to facts. Moreover, as such cases involve factual matters, one might argue that the agency's expertise is more involved than with pure questions. One significant disadvantage to this separate standard for mixed questions, however, is that disputes may arise among judges whether a matter is a pure or a mixed question. Still readers who believe that a lack of circuit court expertise is a problem may favor this separate standard for mixed questions over entirely eliminating *Chevron* deference.

Another argument made for *Chevron* deference is that without deference the courts would disagree excessively as to the meaning of administrative statutes. As a result, the importance of uniformity for federal statutes would require that the Supreme Court resolve these issues. There would, however, on this view be too many cases requiring Supreme Court resolution.

But this argument cannot justify *Chevron* deference for various reasons. First, while uniformity in the interpretation of federal administrative statutes is a value, it is

---

[58] It is mainly under legal realism that these close questions might seem like policy questions. Under that view, law is just policy, and an unclear issue would be a policy question.

[59] *See* Gary Lawson & Stephen Kam, *Making Law Out of Nothing at All: The Origins of the Chevron Doctrine*, 65 ADMINISTRATIVE LAW REVIEW 1, 9 (2013).

not of overriding importance. If the Supreme Court can hear only the most important administrative cases, then those cases will be resolved quickly though others may take some additional time. If different circuits interpret the statutes differently, then there may end up being different interpretations in different circuits for a period. But it is not clear that this is a serious problem. Although uniformity has some value, so does the experimentation and variation that diversity among circuits produces.

Second, even if one believes that uniformity is extremely important, the Supreme Court could decide many additional cases. The Supreme Court docket is at historically low levels and the Court could easily increase the number of administrative law cases involving statutory interpretation it hears.[60] Moreover, even those who believe that the Supreme Court should not increase the number of its cases might still accept that administrative law cases are such an important part of federal law that the Supreme Court should replace other cases it ordinarily hears with administrative law cases.

Finally, even if one rejects all of these approaches, the standard that allows deference for mixed questions but not pure questions would also address any increased need for Supreme Court resolution of administrative law cases. Under this standard, a significant portion of administrative law cases would still receive deference.

B SKIDMORE A second type of deference for legal interpretation is *Skidmore* deference. Under this form of deference, an agency is not legally entitled to deference, but can earn it. If the agency regularly interprets the statute or regulation in question and its interpretation appears to exhibit expertise, the court will recognize that expertise and confer deference on the agency's interpretation.[61]

Skidmore deference is based on an epistemic argument. The idea is that an agency that exhibits expertise should be given deference. In that way, the legal system can make use of the agency's expertise. This justification for deference might seem to be stronger than *Chevron's*, because *Skidmore* is based on exhibited expertise rather than *Chevron's* unsupported inference of congressional intent. But upon closer inspection, this *Skidmore* deference does not withstand scrutiny and turns out to resemble a government privilege.

If *Skidmore* deference is justified based on expertise, then why is such deference applied only to government agencies? After all, private parties can also be quite expert about particular areas. While the Federal Communications Commission may have significant expertise about telecommunications, so will established companies,

---

[60] Deena Shanker, *The US Supreme Court Decides Less than Half as Many Cases as It Did 40 Years Ago – And that's Just Fine*, QUARTZ (July 5, 2015), https://qz.com/443100/supreme-court-decisions/ (Last visited July 21, 2017).

[61] Kristin E. Hickman & Matthew D. Krueger, *In Search of the Modern Skidmore Standard*, 107 COLUMBIA LAW REVIEW 1235, 1258–259 (2007).

such as Verizon or ATT, who regularly must comply with telecommunications statutes and regulations and have access to accomplished lawyers. The failure to accord private parties deference suggests that *Skidmore* confers a privilege on the government.

Moreover, it is not necessary to have *Skidmore* deference to incorporate expertise. If an agency exhibits expertise, then its actions will be more persuasive to the court than if the agency does not do so. The best way to incorporate the agency's expertise into the legal system is simply for courts to evaluate whether the arguments in agency opinions and briefs are convincing. No separate rule of deference is needed. Further, under this method for incorporating expertise, a private party's expertise can also be considered. If the private party's brief exhibits expertise, it will be more persuasive.

Some readers might believe that the courts are not equipped to judge the persuasiveness of the agency's argument. They might think that the courts would reach more accurate results by following a version of the *Skidmore* approach.[62] Under that approach, the court would determine whether the agency exhibits traits often associated with expertise, such as thoroughness, formality, and consistency, and then would confer deference if those traits are present. It is by no means clear that the courts would reach more accurate results by considering these factors. But if one did believe such considerations were relevant, the court could also for look for those in the private party's briefs.

In the end, *Skidmore* deference purports to be about recognizing expertise, but it operates to confer an advantage on agencies. It is not needed to incorporate agency expertise. It should be ended, with courts simply following the more persuasive argument made by the parties.

2 Factfinding

The second type of deference that agencies receive for legislative regulations is for their factual findings. In administrative law, one can distinguish three types of facts: adjudicative facts, legislative facts, and judgmental facts.

Adjudicative facts are the facts that concern the particular parties to a dispute, such as what actions the defendant took. Legislative facts are the facts that are relevant to passing a legislative regulation, such as how often people taking certain types of actions cause damage, which will be relevant to deciding whether to enact a rule prohibiting the action. These legislative facts typically involve the actions of groups of people.[63]

---

[62] *Id.*
[63] 2 Kenneth Culp Davis & Richard Pierce, Administrative Law Treatise 140–49 (3d ed. 1994).

Finally, judgmental facts involve claims that are technically factual, but cannot be established on the current record, either because they are at the frontiers of science or the evidence is not available.[64] For example, evidence of the effects of low dose exposures of a substance may neither exist nor be obtainable. In this situation, the question, which is technically a factual one, will nonetheless be addressed largely as a matter of policy, with the answer turning on considerations such as the agency's policy toward such matters. Since adjudicative facts are not typically implicated by rulemaking, here I discuss only legislative facts and judgmental facts, returning to adjudicative facts when I cover agency adjudication.[65]

At present, legislative facts are reviewed under an arbitrary and capricious standard for informal rulemaking and often a substantial evidence standard for hybrid rulemaking. While the exact relationship between these two standards is a matter of some dispute,[66] one can generally characterize both standards as conferring significant deference on the agency.

The degree of deference that should be conferred on agencies for legislative facts depends on whether or not one adopts the proposal to have independent appellate administrative courts that I discuss later. If one does not adopt that proposal, then the ordinary federal circuit courts reviewing the agency will have considerably less expertise about the matter. By contrast, if one adopts the proposal, then the courts initially reviewing the legislative facts will be expert, although presumably they will know less than the agency that has studied the matter for a long period.

If one does not adopt the proposal and the legislative facts are reviewed by ordinary circuit courts, then the greater expertise of the agency is a strong reason for conferring deference on the agency. But there is a countervailing consideration: the courts are likely to be less biased than the agency in reviewing the facts.

One might respond to this situation in one of two ways. One possibility is simply to retain the existing standard of review that confers substantial deference on the agency. But another possibility is to modestly reduce the degree of deference

---

[64] A GUIDE TO JUDICIAL AND POLITICAL REVIEW OF FEDERAL AGENCIES (John F. Duffy & Michael Herz eds., 2005), at 174 (discussing judgmental facts).

[65] Because usage differs, it should be emphasized that my discussion of legislative facts does not involve any facts that are judgmental. Thus, the legislative facts I am discussing are those which can be established using accepted scientific theories. For example, if science has established that a substance causes harm, then that is a legislative fact that is not a judgmental fact. By contrast, if it is not clear whether a substance causes harm at a particular exposure level, that will be a judgmental fact.

[66] The two standards are often thought to require the same degree of support, but sometimes courts require additional support under the substantial evidence standard. *Compare* ADAPSO v. Federal Reserve, 745 F.2d 677 (1984) (stating that the two standards require the same degree of support under the APA) *with* Corrosion Proof Fittings v. EPA, 947 F.2d 1201, 1213–214 (5th Cir. 1991) (stating that the substantial-evidence standard requires more support than arbitrary and capricious review under the hybrid rulemaking scheme of the TSCA).

to the agency. One might accomplish this by instructing courts to change their attitude about review so as to be a bit less deferential than they are now in reviewing findings of legislative facts.[67]

If one does adopt the proposal and legislative facts are initially reviewed by a court with expertise, then there will be a much smaller difference in expertise between the agency and the reviewing court. Combining this smaller difference in expertise with the reduced bias of the court argues for much less deference. How much deference one ought to confer is unclear, but I tentatively favor something like a midpoint between the existing substantial evidence standard and no deference. I will call this level of deference the modest deference standard.

Finally, under existing law, judgmental facts tend to be reviewed largely as policy statements, with the court inquiring whether the agency asked the basic questions about the issue and whether it gave plausible answers. There is probably no better way of addressing such matters, which are after all essentially policy questions. And thus it makes sense to continue the existing policy review process discussed in the next section.

3 Policymaking

Although some policymaking may be an intrinsic part of executive power, it is difficult to see the extremely broad agency policymaking authority under existing law as anything other than legislative power. Under the extremely lenient nondelegation doctrine, agencies can receive significant authority to adopt the policies that they prefer, without significant legal constraint.

While the congressional approval procedure appears to address the transference of legislative power in the case of major rules, the transference would continue in the case of non-major rules. Thus, it would make sense, especially for nonmajor rules, to reduce the level of policymaking discretion exercised by the agency.

The problem is that it is not clear a feasible way exists to reduce policymaking discretion under existing law. One possibility would be to eliminate all policymaking discretion by having judges review these decisions without deference. But such a transference would be problematic, since it would give the judiciary policymaking discretion that appears inconsistent with judicial power.

---

[67] This would hardly be unprecedented, as it would echo the change in the substantial evidence standard that Justice Frankfurter announced in Universal Camera Corp. v. Labor Board, 340 U.S. 474 (1951). In *Universal Camera*, Justice Frankfurter wrote of the difference between traditional substantial evidence (applicable to reviewing a jury verdict) and the substantial evidence standard he believed the Administrative Procedure Act adopted. He argued that under the latter judges "must be influenced by a feeling that they are not to abdicate the conventional judicial function." Id. at 490. Thus, the court was to be a bit less deferential under the new standard.

Another possibility would be to strengthen the Constitution's nondelegation doctrine. Forbidding Congress from delegating policymaking discretion to the executive would address the problem. But unfortunately establishing a workable nondelegation doctrine has proved to be difficult. It is hard to draw a clear or even reasonably determinate line distinguishing a permissible from an impermissible amount of policymaking discretion.

Under existing law, the principal check on policymaking discretion is the application of reasoning process or hard look review. This type of judicial review attempts to check policymaking discretion by asking whether the agency addressed the most important issues in an acceptable way, while still allowing the agency significant deference about these matters.[68] There is some question as to how strict such hard look review is, with there allegedly being a strong and a version of weak hard look review.[69] If such strong hard look review is now actually employed at least sometimes, then it should be adopted as the governing standard since it reduces agency policymaking discretion and presumably is feasible.

Although there is no feasible way to dramatically reduce the policymaking discretion of agencies in a progressive world of big government agencies, one reform might weakly reduce policymaking discretion. One could place a stronger limitation on congressional delegation of legislative power than the existing law does, while at the same time using a workable standard. One method would be to identify a degree of delegation that is unacceptable. Then delegations of that or a greater extent would be unconstitutional. By contrast, delegations that confer less discretion than this standard (by more than a de minimis amount) would be constitutional.

Under this reform, the standard for an excessive delegation should be defined as the public interest standard. Many delegations are limited by a public interest or public welfare standard – one that requires the action of the agency to be in accord with the public interest. This standard is generally thought to allow an agency broad discretion to pursue its own conception of what is a good policy. It is only extreme actions, such as actions taken for nepotistic reasons, that might be held to violate the standard.

One should declare through constitutional doctrine or a cross cutting statute that delegations to agencies to pursue the public interest standard are impermissible. It is much less difficult to apply this test than most others proposed for the nondelegation doctrine. One merely needs to identify the amount of policymaking discretion that a delegation to pursue the public interest provides and then to prohibit delegations that confer that amount of discretion. For example, a delegation to protect the

---

[68] A Guide to Judicial and Political Review of Federal Agencies (John F. Duffy & Michael Herz eds., 2005), at 177–96.

[69] Adrian Vermeule, Law's Abnegation: From Law's Empire to the Administrative State 159–67 (2016).

public health clearly involves less policymaking discretion than one for the public good, since the public health excludes various considerations, such as costs, that the public good standard would allow.[70]

While this test would have the significant benefit of feasibly limiting delegations, it would nonetheless leave agencies with substantial policymaking discretion. Still, it is better than nothing.

* * *

Overall, then, the changes proposed here would operate as a very significant return of legislative and judicial power from agencies to Congress and the courts. The most significant legislative regulations would be subject to congressional approval. These major rules, as well as the nonmajor rules, would be subject to a much more significant judicial review. Deference for legal questions would be eliminated. There would also be a reduction, although a limited one, in deference for factfinding and policymaking. Together, these changes would move our progressive legal regime as to rulemaking toward a more traditional separation of powers.

C Appellate Administrative Courts

While I have been largely discussing judicial review of agency rulemaking by ordinary Article III courts, one might argue that judicial review would be improved by employing appellate administrative courts that possess more expertise but are independent. Whether such courts would be desirable on balance is unclear, but their virtues justify discussing them here and including them as an option for reform.

At present, rulemakings tend to be challenged in federal circuit courts, which review the rulemaking record. Instead of having the rulemaking directly appealed to federal circuit courts, one might introduce independent appellate administrative courts. These courts would be similar to the independent administrative courts that I advocate in Part III for handling agency adjudication, except that these courts would be appellate. These courts should preferably be Article III courts, but they could be Article I courts so long as they were separate from the agency and the agency did not review their decisions. As with the other independent administrative courts, these courts should have expertise in health, science and economics, should hear cases from multiple agencies, and should employ procedures similar to current agency adjudication to keep costs low.

---

[70] One challenge for this standard is that it would apply irrespective of the scope of the delegation. For example, a regulation that applied across the economy would be subject to the same standard that a much narrower regulation that applied only to a small sector would. But this is the price for adopting a workable standard, since taking into account both the breadth of the regulation and the degree of policymaking discretion conferred is much less clear. Because the public interest standard is so lenient, it should not cause much mischief.

These administrative courts would have significant benefits. The judges would possess expertise about the areas subject to agency regulation, but would be independent. Thus, the administrative courts would have knowledge of the area and fewer of the bad incentives that plague administrative agencies. This combination might be thought to result in uniquely valuable information for the judicial system.

Under this system of appellate courts, judicial review of legislative facts – and possibly of legal interpretation if one believes legal interpreters benefit from expertise about nonlegal subjects – might be much improved. How would such judicial review work? One possibility is to have the administrative courts use the specific standard of review I mentioned earlier – modest deference for agency findings of legislative facts. Then, circuit courts could review the agency's findings under the same standard. This is essentially the way that the Supreme Court reviews circuit court findings. The Supreme Court gives no deference to the circuit court either for fact or law.

But this model is inappropriate. The reason that the Supreme Court gives no deference to the circuit court is that both are thought to have the same degree of expertise and reliability as to the decisions that they review. But the appellate administrative courts have additional expertise and therefore the federal circuit courts should grant them a certain level of deference.

A system with such judicial expertise would represent something of an innovation within American administrative law. But a sense of how it would work could be briefly sketched here. Imagine that an agency found a legislative fact and the administrative court, reviewing it under the modest deference standard, affirmed the agency's decision. If the administrative court's decision were appealed, then what standard of review should the circuit court use? The circuit court should review the appellate administrative court's decision with deference. For example, even if the circuit court disagreed with the appellate administrative court and believed that the agency's decision failed the modest deference test, that should not be sufficient. The circuit court should have to conclude that the agency's decision failed a more deferential test – perhaps the substantial evidence test. In this way, the administrative court would give the agency limited deference and the circuit court would give the administrative court deference. A similar situation could apply when the circuit court seeks to reverse the administrative court's disapproval of the agency.[71]

While these appellate administrative courts would produce a significant benefit, they would also have a significant disadvantage: they would introduce another

---

[71] Suppose that the administrative court concluded the agency's finding of a legislative fact was erroneous and should be reversed under the modest deference standard. The circuit court should not be able to reverse the administrative court simply by concluding that agency passed the modest deference standard. Instead, the circuit court should have to conclude with greater confidence that the agency got the matter correct, thereby allowing the administrative court deference as to its finding.

level of appellate review. Rulemaking would be reviewed first by the appellate administrative courts and then by the circuit court. This would introduce both cost and delay.

Whether the benefits of these courts are worth the additional cost and delay is debatable. In part, it depends on how large the cost and delay are. One might argue that these disadvantages would be limited, because parties would submit similar briefs to each level of the courts. And one might attempt to reduce these costs even further by adopting streamlined procedures, such as discouraging oral arguments at both court levels.

Ultimately, whether it makes sense to employ appellate administrative courts is unclear. But if one did use them, it would move the system one step further in the direction of a separation of powers.

III DELEGATION OF ADJUDICATIVE AUTHORITY

The other major way that modern administrative institutions depart from the separation of powers involves the delegation of judicial power to the agencies. Agencies adjudicate a very large number of federal cases. As with the delegation of legislative power, the delegation of judicial power is justified by the alleged lack of time and expertise of federal courts as compared to agencies. But these arguments, even if they apply to the existing federal courts, are not persuasive against a reformed system of independent administrative courts.

At present, formal adjudications generally occur in an agency with an administrative law judge as the presiding officer and initial decisionmaker. ALJs have limited independence in that they cannot be supervised by anyone involved in the prosecution or investigation of a case and cannot be removed except for good cause as found by the independent Merit Systems Protection Board.[72] This independence, however, is of limited value, because the ALJ's decision does not bind the agency. If the ALJ decides against the agency, the agency can generally appeal the decision to the head of the agency, which can then of course decide the case for the agency.[73] It is true that the agency's decision can be reviewed by a court and the court will take into account the fact that the ALJ decided the case against the agency. But the ALJ's decision will normally not be given significant weight, except as to demeanor evidence.[74]

The limited independence of ALJs is also undermined by several other significant features. First, ALJs hear cases only from a single agency. As a result, ALJs are likely to adopt the perspective (or tunnel vision) of the agency. Second, and relatedly, ALJs

---

[72] Kent Barnett, *Resolving the ALJ Quandary*, 66 VANDERBILT LAW REVIEW 797, 806–07 (2013).

[73] *See* 5 U.S.C. § 557(b) (2006) ("On appeal from or review of the [ALJ's] initial decision, the agency has all the powers which it would have in making the initial decision except as it may limit the issues on notice or by rule.").

[74] Barnett, *supra* note 72 at 807.

are subject to reversal only by that single agency. If ALJs exhibit the normal human reaction of seeking not to be reversed, then they will regularly attempt to predict the agency's decision rather than taking an independent perspective. Third, ALJs are selected by an appointment process that allows the agency a limited, but important opportunity to choose personnel disposed to their agenda. Under the ordinary process, potential ALJs are subject to qualification requirements and a test that results in three top candidates. Because the agency is permitted to choose from these three candidates, it can select the candidate who it predicts is most likely to support its objectives.[75]

A more rigorous separation of powers would replace ALJs with independent administrative judges, who would, under my preferred version of this scheme, be Article III judges. An agency could not then reverse the administrative judge's decision, because the Constitution prohibits an Article III judge's decision from being reviewed by the executive branch.[76] As a result, adjudications would take place before the Article III judge, who would have the final decision. Alternatively, these administrative judges could be made Article I judges, who would be entirely separate from the agency. The statute would then provide that the decisions of the Article I judges are final and cannot be reversed by the agency (even though the Constitution might allow such agency review).

The appointment of these judges would also be taken away from the agencies. It would be best if the Article III or Article I judges were considered superior officers, who would then need to be appointed by the President with the advice and consent of the Senate.[77] This appointment procedure, however, need not significantly depart from the existing method of selecting judges who have scored well on a merit-based test. Congress might instruct the President to nominate from the top three candidates on these tests.[78] While requiring such nominations might be unconstitutional, the President might still comply, especially if the Senate refuses to confirm people not selected by that procedure.

Even though these administrative courts might be filled with Article III judges, the judges who fill these positions should differ from ordinary Article III judges. The administrative courts should be staffed with individuals who have expertise in one of three separate areas: health, science, and economics. These judges could be

---

[75] *Id.* at 804–05.

[76] Hayburn's Case, 2 Dall. 409 (1792),

[77] If these judges were deemed to be inferior officers, then Congress could vest their appointment in either the President alone, the head of the department, or a court of law. U.S. CONST. art. 2, § 2, cl. 2. If Congress did choose to depart from the appointment process for superior officers, then it should vest the appointment in the President alone, thereby taking the decision away from the agencies. For a proposal to appoint ALJs by courts of law, see Barnett, *supra* note 72.

[78] These tests would need to be adjusted to take into account the need for expertise in nonlegal subjects, such as health, science or economics.

selected from people who had developed the expertise either through education, their careers, or both. The judges could then bring this expertise to deciding cases.

The judges would also not decide cases from a single agency. Instead, they would be assigned cases involving their particular areas of expertise. For example, some cases from the EPA might be assigned to health judges, others to economics judges, and yet others to science judges. In exceptional cases, disputes might be assigned to a three judge panel with experts from all three areas.

The system of administrative judges would provide for a more genuine independence. It would avoid the various features of the existing system that undermine the independence of ALJs, because it does not allow agencies to reverse the decisions of the administrative judges, does not limit administrative judges to hearing cases from a single agency, and takes away the agency's power to appoint administrative judges.

After the administrative court heard a formal adjudication, it would reach a final decision on the matter. That decision would bind both the agency and the private party. If either party sought to appeal the decision, the appeal would be heard, much as it is now, by a circuit court. The circuit court would have the advantage of reviewing a decision by an independent entity, but one with some expertise. Thus, the circuit court might be a better position to get an accurate result than at present.

While the administrative courts would possess genuine independence, it would still make sense to employ many of the institutional features that make ALJs an efficient method for resolving large numbers of cases. In particular, many of the informal procedures employed before ALJs should continue to be used in the administrative courts. Many agencies do not use hearsay rules, and cross examination and other procedures are often limited. There would be little reason to change these procedures for the independent courts. Thus, the speed and low cost of formal adjudication could be continued under the administrative courts reform.

In the remainder of this section, I discuss the standards of review and other limitations that would govern agencies under the system with independent adjudicative courts. Some, but by no means all, of the analysis is similar to that in the prior section on judicial review of agency rulemaking.

A *Interpretive Authority*

The same considerations that indicate that agency legal interpretations during rule making should not be given deference also apply to agency legal interpretations reviewed by administrative judges in the adjudicative context. The skill of independent judges in interpreting federal statutes plus the need to constrain agencies strongly supports granting no deference to agency legal interpretations in the adjudicatory context. Moreover, that the administrative judges have non-legal expertise also argues against deference for those who believe such expertise is helpful to statutory interpretation. Thus, there is a strong argument for not conferring either *Chevron* or *Skidmore* deference to statutory interpretations in a formal adjudication.

This argument against *Chevron* and *Skidmore* deference is especially strong in the context of formal adjudications. When an agency adopts an interpretation in a legislative regulation, the public will know the agency's interpretation prior to enforcement. By contrast, when the agency interprets the statute in a formal adjudication, it imposes an interpretation that the public may not know ahead of time. Moreover, the agency can often apply a new legal interpretation retroactively so long as the effect is not deemed too burdensome or unfair.[79]

In addition to *Chevron* and *Skidmore* deference, agencies also enjoy *Auer* deference. *Auer* deference, which applies to an agency's interpretation of its own legislative regulations, is even more of an affront to the separation of powers than *Chevron* deference.[80] *Chevron* deference affords the agency deference as to the interpretation of a statute enacted by Congress. *Auer* deference affords the agency deference as to the interpretation of a regulation enacted by the agency employing legislative power.

The same arguments against *Chevron* deference apply argue against *Auer* deference. The interpretation of both statutes and legislative regulations involves legal issues that should be answered by the courts rather than the agencies.[81] While the agency does adopt the regulations, that does not render them nonlegal. In fact, these legislative regulations are binding not only on the public but also on the agency.[82] For those regulations to function as a limit on the agency, it is important that they be subject to independent review.[83]

---

[79] *See, for example,* Verizon Telephone Companies v. FCC, 269 F.3d 1098, 1109–110 (D.C. Cir. 2001).

[80] Auer v. Robbins, 519 U.S. 452 (1997).

[81] *Auer* deference is also more problematic than *Chevron* in that it applies not merely to agency interpretations in informal rulemaking and formal adjudication, but to interpretations of agency regulations in a wide range of circumstances. *See, for example,* Stinson v. United States, 508 U.S. 36 (1993) (holding that Sentencing Commission "commentary be treated as an agency's interpretation of its own legislative rule" and receive *Auer* deference). While I believe *Auer* should be abandoned in those situations as well, I do not develop the point here since my focus involves informal rulemaking and formal adjudication.

[82] United States *ex rel.* Accardi v. Shaughnessy, 347 U.S. 260 (1954).

[83] *Auer* deference is also thought to give the agency an additional incentive to pass problematic regulations. The passage of legislative regulations requires the agency to go through the rigorous notice and comment process. Without *Auer* deference, the agency would have to enact a regulation that was clear enough to secure the results it desires. That regulation might be subject to serious criticisms during that process, which might lead to it being struck down. By contrast, with *Auer* deference, the agency can enact a vague regulation that will not be subject to such strict scrutiny. Then, the agency can interpret the vague regulations to secure the provision that it desires, receiving deference as to its interpretation. *See* John F. Manning, *Constitutional Structure and Judicial Deference to Agency Interpretations of Agency Rules,* 96 COLUMBIA LAW REVIEW 612 (1996).

B *Policymaking*

The area of policymaking raises serious challenges for an attempt to employ the separation of powers as to formal adjudication. Like legislative rulemaking, policymaking is difficult to eliminate or constrain through judicial review, since drawing a distinction between permissible and excessive delegations of policymaking is difficult and de novo review of policymaking by a court would be inconsistent with the judicial role.

Under legislative rulemaking, the agency's policymaking authority was significantly limited by the congressional approval procedure. One might imagine that agency adjudicatory decisions based on policy could be subjected to a similar procedure that would involve congressional review. But that procedure would not work well for formal adjudication. First, there are likely to be many more agency adjudications than rulemakings. Agencies that set policy by rulemaking often do so through a large comprehensive regulation whereas adjudications tend to cover narrower ground. Thus, a comparable amount of policy change will involve a larger number of adjudicatory decisions than rules. This larger number of adjudications will place a significant burden on OMB and the courts to determine whether they represent the equivalent of major rules. It will also place a burden on Congress to review these adjudicative decisions.

Second, the scope of decisions reached in adjudications is harder to determine than that of those in rulemakings. People very commonly disagree about the scope of a holding. Consequently, it will be more difficult for OMB and the courts to determine whether the holding meets the definition for a major rule. Third, applying the congressional review procedure to an ongoing adjudication would be cumbersome. Once the agency has decided to impose a new adjudicative policy, the decision would be delayed during OMB review for whether it represented a new decision and whether it, along with earlier decisions, met the definition of a major rule. If it did, then the decision would be further delayed to await congressional approval.

Finally, in addition to these practical concerns, congressional review of agency adjudications raises concerns of principle. When Congress reviews a rulemaking, the rule has not yet been applied to the public. Moreover, Congress is reviewing a rule which closely resembles legislation. By contrast, if Congress reviews an adjudicative decision, this review occurs during the agency process applying the decision in a specific case. And Congress will be reviewing quasi-adjudicative behavior, which seems to raise due process concerns. Whether or not such review violates the Constitution, it might conflict with widely held norms about adjudicative behavior.

The difficulty of applying the congressional approval procedure to formal adjudications raises the question of how to police policymaking in those adjudications. One attractive proposal that I support is simply to prohibit agencies from making policy determinations in these adjudications. Agencies arguably do not need to make policy at this stage. Instead, they can enact policy through legislative regulations and then adjudicate in accordance with those regulations.

While I support this proposal, some people might argue that it would hamstring some or all of the agencies that use adjudication to make policy. If one held that view, one could pursue alternative reforms that would allow agencies to make policy during adjudications but would place additional restrictions on the agency to compensate for the lack of a congressional approval procedure. For multi-member commissions, such as most of the independent agencies, the agency might be allowed to make policy, but only with supermajority support. For example, a five-member commission might be permitted to establish policy only if four members of the commission approve it.

Restricting policymaking by single headed executive agencies would be more challenging. But there are various methods that might be employed. One possibility is to require that the policy decision be made in a written opinion issued by the head of the agency, which might then also require formal approval by OMB or even the president. Another possibility is to require that an adjudicative policy finding be followed by a rulemaking adopting the policy. The rulemaking should cover the subject of the adjudication as well as closely related areas. If the agency does not propose a rule that covers a closely related area, then the agency might be precluded from making an adjudicative finding in the future in that area.[84]

C Factfinding

As was the case with delegation of rulemaking authority, factfinding in an adjudication can be divided into three types of facts: adjudicative, legislative, and judgmental.

1 Adjudicative Facts

As noted earlier, adjudicative facts are those that concern the actions of the individuals that are subject of the adjudication, whereas legislative facts are those that are relevant to establishing a regulation that should govern a situation. Since adjudicative facts do not typically arise in rulemakings, I did not discuss the standard of review for such facts in the rulemaking section.

In an adjudication, a strong argument exists that the administrative court should not confer deference on the agency's view of the adjudicative facts. In other words, the administrative court should find the facts on its own as would an ordinary trial court.

---

[84] Another possibility is to enact a default rule that applies to delegations of policymaking in formal adjudications. The most likely possibility is a cost-benefit standard. While this default rule might be desirable for some statutes, it might not work for other statutes where the statute pursues values that seem inconsistent with cost-benefit analysis, such as a statute that protects the public health.

Various reasons support this no deference approach for adjudicative facts even though I recommend some deference for legislative facts later. First, there is generally less expertise required to find adjudicative facts than legislative facts. While finding adjudicative facts can require expertise, the simple determination of what actions were taken by the parties generally requires less expertise than determining how large groups of people have behaved in the past or are likely to behave in the future. Second, administrative courts have expertise whereas ordinary circuit courts do not. Thus, even if some expertise is required to find adjudicative facts, the administrative court will possess it. Third, adjudicative facts are often based on testimony given before the judge. By contrast, legislative facts generally rely upon studies and other documentary materials that will require the expertise and extended study that the agency can better provide.

2 Legislative and Judgmental Facts

The analysis of agency deference for these two types of facts is largely determined by my previous analysis and therefore can be addressed quickly.

In the section on the delegation of rulemaking, I discussed the situation where an agency's legislative facts would be reviewed by an independent administrative court that had expertise. I argued that such legislative factfinding should be reviewed by the administrative court under a modest deference standard. While the expertise of the agency helps with legislative fact finding, the additional expertise of administrative courts as compared to ordinary courts, combined with there being less biased than agencies, argues for reducing the degree of deference that agencies enjoy as to legislative facts. This same modest deference standard ought to apply to agency legislative factfinding reviewed by an independent administrative court in an adjudication.

The approach to judgmental facts can also be resolved by previous arguments. In the section on the delegation of rulemaking authority, I argued that courts should follow the existing law which reviews judgmental facts much as policy findings are reviewed. Here, I would again treat judgmental facts in the same way that policy findings are. If one forbids policy findings from being made in adjudications, then one should also forbid findings of judgmental facts. If one merely restricts policy findings, then findings of judgmental facts should be subject to the same restrictions.

D *Judicial Review of the Administrative Courts*

The final issue to be considered is the standard of review the ordinary circuit courts should use to review the findings of the administrative courts. This issue was touched upon briefly in discussing the appellate administrative courts. Here I further develop that approach.

In the prior section, I noted that higher appellate courts ordinarily use the same standard of review to review an agency decision as the lower appellate courts. For example, the Supreme Court will generally review an agency decision using the same standard of review as the circuit court. By contrast, I noted there is a strong argument for the ordinary circuit courts to grant deference to the administrative courts in areas where the latter have superior expertise.

The standard of review that circuit courts should employ when reviewing administrative courts will depend on the particular issues and the relative expertise of the courts. In the case of legal interpretation, I do not believe that the administrative courts will have more expertise than the circuit courts. To be sure, the administrative courts will have more expertise as to science, health and economics, but the interpretation of statutes should turn not on such policy, but instead on legal matters. Consequently, the circuit courts should review legal issues based on a de novo standard of review. But if one did believe that nonlegal expertise enhanced the ability of administrative judges to make legal findings, then one might provide deference to the administrative courts.

In the case of policy findings, the answer will turn on the regime being employed. If the agency is not allowed to make policy, there will be no opportunity to review such determinations. If the agency is making policy subject to the special restrictions I discuss, then the administrative judge will review the agency findings through an approach of hard look review. Since the circuit court has less expertise as to policy, the circuit court should provide some deference to the administrative court.

For adjudicative facts, the administrative court makes findings without conferring deference on the agency. In this situation, it probably makes sense for the circuit court to review the administrative court's factual findings with some degree of deference – either the degree of deference that the courts give to agency findings (substantial evidence) or that appellate courts give to trial courts (clearly erroneous), depending on how much additional expertise the administrative judges are thought to possess over circuit court judges.

Finally, for legislative facts, the administrative court should apply the same modest deference standard to the agency's findings as I discussed concerning judicial review of appellate administrative courts. That standard is desirable because it would provide some deference to the administrative agency, which has greater expertise than the administrative court. Since the circuit court has less expertise as to legislative facts than the administrative court, the circuit court should also provide some deference to the administrative court.

IV OTHER TYPES OF DELEGATION

While agency authority to enact legislative regulations and to formally adjudicate are the principal type of delegations, there are other important types of administrative decisions. Although there is no space to address these matters in detail, I can briefly discuss two types of decisions: the use of guidances to avoid the requirements of legislative regulations and the use of informal adjudication.

A *Guidance Documents*

One important issue is the failure of administrative agencies to use legislative regulations. Instead, agencies use guidance documents – typically policy statements or interpretive rules. These guidances, which are conceptualized as not having binding effect, provide various advantages to the agency. They avoid the agency's having to comply with the notice and comment procedures of the APA. The guidances also are much less subject to judicial review because they are often not treated as final agency action.

But while guidances are viewed as not having binding effect, they still can have an enormous impact by operating as a threat against those who would violate their prescriptions. If the sanctions for violating the statute or regulation are large, then the regulated party may simply choose to comply with the agency's interpretation and policy to avoid agency prosecution or action. And if the regulated party complies, no judicial review of the agency's guidance will occur. Consequently, guidances often allow agencies to impose their interpretations and policies on regulated parties, without permitting such parties an effective means to seek judicial review.[85] For example, the Office for Civil Rights of the Department of Education has issued various guidances that govern universities. But these guidances have generally avoided judicial review, because universities have been

---

[85] The separation of powers reforms that I have been discussing will have conflicting effects on the use of these guidances – both decreasing and increasing the advantages to agencies of using them. The reforms decrease the advantages to agencies by denying them *Chevron, Auer,* and *Skidmore* deference and thereby make it less likely that the agencies will prevail against regulated parties. For example, if an agency issues a guidance and a person takes action inconsistent with the agency's position in the guidance, the agency can now bring an enforcement action in a formal adjudication within the agency. Because under existing law the agency would receive *Chevron* deference during the formal adjudication, a significant risk exists that the private party will lose in court. Under the separation of powers reforms, however, the agency would not receive deference and thus would decrease its ability to effectively coerce private parties to follow its actions.

But even if these reforms decrease the benefits to agencies of using guidances, they are unlikely to stop agencies from continuing to use such guidances. First, even without deference, a private party might choose to follow the agency's guidance if the party would suffer a large loss if a reviewing court were to agree with the agency's views. Moreover, the reforms will not eliminate all deference. Even under the reforms, the agency would continue to receive deference for legislative facts and policy findings (to the extent such policy findings are allowed). Consequently, the reforms will not prevent agencies from using guidances to induce compliance with their polices. Finally, the separation of powers reforms will also increase the advantages to agencies of using guidances. In particular, if agencies are required to secure congressional approval for legislative regulations, but not for guidances, then this will significantly increase the incentives for agencies to employ guidances.

unwilling to defy them and risk the possibility that the Department will find they violated Title IX or the accompanying regulations, causing them to lose access to federal money.[86]

The use of guidances instead of legislative regulations should be constrained for two important reasons. First, guidances exacerbate the violation of the separation of powers that delegations of legislative power commit. The ordinary processes for enacting and reviewing legislative regulations – notice and comment followed by a significant chance of judicial review of the regulations as a final order – checks this delegated legislative power. The reforms that I propose – in particular, congressional review – impose additional checks. If guidances allow agencies to exercise delegated power without these checks, then they represent more of a departure from the separation of powers and should be limited to the extent feasible.

Second, the use of guidances creates an additional departure from the separation of powers. Guidances create a serious risk that government action, that can severely penalize private parties, will not be subject to judicial review. A strong argument exists that judicial review is required before the government can impose such penalties on the public. Of course, judicial review is not needed to review every government action. But as I argue later, the final decisions of a government agency concerning important matters, such as significant government benefits that a person is entitled to under existing law, should be subject to judicial review.[87] Thus, guidances do not merely allow for the easier transference of legislative power to the agencies. They also eliminate or curtail an essential judicial role.

There is, however, a readily available reform that would limit the ability of agencies to use guidances to regulate private parties. The reform would treat guidances that could impose a significant loss on a regulated party as a binding legislative regulation requiring notice and comment.[88] In this way, the agency could not use the guidances as a way of exercising delegated legislative power without complying with the checks normally imposed on such delegated power. If the guidance would not involve a large loss – for example, if the penalty for violating the guidance were merely an order that the person follow the rule in the future – then the guidance would not require notice and comment and would not be treated

---

[86] Jacob Gersen & Jeannie Suk, *The Sex Bureaucracy*, 104 CALIFORNIA LAW REVIEW 881, 908–10 (2016).

[87] The fact that the regulated party can challenge the action, if he violates it and is prosecuted, does not strongly argue against concluding that judicial power is required. The regulated party should have an effective opportunity to challenge the action in court. He should not have to risk large losses simply to question the action before a judge.

[88] A similar rule was once employed in the D.C. Circuit in the 1970s, called the substantial-impact test. *See* Cabais v. Egger, 690 F.2d 234, 237 (D.C. Cir. 1982). While that rule was reversed as inconsistent with *Vermont Yankee's* rule that courts do not have the power to establish extra-statutory checks on agencies, Vermont Yankee Nuclear Power Corp. v. NRDC, 435 U.S. 519. 524 (1978), the rule I propose would avoid that objection since Congress would enact it.

as binding. In this way, the agency could use guidances to inform the public of the agency's legal and policy positions without coercing the public to conform to those positions.[89]

B *Informal Adjudication*

While there are many types of informal adjudications, one can still make some general statements about reforming this type of agency action. Various agency actions that the APA treats as informal adjudications, such as the decision to start an investigation or to bring a lawsuit, are executive decisions that Congress should not make and that courts should not review under the separation of powers.

But other informal adjudications should be subject to judicial adjudication or judicial review if they purport to be final agency decisions and involve important rights or benefits. Regulatory actions that limit a person's ability to exercise his liberty or use his property should certainly be subject to such judicial review. Similarly, decisions concerning significant amounts of money, to which an individual is entitled under existing law, should also be subject to judicial review.[90] By contrast, agency decisions to deny non-entitlement spending ordinarily should not to be subject to judicial review.

Some commentators argue that providing for less deferential judicial review by Article III courts would pose a problem for programs with a large number of cases. One common example is the Social Security Disability Program, which decides hundreds of thousands of cases every year and has more than 1300 ALJs administering it.[91] It is thought that employing Article III judges to adjudicate these cases would require more elaborate procedures which would overload the courts.

Under my reform proposal, however, the Social Security disability cases could feasibly be heard by independent Article III administrative judges. It is true that

---

[89] A second, narrower reform, would also apply when the agency's action would impose a significant penalty on a private party for violating a guidance. Under this reform, the private party would only be entitled to seek judicial review of the guidance: the guidance would not be invalidated for failure to follow notice and comment. Since this reform would not address the problematic incentive of agencies to employ guidances instead of legislative regulations as well as the broader reform does, I propose only the latter reform.

[90] In mentioning entitlements, I intend to draw upon something like the entitlement standard employed by the Supreme Court in the due process area where property is defined as a legitimate claim of entitlement rooted in a source of law independent from the Constitution. *See* Board of Regents v. Roth, 408 U.S. 564 (1972). For a strong criticism of this approach, *see* Caleb Nelson, *Adjudication in the Political Branches*, 107 COLUMBIA LAW REVIEW 559, 621–25 (2007).

[91] See Paul R. Verkuil, *Reflections upon the Federal Administrative Judiciary*, 39 UCLA LAW REVIEW 1341, 1346 n.18 (1992) (stating that ALJs decided more than 250,000 Social Security cases in 1990); Kent Barnett, *Against Administrative Judges*, 49 U.C. DAVIS LAW REVIEW 1643 (2016).

in such cases the government and the social security applicant are often not represented by attorneys.[92] Instead, the ALJ takes a more active role in resolving the matter.

But there is no constitutional or separation of powers requirement that prevents Article III judges from engaging in this role. First, it is not uncommon for individuals to represent themselves in federal court. Moreover, the federal courts have heard claims for government benefits, that are not contested by the government, since the early days of the Constitution.[93] But if one believes it is a problem that the administrative court is an Article III court, one can make the administrative court an Article I court, and lose little as a practical matter.

CONCLUSION

At present, big government programs operate under a progressive administrative law that employs a very limited separation of powers. This regime is supported in part by the belief that big government is here to stay and can only function with this limited separation of powers. This chapter challenges this belief. Even in a big government world, one could feasibly adopt a much stricter separation of powers that would significantly promote the underlying values of classical liberalism. While this reform may not now be politically feasible, classical liberal ideas have often been promoted as ideals that can only be implemented in the future. Demonstrating that an expanded separation of powers would be feasible in our progressive world is a first step toward a more classical liberal government.

---

[92] FRANK S. BLOCH, BLOCH ON SOCIAL SECURITY § 5:5 (2016) (the government is not represented in Social Security disability hearings); *id.* § 5:6 (many claimants are not represented in Social Security disability hearings).

[93] *See* James Pfander, *Standing, Litigable Interests, and Article III's Case-or-Controversy Requirement*, 65 UCLA L. REVIEW 170 (2018).

9

Political Libertarianism

Jacob T. Levy

PART 1

Benjamin Constant, the great classical liberal theorist and constitutionalist, under-stood the problem. In "The Liberty of the Ancients Compared With That of the Moderns,"[1] his defense and celebration of the modern liberty of pluralism and the private sphere, he warned that the very richness of our modern private lives would lead moderns to neglect what was vital in the liberty of the ancients. Wrapped up in our private lives, we would find democratic politics too burdensome and time-consuming; anxious to protect what is ours, we would find elections too unpredict-able. And so we – by which he meant, especially, the commercial and propertied middle classes – will easily be tempted by the Bonapartist offer: I will take the trouble of governing off your hands and protect you from unpredictable political give and take. Constant was sure that such offers are made in bad faith, and that they would represent a bad exchange even if they were not; they end with even our private modern liberty being at the mercy of strongmen and dictators. But this wouldn't make us immune to the temptation. He worried, in short, that liberals would not be committed enough democrats to make good constitutionalists.

And this would ultimately mean that we are not good enough liberals. For all the transformations of modernity, the regime of religious liberty and free speech, commercial liberty and free trade, and the rule of general law with protection against arbitrary punishment could never be taken for granted. It could always be politically undone. While at first glance Constant's essay seems to turn on progress driven by grand historical change – the rise of commerce, the Reformation, the abolition of slavery – in an important way it's an argument about the fundamental status of politics. All our modern goods are vulnerable to bad politics, and they are

---

[1] Benjamin Constant, "The Liberty of the Ancients Compared with That of the Moderns," *in* BIANCAMARIA FONTANA, ED. AND TRANS., POLITICAL WRITINGS (1989) [1819].

only secure if we secure them with better politics. And it is of course to this task that he devoted the final decades of his life, both as a key liberal parliamentarian and as a public theorist publishing his *Cours de politique constitutionnelle*[2] – a course on constitutional *politics*, aimed at teaching the French citizenry how to practice it. (That the phrase "constitutional politics" sounds as surprising to us today as it does is a good synecdoche for the problems this paper will examine.) While Constant was sometimes (and not very happily) involved in constitution-writing, his constitutional-ism was not ultimately about getting a founding text just right. It was about something more public and more ongoing than that.

A classical liberal constitutionalism that is capable of withstanding the populist, authoritarian, and nationalist threats of our day must find a way to overcome Constant's challenge. It must be able to come to terms with democracy, and must offer a constitutional politics. It must resist the temptation he described: to so prioritize our modern liberty, our freedom of religion and freedom of commerce, that we disdain the time-consuming business of political democracy and try to find shortcuts. I think that the modern classical liberal renaissance that began in the mid-twentieth century has often neglected politics, and that it can no longer afford to do so. The lack of a properly political libertarianism has in some respects left advocates of the liberal order poorly equipped to defend it in light of rising threats, and in other respects has entangled them directly with those threats themselves.

In calling for a political libertarianism I mean a few different, though overlapping, things. The most familiar one to many readers is also probably the least important: an analogy to the political liberalism advocated by John Rawls.[3] Rawls' liberalism is, in his terms, political not metaphysical; it is not grounded in a particular compre-hensive theory of the human good, like Millian or Kantian autonomy, and it is supposed to be compatible with a wide range of such theories, including religious ones. I certainly think the turn to political liberalism was right, and is applicable to classical liberalism as well. But, notwithstanding some occasional arguments about culturally "thick" libertarianism that would exceed the bounds of the Rawlsian "political," I think "political not metaphysical" is not especially controversial in classical liberal thought, and I take it for granted rather than examining it further.[4]

---

[2] Posthumously collected as BENJAMIN CONSTANT, COURS DE POLITIQUE CONSTITUTIONNELLE (1861),

[3] JOHN RAWLS, POLITICAL LIBERALISM (1993).

[4] For more on the relationship between Rawlsian political liberalism and classical liberalism, see GAUS, THE ORDER OF PUBLIC REASON and THE TYRANNY OF THE IDEAL. While he does not put it quite this way, Gaus reconstructs political liberalism to show the importance of liberal *institutions* that can be endorsed by those who espouse a wide range of ultimate visions of justice – a range of visions of the political ideal. In so doing he pushes Rawlsian political liberalism toward the kind of politicalness associated with Waldron and political realism, which will be discussed subsequently.

But the deflationary ambition of Rawlsian political liberalism only goes so far. Rawls insists on the importance of widespread endorsement of liberalism as a "freestanding political doctrine," and maintains that the stability of a constitutional order is not secure if it rests on merely strategic action that generates a *modus vivendi*. Religious liberty might begin in the standoff among religious groups none of which are powerful enough to stamp out the others, but it must eventually be endorsed as a political value in its own right. Without meaning to import the whole Rawlsian apparatus, I do think that this much must be true of a political libertarianism. It should be a thin doctrine about political and legal institutions, not a comprehensive account of the good life; but it should still be a *doctrine* and it cannot do without affirmation by adherents. Although I am much more sympathetic to *modus vivendi* theorizing (and political practice) than Rawls or Rawlsians,[5] I ultimately agree that we cannot simply back into a liberal order through clever balancing of interests or institutional standoffs. There is no constitutional design so clever, no multiplication of veto points so elaborate, that the liberal order can be formally guaranteed. There need to be some actual liberals involved.

A second sense of "political" is the ordinary, everyday sense of the word. Liberalism is a set of ideas and principles, but they are ideas and principles about what is to be done in politics. I have elsewhere referred to liberalism, conservatism, and socialism as "party ideas."[6] In the era of modern politics anticipated by British parliamentarism in the eighteenth century and fully inaugurated by the American founding and the French Revolution, what David Hume characterized as "parties of principle"[7] have been crucial institutional participants, making representative democracy in large states possible and coherent, allowing some measure of political accountability, and extending governmental time horizons beyond the career of one or another ambitious person. I will discuss below the centrality of both parties and representative democracy to a revitalized liberal constitutionalism in Section 3 of this chapter. But for now, I will offer a slogan to parallel "political not metaphysical." This second sense is "political not contractarian." As against the recurring fantasy of being done with political work, of a great supermajoritarian once-and-for-all victory or a hypothetical and imputed unanimity, I suggest that we need a firm liberal embrace of electoral democracy that includes the willingness to work for temporary plurality victories and that understands the legitimacy of temporary plurality losses.

This leads directly to the most important sense of "political" for current purposes: that used by Jeremy Waldron in his call for "*political* political theory," and by Bernard Williams in his recommendation of "realism in political theory" that treats

---

[5] See discussion in Jacob T. Levy, "Contextualism, Constitutionalism, and *Modus Vivendi* approaches," *in* CULTURAL PLURALISM AND POLITICAL THEORY, ANTHONY LADEN AND DAVID OWEN, EDS. (2007)

[6] JACOB T. LEVY, RATIONALISM, PLURALISM, AND FREEDOM 10 (2015).

[7] David Hume, "Of Parties in General," *in* EUGENE F. MILLER, ED., ESSAYS MORAL, POLITICAL, LITERARY (1987).

political conditions and norms as irreducible to *moral* conditions and norms: political not juridical, political not moral-philosophical. Waldron argues that a political political theory must rest on the sense of understanding that we exist amidst people who disagree with us, and we must share institutional space with them, not wish them away. Theories of justice and rights derived philosophically, especially when they are theorized in a way that demands they be constitutionalized and imposed judicially, fail to be properly political.[8] Waldron's recent work in this direction aligns him closely with an important development in political theory in the past decade or so: the turn to, in a specialized sense, "realism" associated especially with Williams and William Galston.[9] I will discuss realism immediately below in Section 2 of this chapter.

Throughout this chapter I will be importing critiques and arguments that have been developed in political theory against nonlibertarian political philosophies, especially Rawlsian ideal theory but also, for example, the kinds of deliberative democratic theory that prioritize consensus.[10] I think that familiar philosophies and habits of thought among libertarians are also vulnerable to these critiques, sometimes even more vulnerable than Rawlsian and other more mainstream theories. Classical liberalism is perhaps especially vulnerable to treating a theory of better political outcomes as a theory of political legitimacy, of trying to dodge the need for politics, of failing to understand the foundational role of political rules and institutions.[11] And because the contemporary crisis is one at the level of foundational political ideas, coming to terms with these critiques offers liberalism valuable intellectual resources for the problems of populism, nationalism, and authoritarianism today.

PART 2

The usual description of realist political theory is that it insists on the irreducibility of politics to morality. Many and varied arguments and theorists have been brought together under that broad idea, as different authors map the realist turn for different purposes. What follows isn't meant as a general survey; I want to emphasize just a few core ideas that I'll develop with reference to two of the realist turn's intellectual precursors and two of the leading current theorists broadly associated with it.

---

[8] JEREMY WALDRON, POLITICAL POLITICAL THEORY (2016); Bernard Williams, "Realism and Moralism in Political Theory," *in* IN THE BEGINNING WAS THE DEED: REALISM AND MORALISM IN POLITICAL ARGUMENT 13 (2005).

[9] William Galston, "Realism in Political Theory," 9(4) EUROPEAN JOURNAL OF POLITICAL THEORY 385–411 (2010).

[10] I give a general criticism of these approaches to political philosophy in "There Is No Such Thing as Ideal Theory," 33(1–2) SOCIAL PHILOSOPHY AND POLICY 312–333 (2016).

[11] I develop this argument more fully in "Toward a Non-Lockean Libertarianism," *in* THE ROUTLEDGE HANDBOOK OF LIBERTARIANISM, JASON BRENNAN, BAS VAN DER VOSSEN AND DAVID SCHMIDTZ, EDS. (2017) and will return to it later.

None of these are classical liberal theorists, though three are liberals broadly understood. While their normative ideas about better political outcomes are more economically egalitarian than mine, that does not matter for our current purposes. The ideas I want to draw out may be summarized as follows, though maybe none of the theorists I discuss would have endorsed all these formulations.

A) Political organizations in general, and the modern state in particular, are social facts, not moral decisions. They *arise* rather than being brought into being by general agreement or by each person's consent. There is no functionalist connection between political organization and moral principles like justice or rights-protection; those might be standards we should use to critically evaluate systems of rule, but those systems don't have any particular tendency toward those norms.

B) In light of (A), and given the fact that political institutions rely on coercive force and the capacity for violence, states have a capacity for organized violence that does not reduce to anything like morally justified coercion and defense.

C) Political life is in part the dispute over how to manage and use these institutions and systems of rule that arise for basically amoral reasons. We share the social and political world with others who disagree with us about such questions; and none of us can win the argument by asserting the truth of our own views, or the tight relationship between our views and the purpose or meaning of the system of rule.

One generally acknowledged precursor of the realist turn is Judith Shklar. In her influential essay "The Liberalism of Fear,"[12] she argued for a liberal political theory whose central commitment was negative: the avoidance of the public violence and cruelty that characterize the modern state. Shklar recognized that, under our current circumstances, we are stuck with the modern state. She does not treat it as a central problem of liberalism to legitimate this political institution; consent theory is irrelevant to the project. But neither is her liberalism one that aims at the abolition or the radical transformation of the state. (This is one of the primary ways in which her thought is a precursor to the realist turn, as we shall see.) Rather, liberalism is an account of how to *manage* the state, how to live with it and under it in a decent and tolerable way. It is a matter of prioritizing: put cruelty first,[13] and aim to limit, monitor, and mitigate the violence and cruelty of agents of the state. A few passages:

"While the sources of social oppression are indeed numerous, none has the deadly effect of those who, as the agents of the modern state, have unique resources of

[12] Judith Shklar, "The Liberalism of Fear," in POLITICAL THOUGHT AND POLITICAL THINKERS, STANLEY HOFFMAN ED., 3–20 (1998).
[13] Shklar further examined this idea in "Putting Cruelty First," 111(3) DAEDALUS 17–27 (Summer, 1982), pp. 17–27; and SHKLAR, ORDINARY VICES (1984).

physical might and persuasion at their disposal." "Given the inevitability of that inequality of military, police, and persuasive power which is called government, there is evidently always much to be afraid of. And one may, thus, be less inclined to celebrate the blessings of liberty than to consider the dangers of tyranny and war that threaten it ... [The liberalism of fear] worries about the excesses of official agents at every level of government, and it assumes that these are apt to burden the poor and weak most heavily ... The fear it does want to prevent is that which is created by arbitrary, unexpected, unnecessary, and unlicensed acts of force and by habitual and pervasive acts of cruelty and torture performed by military, paramilitary, and police agents in any regime."[14]

The liberalism of fear is "entirely nonutopian," unlike Rawls' supposedly "realistic utopianism," and stands apart from both "the liberalism of natural rights" (for example Locke, Paine) or that of "personal development" (Humboldt, Mill).

I should note here that Shklar's liberalism of fear – negative in orientation, concerned to restrain the state, and especially concerned with the arbitrary use of discretionary power – is not entirely unlike F. A. Hayek's insistence on the rule of law in works including *The Constitution of Liberty*, a similarity she acknowledged in one of her (numerous) critiques of him[15]. She thought that he was inheritor to the more attractive, Montesquieuian, tradition of understanding the rule of law, as distinct from the Aristotelian tradition she rejected and identified with Ronald Dworkin. Hayek was rightly concerned with "arbitrariness and ultimately oppression."[16] But she thought that he vastly overstated the connections among the rule of law, his distinctive theory of knowledge, and the spontaneous order of the market. Situating the rule of law in a theory of constitutional democracy rather than a theory of "free-market liberalism," she maintained, could help diminish its abuse as a political football. The protections of due process, immunity from extrajudicial imprisonment and execution, the prohibition against torture, and restraints on police power were too crucial to be allowed to rise and fall with one's theory of economic regulation.

And indeed Hayek's own theory never prioritized the problems of police, military, and paramilitary power. He sometimes emphasized the importance of limiting *the example* of the armed forces – they are necessarily a purposive institution governed by commands, not an abstract order governed by the rule of law, and that distinction had to be protected. But precisely in putting the rule of law on the other side of a bright-line distinction from the state's most violent agents, he arguably deflected attention away from constraining those agents by the rule of law. I think it is fair to say that his *corpus* is marked by more attention to subjecting regulatory and

---

[14] Shklar, "The Liberalism of Fear," pp. 3, 9–10, 11.
[15] Judith Shklar, "Political Theory and the Rule of Law" *in* POLITICAL THOUGHT AND POLITICAL THINKERS, Stanley Hoffman ed., 21–7 (1998); F. A. HAYEK, THE CONSTITUTION OF LIBERTY 196.
[16] "Political Theory and the Rule of Law," p. 28.

administrative agencies to the rule of law than to doing so with the police, even though he certainly acknowledged the roots of English rule-of-law thinking in constraints on extrajudicial punishment. And this, from Shklar's perspective, was backward.

One of the most famous lines from Shklar's "Liberalism of Fear," and one that may make her argument appealing to classical liberals, says that "liberalism is monogamously, faithfully, and permanently married to democracy – but it is a marriage of convenience."[17] She was committed to democracy as a means of holding accountable those with power; but she forcefully denied that liberal liberty *consisted of* democratic participation. Her thought frequently tracks Constant's, but not here. She was so concerned about both majoritarian tyranny and about the claim of the democratic people to speak for each of us as persons that she could not quite embrace democracy as demanded by principle. Constant shared the concerns, but did ultimately see the right to be consulted on how we are to be governed as a mark of the same kind of respect for individual persons as allowing them their private modern liberty.

The second theorist I want to treat as a forerunner of the realist turn (and someone of whom Shklar was sometimes dismissive) is Hannah Arendt.[18] That she has not been received as a contributor to realism seems to me a matter of unfortunate sociology rather than a sensible reading of ideas. Bernard Williams is the key figure in the realist turn, and was a protégé of Isaiah Berlin's; Berlin warmly disliked Arendt and her thought, very plausibly for reasons having more to do with her complicated relationship to Judaism and Israel than with intellectual substance. Probably thanks to Berlin's considerable influence, Arendt has never been taken as seriously in the United Kingdom as she is in the United States, and I suspect Williams' own British students and followers are largely unfamiliar with her.

That as may be, Arendt was firmly committed to the distinction between philosophy and politics that characterizes realism. Her political theory was firmly *worldly*: politics finds its values not in deduction from metaphysical principles but from what the persons engaged in political action bring into the public sphere. And it was foundationally pluralistic and anti-holist: the world is filled with "men, not Man." She distrusted theories that collapsed pluralistic men into a homogenous whole, whether a Marxist species-being or a utilitarian-economistic aggregation of welfare. And she distrusted just as firmly the philosophers' attempt, dating to the Greek critics of democracy, to replace open-ended democratic disagreement and discussion with unity, certainty, and closure.[19]

---

[17] Judith Shklar, "The Liberalism of Fear," *in* POLITICAL THOUGHT AND POLITICAL THINKERS, STANLEY HOFFMAN ED., 3–20 (1998).

[18] See especially HANNAH ARENDT, THE HUMAN CONDITION (1958) and HANNAH ARENDT, ON REVOLUTION (1963), though the broad ideas I describe here recur throughout her work in political theory.

[19] ARENDT, THE HUMAN CONDITION.

Arendt had a clear skepticism about the modern, bureaucratic, administrative state, and about its attempt to reduce all of large-scale political life to a manageable and calculable social economy. But this derived not at all from any particular appreciation of the self-organizing spontaneous order of economic life. Rather, she was concerned with the way that the machine-like modern state quashed the possibility of agency, spontaneity, and free action *in politics itself*. She perceived an affinity between the machine-like character of the modern bureaucratic state and that of advanced capitalism; she took Weber's "iron cage of modernity" very seriously and, like him, was concerned to find space for free action within it.

Arendt was the most interesting and important twentieth-century advocate of what Constant described as "ancient liberty." And she was so without giving an inch to the Rousseauian absorption of the individual into the whole that so concerned both Constant and the twentieth-century antitotalitarian liberals like Popper, Berlin, and Shklar. Her theory of political foundings was not one of a whole, unified people giving itself a constitution once and for all, nor of a people passively receiving its law from a Rousseauian Legislator. Rather, she emphasized that institutions take shape interpersonally, filling the social world precisely because men – different, pluralistic men – create them to give them common rules, structures, and points of reference.

These are among the features of Arendt's thought picked up and celebrated by one of the contemporary realists, Jeremy Waldron. In *Political Political Theory* he offers an explicitly Arendtian account of political constitutionalism meant to rival the moralistic and juridical consitutionalism of Dworkin, and the negative constitutionalism of classical liberal rights theory. With more institutional detail than Arendt, Waldron emphasizes the institutions that make up constitutional representative democracy, and the roles they serve beyond mere naysaying. He recasts bicameralism, the separation of powers, the existence of a loyal opposition party, and the contestatory face of the rule of law, not as a series of blocks or checks on state action, but as the way that we structure and organize the fact of our coexistence with people with whom we have disagreements and yet we face the necessity of joint action, or at least joint decision about whether and when to engage in joint action.[20]

This is an important point, and goes to one of the reasons why classical liberal thought has sometimes been slow to take democracy as seriously as it should. The standard liberal institutional moves in response to disagreement are exchange and property, association and disassociation. In the face of disagreements about how to use resources, liberals ask: to whom does the initial right to decide belong? And: Are the channels of exchange clear to make it possible for disagreements to turn into trades? If I disagree with you about the best use of my house – I want to live in it, you want to knock it down to build condos – we have a peaceful dispute resolution mechanism: I decide, until and unless you persuade me, primarily by paying me

[20] JEREMY WALDRON, POLITICAL POLITICAL THEORY (2016)

enough, to let you decide instead. We never have to agree about the right answer; we just rely on property and exchange to peacefully allocate authority to choose. Many other kinds of disagreements are managed with the combination of free association and free disassociation: if your group and my group disagree about the nature of salvation, we schism and each create our own new church.

Waldron doesn't deny the importance of such mechanisms. But he maintains that they do not allow for the management of all disagreements, and that we disagree *about when those mechanisms hold.* Even in those examples, we disagree about who holds the initial allocation of property rights, and about which of the two new churches gets to act as the successor to the old unified church and keep its stuff. More generally, we disagree about what to do with the apparatus of the state, including how to conceptualize and operationalize our liberal rights. So, he says, inhabiting "circumstances of politics" analogous to the Humean/Rawlsian "circumstances of justice," we face the ongoing need to decide things together in the face of disagreement, even if only deciding which things to forego deciding together. And in the face of those disagreements, *just as with disagreements over the use of resources or the nature of religious truth,* neither side can just assert its own correctness as a way to win the argument. We are stuck here on earth with no direct, uncontroversial access to the truth about hard disputed questions. He argues that democratic procedures, like liberal rights, offer procedural solutions when substantive questions are under this kind of dispute. Waldron is a liberal, as Arendt was not; but his liberalism, like Constant's and unlike Shklar's, has room for a strong principled commitment to democracy. And, like Arendt, his commitment to democracy is not at all tied up with the rightness of the majority, still less with any claim that it makes to speak for the people as a whole.

Rather, he endorses something like the claim made by the final thinker I want to mention in this section, Bernard Williams, who insists that political realism:

> does not mean that we throw our political convictions away: we have no reason to end up with none, or with someone else's. Nor does it mean that we stare at our convictions with ironical amazement, as Rorty suggests. But we do treat them as political convictions which determine political positions, which means, for one thing, that we acknowledge that they have obscure causes and effects. It also means that we take certain kinds of view of our allies and opponents. Even if we were utopian monarchs, we would have to take into account others' disagreement as a mere fact. As democrats, we have to do more than that. But remembering the points about the historical conditions, we should not think that what we have to do is simply to argue with those who disagree: treating them as *opponents* can, oddly enough, show more respect for them as political actors than treating them simply as arguers – whether as arguers who are simply mistaken, or as fellow seekers after truth. A very important reason for thinking in terms of the political is that a political decision – the conclusion of a political deliberation which brings all sorts of considerations, considerations of principle along with others, to one focus of

decision – is that such a decision does not in itself announce that the other party was morally wrong or, indeed, wrong at all. What it immediately announces is that *they have lost.*[21]

This is one piece of Williams' general defense of "realism" against "moralism" in political theory. He maintains that normative political questions are not reducible to questions of moral philosophy, that they have a logic of their own that begins by taking the facts of political life for granted. He shares with Waldron a sense that these facts crucially include coexistence amidst disagreement. But he emphasizes as Waldron does not the amoral, factual character of our political condition. The provision of order and safety, the organization and channeling of violence and domination: these are politically fundamental. The attempt by Rawls – but also by consensus-oriented deliberative democrats and by utilitarians – to govern political life only in terms of values outside of it, such as "justice" or "welfare," is misguided.

Williams made these arguments in a brief and somewhat elliptical essay published posthumously;[22] political theory was not his main intellectual concern. The essay has sparked a tremendous outpouring of interest that has not yet converged on quite how to think about this distinction between political and moral normativity. My own gloss is, in part: political normativity does not rest on moral microfoundations. Political obligation is not built out of micro-level concepts like consent and contract; territorial sovereignty is not built out of the aggregation of individual property rights and holdings. Justice is the first virtue of a judicial decision about the rights of two parties; it is not, *pace* Rawls, the first virtue of "social institutions." Political phenomena, like other large-scale social phenomena, have to be recognized as facts that our normative ideas work with and around, not legitimated as creations from the moral ground up. The idea of moral microfoundations is mine, not Williams, and it rests in part on a characteristically classical liberal understanding of rights, justice, and private law categories like property and contract. But I think (and argue elsewhere) that it does a reasonably good job of letting us make sense of Williams' distinctions. If he's intuitively identified a genuine joint at which to carve the normative world (and I think he has), irreducibility to moral microfoundations does a pretty good job of letting us make sense of it.[23] And here we might recall Shklar's distinction between the liberalism of fear (which Williams elsewhere endorsed) and the liberalism of natural rights. The latter is a theory of justice, but one that has a hard time making sense of the existence of the state, or of any other large-scale political institution that governs people involuntarily. The former takes our political circumstances for granted: in modernity, we live under states, which have a tremendous capacity for organized violence. It then asks how we

---

[21] WILLIAMS, IN THE BEGINNING WAS THE DEED, p. 13.
[22] Ibid.
[23] Jacob T. Levy, "Political Realism and Moral Microfoundations," unpublished.

can manage it. Shklar does not ask how the existence of the military, paramilitary, and police might be justified. She asks how we should politically engage with the fact of their existence and power.

There's considerable overlap among these four thinkers (though perhaps the least between Shklar and Arendt, who derived very different lessons from their experiences as Jewish refugees from totalitarian Europe). But we might identify at least two key lessons, one primarily from Arendt and Waldron, one primarily from Shklar and Williams. First, disagreement is fundamental and ineradicable in politics, and we cannot escape it with recourse to claims of philosophical truth; we must live with it, as democracy can help us do. Second, the organized use of violence and domination is fundamental to political life, and even when it is channeled in ways that helpfully establish local zones of peace, it's not basically peaceful. Political normativity is a matter of responding to the fact of a social landscape that is thick with power, not a matter of legitimizing that power or wishing it away.

PART 3

Political realism so construed thus calls for attention to the facts of political life, including *both* disagreement that should be managed democratically, and organized violent power – under our current circumstances, state power. I now want to lay out a more elaborate set of claims, incorporating these basic facts but building on them with special reference to developments in modernity and to the relationship between politics and economics. I suggest that we treat all of the following as facts in political theorizing – fixed points in our social analysis to work with, not objects for decision, legitimation, or delegitimation.

A. The emergence of the modern state – domestically Weberian and internationally Westphalian, possessed of a corporate legal personality and juridical permanence, of a domestic (near-enough) monopoly on the legitimate use of force or the right to authorize it, and of external sovereignty vis-a-vis other similarly-situated states in a transjurisdictional order.

B. The tight connection between the development of the modern state and the development of modern markets, financial markets in particular. States were always centrally capital-accumulation and capital-borrowing organizational forms, dependent on their ability to tax and to issue debt. In turn, the large scale of states' capital needs seeded the emergence of large-scale trade in financial instruments, from the Amsterdam stock exchange and its trade in shares of the (parastatal) Dutch East India Company to the Bank of England and the development of a permanent national debt widely traded in the form of a bond market.

C. The *particularly* tight connection between liberal market capitalism and what North, Wallis, and Weingast[24] call the *open-access order* of broad-based access to legal institutional tools that had previously been elite privileges: the tools of contract and corporation as well as of political organization. The massive economic takeoff that began in the late eighteenth century in England and that spread to other regions of Europe and to the United States in the nineteenth century was growth in democratic contexts. I'm not committed to a tight causal relationship here, but there is *at the very least* an elective affinity between the development of liberal capitalism characterized by long-term ongoing growth and the emergence of modern representative constitutional democratic government. And I am persuaded by North, Wallis, and Weingast that it is more than an elective affinity. The transformation of, for example, the corporate form from an elite privilege that offered monopoly rents to a democratized organizational tool open to all was part of the same phenomenon as the transformation of the political party from a caucus of parliamentary elites to a democratized vehicle for mass political participation.

D. Separate from that connection between liberal capitalism and democracy, the universal pattern is that successful democratic politics in modern states is *party* politics. There are no modern democratic states larger than island microstates (and few even of those) without parties, indeed without parties as fundamental pillars of electoral politics. Parties are not sufficient for democracy, of course. The one-party state is a distinctive modern genus of autocracy, with the totalitarian state as its most extreme species. But they are necessary: non-party states are either military dictatorships, theocracies, or patrimonial monarchies.

If these claims are right, and political realism is broadly right, then a great deal follows for the shape of classical liberal or theories about politics. It means that we should understand liberalism as, at its core, a theory *within* the circumstances of political disagreement about what the state should and should not do. It is not a theory of political legitimacy. As such, it need not be a theory about the constitutionalization, entrenchment, or securing for all time of its policy prescriptions. It need only argue for the normative superiority of state action and inaction that favors, for example, a regime of free and open commerce, speech, and religious and cultural practices. An excessive concern with foundational questions of state legitimacy, guaranteed rights, and social contractarian foundations interferes with the development of a set of ideas suited for ongoing democratic contestation, ideas that don't on their own terms equate a temporary political loss with the end of legitimate government.

---

[24] NORTH, WALLIS, AND WEINGAST, VIOLENCE AND SOCIAL ORDERS (2009).

Now, I think this reunderstanding of liberalism in light of realism ought to be congenial to classical liberals for at least a number of reasons. One is that we have social-theoretical resources for understanding phenomena that are the result of human action but not human design, orders that arise emergently, social facts that are explained in nondecisionistic ways. It is anomalous to treat political social facts asymmetrically from all other social facts – economic, technological, cultural, linguistic. But this is what classical liberals do when they are (for a shorthand) Lockeans about politics but Hayekians about everything else.[25]

Or, to put it differently: libertarians rightly understand the idea that, as Nozick put it, resources come into the world already owned, not like manna from heaven.[26] We simply don't encounter new resources with a blank moral slate, able to decide "who should get this, on the basis of need, or desert, or utility?" And this is true even if the new resources are created in ways that draw on some existing resource the ownership of which is not morally untainted back to the beginning of time, even if they are created on land whose ownership began in violence and theft. Both prescription and the value of the new creation or innovation have their legitimate place; we are not doomed to *never* have legitimate ownership over new things because all the old things have illegitimacy somewhere in their title chain. What political realism offers is a similar way to think about politics: we come into the world *already governed*. We don't face the *tabula rasa* problem of legitimating political rule from scratch, nor the *tabula rasa* opportunity to organize our lives without it.

The second is that by eliminating the need for a theory of legitimacy that grounds all of political life in the wills and decisions of those who are ruled, realism opens critical space between the self and the state. Consent theory always concludes in imputing the acts of the state to the will, choice, or authentic self-individual persons. What Rousseau famously articulated as being "forced to be free" characterizes *every* consent and contract theory of legitimacy; after all, it *accurately* characterizes what happens when I am constrained to fulfill an actual contract to which I have actually agreed. The same is true for Hobbes' denial that the sovereign can act unjustly, since after all the subject is the true principal to the sovereign's agent, the true juridical author of the sovereign's actions. Treating contract and consent as the microfoundations for politics always deprive us of the ability to criticize political rule as alien to us, as something that happens to us rather than something we do to ourselves.

This means that political libertarianism based on realism offers us grounds for denying populism, nationalism, holism, and organicism, grounds that Lockean contractarian foundations does not offer. The "forced to be free" imputation of the will of the powerful to the will of everyone is especially characteristic of nationalism and populism: the assertion that those who agree with me make up

---

[25] On this, see my "Toward a Non-Lockean Libertarianism," *in* THE ROUTLEDGE HANDBOOK OF LIBERTARIANISM, JASON BRENNAN, BAS VAN DER VOSSEN AND DAVID SCHMIDTZ, EDS. (2017).

[26] ROBERT NOZICK, ANARCHY, STATE, AND UTOPIA, p. 219.

the true People, that minorities, dissenters, and rivals are alien invaders of the organic body politic. But if liberalism is a constitutional settlement that rests for its legitimacy on something like initial unanimous consent, then it *requires* such an image of a unified people, and so contributes to the ideational soil in which populist nationalism grows. (To strike a nonscholarly note: I think this has a great deal to do with the apparently strong connections between popular libertarianism and the racist alt-right in the United States, as well as with the frequent turn by *soi-disant* classical liberal political parties elsewhere toward xenophobia.)

All of this particularly means that this kind of realism undercuts what can be morally claimed on behalf of democratic political decisions. Recall Williams's comment that losing an election doesn't mean that one is morally wrong, or indeed wrong at all; it only means that one has lost. That intellectual space for acknowledging the vicissitudes of politics but still believing in the minority's (or the individual's) rightness on a question ought to make a great deal of sense to classical liberals.

So too does the understanding of the state as distinctively a locus of violent power, something that the exaggerated claims on behalf of democracy often obscures. Of the four theorists I surveyed, only Waldron at all seems to slip into treating state decision making as a realm of principle rather than a matter of the social organization of power – and this is true only because he often deliberately focuses on democratic *legislatures.* His fuller theory is deeply concerned with the use of coercive force by the executive, and with restraint on the armed agencies of the state by legislative and judicial authority alike.[27] In Shklar, Williams, and Arendt in their different ways it is even clearer that no state, including a democratic state, acts as the transparent agent of the moral principles of the governed. States *rule*, and one of the key normative tasks of politics is to manage and limit the mechanisms of that rule.

Finally, I think that this vision of politics ought to appeal to classical liberals because it abolishes the myth of sovereign state action. Populists of the left and right alike attack the market as being outside the sphere of deliberate control. Markets make us vulnerable to the decisions of outsiders, to forces beyond our ability to decide. They make us globally dependent rather than politically independent. Bond and currency markets come in for special abuse: they make our political decisions for us, taking away the authority of we the sovereign people to make our social world. This is all so much nonsense. The state, and later the representative democratic state, was a successful organizational form in part precisely because it was a better credit risk than other political organizations. The state was born interdependent with financial markets; it never was and could never be the site of sovereignty in the sense that these critics of markets mean. The social world as a whole is always beyond our ability to plan it and control it; indeed, even the *political* world is

---

[27] JEREMY WALDRON, TORTURE, TERROR, AND TRADE-OFFS: PHILOSOPHY FOR THE WHITE HOUSE, (2010).

beyond such control, as we understand once we stop thinking about it decisionistically and start thinking of it as something that happens to us. So, the untrammelled sovereignty, the control that the populist democrat is always complaining about the people having lost and needing to take back, is a phantasm. There is plenty of room to debate how such deliberate control as we *do* have should be exercised. But realism abolishes the argumentative high ground claimed by those who say that we face a choice between *having* control and not, where the former means something like the radical ability to make our world (including our economic world) as we see fit.

But of course that is not how things have worked out; classical liberal and libertarian understandings of politics have been highly resistant to thoughts like these, and remain firmly in the grip of a combination of Lockean decisionism about political legitimacy (only governments we choose, governing by our consent, which is simultaneously collective and individual), ideal theory moralism about the acceptable content of politics (only to protect and respect our rights), and legalism about constitutionalism.

Liberal theories of justice in general and libertarian rights theories in particular often make recourse to an idea of purpose that is genuinely quite strange: it is the *purpose* of the state to instantiate justice or to protect rights. "To secure these rights, governments are instituted among men," said Jefferson. This is faithful to Locke, but is quite absurd. It identifies one kind of thing we would morally like to see governments do as being central to the explanation, emergence, and ongoing functioning of them. It leads us to see rights-violations as not only wrong but anomalous – so anomalous that they cast the legitimacy of the entire legal and political system into doubt. "Governments are instituted to protect rights, but everywhere they violate them" is no more sensible than Rousseau's "man is born free but everywhere he is in chains."[28] It similarly invites Alexander Herzen's famous rejoinder by analogy: "Fish are born to fly – but everywhere they swim."[29]

This also means that when we are reluctant to call the legitimacy of legal and political systems into doubt – as most people are, most of the time, just as a matter of moral psychology – it becomes difficult for us to perceive and challenge rights-violations and other injustices. It is thus plausible that the end result of the idea that the purpose of governments is to protect rights and that their legitimacy depends on this is perverse: a reluctance to identify rights-violations where they exist. By distinguishing legitimacy from morality, realism opens the space to call systems of rule, violence, and abuse what they are rather than morally dressing them up as something nicer.

---

[28] Jean-Jacques Rousseau, The Social Contract and Other Later Political Writings, ed. Victor Gourevitch (1997).

[29] Alexander Herzen, From the Other Shore and the Russian People and Socialism, Moura Budberg and Richard Wollheim trans., 108 (1979).

The emphasis on contestatory partisan democracy offered by these realist approaches often seems particularly unattractive to classical liberals. Some would object that libertarian policies will tend to lose out in day to day contestation for predictable, for example public choice, reasons, and therefore if those policies are correct they must be constitutionalized. This, it seems to me, is more or less hopeless as a reply. It imagines that supermajorities are easier to come by than majorities, that what can't be won in elections could be won in constitution-writing. This is made to seem plausible in something like *The Calculus of Consent*[30] by imagining constitution-writing as a social contractarian moment entered into by people who *ex ante* don't have power relations among themselves. But there is no such moment, and constitutions aren't like that.

While libertarian theory has never been as anti-democratic as its reputation sometimes suggests, its embrace of democracy has often been half-hearted, even before the current vogue for books like Jason Brennan's *Against Democracy*.[31] Nozick famously and provocatively traced a step-by-step series of changes in a slave's condition through slavery to a many-person collective master to a many-person collective master that would allow the slave to cast tie-breaking votes about what would be commanded to having a full vote in deciding what would be commanded, and asked at which step on the way to democracy the slave ceased to be a slave.[32] The device does teach us something interesting and valuable about democracy; but it's not the only thing worth knowing.

If, as I suggested above, the regimes of modern liberty, the free societies of something like liberal commercial capitalism with freedom of religion and the rule of law developed in a tight relationship with partisan contestatory democracy, then that seems important to know, too. The desire to make an end-run around politics – by the perfect one-time constitutional design, by getting judges who will constitutionalize our best understanding of rights theory, by the enlightened liberal autocrat who will keep the forces of the mob at bay – has significantly impaired the theoretical appreciation for democratic politics. Shklar's liberalism has only a marriage of convenience with democracy; too often classical liberalism seems to be only casually dating it.

I also think classical liberal social and political theory has remained very committed to moral microfoundationalism in a way that impedes its reception of political realism. (Again, remembering that this is my own gloss on what political realism means.) This is true in arguments ranging from traditional Lockean consent theory to Nozick's attempt to ground political legitimacy in an invisible hand explanation arising out of bilaterally just commercial exchanges. We see it more recently in

[30] James M. Buchanan and Gordon Tullock, The Calculus of Consent: logical foundations of constitutional democracy (1965).
[31] Jason Brennan, Against Democracy (2016).
[32] Robert Nozick. Anarchy, State, and Utopia 276–94 (1974).

Michael Huemer's work disputing political authority and obligation on the grounds that they cannot be constructed out of common-sense morality at the micro level, and Jason Brennan's defense of "moral parity" between state agents and private users of violent force such that one may defend oneself against either with the same moral legitimacy.[33]

We might take two famously ungenerous readings of libertarian thought as asserting that libertarianism is *as such* committed to the reduction of the political to the moral, and is incompatible with recognizing the distinct normative status of the public sphere, though the authors were certainly not Williams-style realists. I refer to John Rawls' claim that libertarianism cannot make intellectual space for what he refers to as "the basic structure" of a social order,[34] and Samuel Freeman's account of it as intrinsically illiberal because it cannot accommodate the distinctiveness of public political power. ("Like feudalism, libertarianism conceives of justified political power as based in a network of private contracts. It rejects the idea, essential to liberalism, that political power is a public power, to be impartially exercised for the common good."[35]) That these were ungenerous and probably unfair even to the authors under discussion doesn't however, mean that there's not a reason why libertarianism struck them this way.

The possible reasons for this resistance are many – the continuing influence of Locke and consent theory, but also a misapplication of the idea of methodological individualism borrowed from economics, and the understanding of justice derived from common law and legal theory as essentially micro-scale and bilateral respect for rights. While the shift I'm urging requires rejecting Lockeanism about politics, it does *not* require rejecting methodological individualism about social explanation, once we firmly remember that emergent phenomena and "the products of human action but not human design" are *very complicated* from a methodologically individualistic standpoint. Neither does it require rejecting the juridical concept of justice (which indeed I endorse), so much as it requires overcoming the prejudice that states and politics are purposively centrally about justice at all.

PART 4

Constitutionalism is a balancing act. Madison understood that much: If men were angels, if governments were made up of angels. But the balance is more complicated

---

[33] Michael Huemer. The Problem of Political Authority: An Examination of the Right to Coerce and the Duty to Obey (2012); Jason Brennan, "When May We Kill Government Agents? In Defense of Moral Parity," 32 Social Philosophy and Policy 40 (2016); Jason Brennan, When All Else Fails: Resistance, Violence, and State Injustice (forthcoming 2018).

[34] John Rawls, Political Liberalism 262–65 (1993).

[35] Samuel Freeman, "Illiberal Libertarians: Why Libertarianism Is Not a Liberal View," 30 Philosophy and Public Affairs 105 (2001).

than the one he described, because the relationship between governments and those they govern runs both ways. A free society requires:

A. a government that is able to restrain private persons from aggression against others (including ordinary private crime but also organized private violence, power, and domination); this is Madison's "you must first enable the government to control the governed;"[36]
B. a government that will not tyrannize over private persons, individually or collectively; as Madison had it, we must "oblige [the government] to control itself;"[37] but also
C. a government that cannot be used as an instrument by some private parties to aggress against or dominate others.

For short, I will refer to these as the problems of (A) private power, (B) general public power, and (C) particular public power. The balance between private power and general public power was treated as fundamental by Madison, as it had been by Locke. But, inspired by North, Wallis, and Weingast, I want to suggest that it is the balance between general and particular public power that is both more crucial and far more difficult. The open-access order of liberal, democratic, constitutional, market society was not built out of individuals contracting to avoid the violence of the state of nature. It emerged out of what North, Wallis, and Weingast refer to as the "natural state": the general condition in which political power is reserved to a coalition of powerful elites who use it to organize their dominance over, and profits from, the society they rule.[38] In other words, *particular public power is the normal historical condition*, and constitutional politics must be at least as concerned with it as it is with private power.

I could discuss particular public power under the labels "rent-seeking" or the "capture" of the state by private interests. But I worry that these terms have become (among libertarian social theorists and social scientists) the kind of cliché that inhibits thought rather than helping it. "Rent-seeking" in particular calls to mind more banal kinds of private use of state power than I intend. And so, I will instead describe the balance of constitutional politics using the terms just given, and with stylized examples.

First consider religion. The American balance of free exercise and nonestablishment is a pretty successful balance of solving the problems of both general and particular public power, but its familiarity can mislead us about how rare and fragile it is. Free exercise, private religious liberty, has of course often been violated by state elites hostile to the religious beliefs of those they rule: in Communist states, in

---

[36] James Madison as Publius "No. 51" in THE FEDERALIST PAPERS 319 (2003) [1788].
[37] *Ibid.*
[38] NORTH, DOUGLASS C., JOHN J. WALLIS, AND BARRY R. WEINGAST, VIOLENCE AND SOCIAL ORDERS: A CONCEPTUAL FRAMEWORK FOR INTERPRETING RECORDED HUMAN HISTORY (2009).

secularizing republican France and Turkey, in dictatorships in Arab Muslim countries worried about religion as a source of political resistance. But by far the more common arrangement through history has been that the clergy of the dominant religion are members of the elite coalition that shares governing power, and they use that power to suppress religious dissent of all kinds: heresy, apostasy, the existence of religious outsiders, or even just challenges to status quo church governance. This is the stuff of religious establishment, dissected at length in Book V of *The Wealth of Nations*,[39] and it is not best understood as simply an imposition by an alien state on a passive society. What exists today in an extreme form in Saudi Arabia and Iran – state power as a tool of the dominant religious hierarchy – has been very common over history and around the world. And some of the cases in which free religious exercise has never taken full hold in constitutional democracies – such as France – arose out of particularly difficult struggles to pry political power out of the clergy's hands.

Now consider wealth. In the contractarian libertarian tradition, the Lockean thought behind Madison's dictum comes out as: we need a government that can (1) prevent private people from taking one another's property, but (2) not so powerful or unrestrained as to itself take private property. The property-owners are the potential victims of both private theft and public expropriation. The possibility that (3) the wealthy hold and use state power for their own benefit is shuffled out of sight. But it has been, by far, the most common case through history. Here is where I think it becomes especially important not to think first about the cases most easily called to mind by "rent-seeking": a subsidy for football stadium owners here, a mercantilist tariff against imports there, some eminent domain to take land and give it away to a private developer, occupational licensing or excessively strong intellectual property, all publicly approved through regular due process in a system still more or less governed by the rule of equal law. The normal sense in which the wealthy hold and use governing power is much more pervasive. It includes, for example, the direct enrichment of office-holders via what we would now identify as corruption, self-dealing, and conflicts of interest, none of which even make sense as complaints until modern ideas about the impartial responsibilities of public office take hold. We can think of such cases as the normal case of rent-seeking precisely insofar as we live in societies that have crossed what North, Wallis, and Weingast characterize as the "threshold" separating natural states from open-access orders.[40]

The illusion that we are faced only with Locke-Madison problems yields the temptation to think that we are faced only with problems of general public power, plus some relatively minor problems of particular public power (the problems of familiar kinds of rent-seeking within consolidated constitutional democracies).

[39] Adam Smith, An Inquiry into the Nature and Causes of the Wealth of Nations: Volume II (1979) [1776].
[40] North, Douglass C., John J. Wallis, and Barry R. Weingast, Violence and Social Orders: A Conceptual Framework for Interpreting Recorded Human History 23–5 (2009).

We think that the problem of private power is already solved, because we inhabit Weberian states and we take for granted the connection of that institution to the prevention of interpersonal crime and coercion. (I will return to this point.) And we ignore the genuinely deep problems of particular public power, because we treat the impartiality and stability of the state as reasonably fixed background conditions.

This results in a serious bias in the analysis of constitutional politics. It means that we treat the only serious problem to be solved as that of blocking the use of general public power. We imagine that it can be solved legalistically, with a sufficiently clear and specific constitution that emphasizes veto points and blocks on state action, especially legislative state action. This feeds the fantasy of solving politics once and for all at the moment of constitutional design, and it neglects the difficult ongoing task of constituting political power as public, accountable, and constrained. This has the only-apparently paradoxical effect of leaving classical liberal theory blind to the *unconstrained*, but not as a matter of principle socialistic, use of state power and especially executive power for private enrichment and violent domination – or, if not blind, too quick to think that the problem is solved by a *general* reduction of state power.

Realism counsels us against thinking that there's anything very much like such a reduction. Power is *potentia*; it exists in potential form even when not being exercised. This means that, say, a general tax and budget cut is not actually a *reduction* in the power, in a meaningful sense, of the modern state. I suggest that we think of the awesome scope of that power as something more like a fixed social fact at any moment in historical development; in the era of the Weberian modern state, the power is fixed at a very high level.[41] The Weberian modern state hasn't always existed and won't always exist, but a budget cut doesn't turn it into something else. It doesn't facilitate any newfound control over the police, paramilitary, and military, for example, and it may impede such control.

With Hayek, I think that there are deep features of our evolutionary moral psychology that will always sit uneasily with the demands of the extended liberal order or the open-access society. We are tribal animals living in a social world that can be destroyed by tribalism. I would characterize these problems somewhat differently from Hayek. We are, as he emphasized, drawn to communal sharing in small kinship groups; this extends to considerable favoritism for our extended kin. (Nepotism is as much an intrusion into modern institutions by a moral psychology alien to them as socialism is.) We are concomitantly drawn toward intense rivalry with outside groups, toward not only a zero-sum competition with them over resources but also negative-sum violent conflict with them over existence. These tendencies manifest, under modern conditions, as nationalism, mercantilism, xenophobia, and militarism. (I emphasize *under modern conditions*; nationalism is not

---

[41] See Jacob T. Levy, "*Contra* Politanism," European Journal of Political Theory, forthcoming.

just the same as extended-kin-group tribalism, but is a distinctively modern political appropriation and transformation of those sentiments.) And, finally we are status-seekers but also status-followers. That there should be a dominant figure leading and commanding our group of insiders, that there should be occasional challenges over who is dominant followed by a strong sense of identification with the winner, is as basic to us as the communal identifications. It is not in tension with them; when we cohere as a group under powerful leadership, we have the best chance of victory against outsiders and of increasing the spoils for us to communally (though not *equally* – the leader claims a larger portion) share. Strongman rule, demagoguery, cults of personality, the allure of the man on white horseback: these, too, are eruptions of old moral psychology into circumstances for which they are unsuited. This is of course all wildly speculative, as much as Hayek's reflections on the roots of socialism in *The Fatal Conceit*.[42] But I do not think it any *more* speculative.

What follows from this is that populism, nationalism, and the draw of the strongman who embodies the will of the whole society are just as constant threats to the abstract liberal order, to the open-access society, as the socialist excess of public power, the atavistic demand for too much communal sharing. In an era when the liberal order faces resurgent populist, nationalist, and authoritarian challenges, classical liberalism as an intellectual system cannot afford to remain tied up with the pre-political holism of social contract theory, or with the anti-political dream of victory through constitution-writing or judicial appointments. The liberal, extended, open-access order isn't a natural state of affairs that will simply happen when the state is hemmed in to its natural limits as an enforcer of justice and natural rights. It arises within, and requires defense by, pluralist, contestatory, democratic political action.

PART 5

I conclude with an example of the importantly different approach to contemporary questions that I think a political libertarianism makes possible. Consider the United States' paired problems of mass incarceration and police violence. Now, one of the proximate causes of these problems is the so-called war on drugs begun in the 1970s and accelerated in the 1980s. Libertarians have always been justifiably critical of drug prohibition, and have often been among the leading critics of it. But the drug war has not been the only contributing factor. A great deal of the tremendous surge in incarceration is directly attributable to changes in charging and sentencing practices for offenses that are not (or not only) victimless-crime drug offenses: prosecutors increasing the severity of the charges they bring and the sentences they seek, judges – sometimes constrained by sentencing guidelines or mandatory min-imum rules – increasing the sentences they hand down. Insofar as the underlying

---

[42] FRIEDRICH HAYEK, THE FATAL CONCEIT (1989).

crimes include some offenses against person or property, traditional libertarianism has little to say about these phenomena, and shows little willingness to prioritize them. Policing and imprisonment are among the few state functions that *don't* trouble libertarians at the level of principle: the purpose of the state (in that odd sense of "purpose" I discussed above) is to protect persons and their property against crime, and police and prisons are central to that.

But policing and incarceration, *even if in the service of the prevention and punishment of genuine crimes,* can be a real source of unfreedom. Shklar was right to distinguish her liberalism of fear from a liberalism of natural rights, partly for this reason. Her focus on the police, the military and paramilitary branches, and the intelligence services doesn't depend on an argument about what the content of the criminal law happens to be. When police brutality is a constant risk, when large fractions of a local population are on parole or probation or have prior convictions, or simply when there is a great deal of uncertainty about how many minor crimes are on the books, whole neighborhoods and communities live in fear of the arbitrary power of the police, and that fear further increases their power. Even those innocent of all crimes fear interactions with the police, and to that degree become unwilling to report even violent crimes. None of this depends on the offenses being nonviolent drug offenses, and none of it would disappear (even if it might diminish) in the wake of drug legalization.

Much the same is true for mass incarceration. The acceptance in principle of imprisonment as legitimate risks obscuring the large-scale change in the character of a society as incarceration rises. The United States imprisons at least four times as large a share of its population as other developed constitutional democracies; it imprisons more people than contemporary China does or than the Soviet Union did in the era of the gulags. I suggest that any reasonable understanding of an idea like "free society" should tell us that the United States *is a less free society, on this basis,* than other developed constitutional democracies. An American political program concerned with liberty ought to be centrally concerned with unwinding mass incarceration, even if it turns out that charging and sentencing practices with respect to non-victimless crimes are the primary drivers of it, even if prison is in principle legitimate. But this requires a willingness to think about social and political patterns without too much concern about either their microfoundations or their contractarian-constitutional legitimacy.

Finally, thinking in realist terms, giving up on the idea of the state as a justice machine and on the ideal-theory understanding of state purposes, allows us to pay attention to the social *sources* of overpolicing and overincarceration, rather than naturalizing policing and incarceration as unremarkable responses to the fact of violent crime. I cannot here do the work of *showing* that these social sources in the United States include structural racism, that the modern American carceral state is an effect of underlying racist power, though I think that is true. But it ought to be the kind of thing that those concerned with human liberty can at least ask about: is racism a cause of abusive and coercive state power in the United States? And asking about it requires thinking about state power as a phenomenon to be explained, understood, and mitigated – as *caused*, not *decided*.

I have emphasized the difference between libertarianism as a theory of political legitimacy and libertarianism as a theory of better and worse political outcomes, the former of which prioritizes questions that seem amenable to being solved as a matter of principle, outside political contestation. But overpolicing, overly violent policing, and overincarceration aren't like that. The courts enforcing general constitutional rights can certainly curb some of the worst and most arbitrary abuses, but they cannot eliminate the need to make decisions about how much, of what kind, in what spirit, policing and imprisonment will take place. If they pass the bar of legitimacy, they do not thereby become non-issues for classical liberalism. They demand a willingness to engage in ordinary political contestation about matters of judgment rather than formulaic principle, a constitutional politics about how free a society we wish to inhabit.

10

The Bourgeois Argument for Freer Immigration

Fernando R. Tesón

In this chapter, I offer a classical-liberal argument for freer immigration: the state should liberally admit immigrants because they are entitled to better themselves by trading their skills and entrepreneurship with willing trading partners across the border. I borrow the underlying principle, the ethics of trade-tested betterment, from Deirdre McCloskey, who developed it recently (albeit as a historical, not normative, thesis) in her massive volume *Bourgeois Equality*.[1] She calls it the bourgeois ethics, and for that reason I call my thesis here the Bourgeois Argument for immigration. The idea is that persons who seek to better themselves by offering their labor or entrepreneurship to willing buyers across borders should be accorded the same dignity and respect to do so that natives enjoy. The argument is consistent with, though not reducible to, two standard pro-immigration arguments: the recognition of migrants' moral right to free mobility, and the recognition of the immense economic benefits of immigration. In fact, if McCloskey is right, societal acceptance of the bourgeois ethics was the main cause of the societal enrichment in the last two hundred years or so.

On the other hand, the Bourgeois Argument is at odds with a specific pro-immigration argument found mostly in the popular press: that we must liberalize immigration because doing so improves the political demographics of society. In the United States, the idea is that because immigrants are likely to vote for the Democratic Party, and this party is thought to provide better governance, immigrants should be freely admitted so that eventually they can become voters. Call this the Demographic Argument for immigration. Interestingly, there is a symmetrical *anti*-immigration demographic argument: we should *not* allow immigrants *precisely*

---

[1] DEIRDRE McCLOSKEY, BOURGEOIS DIGNITY: HOW IDEAS, NOT CAPITAL OR INSTITUTIONS, ENRICHED THE WORLD (2016). This book is part of a trilogy. The other two volumes are BOURGEOIS DIGNITY: WHY ECONOMICS CAN'T EXPLAIN THE MODERN WORLD (2010); and THE BOURGEOIS VIRTUES: ETHICS FOR AN AGE OF COMMERCE (2006).

because they will vote for the wrong party.[2] I consider the Demographic Argument essentially flawed, *even* if it were true that immigrants would in fact vote for the better political party. This is because the Demographic Argument fails to treat immigrants with proper respect.

I proceed as follows. I start with a brief description of the domestic and international law of immigration. I will then discuss and reject three *nativist* arguments. I then address two central pro-immigration views and show that they converge in supporting liberal immigration policies. I reject the Demographic Argument for liberal immigration before defending the Bourgeois Argument. And finally, I address the national-security exception to liberal immigration laws.

IMMIGRATION IN NATIONAL AND INTERNATIONAL LAW

The immigration debate often proceeds in a vacuum, almost as if the issue would be how to design immigration laws starting afresh, from a clean slate. The truth is that institutions are already hostile to immigration. Every single national constitution grants the state the power to control borders and thus to exclude aliens for virtually any reason. In the United States, the Supreme Court has consistently held that the federal government has plenary power to exclude aliens.[3] In the words of the court:

> The power of the government to exclude foreigners from the country whenever in its judgment the public interests require such exclusion has been asserted in repeated instances, and never denied by the executive or legislative departments.[4]

In recent years, this doctrine has eroded a bit: although the matter is disputed, most scholars think the federal government may not implement immigration policies based on race or religion, and immigrants *in American soil* enjoy a wider due process than before.[5] What is important for my purposes is that the federal government can

---

[2] Brian Doherty discusses and rejects this reverse demographic argument in Brian Doherty, "Is Being for Immigration Inherently Unlibertarian?" REASON MAGAZINE, March 3, 2017, at http://reason.com/blog/2017/03/03/is-being-for-more-immigration-an-inheren.

[3] The doctrine has been strongly criticized by scholars, but has not been repealed by the Supreme Court. See, for example, Peter J. Spiro, "Explaining the End of Plenary Power" 16 16 GEORGETOWN IMMIGRATION LAW JOURNAL 339 (2001); and Ilya Somin, "Yes, Obama's Executive Action Deferring Deportation for Millions of Immigrants Is Constitutional," REASON *Magazine*, April 19, 2016, at http://reason.com/archives/2016/04/19/yes-obamas-executive-action-deferring-de.

[4] *Chinese Exclusion Case*, U.S. 581, 607 (1889). This case is rightly derided for validating overtly racist immigration legislation, but the principle behind the case remains largely untouched.

[5] SEE CURTIS BRADLEY AND JACK GOLDSMITH, FOREIGN RELATIONS LAW: CASES AND MATERIALS, 5TH ED. 155 (Aspen, 2017). The current debate over President Donald Trump's executive order turns on whether it is a pretext for religious discrimination, not on the validity of the general power of the government to exclude. See www.npr.org/sections/thetwo-way/2017/03/15/520171478/trump-travel-ban-faces-court-hearings-by-challengers-today.

exclude persons known as economic refugees, that is, those seeking opportunity in the United States for themselves and their families.

International law is equally restrictive. While international conventions place important limits on the right to exclude, otherwise international law grants broad discretion in the control of national borders. A state is legally free to close its borders altogether.[6] Even the relatively generous rules of the European Union start with the following statement: "As a general rule, states have a sovereign right to control the entry and continued presence of non-nationals in their territory."[7] Protocol 4 to the European Convention establishes freedom of movement for persons *lawfully* within the territory of a state *within* that territory.[8] True, international law has made great strides in protecting immigrants and facilitating greater movement of persons across borders. But the sovereign power to exclude foreigners recognized by international law remains virtually unchanged.

JUSTIFICATIONS FOR RESTRICTIVE IMMIGRATION POLICIES

How can these restrictive policies, well settled in the law, be morally defended?[9] Writers have given a number of justifications for restricting immigration. I will discuss three: the view that admission of immigrants hurts the domestic poor, the view that nations are self-determining units and therefore may exclude aliens virtually at will, and the argument that nations have a right to protect their culture.

The Priority of the Domestic Poor

Surely the view that domestic *rich* persons should be protected from foreign competition cannot be seriously maintained. Such measures would amount to a reverse international subsidy, where the less rich foreign professionals are prevented from competing with their wealthier counterparts. But defenders of national borders point out that this does not apply to the protection of the poor in society. They may rely on John Rawls's famous difference principle and claim that the immigration policies of a nation are permissible on grounds of justice only to the extent that they

---

[6] International case law usually focuses on the treatment of aliens once they are in the state's territory. For example, the *Abdulaziz* case declared invalid the United Kingdom's exclusion of husbands of lawful immigrants on equality and privacy grounds. It did not challenge the right of the United Kingdom to exclude *everyone* if it so wished. *European Court of Human Rights, Abdulaziz, Cabales and Balkandali* v *The United Kingdom*, Application nos. 9214/80, 9473/81, and 9474/81, 28 May 1985.

[7] *Handbook on European Law Relating to Asylum, Borders, and Immigration* (Council of Europe, 2014), 26.

[8] European Convention of Human Rights, Protocol 4, Article 2.

[9] This section draws loosely from LOREN E. LOMASKY AND FERNANDO R. TESÓN, JUSTICE AT A DISTANCE: EXTENDING GLOBAL FREEDOM ch. 4 (2015).

do not diminish the prospects of the poor in that same country.[10] It is not strictly relevant to questions of justice in the United States whether the effect of these policies damages the prospects of the poor in Mexico, not even if Mexicans are on average much poorer than Americans. Here's the philosopher Thomas Nagel:

> Every state has the boundaries and population it has for all sorts of accidental and historical reasons; but given that it exercises sovereign power over its citizens and in their name, those citizens have a duty of justice toward one another through the legal, social and economic institutions that sovereign power makes possible. This duty is *sui generis*, and is not owed to everyone in the world ... Furthermore, though the obligations of justice arise as a result of a special relation, there is no obligation to enter into that relation with those to whom we do not yet have it.[11]

While Nagel does not say it expressly, his view here implies the permissibility of restrictions to access. Because low-skilled immigrants compete with the domestic poor for the limited number of low-end jobs, they can be permissibly excluded. Stephen Macedo draws exactly that conclusion:

> [I]f high levels of immigration have a detrimental impact on our least well-off citizens, that is reason to limit immigration, even if those who seek admission seem to be poorer that our own poor whose condition is worsened by their entry. Citizens have special obligations to one another: we have special reason to be concerned with the distribution of wealth and opportunities among citizens. The comparative standing of citizens matters in some ways that the comparative standing of citizens and non-citizens does not.[12]

This view is open to several objections. First, there is good reason to think that to an important extent justice is global, not merely domestic. This is not the place to summarize the rich literature on global justice that has emerged in the last twenty years or so, but most writers agree today that justice requires at the very least *concern* for the global poor. Indeed, "[t]hat those who are relatively well off with regard to nutrition, shelter, health care and access to educational services should be protected against competition from people markedly worse off along all these dimensions does not plausibly present itself as any kind of egalitarianism worthy of respect."[13] With respect to migration, the universality of justice entails the position that all persons have a presumptive right to mobility (subject to the property rights of others), and that coercive interference with that right bears a significant justificatory burden.

---

[10] John Rawls' difference principle states in relevant part: "Social and economic inequalities are to be arranged so that they are ... to the greatest benefit of the least advantaged," JOHN RAWLS, A THEORY OF JUSTICE 83 (1971).

[11] Thomas Nagel, "The Problem of Global Justice," 33 PHILOSOPHY & PUBLIC AFFAIRS 121 (2005).

[12] Stephen Macedo, "The Moral Dilemma of US Immigration Policy: Open Borders versus Social Justice," in DEBATING IMMIGRATION, ED. CAROL M. SWAIN 64 (2007).

[13] LOMASKY AND TESÓN, JUSTICE AT A DISTANCE, 106.

Second, the empirical claim that immigrants harm the domestic poor is highly contentious.[14] Recent studies suggest a negative reply both with respect to wages and employment.[15] And, if basic comparative cost analysis is correct, the supply of immigrants for low-end jobs means that complementary jobs will be greater. Nor do immigrants impact negatively on government's budgets. As Alex Nowrasteh summarizes his study on the subject: "Even in situations where immigrants decrease government benefits, those negative effects are likely swamped by the large economic benefits elsewhere in the economy."[16]

Third, just as erecting trade barriers is an inefficient way to help people hurt by trade, so closing borders is an inefficient (and morally problematic) way to protect the domestic poor. The state could provide compensation in cash or in job training to those disadvantages by immigration flows.

Fourth, this whole debate is an embarrassment to the domestic welfare state. Compare the marginal American worker with a typical Mexican immigrant. That worker, unlike the immigrant, speaks English, has benefitted from relatively good schools, health care, and the myriad benefits offered by the welfare state, and *still* he fears competition from his Mexican counterpart. This stands, at the very least, as an indictment of the modern welfare state. And properly so: despite expenditures on the poor that are quite enormous by world standards, the United States welfare apparatus has not fared particularly well. It is hard to avoid concluding that "the proposal to show solidarity with the domestic least well-off by excluding desperate people from abroad is a desperation move from an ideology at the end of its tether."[17]

Self-Determination

Another objection is that natives are entitled to decide democratically to associate with whomever they want, and this includes the freedom not to associate with immigrants. Just as individuals by right are at liberty to refuse or admit whomsoever they choose into their homes, so too democratic electorates through their chosen representatives decide who to admit and who to exclude. How many immigrants the United States admits is purely its own decision. It can be faulted on grounds of economic efficiency, perhaps, but not in terms of any injustice done to those stopped at the border. According to Christopher Wellman, "legitimate states are morally entitled to unilaterally design and enforce their own immigration policies,

---

[14] See Howard F. Chang, "The Economic Impact of International Labor Migration: Recent Estimates and Policy Implications," http://papers.ssrn.com/sol3/papers.cfm?abstract_id= 946204; and "Migration as International Trade: The Economic Gains from the Liberalized Movement of Labor," 3 U.C.L.A. JOURNAL OF INTERNATIONAL LAW AND FOREIGN AFFAIRS 371 (1998).

[15] See Peter T. Leeson and Zachary Grochenour, "The Economic Effects of International Labor Mobility," *in* THE ECONOMICS OF IMMIGRATION, BEN POWELL ED., 11–37 (2015).

[16] Alex Nowraseth, "The Fiscal Impact of Immigration," in *The Economics of Immigration*, 38.

[17] LOMASKY AND TESÓN, JUSTICE AT A DISTANCE, 108.

even if these policies exclude potential immigrants who desperately want to enter."[18] The reason is that, because citizens have in some sense associated with one another, they are entitled to exclude those with whom they do not want to associate. A state, on Wellman's view, is like a private club: outsiders have to be admitted as new members; they cannot impose themselves on the association already formed.

The analogy of a nation to a private club is faulty. Most land in the United States is not owned by the government but by private parties. On the other hand, all persons have the right to free mobility, and any majoritarian attempt to restrict them bears a heavy burden. Current migration restrictions violate those rights. They interfere with the free movement of non-citizens and also with the choices of citizens. Electoral majorities are not permitted to establish rights-violating policies, or, at the very least not without a weighty justification. If individuals have the right to free movement, then it is dubious that such right can be cancelled by majority vote. It can be limited only by a legitimate property title. But a nation's majority does not have a property title over the territory of the state.[19] The assertion "the people can democratically exclude foreigners" is disanalogous to the assertion, "I can exclude trespassers from my property."

Moreover, states are not voluntary associations; they are coercive institutions. This means that the idea of self-determination cannot be cashed out, as Wellman does, in terms of freedom of association.[20] Simply put, citizens have not associated voluntarily with one another, and therefore the reasons that apply to private clubs are inapplicable to the state. The value of freedom of association resides in the voluntary nature of that association, a freely agreed-upon relationship that third parties are not entitled to disturb. Those reasons do not apply to states, where most individuals have been coercively recruited into citizenship.

Contrary to Wellman's suggestion, freedom of association supports a generous immigration policy. If a democratic majority enacts immigration restrictions it violates the freedom of association of *both* potential immigrants and *those who want to associate with them.* Land owners have the right to exclude others. But the democratic majority does not have the power, over and above the owner's property right, to impede access to the owner's land of *additional* classes of persons, persons that the owner herself is willing to admit. Freedom of association is an individual right; it is not a right of collectivities. When the state coercively prevents me from associating with someone, it is violating that individual right. The right to exclude, therefore, cannot be based on freedom of association but in some other property ascribed to the coercive apparatus of the state (such as the

---

[18] CHRISTOPHER HEATH WELLMAN AND PHILLIP COLE, DEBATING THE ETHICS OF IMMIGRATION: IS THERE A RIGHT TO EXCLUDE? 13 (2011).

[19] See my article "The Mystery of Territory," 32 SOCIAL PHILOSOPHY AND POLICY 25 (2015).

[20] See Bas van der Vossen, "Immigration and Self-Determination," POLITICS, PHILOSOPHY, AND ECONOMICS, July 3, 2014, online version, p. 9, accessed November 30, 2014, http://ppe.sagepub .com/content/early/2014/07/02/1470594X14533167.

power to coercively determine the future direction of the society.)[21] I am skeptical that such property can be defended in a manner consistent with respect for individual freedom.

Ryan Pevnick's views are flawed for similar reasons. Pevnick rejects Wellman's freedom of association argument (as do I) and says instead that citizens own their institutions and "have a prima facie right to make their own decisions about the policies under which they live (including policies regarding membership.)"[22] But from the claim that persons own the fruits of their labor one cannot conclude that citizens own institutions, over and above their private rights of property. Surely, this must be a different sense of ownership. And if it is different, it is dubious that the rules that allow owners to exclude others from their property can apply to states, at least when that exclusion infringes important liberties on both sides of the border.

Cultural Nativism

Cultural nativism holds that a state has an interest in controlling its culture, and that it may therefore democratically determine the future direction of that culture, especially, but not only, the public culture.[23] It is a special case of the self-determination argument just discussed, but it focuses on culture. Because freer borders may significantly alter the native culture, citizens can reasonably control immigration to avoid undesirable changes. There are, of course, wildly implausible versions of this view (those that border on racism and xenophobia), but here I consider a more plausible version.

The plausible version of cultural nativism is that culture is a public good. Like any other public good, it is likely to be underproduced. Public goods are defined by nonexcludability and nonrivalry in consumption. Consider Joseph Raz's example: the architecture of the city of Oxford. Locals and tourists alike enjoy the quaint narrow streets and the architectural beauty of the houses, colleges, and churches.

---

[21] Michael Blake likewise criticizes Wellman by pointing out that freedom of association is part of a package of liberties that must be considered as a whole, and that therefore freedom of association cannot be a trump card when other liberty considerations are at stake. Michael Blake, "Immigration, Association, and Antidiscrimination," 122 ETHICS 748 (2012). But Blake concedes too much: I believe that freedom of association is *inapplicable* at the state level.

[22] RYAN PEVNICK, IMMIGRATION AND THE CONSTRAINTS OF JUSTICE: BETWEEN OPEN BORDERS AND ABSOLUTE SOVEREIGNTY 27, 33 (2011).

[23] See David Miller, "Immigration: The Case for Limits," *in* A.I. COHEN AND C.H. WELLMAN, CONTEMPORARY DEBATES IN APPLIED ETHICS, 363, 369–372. Margalit and Raz similarly endorse the view that goups are entitled to self-determination when they have a "comprehensive culture." Avishai Margalit and Joseph Raz, "National Self-Determination," 87 THE JOURNAL OF PHILOSOPHY 439 (1990). They do not address the consequences for immigration, however.

Neither the owners of these buildings nor the city government can exclude non-paying consumers of the good. We enjoy it for free just by walking by. Nor does my enjoyment of the good detract from your enjoyment: consumption is nonrivalrous. Now imagine an owner wants to sell her Georgian house to someone who intends to build a video game arcade painted in pink. This transaction would destroy the public good, which is based on the stunning architectural ensemble. The owner would, it may be hoped, agree that the good has to be preserved, but she is seeking a profit and hopes that others will do whatever is needed to preserve the character of the neighborhood. She is a free rider. Everyone reasons similarly, so the good is under-produced or not produced at all. The government, then, can permissibly prohibit the sale in order to preserve that public good, Oxford's beauty, that all want but the market cannot salvage.

Now let us apply this reasoning to immigration. Our culture is a public good in the same sense as Oxford's architecture. The market cannot preserve culture because some people will opportunistically undermine the efforts to preserve it. Suppose most people in my small border town believe that the English language is an essential feature of our public culture. Suppose further that a business owner wants to hire a number of Spanish-speaking immigrants who, the neighbors fear, would alter that feature. The public-good justification of prohibiting the immigration of these workers is that the business owner is free-riding on the efforts of the rest of the town folks to preserve the English language. Therefore, it is thought, the government can permissibly prohibit immigration to preserve this cultural trait, language purity.

Loren Lomasky and I have elsewhere offered four responses to this line of argument.[24] The first one is that the public-goods justification of state coercion requires that the defector really be a free rider. But whether or not she is a free rider cannot be presumed: maybe she does not care about the public good at all. Maybe she is what David Schmidtz has called an "honest holdout." It is one thing to prevent free riding; it is quite another to impose a cultural project on persons who do not share it and are thus not free riders at all. The second reply denies that cultures can be coercively imposed, even on free riders. People do not have a right to a state that reflects their culture. They do not have a right that their cultural environment remain unchanged. Cultures are valuable to the extent, and only to the extent, that they are the result of voluntary interactions. This is because only individuals, not groups or communities, are proper moral claimants. Third, the future direction of the country will be determined by many internal factors besides immigration, such as economic policy, birth rates, and different social equilibria between cooperators and defectors, to name a few. If the reason to close the borders is that citizens are entitled democratically to control the future, then they should be equally entitled

---

[24] JUSTICE AT A DISTANCE, 114–118.

(democratically) to impede internal movement, control birth rates, impose school curricula, prohibit ethnic restaurants, and so forth – measures that, we presume, few people would support. And finally, there is little question that cultural change is largely *beneficial,* not harmful.[25] I add one more consideration: it seems unlikely that a robust political culture like the one obtaining in the United States will be threatened by immigration. While this is of course an empirical issue deserving of a serious study, anecdotal evidence suggests that migrants enthusiastically adopt American civic culture.

STANDARD ECONOMIC PRO-IMMIGRATION VIEWS

I have already sketched the central ethical argument for immigration: people have a moral right to free movement. Preventing them at gunpoint from moving from one place to another is presumptively unjust, and the justifications that are usually given fail to overcome that presumption.[26]

But even ignoring the moral dimension, there is every indication that immigration controls are exceedingly costly. Michael Clemens has estimated that the global gains from eliminating immigration controls may reach 50 to 150 percent of the world's gross national product.[27] As we saw, the extensive literature on the effect of immigration on wages converges on the finding that those effects are virtually nul. Both theory and empirical evidence support the conclusion, predicted by the law of comparative advantage, that "getting the most of our of the world's labor force requires permitting labor to move to those areas where it is more productive."[28] Jason Brennan and Bas van der Vossen nicely summarize the economic case for free immigration:

> At first glance, then, the idea that freeing up immigration might lead to disastrous economic consequences seems exactly the opposite of the truth. What is disastrous, economically speaking, is our current system of restrictions to the free movement of labor around the world. Opening the borders would not only provide a staggering benefit to migrants themselves, who would see their earnings multiply in ways that would otherwise be near impossible, but also to the rest of the world.[29]

---

[25] A particularly insightful account can be found in Tyler Cowen, Creative Destruction: How Globalization Is Changing the World's Cultures (2002).

[26] For a cogent defense of open borders along these lines see Joseph Carens, The Ethics of Immigration 225–254 (2013).

[27] Michael Clemens, "Economics and Emigration: Trillion-Dollar Bills on the Sidewalk?" 25 Journal of Economic Perspectives 83, 84 (2011).

[28] Leeson and Grochenour, "The Economic Effects of International Labor Mobility" *in* The Economics of Immigration (2015).

[29] Jason Brennan and Bas van der Vossen, In Defense of Openness (forthcoming).

The Demographic Argument

Some people recommend liberal immigration laws because they think immigrants will eventually vote for the better-governing party.[30] This better governance is usually cashed out in terms of welfare benefits. The idea is that the state should liberally admit immigrants because they will become likely beneficiaries of welfare benefits, which in turn will help these immigrants become productive members of society. Once enabled to vote, immigrants will most likely vote for the party that promises welfare benefits, since they will recognize the importance of those benefits in their own lives. The welfare state is good; the party that promotes and enlarges the welfare state is the better governing party; and freer immigration will enlarge the pool of persons who will help this party remain in power.

I think this is a bad argument for freer immigration. At best, it treats immigrants as passive recipients of welfare benefits, not as individuals entitled to work, trade, and prosper on the same footing as natives. At worst, the Demographic Argument is a crude manipulation of immigration laws aimed at winning elections. Notice that even under the best reading of the Demographic Argument, the chief aim of free immigration is not to help the immigrant, but the politicians who would be presumably be elected with the immigrant vote. Proponents of the Demographic Argument want to groom the immigrant into voting for the party that will establish the policies that, they think, would help everyone. The idea is that the immigrant, as a recipient of state benefits, will appreciate them enough to be convinced that welfare policies are the right policies. The Demographic Argument, then, promotes instilling in people the belief that they can only thrive with subsidies provided by the native taxpayers.

There is every reason to doubt the view that immigrants invariably need the welfare state to prosper. Most immigrants seek opportunity for themselves and their families. They flee societies saddled with bad institutions, war, poverty, famine, and the like. By and large, immigrants want to work. They search for a healthy institutional home that will allow them the freedom to offer their skills in the market, something they did not enjoy in their dysfunctional countries of origin. It is simply false that a necessary condition for the immigrant's prosperity is for her to collect welfare benefits from the state. And it is equally false that they, the immigrants, wish to come here in order to get these benefits (I suspect education and basic healthcare may be partial exceptions). This conjecture could be easily tested by attaching a prohibition from receiving state benefits for a period of time as condition of

---

[30] I have not seen a sustained scholarly defense of this argument, maybe because it would be quite embarrassing for the proponent. But in the United States the political press routinely assumes that Democrats want freer immigration, and Republicans the opposite, for electoral reasons. For an analysis of these presumed political effects, see James G. Gimpel, "Immigration's Impact on Republican Political Prospects, 1980–2012," BACKGROUNDER, (Center for Immigration Studies, April 2014), at http://cis.org/immigration-impacts-on-republican-prospects-1980–2012.

admission. I predict that most prospective immigrants will accept such condition. This is because they do not seek government giveaways but the opportunity to work, to better themselves and their families by offering to natives their skills and entrepreneurship – in short, by trading.

But suppose it is true that immigrants can only prosper in their adoptive land through subsidies granted by the state from general taxes. That is: persons can only better themselves with the subsidies coercively exacted from native citizens. Even then the demographic argument fails to treat immigrants with respect. For the Demographic Argument is not interested in the betterment of immigrants as such. It is interested in them only for electoral reasons. The Demographic Argument *uses* immigrants for political purposes. Indeed, someone making this argument doesn't care about whether immigrants do well or badly, as long as they vote for the favored political party. Luring them with welfare benefits is just a means to get them eventually to cast the right vote.

There is another reason to cast doubt on the propriety of the Demographic Argument. As is well known, the influx of immigrants can exert considerable pressure on the welfare state. This is a common argument against freer immigration laws. Welfare benefits have been built over time by native citizens who have contributed with their taxes. It seems unfair now to allow immigrants who have not contributed to free ride on the system and cause its depletion. That is why proposals for freer immigration often include a prohibition for the immigrant to collect welfare benefits. But such a move is unavailable to the proponent of the Demographic Argument. For he needs to bestow such benefits to the immigrant in order to lure him to vote for the political party that promotes the welfare state. Put differently: the supporter of the Demographic Argument is prepared to allow unfair free riding and depletion of the welfare system in order to create a pool of future voters that will eventually elect him to political office.

The Bourgeois Argument

In a trilogy completed in 2016, the economist Deirdre McCloskey has argued that the enormous jump in global prosperity (the Great Enrichment) between sometime in the early or mid-eighteenth century to the present day was caused, not by technological advancement or the establishment of property rights, but by a Gestaltic change of ideas originated in northwestern Europe. She argues, first, that contrary to the conventional wisdom advanced by the intellectual and artistic elite (which she calls the "clerisy"), the middle class of traders, inventors, and managers, far from being selfishly materialistic, is "pretty good", and has been so for much of human history. Second, she claims that institutions and innovations alone cannot have caused the Great Enrichment, because good institutions such as robust property rights have existed at several other times in human history when the enrichment had been much less intense. And, third, she claims that a radical change in social mores was the real cause of the Great Enrichment. This novel ethical outlook is simply the recognition of a new liberty and dignity of commoners and the activity on which they specialized: the ethics of trade-tested betterment. The idea is that the Great Enrichment was triggered by the abandonment of fixed social classes characteristic of feudalism and societal recognition of, and admiration for, the liberty and dignity of all persons to prosper through trade and innovation.[31]

I borrow this idea with three friendly amendments. First, I treat the bourgeois ethics as a *normative* principle, and not just as a historical ethical development that had enormous beneficial consequences (although I largely agree with McCloskey's account). The bourgeois ethics is, I think, a proper way to treat others above and beyond whatever relational bonds (compatriots, friends, family) we may have with them. Respecting their right to better themselves though trade is a special case of according them dignity and respect. Second, borrowing the bourgeois ethics does not commit me to accept McCloskey's controversial claim that institutions had a minor causal role in the improvement of people's lives around the globe. I suspect (but will not argue here) that McCloskey exaggerates the differences between her approach and that of institutionalists like Acemoglu and Robinson.[32] Be that as it may, my argument here is ethical, not historical, so I don't need to take sides in that dispute. And finally, I extend the Bourgeois Argument to immigrants. McCloskey, I think, is content to describe the surge of the bourgeois ethic in Europe and then the world but *within nations*. It is entirely unclear that those who promoted and practiced the bourgeois ethic were thinking of elevating foreigners to the equal treatment that local traders now enjoyed.

The Bourgeois Argument, I said, is a special case of a principle that mandates treating others with dignity and respect, which means treating them as rational, autonomous agents. But the literature abounds in divergent interpretations of the principle. Ronald Dworkin, for example, thinks that the state has a duty to treat everyone with dignity and respect, and that the way to do this is to enhance equality in order to erase the unfair effects of citizens' differing starting points. A redistributive tax policy secures to people the material benefits that would equalize such unfairness and allow them to pursue their life plans with chances of success.[33] Whatever the other merits of this approach, it treats persons as *passive beneficiaries* of the transfer of resources. As such, the state's bestowing benefits cannot in itself represent or embody *respect* for the beneficiary, since such transfer has at best an *indirect* relationship with the beneficiary's agency, dignity, or autonomy. The thought is that, thanks to the benefit, the beneficiaries' prospect will be equalized, as it were, and they will eventually be capable of functioning as productive members of society.

---

[31] See Bourgeois Equality, xi–xii.
[32] See Daron Acemoglu and James A. Robinson, Why Nations Fail (2013).
[33] See Ronald Dworkin, Sovereign Virtue: The Theory and practice of Equality (2000).

In contrast, the bourgeois ethics sees persons as agents, as masters of their own destinies. Instead of payments, individuals receive the recognition of their agency and the encouragement to offer their skills in the market to better themselves and their families. The bourgeois ethics sees persons, not as passive beneficiaries, but as *active agents*. In contrast to Dworkin's view, the Bourgeois Argument emphasizes ethical equality: the equal freedom of every person, native or not, to offer their skills and talents in the market. For that reason, the bourgeois ethics is, I believe, closer to the core notions of dignity and respect than the mainstream egalitarian ethics. It encourages persons to work and innovate, and it discourages resentment and misplaced feelings of entitlement. If McCloskey is right that the bourgeois ethics has been a main factor in global prosperity even with relatively closed borders, then affirming the Bourgeois Argument for immigration is a modern imperative for even greater things to come. This is where the Bourgeois Argument nicely dovetails with economic findings on immigration. Recognizing the migrants' right to better themselves through trade is the right thing to do, and it is also a sure recipe for significant (indeed, massive) increase in prosperity and the corresponding alleviation of poverty.

The bourgeois ethic replaced the old hierarchical ethic that forced traders to remain in their assigned social places.[34] This is why Joseph Carens defends open borders by pointing out that immigrant status is "the modern equivalent of the feudal class privilege."[35] A person who has immigrant status lacks standing to better herself through trade with the natives. Immigration status *means* denial of bourgeois status in McCloskey's sense and it is in that sense, as Carens suggests, a remnant of the feudal hierarchical ethic. Notice that this objection is different from the "luck-egalitarian" objection given by progressive supporters of freer immigration.[36] The luck-egalitarian argument for free immigration is that someone born in a poor country does not *deserve* such fate, and therefore immigration controls should be relaxed to somehow undo the initial arbitrariness of having been born there rather than here. I do not pass judgment on this argument, although I am generally skeptical of luck egalitarianism.[37] Here I simply notice that the kind on inequality created by immigration laws is a *legal* inequality, not an inequality caused by the accident of birth. This is why the luck-egalitarian argument is not needed to condemn these laws. The reason we should allow access to the immigrant is that at the moment such access is denied him by armed guards at the border. The reason is *not* that we should grant him access to nullify accidents of birth. Maybe that consideration applies, maybe not, depending on

---

[34] The classical source is Henry Sumner Maine, Ancient Law (extract from chapter V), at www.panarchy.org/maine/contract.html.

[35] The Ethics of Immigration, 226.

[36] See, for example, Kok-Chor Tan, "Luck, Institutions, and Distributive Justice: A Defence of Global Luck Egalitarianism," European Journal of Political Theory 10 (2011), at http://journals.sagepub.com/doi/abs/10.1177/1474885111406391.

[37] See Lomasky and Tesón, Justice at a Distance, 130–136.

one's evaluation of luck egalitarianism as the basis of a sound political theory. But regardless, surely every liberal, progressive or classical, will agree that coercively enforced inequality of this kind is presumptively wrong.

National Security

I spoke of freer immigration, not of open borders. The Bourgeois Argument disallows the mercantilist idea that migrants seeking betterment (so-called economic refugees) can be legitimately stopped at the border to prevent them from competing with natives. Migrants seeking to better themselves through trade should be allowed to cross borders freely.

But I also think a liberal democracy is entitled to stop criminals and terrorists at the border.[38] This should be done, of course, in a reasonable way and in a manner consistent with liberty, including bourgeois liberty.[39] This view has been challenged recently by Jason Brennan. He argues that closing international borders on the grounds that crime will increase is unjustified because the same position applied to internal migration is clearly wrong. There is no more justification to prevent poor Mexicans from coming to Arizona than there is to prevent poor Californians coming to Arizona, even if in both cases crime will predictably increase.[40] Therefore, Brennan thinks, not even the prospects that some immigrants will commit crimes entitles the state to stop them at the border.

I have two replies. The first one requires a brief foray into the philosophical foundation of the concept of state territory. A classical-liberal theory of immigration should start with private property rights. The territory of the state derives from these property rights in land. Individuals have created a protection agency to which they have delegated limited powers. But owners have not delegated their private property rights beyond the land required by the state to function, so the state lacks the power to exclude foreigners (or anyone else) if owners wish to admit them into their property. Thus, if an owner in Tucson wants to hire a Mexican from Hermosillo to mow her lawn, she is free to do so and the state lacks the power to prevent the entry of the employee. Immigration controls infringe the right to contract, itself an incident of property rights.

---

[38] For a defense of the exception, see Lomasky and Tesón, Justice at a Distance, 100–105.

[39] Current objections, including judicial rulings, against President Trump's immigration executive orders say that they are clumsy, counterproductive, or worse. They do not question the government's power to exclude criminals and terrorists. See, for example, the judicial decision blocking the order: (with full text): www.vox.com/2017/3/15/14940946/read-full-text-hawaii-court-order-trump-refugee-travel-ban. On the other hand, the constitutionality of the revised order is highly disputed. For a view that the order is wrong as a matter of policy but (alas) constitutional, see Fernando Tesón, "Does Constitutional Law Exist?," at http://bleedinghear tlibertarians.com/2017/03/constitutional-law-exist/.

[40] See Jason Brennan, "The Crime Objection to Open Borders," at http://bleedingheartlibertar ians.com/2016/01/the-crime-objection-to-open-borders/.

However, the state has the power to prevent the entry of persons who predictably intend to kill, rape, or steal. The parties to the social contract have delegated to government the power to protect them, and this includes the power to prevent crimes. I am not suggesting that people can be arrested preventively. I am only suggesting that they can be stopped from moving to the scene of their planned crimes, from reaching their intended victims. Conceived in this way, Brennan's objection is less powerful, for I would apply the same rationale to domestic migration. If poor folk from inner-city Miami want to move to my Tallahassee neighborhood they can do so by buying or renting land here. But suppose that these persons are members of a gang that predictably plans to murder and assault the neighbors. I do not think they can be arrested for planning crimes, but I think they may (indeed, should) be stopped from moving to the neighborhood.

Secondly, the national-security exception to free immigration sits comfortably with the Bourgeois Argument. On the classical-liberal vision, immigrants should be allowed the opportunity and the freedom to participate in the global economy and thus seek a better future for themselves and their families. The Bourgeois Argument protects free, voluntary exchanges across borders. It does not protect predatory behavior. That is why the Bourgeois Argument is more restrictive than a straightforward defense of open borders. The argument puts the emphasis where it should be: the desire for, and benefits of, peaceful, voluntary cooperation. A straight open-borders argument, based at it is solely on freedom of movement, ignores the problems raised by predatory behavior.[41]

CONCLUSION

Traditional views on immigration are anchored in false theoretical and empirical premises. One is the idea of national sovereignty, the notion that the body politic has a will and, like a flesh-and-blood person, can decide freely not to associate itself with others, and to exclude foreigners from its soil at its discretion. Another one is the mercantilist notion that immigration and trade are zero-sum games, which implies that what the immigrant gains the natives lose. Once we realize that, first, there is no such thing as a nation distinct from the people who compose it, and second, that allowing all persons to better themselves by trading their skills, ingenuity, and entrepreneurship is the key to individual and collective flourishing, most objections to strong immigration controls vanish.

---

[41] I ignore here the problems of implementation of any system to scan for criminals. But the principle is simple enough, and a sound vetting system should be respectful of liberty and proportionate to the threat that it is intending to address.

11

Rationality – What?

Misconceptions of Neoclassical and Behavioral Economics

Mario J. Rizzo

Reason is large. To ask the question whether some instance of human behavior is rational is tricky. Definitive answers that the behavior is not often rest on some technical narrowing of the meaning of rationality designed for a specific purpose in some other context. Often that specific purpose gets lost in the discussion. Statements about instrumental rationality need to be tied down to specific meanings, contexts and consequences.

And then there is the normative-positive distinction. Concepts of rationality may be useful when applied to understanding actual behavior. When they fail, it doesn't necessarily mean that the agents are in error and that must correct themselves or be corrected. The economist may simply be using the wrong model. On the other hand, applying a normative standard to human behavior is a sensitive task for economists. Unless they are going to replace the value-judgments and perspectives of the agents with their own, they must have a broad view of what constitutes their agents' interests.

What misleads economists is that the "normative" criteria they have developed – the axioms of rationality – were developed in the service of giving choice theory a firm logical foundation. This foundation was designed to rid economics of any specific psychological presuppositions and thus increase the generality of the theory. Then economic theory could understand choice as such regardless of the agents' sources of motivation. This axiomatization of economic theory became intimately tied to the construction of the utility function. The axioms of completeness and transitivity, for example, were shown to be necessary and sufficient conditions for a conventional utility function to exist. Thus, these axioms began to be called "norms."

Nevertheless, they are norms only in the sense that if you want model behavior in terms of a utility function or as "rational" in the sense constructed, then the axioms must be followed.

Norms in this technical sense are not necessarily *prescriptive*. To clarify, let us adopt the distinction made by Searle (1969).[1] There are constitutive rules and prescriptive rules. In the first category, for example, there are rules of playing chess. You are not obligated to play chess; it may not be in your interests to play chess (unless, of course, you have already committed to be in a chess match). The rules of chess are *constitutive* of what it means to play chess. If you do not follow these rules, you are not playing chess. You may be paying checkers. That's all. On the other hand, if you are driving and you do not follow the rules of the road (for safety, for example) you are still driving but you are not driving correctly or safely. Here the rules prescribe a certain type of behavior based ultimately on what we believe the agent is trying to accomplish.

Economists – both neoclassical and behavioral – have confused the status of the axioms of rational choice. They have transformed the constitutive norms of economic theory into prescriptive norms. It is said that agents who do not conform to the axioms are not simply failing to behave as "neoclassical agents" they are acting erroneously. In the neoclassical approach, they always behave as if they conform. In the behavioral, they often do not and when that is the case, their decisions ought to change.[2] Dr. Economist must provide a prescription for that change.

WHY IS THIS IMPORTANT?

Over many decades, economic critics of unregulated markets based their criticisms on grounds of *market failure*. Most agreed that markets generally "worked" especially when compared to socialist systems. Their failure was due to externalities, public goods, monopoly, incomplete markets, asymmetric knowledge, and perhaps a few other factors. All of these were problems of interpersonal interactions that did not occur in normal, competitive markets. But "everyone" thought the agents made individually rational decisions. On the other hand, the advent of behavioral economics has supplemented the market-failure arguments with *decision-making–failure* arguments. Just as markets can break down, so can individual decision-making processes.

The policy arm of behavioral economics is a paternalism-generating machine. It finds, not without substantial disagreement however, that agents sometimes, often or most of the time (the overall claim is unclear), do not behave in accordance with strict rationality. This is interpreted as showing that they do not behave in accordance with their own best interests because their preference-expression is distorted for

---

[1]   J. R. SEARLE, SPEECH ACTS: AN ESSAY IN THE PHILOSOPHY OF LANGUAGE (1969).
[2]   For the view that actual optimization is too strict a condition for rationality, see Richard A. Epstein, "Behavioral Economics: Human Errors and Market Corrections," 73 UNIVERSITY OF CHICAGO LAW REVIEW 111 (2006).

"behavioral" reasons. Again, Dr. Economist must come to rescue with a prescription to induce change in their behavior.

The purpose of this chapter is to give the reader compact analysis of misconceptions about rationality that have produced the current state of affairs in the policy area. It is beyond any doubt important to engage behavioral paternalists on the ground of the specific issues and policies they have studied. Nevertheless, it is crucial to go to the roots of their errors in the manner in which they employ the concept of rationality in economics.

The thesis is simple: Both behavioral and neoclassical economists maintain a concept of strict rationality that is exceptionally narrow. Neoclassicists use it as a tool both to explain what agents actually do and as a prescriptive framework. Behavioralists do not believe it adequately explains actual behavior but that it is still a good prescriptive framework. My view is that whatever the technical virtues of strict, narrow rationality in providing a foundation for useful economics constructs, *it is completely inadequate as a prescriptive standard*. The appropriate concept of rationality for evaluation purposes must be "liberal" or broad reflecting the complexities of human decision making. Behavioral economists are blind to much of this at a normative-prescriptive level. So, their critique of market or other outcomes is impoverished.

In the Part One we examine the idea of rationality. We find that the standard neoclassical concept is extremely narrow and limited in what it can explain. It doesn't acknowledge that individuals can be rational in some respects but not in others, in other words, that there are levels of rationality. The conventional view also tends to overlook the subjective meaning or interpretation that agents bring to a choice-situation. Furthermore, since the neoclassical framework remains abstract or context-free the specific ecological validity of a cognitive tool or "bias" escapes notice.

In the Part Two we examine the idea of irrationality (or what is now more fashionably called "bounded rationality"). Just as the standard conception of rationality is too narrow, the behavioral conception of violations of rationality is too broad. Normative behavioral economics is too quick to jump to a conclusion of decision-making failure. On the contrary, there is a failure to see the sometimes subtle ways in which "irrational" behavior is adaptive to the circumstances at hand and can increase the agent's welfare.

Obviously, a relatively short chapter cannot settle every issue and must of necessity be preliminary in many respects.[3] But the time is long past to remedy those

---

[3] For my (and my coauthor's) further criticisms of the behavioral approach to rationality and policy, see Mario J. Rizzo, "Behavioral Economics and Deficient Willpower: Searching for Akrasia," 14 GEORGETOWN J. LAW & PUBLIC POLICY 789 (2016); Mario J. Rizzo "The Four Pillars of Behavioral Paternalism," *in* S. ABDUKADIROV (ED.), NUDGE THEORY IN ACTION 37–63 (2016); Mario J. Rizzo and D. G. Whitman, "The Knowledge Problem of New Paternalism," 2009 BYU L. REV. 103 (2009); Mario J. Rizzo and D. G. Whitman, "Little Brother Is Watching You: New Paternalism on the Slippery Slopes," 51 ARIZ. L. REV. 685 (2009).

imbalances and confusions at a fundamental level that are the joint responsibility of neoclassical narrowness and behavioral impetuosity.

PART ONE: RATIONALITY

Rationality, in its most fundamental sense, is not a precisely defined concept nor can it be. It is too large because it has many possible manifestations in different contexts. At the very least, the human ability to reason about rationality puts us in the position of discussing rationality at many different levels.

Our particular interest in rationality lies in what it means to say that certain behavior is rational or, relatedly, that to hold certain beliefs is rational. Perhaps this should be rephrased. What *should* it mean to say that certain behavior or beliefs are rational? This is related to yet another question: How is it best for us as scientists to understand human behavior?

The problem of rationality in the social world concerns understanding the behavior of individuals in social or interpersonal contexts. The general rationality principle (and even the more specific rationality axioms of standard economics) is a *tool* for our understanding. The task before us is not to discover some intrinsic truth about whether people are "rational" or not. Of course they are, and of course they are not. It depends on how we look at behavior and by what criteria we assess the rationality of behavior and beliefs. This in turn depends on the purposes for which we are constructing our models. What exactly do we wish to understand?

Thus, the attribution of rationality or irrationality to agents is as much as statement about the scientists' mode of understanding as it is about the agent itself.

The Rationality Hermeneutic in Human Behavior

Standing behind both standard and behavioral economics explanations of human behavior lies a common principle, that is, the understanding of human action by desires (preferences) and beliefs. This is often called "folk psychology" because it is the way that ordinary people ("the folk") understand each other's behavior. It is not strictly a theory but a broad framework within which testable theories are created.[4]

---

[4] There are different views of the epistemic status of folk psychology. See, for example, the discussion of several of these in the entry "Folk Psychology" in ROBERT AUDI, ED., THE CAMBRIDGE DICTIONARY OF PHILOSOPHY, 2ND ED. (1999). As a framework for theories, folk psychology makes no testable generalizations about human behavior. Nevertheless, as a framework it seems compelling. It is supported by reasoning that most researchers in the social sciences would at least implicitly accept: "... [T]he notion of action is folk-psychological – that a behavioral event counts as an action only if it is caused by propositional attitudes that rationalize it (under some suitable act-description). If so, and if humans never really undergo propositional attitudes, then they never really *act* either. In particular, they never really *assert* anything, or *argue* for anything (since asserting and arguing are species of action)" Audi, 313–14.

The framework is treated by scientists as untestable or maintained for the purposes of certain kinds of research.[5]

While standard economics says, for example, that people are motivated by expected levels of wealth (or expected levels of utility) in risky or gambling situations, behavioral economists say that, in many cases, they are motivated by relative changes in wealth (losses or gains relative to some base line). In each case, there is a desire or preference that can be readily understood in terms of folk psychology. In neither case are the individuals crazy or irrational in any non-specialized sense of the term.

Many standard economists assume that agents are rational in their expectations, that is, they expect just what the model in which they "live" says about the stochastic structure of the world. On the other hand, behavioral economists claim that expectations are affected by all sorts of "biases,"[6] including the availability bias. The perceived probability of an event may be higher than its actual relative frequency because the event is uppermost in the individual's consciousness. When airplanes crash, some people believe they are most likely than they really are. Of course, if individuals have a lot on their minds certain kinds of information may be costly to ascertain. Individuals subject to availability bias do not hold fundamentally irrational beliefs. In any event, whether their beliefs are rational in the technical sense or behavioral, the agents act on the basis of desires and beliefs.

The Rational-Irrational Dichotomy

Let's us move beyond the general framework of desires and beliefs to the level of potentially falsifiable theories about individual rationality. Here any sharp dichotomy between rational and irrational behavior is an error.[7] There are, instead, degrees and levels of rationality. Consider the following four levels:

(1) Goal directed conduct in light of given beliefs.
(2) Choice of beliefs in light of a given standard.

---

[5] Even neuroeconomics does not dispense with desires and beliefs but attempts to show the neuro-chemical roots of desires and beliefs. See P. W. GLIMCHER, DECISIONS, UNCERTAINTY, AND THE BRAIN: THE SCIENCE OF NEUROECONOMICS (2004). However, human beings can be studied without reference to desires and beliefs by brain science. This is not at issue here.

[6] The word bias is value-laden. It implies that some error or mistake has been made. Whether the behavior (including thought processes) exhibited by the individual subject to the bias is a mistake depends on the specific criterion of rationality used. If one objects to the appropriateness of the criterion, the agent's "mistake" vanishes. The situation then becomes an example of the analyst's mistake. See, for example, Vernon L. Smith, "Behavioral Economics Research and the Foundations of Economics," 34 J. SOCIO-ECONOMICS 135, 145–6 (2005).

[7] I. C. Jarvie and J. Agassi, "The Problem of the Rationality of Magic," 18 BRITISH JOURNAL OF SOCIOLOGY 55 (1967); J. Agassi and I. C. Jarvie, "Magic and Rationality Again," 24 BRITISH JOURNAL OF SOCIOLOGY 236 (1973).

(3) Choice of beliefs in light of the best available standard.
(4) Choice of the standard (of choosing beliefs) itself. What is the appropriate standard?

First, suppose we observe a culture in which people have a grasp of the ordinary scientific principles of farming – they know how to plant seeds properly, at the correct time of the year, and so forth. But we also observe that they engage in all manner of magical rituals to assist the growth of their crops. Are these people rational or irrational?

Clearly, given that they use "scientific" principles of crop management they must be rational. On the other hand, their continual invocation of magical rituals and spells speaks to their "irrationality." Let us ignore their scientific side since there seems to be no issue there.

The people in the culture know when to call the "priest." They know how to participate in the relevant rituals – what to say and do and the appropriate time. The priest is meticulous about the detail involved in the appropriate rituals. When in doubt he consults the tribal elders, who draw on their memory of what others have told them. If the rituals are not performed strictly according to traditional procedure, they will not be effective. The ritual will have to be redone.

Clearly, these individuals are highly goal-directed within their given set of beliefs.

Second, do these individuals have a standard by which they determine whether these magical beliefs ought to be held? We would imagine that they are not held arbitrarily or because just anyone told them. Suppose their beliefs are based on what successful farmers in the past have done. All successful farmers, as far as these people know, followed the rituals. Indeed, from their perspective it might look that performance of the rituals is a necessary – though not sufficient – condition for success. Are these individuals irrational in having this standard? In a primitive world where much about natural processes is not understood, relying on the tried and "tested" is rational.

Third, suppose now these people have been visited by a scientist. He has convinced them to hold as the standard by which they hold beliefs the principle of falsifiability. They ought not to believe any statement that is in principle not falsifiable. Applying this to their magic rituals they find that they have not been "rational" with respect to investigating the claims of their priests. They now simply apply scientific farming and find that they are no less successful. They also can have more leisure time since rituals performances are unnecessary. Now they are rational in light of (let us suppose) the best available standard of belief.

Fourth, matters need not stop there. As their society prospers and more and more people devote themselves to philosophical discussion, they begin to question whether falsifiability is the best possible standard of belief. Perhaps it needs to be supplemented with other considerations and modified in view of the difficulty in knowing why hypotheses fail. Now they will have to choose which standard of belief acceptance is best or better. They will have to engage in careful reasoning. They will use more fundamental and more general principles of rationality to evaluate the candidate-standards.

Rationality is present throughout these scenarios. But there also "irrationality" if by that we mean the acceptance of dogmas or principles beyond question. True, we can hold that no set of beliefs should be *permanently* beyond criticism and perhaps that is the ultimate level of rationality. But surely we cannot confine rationality *only* to people who accept this standard.

Rationality and Meaning Context

Standard economics has developed a highly abstract axiomatic approach to choice in revealed preference theory. This abstractness is considered a strength insofar as it establishes criteria for rational choice that are independent of content. Even the notion of preference also is not precisely defined so as to make room for individual evaluations that may proceed across many dimensions or only a few. Whether the economist wants to incorporate mental states (preference as a determinant of choice) or whether he wishes to minimize "unobservable" entities (preference as identical to choice) can also be accommodated.[8]

There are many difficulties with this approach that are usually swept under the rug. In the first place, the idea of content-free axioms of rationality is completely atemporal. Consider, for example, the basic criterion of choice consistency. If A is revealed preferred to B, then B *cannot* be revealed preferred to A. Quite true if time has not passed. But if time has passed, then the statement is false. Consistency will hold over time only when the overall pattern of preferences (or utility function) has not changed. But to say that the agent in two time periods can be represented by the same pattern is to say in different words that, among other things, the criterion of consistency is satisfied between the two periods.[9] Therefore, the statement of choice consistency will be true when it is true.[10]

The most important problem, however, is the complete abstraction from *context*. To observe inconsistency or intransitivity requires that the economist know what the choices mean to the agents. To put it another way, the objects of choice are not simply the entities described in purely physical terms or in the terms that the economist personally considers relevant.[11]

---

[8] The original version of revealed preference was explicitly developed to rid choice theory of reliance on unobservable entities like *mental* or *attitudinal* preferences. See Paul A. Samuelson, "A Note on the Pure Theory of Consumer's Behavior," 5 ECONOMICA 61 (1938).

[9] Choices must exhibit consistency if they are to be represented by a utility function.

[10] Much the same can be said about the criterion of transitivity. (If A is revealed preferred to B and B is revealed preferred to C, then A must be revealed preferred to C.)

[11] "Is it not the 'behavior of prices' rather than the behavior of men in the market situation which is studied by the economist . . .? Does not the economist investigate successfully subject matters such as savings, capital business cycle wages and unemployment, multipliers and monopoly as

Suppose that an individual chooses the medium-sized piece of cake when both a big and a small piece are also available.[12] *Why* he chose this piece is strictly irrelevant to the revealed preference approach. We simply observe that he chose the middle-size piece. Now suppose the individual is faced with a contracted choice set. He can have either the medium size piece or the small size piece. He chooses the small piece. Why he has done so is again none of our concern. He has violated the consistency axiom. The elimination of an irrelevant alternative – the big piece – should not make a difference to his ultimate choice.[13]

The problem (if there is one) is not with the agent but with the economist. He has tried to apply an abstract criterion of rationality in the absence of any idea of what the agent is trying to do or what the options mean to the agent.

In the first case, the economist may have surmised that the agent wanted to balance the pleasure of cake with the costs of high caloric intake and so he chose the medium piece. But in fact, let us suppose, the options did not simply mean or represent pleasure-calorie composites. They may have represented pleasure-politeness composites. If the agent believed that taking the biggest piece of those available is impolite, he was really balancing eating pleasure with politeness costs.[14] In that case, the medium piece becomes the largest piece in the second choice-situation. The contraction inconsistency vanishes.

The general difficulty to which this example points is that, in the absence of knowing the agent's criteria of choice (mental preferences) and his beliefs about the consequences of choosing particular objects, we shall be at a loss to ascertain whether choices are consistent or not. The agent is not choosing the pieces of cake for their own sake, pure and simple.[15] He has something in mind. We need to know what.

Analysis of the revealed preference approach shows that it is impossible to have an atemporal and acontextual theory of rational behavior. The first problem

---

if these phenomena were entirely detached from any activity of the economic subjects, and even less without entering into the subjective meaning structure such activities have for them? . . . Closer investigation however, reveals that this abstract conceptual scheme is nothing else than a kind of intellectual shorthand and that the underlying subjective elements of human actions involved are either taken for granted or deemed to be irrelevant with respect to the scientific purpose at hand . . . Correctly understood, the postulate of subjective interpretation as applied to economics as well as to all other social sciences means that we always can – and for certain purposes must – refer to the activities of the subjects within the social world and their interpretation by the actors in terms of systems of projects, available means, motives, relevances, and so on." A. Schutz, Collected Papers, Vol. 1 ("The Problem of Social Reality") 34–5 (1964).

[12] Amartya Sen, "Internal Consistency of Choice,"61 Econometrica 495 (1993).

[13] This is the idea of contraction consistency. It is related to the principle of the Independence of Irrelevant Alternatives.

[14] He may have also been concerned about too many calories. In that case, his preferences will have to be defined over three characteristics.

[15] Once we identify the objects of choice as pieces of cake rather than in some equivalent physical or chemical terms, we are implying that the objects of choice are simply food. But if the agent's purposes and beliefs are as outlined above, this is an incorrect description or, at least, an incomplete description.

undermines the usefulness "logical" criteria themselves. A judgment must be made whether the analyst is truly dealing with an unchanging preference structure. Observation of actual choices is not enough here.

The second problem points to an even more basic issue. Identification of the choice-situation *as the agent sees it* cannot be captured within austere behaviorist strictures. This approach tends to lead to excessive findings of irrationality relative to what a more contextually sensitive application of the axioms would find.

We cannot reduce the agent to the grabbing of objectively defined things. This is why the original behaviorist revealed preference project in untenable. Behaviorist rationality is a mirage.

Behavioral Economics and Context

We must distinguish between the *behaviorism* that motivated Paul Samuelson's theory of revealed preference and the modern *behavioralist* movement. The former tried to extricate mental states from economics; the latter explicitly tries to bring them back in. On the one hand, a central task of behavioral economics is directed toward bringing the preferences, beliefs, and contextual understanding of actual agents into the discussion of rationality. On the other hand, it is wedded to the standard axiomatic approach to rationality as the normative ideal. Behavioralists claim that the behavior of "real" agents does not satisfy the rationality axioms, *but it should.*

Behavioral economists do not seem to understand that in holding the axioms of revealed preference as the normative standard of rationality they are saying that the meaning context of the choice-situation *ought* to be irrelevant. But since consistency and transitivity of choice cannot be meaningfully identified outside of such a context, the norm makes no sense.

Perhaps because of their ambivalence about the important of context at the descriptive and normative levels, behavioral economists have failed to give adequate attention to the matter of context in their research. Ironically, they make the same general error, albeit in different ways, that is made by standard economics.

On the one hand, behavioral economics argues that because of the importance of context the austere axioms of choice are irrelevant or inapplicable to under the understanding of actual behavior. On the other hand, the behavioralists argue that the departures from "rationality" are systematic, persistent and widespread – that across a wide variety of contexts people made the same types of errors. As we point out subsequently, modern psychology does not support this view. The results of psychological research and experiments are far more context and measurement-procedure specific than behavioralists believe.[16]

---

[16] "Psychologists have encountered the greatest difficulty generating concepts that applied to settings that were very different from the one that gave rise to the original observation because most concepts refer to the behavioral or physiological reactions of animals and humans to

At this point we can consider two examples of this error in behavioral economics: (1) abstracting from the meaning individuals give to experimental problems and (2) abstracting from the real-world problem context, that is, the ecology in which the individuals' tools of cognition and decisionmaking have developed.

Meaning in Experiments

The problems that arise from the experimental subjects' confusion over the meaning of the problem they are supposed to solve can be significant. A good example of this is the famous "Linda Problem," which supposedly illustrates the "conjunction fallacy."

This is the description given to the subjects in a famous experiment by Tversky and Kahneman (1983):

> Linda is 31 years old, single, outspoken and very bright. She majored in philosophy. As a student, she was deeply concerned with issues of discrimination and social justice, and she also participated in antinuclear demonstrations.

They were asked which of these statements is more probable: (1) Linda is a bank teller (T) or (2) Linda is a bank teller and is active in the feminist movement (T&F)? The uniquely correct answer, according to Tversky and Kahneman, is the first: Linda is a bank teller.

If the reader had guessed the second, he should be forgiven because many an intelligent – (rational?) person will not give the "correct" answer. Kahneman and Tversky report that more than eighty percent of the participants in the experiment got the wrong answer. Why is the second answer incorrect? The answer is simple: There are many more bank tellers than they are bank tellers who are feminists. The conjunction of tellers and feminists can never be more than the number of tellers alone. Hence the subjects commit the "conjunctive fallacy."

There are many things wrong with the conclusion that the subjects were guilty of a cognitive mistake.[17] In the first place, what did the participants understand by "probability"? They were not being specifically asked about relative frequencies. So, it is natural that they interpreted the question as their degree of belief, given the description. If we look closely at the description it is not at all unreasonable to conclude that the experimenter is *almost* telling us that she is a feminist. Furthermore, if the subjects believe that the experimenter is cooperating, rather than trying

---

specific situations, rather than to the relatively stable, inherent features of these agents, such as their body mass, pigmentation, or blood type. As a result, many psychological concepts refer to phenomena that are necessarily influenced by the context. . . . A frustrating consequence of the influence of the local context is that few psychological concepts intended to represent a person's tendency to react in a certain way apply across diverse settings ..." J. KAGAN, PSYCHOLOGY'S GHOSTS: THE CRISIS IN THE PROFESSION AND THE WAY BACK 3–4 (2012).

[17] G. GIGERENZER, ADAPTIVE THINKING: RATIONALITY IN THE REAL WORLD 248–51 (2000).

to "trick" the subject, the inference is even more natural.[18] Of course, some versions of probability theory would claim that the single-case probability and the long-run relative frequency should be identical. And yet that is far from uncontroversial. So much for the view that there is only one correct answer.

When Hertwig and Gigerenzer (1999) redid the study asking specifically about natural frequencies,[19] the subjects *overwhelmingly* gave the answer Tversky and Kahneman were looking for: Linda is a bank teller.[20]

The problem with the attribution of cognitive mistake is that the experiment did not take sufficient account of not only what the term probability meant to the subjects but also the social meaning that the subjects attributed to the experimenters' question. Were they basically being told the "right" answer or were the experiments trying to deceive or manipulate them? We cannot abstract from the meaning individuals attribute to the experimental situation.

Ecological Meaning

Another sense in which context matters is when we try to understand a cognitive process or behavior characteristic in terms of the function it has in its usual environment. In fact, in most cases it is necessary to the understand in this way in order to get a full sense of what is happening in experimental and field situations.

Let us take two examples. The first has to do with the "peak-end" rule or heuristic that Kahneman et al. (1993) find is characteristic of memory in hedonic situations.[21] This rule says that individuals will remember, for example, a colonoscopy or episode of a hand emerged in cold water by averaging the peak pain (pleasure) and the ending pain (pleasure) of a temporally extended experience. The problem with this heuristic is that it violates "temporal monotonicity." If the experimenter adds a longer period of pain to the experience but ends on a better note than in the shorter episode, the individual will remember the longer as "better." In cases with this

---

[18] H. P. Grice, Logic and Conversation 41–58 (1975).

[19] The question was reworded: "Imagine 200 women who fit the description of Linda. How many of the 200 women are: Bank tellers (T). Active in the feminist movement (F). Bank tellers and are active in the feminist movement (T&F)" Gigerenzer et al., Cognitive illusions recon- sidered," *in* Charles R. Plott and Vernon L. Smith, Eds., *Handbook of Experimental Economics Results* (Vol. 1), 1028 (2008).

[20] In Tversky and Kahneman (1983) 85 percent of subjects committed the "conjunctive fallacy." A. Tversky, and D. Kahneman, "Extensional versus Intuitive Reasoning: The Conjunction Fallacy in Probability Judgment," 90 Psychological Review 293 (1983). In Hertwig and Gigerenzer (1999), when the experiment asked people to report on the frequency of each of the categories, the number of "fallacious thinkers" was zero in two substudies and 13 percent in two others. R. Hertwig, and G. Gigerenzer, "The 'Conjunction Fallacy' Revisited: How Intelligent Inferences Look Like Reasoning Errors," 12 Journal of Behavioral Decision Making 275 (1999).

[21] Daniel Kahneman, et al., "When More Pain Is Preferred to Less: Adding a Better End," 4 Psychological Science 401 (1993).

particular profile of affect, the rule will produce an error (*if* this kind of memory is used to evaluate similar future courses of action) from the normative standpoint of maximizing experience utility over time.

If, however, we ask the question, "What is memory for?" we may get a different perspective. In the first place, from a contextual perspective it should not be odd to observe that ordinary people do not have a "Newtonian" or spatialized conception of time. They do not treat all periods or time as homogeneous and equal. They perceive time in terms of personal relevances. Events or experiences that are more important to them will be weighted more than those that are less important. Memory is not a motion picture of what happened in the past.[22]

Fredrickson (2000) suggests a number of reasons why the peak-end heuristic makes sense in the context of the typical problem situation with which memory copes.[23] The problem situation is this: Can I cope with the stress of the pain and is it all worth it in terms of the cost? The peak reveals the capacity necessary for enduring or coping with the episode. What resources are needed? The end is important for several reasons. The most obvious is that the end point is the conclusion; nothing more will happen. The peak cannot be determined without reference to the end point. More fundamentally, however, the end represents the outcome in goal-directed experience. It directs the individual to a determination of whether this outcome was worth the cost. In some cases, the ending reveals the whole character of the episode as when a person thought to be a good friend leaves town without saying goodbye.

In a world in which memory is limited and people do not have the capacity to run motion pictures of the past in their heads, peak-end averaging makes sense as a summary statistic.[24]

We should note that the experiments in which Kahneman (1993) observes the peak-end heuristic are extremely artificial ones in which the experience is arbitrarily truncated at a point where no apparent purpose has been served.[25] The true end of a colonoscopy is only trivially the conclusion of the mechanical process. More relevantly, it is the purpose served. Did the test eliminate potentially harmful polyps? Did the doctor provide good post-test advice? Did he appear to be competent? Of course, these are not hedonic experiences. But rarely is hedonic experience the *only* thing that individuals care about. The heuristic is meant to solve problems in the

---

[22] Kahneman's (2003) comparison with a moment by moment record of what the subjects are feeling suggests that this is what memory should be. Daniel Kahneman, "Experienced Utility and Objective Happiness: A Moment-Based Approach," *in* I. Brocas and J. D. Carrillo, The Psychology of Economic Decisions, Volume 1, Rationality and Well-Being (2003).

[23] B. L. Fredrickson, "Extracting Meaning from Past Affective Experiences: The Importance of Peaks, Ends, and Specific Emotions," 14 Cognition & Emotion 577 (2000).

[24] "The personal meanings carried by peak and end affect also make us question whether and when reliance on the peak-and-end rule should be considered a mistake." Id at 593.

[25] Daniel Kahneman, et al., "When More Pain Is Preferred to Less: Adding a Better End," 4 Psychological Science 401 (1993).

world where evaluation is complex. Applying the peak-end rule outside of its typical problem situation is bound to give misleading or, at least, hard to interpret results.

The second set of examples reveals that expert traders will do less well in avoiding pitfalls and biases than student subjects when the experimental environment does not match the natural environment in which the experts have developed their heuristics. Several of these examples are discussed by Levitt and List (2007).[26] When, for example, both wool traders and students were placed in experimental progressive oral auctions, the wool traders relied on heuristics they had used in actual markets. These heuristics failed because the incentives in the experiment penalized the heuristics.[27] Students tend to follow more abstract rules and use "test taking" skills that can payoff in experiments.[28] People enter experimental situations with propensities that they have developed outside of the laboratory and which, often, have become adapted to that outside environment. Ecologically rational behavior can give the appearance of biased or "irrational" behavior in the laboratory.

Summary and Conclusions of Part One

Rationality is a tool that social scientists use to understand the world. The term rational is not a description of a person but a way of looking at some or all of his actions, including the beliefs he holds.

Rationality is not just one thing. It operates on different levels and is present or absent in different degrees. People can be rational in one respect and not in another respect.

Most importantly, however, rationality cannot be adequately understood outside of its context, that is, the meanings that people attach to their environment and the problems they typically face. The attempts by revealed preference theorists to create a series of axioms that embody rational choice criteria are flawed by the very abstractness of the project. We cannot identify the satisfaction or violation of these axioms without paying significant attention to the content or meaning of the choice-acts. There is much room here for analysts' confounding of contextually rational behavior with inferences of irrationality based the violation of formal axioms. Even among behavioral economists who explicitly reject the idea that behavior can be understood outside of its context, have paid insufficient attention to meaning,

---

[26] Steven D. Levitt and John A. List, "Viewpoint: On the Generalizability of Lab Behaviour to the Field," 40 CANADIAN JOURNAL OF ECONOMICS/REVUE CANADIENNE D'ÉCONOMIQUE 347 (2007).

[27] P. Burns, "Experience and Decision Making: A Comparison of Students and Businessmen in a Simulated Progressive Auction," *in* RESEARCH IN EXPERIMENTAL ECONOMICS, VOL. 3, 139–53 (1985).

[28] D. J. Cooper, et al., "Gaming against Managers in Incentive Systems: Experimental Results with Chinese Students and Chinese Managers," 89 AMERICAN ECONOMIC REVIEW 781 (1999).

personal relevances and the ecology of decision making and belief. Thus, in each case, it is "easy" to find violations of the standards of rational behavior.

The normative issue is even more disturbing. Both standard and behavioral economists accept the axioms of revealed preference as the normative standard of rational choice. At one time, most standard economics affirmed the view that, by and large, the axioms were satisfied by real world behavior. Today, doubts have been raised by behavioral economics. Nevertheless, both are in agreement that these *norms* for rationality are intact. But what can that mean?

Does it mean that if a pattern of choice appears inconsistent in terms of the transitivity axiom, the agents must reform some of the choices? And yet since action takes place in time, why should criteria that apply to a timeless "logical" world be impressed upon actors operating in time? Furthermore, does it mean that the construal of a problem situation – for example ascertaining the "probability" of Linda's identity – must be construed in the way the experimenters intend? These are important problems.

PART TWO: IRRATIONALITY

What does it mean to say that a person's behavior is not rational? It could mean that it is *non-rational* in the sense that it is not an action – that is, not intentional, not purposeful and therefore not explicable in terms of desires (preferences) and beliefs.[29] Perhaps the behavior is generated by biochemical processes or is a motor reflex. We are not concerned with the purely nonrational.

Normally, however, it means that while an action is associated with certain desires and beliefs, there is a failure or a gap between these and the action. For example, the individual may suffer from weakness of will or his preferences may be inconsistent with each other or his beliefs may be incorrect because he does not learn "properly." This is a "failure within the house of reason" or a failure *within* the interpretive framework of desires and beliefs.[30]

Since rationality is a tool we use to understand the social world, irrationality represents a failure of that tool in a particular respect or at a certain level of analysis. It does not preclude understanding behavior that can be seen as irrational in one respect as rational in another. Irrationality is incomplete rationality or, in many cases, a form of rationality in process.

As we have seen, there are different levels or degrees to which we can characterize a person's behavior, preferences or beliefs as rational. When they fail one or more of these tests of rationality but satisfy others, we can say that the behavior, preferences

---

[29] Explanations that proceed in terms of looking at behavior *as if* it were the pursuit of some particular goal cloud this issue.

[30] D. Davidson, "Paradoxes of Irrationality," *in* P. K. MOSER, RATIONALITY IN ACTION: CONTEMPORARY APPROACHES 449–464 (1990).

or beliefs are incompletely rational. There is no implication here that anything can be *completely* rational in all interesting respects, but the appellation "incompletely rational" is of heuristic importance since it focuses attention on the complex nature of rationality.

Superstitious Prior Beliefs

In the previous part, we outlined several levels of rationality relative to beliefs. The least demanding level is that of "goal directed conduct in light of given beliefs." In recent papers Peter Leeson has shown how behavior centered around or coordination by "irrational" beliefs can serve important social functions among individuals who are otherwise rational. For example, in medieval Europe where people believed that clerics of the Catholic Church could cast curses upon violators of the Church's property rights, this belief could serve as a protection of those rights.[31] Monks could credibly curse people who violated the Church's rights.

On the one hand, the belief in malediction was unfalsifiable. This maintained people's prior probabilities of efficacy. Thus, if a predator expected with probability p that a cost c would result from the curse, then the expected cost of the predator's activity would rise by $p \cdot c$. The deterrence of predation depends, at the most basic level, on all of the agents acting rationally with respect to this cost imposition.[32] The clerics assess the cost of casting a malediction which is near zero. The potential predators assess both the costs imposed by cursing which vary by their degree of belief as well as the physical costs of predation and then compare the sum of these with the value of the property.

Once predator-agents have accepted that cursing-costs are real, they continue as rational optimizers to make their decisions. Insofar as clerics believe that they have this spiritual power (or at least believe that others believe they have) they will impose the costs because they wish to create the proper incentives. *All* agents are rational, given their prior and unfalsifiable beliefs.[33] The social consequence of this form of rationality is to protect property rights in a world where alternative methods are not available. Thus, defects in rationality, relative to a scientific standard of criticism or evaluation, need not reduce social welfare when taken in their social context. Both the meaning and function of beliefs cannot be assessed outside of their relevant contexts.

---

[31] Peter T. Leeson, "God Damn: The Law and Economics of Monastic Malediction," 30 JOURNAL OF LAW, ECONOMICS, AND ORGANIZATION 193 (2012).

[32] In a certain sense the costs are not real but imaginary (to us). Yet in the relevance sense that determines choices they are real as long as the acting parties think they are real. Undertaking or not undertaking a certain course of action will be affect by this perception.

[33] This is consistent with Bayesianism insofar as no restrictions are placed on prior beliefs or probabilities. On the other hand, it is not consistent with Bayesian updating because no data is considered relevant. The belief is unfalsifiable. Thus the "irrational" belief structure that is given in the analysis is (1) an "unscientific" *prior* belief in cursing that is (2) unfalsifiable. So it remains in place as a constraint.

Limited Cognitive Abilities

Just as we can have incompletely rational agents adapting to a shared set of "false" beliefs in quite rational and social welfare-enhancing ways, we can often think about agents with limited cognitive abilities as "simply" making decisions under constraints that, in principle, are not very different from any other constraint. We could look at the beliefs underlying the cursing institution, discussed above, as a shared manifestation of a cognitive limitation.

Is costly information a manifestation of a cognitive limitation? Beginning with Stigler (1962) economists have systematically treated information as something costly to acquire.[34] But in a perfect world the mind would already know what it needs to know to make individually optimal decisions. Economists would agree but then say we must deal with the world as we find it. Information is costly.

So, where does it get us to say that while information is costly to acquire it is costless to process or costless to retrieve? Perhaps there is an illusion that in the former case "everything" is objective. We just sample prices that exist objectively in, say, an urn. But when the individual stops sampling is going to depend on his estimate of what he will gain if he continues sampling. And that will depend ultimately on his subjective prior on the distribution of prices in the urn.

In any event, there are cases when information might be in the hands of people but not in their minds. Consider the oft-cited case of American tourists crossing the street in London.[35] Let us suppose they all "know" that cars will be coming from right as they cross the street. Nevertheless, over years of experience as pedestrians in the United States they have built up the useful habit of, without much thought, looking left as they cross streets. This habit is hard to break in a few days on vacation.

Nevertheless, they were told the facts. They have the information. If we see them crossing and looking in the wrong direction, subsequently being hit and killed by an oncoming car, do we conclude that they wanted to commit suicide? Some economists have claimed that on a literal revealed preference approach one would have to say yes.[36]

From there they are able to suggest the absurdity of the revealed preference approach to choice and rationality. They conclude from this example that people do not always reveal their preferences in their choices. They can prefer to do the better (look right) and yet do the worse (look left). They are not behaving rationally.

[34] George J. Stigler, "Information in the Market," 70 JOURNAL OF POLITICAL ECONOMY 94 (1962).
[35] B. D. Bernheim and A. Rangel, "Behavioral Public Economics: Welfare and Policy Analysis with Nonstandard Decision-Makers," *in* P. DIAMOND AND H. VARTIAINEN, H. (EDS.). BEHAVIORAL ECONOMICS AND ITS APPLICATIONS 7 (2007).
[36] Id.

This position is a tissue of misconceptions. The revealed preference theory is indeed defective for many reasons, some of which were outlined in the previous Part. But this story does not illustrate one of its inherent defects.

Our American tourists in London have a habit that is ecologically rational. It is adapted to the environment of the United States and most other countries. The habit enables them to implement their knowledge in a rapid and highly effective way. In fact, the knowledge is almost embodied – their heads pretty much move on their own, so to speak, in the correct direction. So now give them a new environment and new knowledge. The cost of "retrieving" the new knowledge at the appropriate moment in London is now high. In some cases it may be so high that the set of *feasible options* faced by the individual does not include looking in the correct direction. Practically speaking, it is no different from a high cost of acquiring the information about the direction of traffic.[37]

In either case – costly acquisition of information or costly retrieval of knowledge – the individual does not violate any axioms of rational choice or act contrary to revealed preference. In both cases the social policy is obvious: paint a sign in the street indicating the direction in which pedestrians should look. This reduces the cost of information acquisition or knowledge retrieval and thus expands the set of feasible actions.

We are free to *define* rational behavior as incorporating the costless retrieval of information. Economists, under the sway of perfect competition, used to model *homo economicus* as a decisionmaker with perfect knowledge. In either case, we are dealing with a specific conceptualization or model within the "house of reason." Nothing profound is at stake. Which model we choose depends on the problem-situation we as economists face. Whether the agents have costs of acquiring information or retrieval depends on the problems they face. The manifestations of rationality are contextual.

The Rational "Choice" of Bias

The behavioral economics literature portrays cognitive biases as departures from rational thought as defined by certain abstract criteria. The contrast is made between deliberate thought in accordance with scientific methods of sampling, data gathering, and Bayesian updating. Departures from this kind of thinking arise from a different brain "system" – one that is more intuitive, perhaps impulsive, and associative rather than conceptual.[38] It appears as if this kind of biased thinking and the choices to which it may give rise are breakdowns in rationality.

---

[37] F. Gul and W. Pesendorfer, "The Case for Mindless Economics," *in* A. Caplin, and A. Schotter (Eds.) THE FOUNDATIONS OF POSITIVE AND NORMATIVE ECONOMICS: A HANDBOOK 3 (2008).
[38] DANIEL KAHNEMAN, THINKING, FAST AND SLOW (2011).

Of course, the breakdown, if there is one, is in a certain kind of rational thinking – the deliberate "constructivist" form. But rationality, as we have seen and will further see, is bigger than that. The rules of rationality are sometimes the embodiment of specific abstract axioms but also encapsulated in the heuristics and rules-of-thumb that enable people to make good decisions in many kinds of environments.

Consider now the bias of overoptimism. In a sense, overoptimism is a form of wishful thinking. I want to be more efficacious so I think I am. I want more favorable states of the world to occur so I think they will. Wishful thinking is often cited as a form of irrationality.[39] But suppose wishful thinking as overoptimism helps the individual overcome certain other biases or provides a degree of hedonic utility, is it then irrational? To get a clearer picture of what is or is not rational we must understand cognitive tendencies in their context.[40]

Optimism against Procrastination

Let us assume that an individual has a present bias, that is, he discounts short-run benefits more heavily than long-term benefits. Therefore, if asked to choose between $100 today and $110 tomorrow he will choose $100 today, and if asked today to choose between $100 in thirty days and $110 in thirty-one days he will choose $110 in thirty-one days. But then when the thirtieth day becomes today and the thirty-first becomes tomorrow, he chooses $100 over $110. The present bias consists in the preference reversal that he exhibits.[41] This individual sees time-delay in terms of distance from him in the present thus a delay of one day is reckoned differently if it is "immediate" than if it is distant.[42]

---

[39] Wishful thinking violates what Binmore (2008, 5) calls Aesop's Principle. K. BINMORE, RATIONAL DECISIONS (2008). In Aesop's fable the fox decides that when (because) he could not reach the grapes that they were sour and therefore he did not want them. The principle requires that an agent's preferences and beliefs that is, her assessments of what is feasible, must be causally independent of each other.

[40] For a brief but insightful analysis of whether overoptimism leads to inferior decisions, see RICHARD A. EPSTEIN, SKEPTICISM AND FREEDOM: A MODERN CASE FOR CLASSICAL LIBERALISM 244–5 (2003).

[41] Unfortunately, almost all of the evidence of preference reversal is from latitudinal (cross sectional) studies. In this approach the individual is asked to make a decision, *at a given point in time*, between smaller-sooner and larger-later in both an immediate and distant set of options (each with the same delay from the earlier to the later reward). What this may tell us is that the individual's current intentions are inconsistent. It does not show that *in the passage of time* the individual will reverse the distant decision. To demonstrate this a longitudinal study is required. Unfortunately for the standard hypothesis, people do not uniformly become more impatient as the distant decision become immediate in real time. About the same number become more patient. For a fuller discussion see D. Read, et al., "Four Days Later in Cincinnati: Longitudinal Tests of Hyperbolic Discounting," 140 ACTA PSYCHOLOGICA 177 (2012).

[42] The individual is supposed to accept the Newtonian view of units of time as homogeneous and empty. The idea is that these units are loci for the allocation of resources and that elapse of time means the same thing regardless of when it happens.

Such a person is subject to immediate gratification in cases where benefits are upfront as in the example just presented. He is also subject to procrastination when costs are upfront and benefits come later. In the latter case, he prefers not to incur the cost because costs are overvalued relative to what they would be valued by someone without present bias.[43] His perception of the cost-benefit ratio is too high to undertake the project. Hence the present biased individual will make plans but procrastinate in the implementation.

Overoptimism can help offset the tendency to procrastinate.[44] It can do this by raising the expected return on effort relative to the "exaggerated" cost. Think of θ as the perceived probability of successfully completing the task and bringing about the benefits associated with it.[45] Overoptimism about the probability of success, that is, having a θ that is greater than the true probability of success, would raise the expected benefits relative to the exaggerated costs. This could overcome the tendency to procrastinate.[46] Thus the individual could have an interest in building his self-confidence or optimism beyond that which is "rationally" justified in order to overcome his "irrational" procrastination bias.

Is Overoptimism a Bias? Even If So, Is It Irrational?

In keeping with our general view of the contextual nature of rationality, overoptimism here seems to function quite differently than in the free-floating case. It has an adaptive role in the full context of the individual's cognitive functioning. In other words, cognitive biases can not only adapt to the external environment but they can adapt to the rest of the internal environment, that is, to each other.

In some cases, the individual will explicitly try to "pump up" his confidence through motivational programs, talking with optimistic friends, recalling his previous successes and so forth. It would stretch credulity, however, to say that he *consciously* overestimates the probability that he will succeed in a given project, although people do sometimes holds two contrary thoughts in their minds. Nevertheless, the explicit modeling in this area is less important than the idea that the rationality of biases cannot be assessed outside of the full cognitive profile of the individual.

---

[43] The person with present bias would perceive the costs (c) as c/β where β is the present discount factor less than one. The person without present bias would perceive the costs just as c.

[44] Jean Tirole, "Rational Irrationality: Some Economics of Self-Management," 46 EUROPEAN ECONOMIC REVIEW 633 (2002).

[45] It could also be viewed as the degree of self-confidence.

[46] The more general picture is more complex. At very high levels of self-confidence, there is no procrastination because the expected benefits are very high. At very low levels, both the planning self and the acting self are in agreement that effort is not worthwhile. But at intermediate levels the degree of self-confidence may not be sufficient to induce the acting self to act (not procrastinate) while the planning self finds the project and effort worthwhile. This is when overoptimism is useful.

Overoptimism as Utility Enhancing

Even when overoptimism appears to serve no offsetting function unlike in the above discussion, it can be directly utility enhancing. This is an essential element in the theory of "optimal expectations."[47] There is anticipatory utility associated with optimistic expectations. People like looking forward to good things and successes.

The agent faces a mapping from actions to payoffs in different states of the world. Payoffs are higher or lower in different states. Each of these states, we shall suppose, has an objective probability of coming about. If there were no such thing as anticipatory utility the agent would have no incentive to depart from these objective probabilities. But, as things stand, he would be happier if he believed that the probabilities of the higher payoff states were greater than they actually are. There are benefits to him in distortion of the probabilities and thus from overoptimism.

Optimal expectations are "a set of subjective probabilities ... that maximize well-being."[48] However, well-being is not maximized by ignoring the behavioral distortions (savings, investment) that will occur if expectations are not rational in the technical sense of consistency with objective probabilities. There are costs to fooling oneself. In this model, unlike in the previous one, optimistic distortions of probabilities do not offset other distorting tendencies, but create them.

If it is true that people have biased expectations because these produce utility, then the assumption of rational expectations is violated. While one can call an equilibrium in which the subjective probabilities (of future states of the world) coincide with their objective probabilities "rational," it cannot be simply a matter of definition. If rationality is fundamentally manifested in the relevant context, optimal expectations have greater claim to rationality because they are rooted in the maximization problem that is faced by the agent.

There is a tradeoff between gains in anticipatory utility and the costs of behavioral distortion. When the distortion costs are low the agent can afford to indulge his pleasant optimistic fantasies; when they are high he must come to his senses and face reality. We should expect expectations to be less optimistic and more nearly realistic ("rational") as the costs rise.

The Brunnermeier-Parker model is not entirely clear on the actual mechanism by which optimal expectations are generated. A literal interpretation of the model suggests the agent applies deliberate effort to balancing the costs and benefits. But they do not view this as essential since the "system" generating the distorted probabilities operates below the level of consciousness. But the conscious deliberative system will

---

[47] M. K. Brunnermeier and J. A. Parker, "Optimal Expectations," 95 AMERICAN ECONOMIC REVIEW 1092, 1096 (2005).
[48] Id.

make an effort to assess probabilities correctly to the best of its ability although it is being pulled in the optimistic direction.

Is overoptimism simply as a source of anticipatory utility "irrational"? It is hard to see why. In the first place, do we not usually take the sources of utility as given? If an individual derives hedonic utility from a steak, do we question it? It is has not been the practice of economists to do so. So why should we question or rule out anticipatory utility from thinking about eating the steak tomorrow night? If we allow this, then it is a short step from deriving utility from overly optimistic assessments of the probability of success. In general, we begin – as with intrinsic preferences – with nonrational givens.

Summary and Conclusions of Part Two

The role of rationality is to "process" what we start with. In the case discussed here the individual has a well-defined problem; he once-and-for-all revises his initial overoptimism by balancing costs and benefits;[49] he maximizes the present value of the utility streams in an exponential way. Thus, as we have seen before, the "irrationality" of the agent lies in a particular, acontextual, view of rationality. The assumption is that expectations of a rational kind serve only one purpose: to maximize the present value of the sum of utilities experienced at the various points in the future – the so-called instantaneous utility. In a world in which people derive anticipatory utility it is not reasonable to call optimal expectations "irrational." Would individuals in such a world be rational if they neglected this source of utility?

In the above discussion, we saw that behavior is often usefully viewed as incompletely rational, that is, as violating some criteria of rationality while satisfying others. Specifically, individuals may accept non-falsifiable beliefs that according to modern science are false; they may be trapped in old habits and have difficulty accessing new relevant information; they may overestimate, even to some extent consciously, the probability of their own success; and they may simply enjoy optimistic expectations even at the expense of behavioral distortions. And yet their behavior is rational or, at least, it adapts and transforms what, taken individually and out of context, appear to be irrationalities into sensible, reasonable behavior. Furthermore, this behavior will often have social-welfare and individual-welfare enhancing properties.

Are the agents described in the aforementioned examples rational or irrational? As before, the answer is both. They are incompletely rational.[50]

---

49 Because the individual does not continually update his probabilities as he gets more experience, he is incompletely Bayesian.

50 And yet who among us is completely rational (except in some artificial model construct)? It is difficult to imagine what this could mean.

Overall Conclusions

The standard neoclassical construct of rationality is very narrow. This narrowness has served the function of providing a firm (read: axiomatic) foundation for a "psychology-free" choice theory, including the rigorous derivation of the utility function. Violations of this rationality construct, to the extent they occur, should be viewed as the failure of a model to explain instances of behavior and not, more broadly, as the failure of agents. Prescriptive rationality is a difficult business. It requires a broader view of rationality – one that is sensitive to the particular context and content of decisions.

The lesson that I have attempted to convey here is a rather basic one that is often forgotten or neglected. Intellectual constructs, such as neoclassical rationality, are *for something*. In a sense, there is no "rationality in the air," no all-purpose concept that can be used to evaluate all instances of individual or aggregate behavior. To believe the contrary is to reify a construction and to ignore its function. It is no doubt true that rationality in economics is instrumental rationality but that in itself does not require that the agents' behavior must in all circumstances obey the standard neoclassical rationality axioms. Reason is large.

12

Property, Intellectual Property, and Regulation

James Y. Stern

"At the high point of classical liberal thought," wrote Thomas Grey in his well-known essay *The Disintegration of Property*, "the idea of private property stood at the center of the conceptual scheme of lawyers and political theorists."[1] It was not to last, however. By the late twentieth century, Grey declared, property could no longer be considered "a coherent or crucial category in our conceptual scheme."[2] And the demise of property necessarily meant the demise of classical liberalism.

The argument was audacious when it first appeared and it has become even more provocative with the passage of time. In the decades since Grey wrote, property's institutional standing has arguably improved on a number of fronts, political, theoretical, and practical. One of the more obvious of these is the growth of the field referred to as intellectual property, or IP, which has emerged as a principal frontier of modern law and a major object of economic attention around the world. Unsurprisingly, the status and role of intellectual property are contested on a variety of grounds, but the fact of its significance today cannot seriously be gainsaid.

This chapter examines both property and intellectual property. It will offer some general comments about IP rights in an effort to help situate them within the larger domain of property and private law. Its ultimate aim, however, is less to explore whether IP rights are or resemble property rights than to consider what IP might tell us about property generally. It will suggest that the path taken by intellectual property law is an indication of the continued vitality of property as a fundamental legal concept, notwithstanding the collapse described in Grey's gloomy elegy.

---

[1] Thomas C. Grey, *The Disintegration of Property*, in NOMOS XXII: PROPERTY 69, 73 (J. Roland Pennock and John W. Chapman eds., 1980).

[2] *Id.* at 74.

I

Nearly four decades and several hundred citations later, it is worth revisiting the central claims in Grey's *Disintegration* essay. The best known of these, expressed in its title, was that the very concept of property had fallen apart. Property in its classical manifestation comprised two central elements, (a) *ownership* of (b) *things*, and both had become conceptually obsolete. Grey concentrated most of his fire on ownership. Blackstone famously equated property with "sole and despotic dominion which one man claims and exercises over the external things of the world ..."[3] But for today's specialist, Grey wrote, this hearty and simple understanding had been supplanted by a "more shadowy" notion of property as a bundle of rights.[4] As Grey acknowledged, this argument was anticipated in many respects by Legal Realism, which promoted the bundle-of-rights view of property.[5] The Legal Realists, though, were motivated in part by a desire to "remove the sanctity that had traditionally attached to the rights of property" because private property stood as an obstacle to the regulatory and welfare state.[6] Grey argued, however, that the Realists' program was basically superfluous. Something like the bundle-of-sticks conception of property was bound to emerge as a natural result of pressures generated by market capitalism itself, without any help from its critics.

At any rate, whether natural or intentional, the result of the bundle conception of property is the same, according to Grey. As the traditional notion of property as thing-ownership recedes, "the neutrality of the state as enforcer of private law evaporates: state protection of property rights is more easily seen as the use of collective force on behalf of the haves against the have-nots."[7] The conflict between capitalism and socialism, he wrote, can no longer be seen as a clash between liberty and equality but as a matter of finding the appropriate blend of two institutional techniques that advance liberty by different means. Property as such cannot be understood as a manifestation or a component of freedom. Property is itself a form of regulation.

* * *

Time hasn't been entirely kind to Grey's thesis. The fall of the Soviet Union, a geopolitical empire founded on antipathy to private property, eliminated the most direct political challenge to property-based liberalism and exerted powerful effects on the philosophical treatment of property. Though the aftermath was in no sense a runaway victory for classical liberalism, the triumph of the capitalist West

---

[3]   2 WILLIAM BLACKSTONE, COMMENTARIES *2.

[4]   Grey, *supra* note 1, at 69.

[5]   The realist project was also carried forward by the Critical Legal Studies movement.

[6]   Grey, *supra* note 1, at 81.

[7]   *Id.* at 79.

encouraged a wave of "neoliberalism" and a general shift in favor of markets, deregulation, and privatization.[8] No less significant, the notion of ownership continues to structure many of basic social relationships, and it plays a fundamental role in more complex economic arrangements as well. Rights in assets may be fragmented, recombined, and fragmented again, but those fragments of ownership are themselves owned. Whether or not a corporate shareholder is properly thought of as a fractional owner of the corporation, at the very least the shareholder is assuredly an owner of her shares.[9]

Within the technical arena of legal doctrine, meanwhile, constitutional protection of property was strengthened in a series of Supreme Court decisions involving the Takings Clause, adding a certain prestige to the subject in the American context.[10] Indeed, the Court's unwillingness to go further in one much-publicized case,[11] provoked a nationwide backlash, suggesting that private property still has considerable hold on the popular political imagination.[12] At the same time, property scholars have undertaken careful examinations of the characteristics of the institution they study and in doing so provided sophisticated accounts of how property works – which implies, of course, that it can and often does.[13] These and other developments cast doubt on Grey's suggestion that property is no longer a legal or social institution of operational or theoretical significance.

At the same time, however, Grey's claims find some support in unexpected quarters. Much of the revivification of property within the American academic context has been utilitarian and consequentialist in character and in various degrees aligned with the wider law-and-economics movement. A central concern of this

---

[8] It is these effects, rather than the collapse of communism itself, that cuts against Grey's thesis.

[9] *Cf.* James Y. Stern, *Property's Constitution*, 101 CALIFORNIA LAW REVIEW 277, 303–04 (2013) (arguing that rights are themselves things and that rights-holders have property rights in their rights).

[10] *See, e.g.*, Horne v. Dep't of Agric., 135 U.S. 2419 (2015); Lucas v. South Carolina Coastal Council, 112 U.S. 2886 (1992); Nollan v. Calif. Coastal Comm'n, 483 U.S. 835 (1987); Loretto v. Teleprompter Manhattan CATV Corp., 458 U.S. 419 (1982).

[11] Kelo v. City of New London, 545 U.S. 469 (2005).

[12] *See generally* Ilya Somin, *The Limits of Backlash: Assessing the Political Response to* Kelo, 93 MINNESOTA LAW REVIEW 2100 (2009).

[13] *See, e.g.*, J. E. PENNER, THE IDEA OF PROPERTY IN LAW (1997); CAROL M. ROSE, PROPERTY AND PERSUASION: ESSAYS ON THE HISTORY, THEORY, AND RHETORIC OF OWNERSHIP (1994); ROBERT C. ELLICKSON, ORDER WITHOUT LAW: HOW NEIGHBORS SETTLE DISPUTES (1991); ELINOR OSTROM, GOVERNING THE COMMONS: THE EVOLUTION OF INSTITUTIONS FOR COLLECTIVE ACTION (1990); GARY D. LIBECAP, CONTRACTING FOR PROPERTY RIGHTS (1989); Thomas W. Merrill and Henry E. Smith, *The Property/Contract Interface*, 101 COLUMBIA LAW REVIEW 773 (2001); Michael A. Heller, *The Tragedy of the Anti-Commons: Property in Transition from Marx to Markets*, 111 HARVARD LAW REVIEW 621 (1998); Dean Lueck, *The Rule of First Possession and the Design of the Law*, 38 JOURNAL OF LAW & ECONOMICS 393 (1995); Richard A. Epstein, *Holdouts, Externalities, and the Single Owner: One More Salute to Ronald Coase*, 36 JOURNAL OF LAW & ECONOMICS 553, 557 (1993); James E. Krier, *The Tragedy of the Commons, Part Two*, 15 HARVARD JOURNAL OF LAW & PUBLIC POLICY 325 (1992); Margaret Jane Radin, *Property and Personhood*, 34 STANFORD LAW REVIEW 957, 957 (1982).

mode of analysis is the effect legal rules and institutions have on human behavior. Law will create incentives to act in particular ways, and these effects can be predicted on the assumption that human beings are to some considerable extent rational and self-interested. So far as property is concerned, the goal is to shape legal incentives in order to make the most of the use of the world's scarce resources. This can be accomplished by ensuring that individuals are able to reap the rewards that flow from whatever choices they make concerning the use of particular resources and are prevented from projecting the costs of their behavior onto others. Equally if not more important, property can reduce waste by directing resource rights to higher-valued users, either by direct assignment or by reducing costs of transacting and thereby unlocking gains from trade.

Law and economics are different disciplines that can point in opposite directions, and while law may come first in the movement's name, economics is primary. So far as economic analysis of the law is concerned, law is the means by which the ends specified by economic thought are pursued. The resolution of a given legal problem is to be ascertained not by deducing the answer from legal materials through the techniques of legal reasoning but by recourse to the expected consequences of various outcomes on human behavior – that is, by reference to sound policy.

This perspective can be refreshing both for its practicality and often its apparent clarity. Even where the real-world consequences of a given legal regime cannot be assessed, the indeterminacy of this mode of analysis is often at least theoretically soluble – the problem is "merely" epistemic, not conceptual. At the same time, however, however, this approach is in obvious tension with the role of law to the extent it suggests the driving consideration in the actual resolution of legal problems should be efficiency, rather than the law's demands on its own terms. Even as a matter of positive description, without implying anything about how particular cases ought to be resolved, the emphasis on practical consequences over legal reasoning can result in a failure to appreciate how the law actually operates.[14]

Of course, sensible economic analysis cannot altogether neglect the role of institutions within the overall legal system. And in recent years, some leading scholars associated with the law-and-economics tradition have mounted a qualified defense of certain conceptual and doctrinal constraints in property law, suggesting that an excessive commitment to function over form may overlook and undermine the functional advantages that formalism can offer.[15] Nevertheless, even this

---

[14] For example, the simple view that an award of purely compensatory damages for violation of an entitlement is equivalent to a transfer of the entitlement (or portion of it) has a way of obscuring the fact that such damages are generally limited to cases in which the violation was accidental. It's also hard to square with, say, recordation procedures or tax law – as though the defendant in a case of accidental trespass were required to pay income or property tax on the "license" so received.

[15] *See, e.g.*, Thomas W. Merrill and Henry E. Smith, *Optimal Standardization in the Law of Property: The* Numerus Clausus *Principle*, 110 YALE LAW JOURNAL 1 (2000).

neo-formalist turn in property scholarship necessarily looks beyond the horizon of property itself to what is implicitly recognized as a superior normative aspiration and frames property within a paramount structure of legislation and regulation. Economic analysis has helped revitalize the study of private law in the United States but it has done so in part by treating property as wholly subordinate to an independent notion of social welfare, devoid of an internal logic that generates normatively compelling demands of its own force.

* * *

Recall that in arguing property had disintegrated, Grey emphasized a "bundle of rights" account of property, which he considered a more accurate characterization of contemporary property law than the classical vision of ownership. Much has been written about the bundle-of-rights metaphor, and rather than wade into that well-developed debate,[16] the goal here is simply to clarify and point out some features of the view of property typified by bundlism.

At the outset, it's worth observing that the bundle metaphor gains a good deal of its traction because it is ambiguous in important respects. There are two basic versions of the bundle, only one of which is a significant source of dispute and debate. The weaker and relatively uncontroversial version treats the idea as simply an analytic device – a conceptual technique – that may sometimes be helpful insofar as it makes it easier to understand the specifics of particular configurations of property rights. Ownership applies in different ways for different types of resources and different contexts, ownership is only one type of property entitlement, and individuals can alter the rights they and others have in particular resources through transfer. The notion of property as a bundle of rights can help to describe these aspects of variation in property as a legal type. Thus, for instance, when a landowner grants an easement to her neighbor, she is thought to have transmitted a portion of her larger ownership right to the neighbor. The purely analytic version of the bundle metaphor treats that fragment as one member in a larger set of sub-rights that collectively add up to ownership.[17]

The stronger and controversial version of the bundle of rights account, however, is more normatively loaded. It suggests not that our understanding of particular

---

[16] *See, e.g.,* Thomas W. Merrill and Henry E. Smith, *Why Restate the Bundle? The Disintegration of the Restatement of Property,* 79 Brooklyn Law Review 681 (2014); Jane B. Baron, *Rescuing the Bundle-of-Rights Metaphor in Property Law,* 82 University of Cincinnati Law Review 57 (2013); Eric R. Claeys, *Property 101: Is Property a Thing or a Bundle?,* 32 Seattle University Law Review 617 (2009) (book review); J.E. Penner, *The "Bundle of Rights" Picture of Property,* 43 UCLA Law Review 711 (1996). *See also generally* Symposium, Property: A Bundle Of Rights?, 8 Econ J. Watch 193 (2011).

[17] *Cf.* James Y. Stern, *The Essential Structure of Property Law,* 115 Michigan Law Review 1167, 1182–83 (2017) (suggesting property may be better understood in terms of a pie than a bundle for this reason).

property arrangements can often be improved by mentally subdividing individual entitlements, but that there is really nothing to subdivide in the first place; property has no necessary structure or form and that consequently property cannot or should not impose constraints on government regulation. The essential difference between the weak and the strong version of the bundle metaphor is that the weak version leaves open the possibility that property has default positions – molecules as well as atoms – and that its idealized forms do real work in structuring its everyday operation. The strong version of the bundle metaphor, by contrast, conceptualizes property as fundamentally ad hoc, if it is anything at all. It was this second sense in which Grey, following on the Legal Realists, described property as a bundle of rights. While Grey disclaimed any ideological motivation, his ultimate point was that the fragmentation of property undermined the conceptual foundations of classical liberalism and its suppositions about individual liberty precisely because there was no longer any there there where property was concerned.

Often as not, talk of property as a bundle is essentially atmospheric, rather than descriptive in any serious way. Whether the concept of ownership really does affect how the law plays out should be subject to empirical investigation (with further questions to be resolved about how big that impact would have to be for the bundle metaphor to be called into question). In practice, however, the strong form of the bundle often serves more as a kind of slogan.[18] The exaggerated Blackstonian notion of something that is *mine-all-mine* is countered by the notion that property is *just* a bundle of rights. The false proposition that one can do absolutely anything with what one owns is met by the equally false proposition that because property is subject to some limitation, it is therefore subject to any limitation. The recurring opposition of these two tropes amounts to a wrestling match between strawmen that would be too tedious to watch were the consequences not so important.

The real point here isn't about the bundle of rights metaphor itself. At the end of the day, it seems unlikely that an institution as significant as property, much less a general philosophy of politics, would turn on a single figure of speech, itself susceptible to opposing interpretations. In reality, the bundle of rights debate is a kind of proxy war in a larger struggle, the terms of which Grey outlined fairly accurately. The strong version of the bundle metaphor represents a rejection of the idea of property as an institution with formal integrity or normative weight – and is rightly understood as an attack on the institutional framework of classical liberal politics.[19]

---

[18] *Accord* J. E. Penner, *The "Bundle of Rights" Picture of Property*, 43 UCLA LAW REVIEW 711, 714 (1996).

[19] *See* Gary Peller, *Privilege*, 104 GEORGETOWN LAW JOURNAL 883, 885 (2016) ("Seeing property interests as a necessarily ad hoc bundle of rights against injury and privileges to injure was an important dimension of the more general realist point that purportedly private fields of law such as contracts, torts, and property actually involved public regulation (and distribution) rather than merely facilitative private law.").

It is not, however, an attack on property per se. There is an important irony in the essentially critical approach represented by the ad hoc bundle conception of property. If property is plastic enough to allow for any bundle of rights the law might care to fashion, then by the same token *any* bundle of rights is property – which might suggest, for instance, that constitutional protection is appropriate for every legal entitlement a person holds.[20] This formal conundrum might perhaps be evaded by weakening the implications of classifying a legal relationship as property – watering down the demands of just compensation or due process, for instance – but that in turn brings more fundamental difficulties into view.

The classical liberal understanding of politics presupposes an opposition between private rights and public regulation. In characterizing the existence and shape of property as fundamentally arbitrary, the ad hoc bundle school implies the negation of the pivotal distinction between private and public. Property is treated as a choice, socially determined, and, as Grey suggested, to see property as a type of regulation is seen to deny private property a role in limiting the sphere of public regulation. Yet by the same token, this perspective makes it hard to identify principles of public power that would necessarily limit private property. If, for example, legislation is presumptively justified as the outcome of a struggle between competing interest groups, as various influential theories of democratic politics would have it, then the bundle conception opens the door to an expansion of property entitlements.[21] When the result yielded by the democratic process is a proliferation of private rights, that's just the way the democratic cookie crumbles.[22] For its part, law-and-economics scholarship also adopts the view of property as a form of regulation.[23] But where regulation of every kind is to be measured against the common metric of efficiency, it is perfectly plausible the result would be more, rather than less, property. Thus, conclude William Landes and Richard Posner, "so far as is feasible, all valuable

---

[20] *Compare* RICHARD A. EPSTEIN, TAKINGS: PRIVATE PROPERTY AND THE POWER OF EMINENT DOMAIN 57–62 (1985) *with* Margaret Jane Radin, *The Liberal Conception of Property: Cross Currents in the Jurisprudence of Takings*, 88 COLUMBIA LAW REVIEW 1667, 1674–78 (1988).

[21] For a vivid articulation of this perspective on democratic theory, see EARL LATHAM, THE GROUP BASIS OF POLITICS 35–36 (1952) ("The legislature referees the group struggle, ratifies the victories of the successful coalitions, and records the terms of the surrenders, compromises, and conquests in the form of statutes."). *See also* Kathleen M. Sullivan, *Unconstitutional Conditions*, 102 HARVARD LAW REVIEW 1413, 1469 (1989) (stating that "interest-group pluralism is the unofficial theory of the Supreme Court – at least since the New Deal with respect to review of socioeconomic legislation."). Interest group pluralism is in the first instance a positive theory, but it has tended to support a generous normative stance toward democratic legislation.

[22] *Cf.* U.S. R.R. Ret. Bd. v. Fritz, 449 U.S. 166, 179 (1980); Williamson v. Lee Optical Co., 348 U.S. 483 (1955).

[23] *See* RICHARD POSNER, ECONOMIC ANALYSIS OF LAW, 389 (7th ed. 2007) ("The choice is rarely between a free market and public regulation. It is between two methods of public control–the common law system of privately enforced rights and the administrative system of direct public control ..."); Robert C. Ellickson, *Three Systems of Land-Use Control*, 13 HARVARD JOURNAL OF LAW & PUBLIC POLICY 67, 68 (1990) ("What we ordinarily think of as private property ... is a form of regulation.").

resources ... should be owned."[24] Of course, feasibility is potentially an important constraint. But in practice it is more than a little elastic for both conceptual and epistemic reasons.

The strong version of the bundle metaphor is generally offered as a critical tool, in the deconstructionist sense of "critical studies." But deconstruction is an intrinsically negative enterprise and can only go so far. Discrediting the sanctity of property does not also establish its damnation. The irony is that the attack on the integrity of property – the disintegration, as Grey called it – could easily result in a property expansion, rather than an implosion.

                                        II

One of the more curious aspects of Grey's essay was the second prong of his disintegration argument: his claim that property could no longer be understood as rights to *things* because "most property in the modern capitalist economy is intangible."[25] These nonphysical assets include not only abstract claims to resources like bank accounts and share certificates but also "more arcane intangibles such as trademarks, patents, copyrights, franchises, and business goodwill," which is to say, intellectual property.[26] IP was hardly novel at the time of Grey's writing, but its significance has increased exponentially in the decades since his essay appeared. If Grey is correct that the growth of intellectual property contributes to the disintegration of property, then property has endured quite a drubbing over the last forty years. That, however, simply doesn't ring true. To be sure, one could imagine that the kinds of limitations placed on IP rights – the temporal expiration of copyrights and patents, for instance, or the fair use defense in copyright law – might bleed over to the law of real and personal property.[27] By and large, however, this has not happened,[28] and it is worth considering why.

Grey's bundle-based attack on the notion of ownership was developed more fully than his attack on the notion of rights in things, and his argument against thing-rights was quite weak. Even if it is true that "most property"[29] is now intangible, so what? The capacity of the property concept to extend to intangibles might seem like an indication of its durability, rather than its obsolescence. Perhaps what Grey really meant is that these rights aren't really property rights at all – that there is something un-thinglike about intangible things. But the sentence refutes itself. Although

---

[24] William M. Landes and Richard A. Posner, *Indefinitely Renewable Copyright*, 70 University of Chicago Law Review 471, 475 (2003).

[25] Grey, *supra* note 1, at 70.

[26] *Id.*

[27] *See* Peter S. Menell, *The Property Rights Movement's Embrace of Intellectual Property: True Love or Doomed Relationship?*, 34 Ecology Law Quarterly 713 (2007).

[28] *Cf.* Ben Depoorter, *Fair Trespass*, 111 Columbia Law Review 1090, 1094 (2011) (proposing that it should).

[29] Grey, *supra* note 1, at 70.

intangibles are often less immediate than physical objects,[30] it isn't clear how intangibility detracts from thinghood in any categorical sense, much less one relevant to the concept of property. "Grey cannot grasp the concept of a thing that he cannot grasp," as Jeanne Schroeder puts it.[31] Many others, however, are more dexterous.[32]

So far as the relationship between property and intellectual property is concerned, the more common position is that intellectual property is influenced by the concept of property – indeed, too much so – than the other way around. Academic commentary in the United States generally accepts the view that IP is a form of regulation.[33] The dominant position, by and large, is that IP *should* disintegrate more than it does.

The language of "intellectual property" arises in part out of the resemblance in form between IP rights and classical manifestations of property – the notion of rights against the world defined in terms of control over the use of discrete things. In a purely formal or conceptual sense, IP testifies to the enduring power of this institutional structure. That fact, however, only partly refutes Grey's assertions. Grey's ultimate point about property concerned its role within a larger set of beliefs about liberty and politics. Here, too, the development of intellectual property is revealing, but the story is a little longer in the telling.

* * *

The starting point in the standard academic analysis of intellectual property, at least within the United States, is the proposition that ideas and information are non-rivalrous.[34] In essence, what this means is that these information goods are shareable: One person's consumption doesn't diminish another's. Two people can't swallow the same pill or play the same violin, but they can take the same kind of medicine or play the same sonata.

Because of this, intellectual property law is thought to be something of a misnomer, or at least an uneasy fit, so far as property is concerned. In purely formal or conceptual terms, property in what are largely rivalrous physical resources resolves conflicts over how those resources are to be used. Neoclassical economic theory goes a step farther, suggesting that waste can be minimized by assigning property

---

[30] Even so, intangible things can be quite important, meaningful, and visceral – think, for example, of God, the United States, a marriage, or Haliburton.

[31] Jeanne L. Schroeder, *Chix Nix Bundle-O-Stix: A Feminist Critique of the Disaggregation of Property*, 93 MICHIGAN LAW REVIEW 239, 274 (1994).

[32] *See* Felix S. Cohen, *Dialogue on Private Property*, 9 RUTGERS LAW REVIEW 357, 360, 369 (1954).

[33] *See, e.g.*, Mark A. Lemley, *Taking the Regulatory Nature of IP Seriously*, 92 TEXAS LAW REVIEW SEE ALSO 107 (2014) ("Intellectual property (IP) is a form of market entry and price regulation."); Shubha Ghosh, *Patent Law and the Assurance Game: Refitting Intellectual Property in the Box of Regulation*, 18 CANADIAN JOURNAL OF LAW & JURISPRUDENCE 307 (2005).

[34] *See* Dan L. Burk, *Law and Economics of Intellectual Property: In Search of First Principles*, 8 ANNUAL REVIEW OF LAW & SOCIAL SCIENCE 397, 406 (2012).

rights to those most value individual resources – in other words, by seeking to ensure that resource conflicts are resolved in favor of whomever would derive the greatest benefit from prevailing. The simplest version of this form of analysis is simply a snapshot picture of the world, or what is referred to as static efficiency. If A derives greater benefits from a resource than B or C, overall social wealth would be maximized if the resource is given to A.

If information goods are non-rivalrous, however, they do not slot into the conceptual role of traditional property rights because they don't generate the conflicts that traditional property rights resolve.[35] And from the standpoint of static efficiency, there's no need to ascertain the highest-valuing user since all users can be accommodated. The optimal allocation of a non-rivalrous information good is to give it to everyone who wants it. Rather than a tool that can be used to maximize overall welfare through a more efficient distribution of scarce goods, a system of property in information goods is necessarily inefficient from a static perspective.[36] If IP rights can be justified, the thinking goes, it is only as a form of incentive that will encourage the production of information goods. Intellectual property is functionally equivalent to a system of subsidies or bounties, offering a reward to creators in the form of a kind of artificial property – or what is often described as "monopoly" in the sense that the exclusivity that IP rights provide prevents competition by others. There is nothing natural or conceptually intuitive about intellectual property rights; they represent a conscious decision to distort natural market conditions of free competition.[37]

This view tends to dominate the theoretical treatment of intellectual property in the United States, but it doesn't align as neatly with actual intellectual property law. Of course, theory and practice are seldom if ever in perfect harmony, but the source of the disconnect runs deeper because the non-rivalry story misses the mark in a fundamental way. As I have explained in greater detail elsewhere,[38] the possibility of sharing a resource as a brute technical matter doesn't necessarily translate to an absence of resource conflicts and it doesn't necessarily mean that static efficiency is achieved by allowing everyone who wants access to a resource to have it. While it is often true the same information good can be consumed by more than one person, that fact is not itself sufficient to preclude the concept of property. In terms of simple resource conflict, one person may oppose another's use of a resource. If A would like to publish a letter B once wrote to an old flame and B would like the letter to remain private, the fact that A might be able to copy the letter without preventing B from

---

[35] *See* C. Edwin Baker, *First Amendment Limits on Copyright*, 55 Vanderbilt Law Review 891, 907 (2002).

[36] *See* Matthew Sag, *Copyright and Copy-Reliant Technology*, 103 Northwestern University Law Review 1607, 1614 (2009).

[37] *See* Mark A. Lemley, Property, *Intellectual Property, and Free Riding*, 83 Texas Law Review 1031, 1055 (2005).

[38] *See* James Y. Stern, *Intellectual Property and the Myth of Nonrivalry* (unpublished).

having a copy of his own is beside the point, which is that their preferences concerning the use of the information contained in the letter are incompatible. Instinctively, the law recognizes this fact and it is for this reason that intellectual property rights are in many ways more generous toward rights-holders than the incentives-only theory of IP allows.

To translate this conceptual point to efficiency terms, lessening others' consumption opportunities is only one way a person's use of a resource might generate negative external costs. And where one person's action imposes costs on another, economic analysis calls for a comparison of the relative costs and benefits. If A is harmed by B's use of an information good more than B is benefitted by it, then granting B an entitlement to use the resource would not maximize overall social welfare, assuming positive transaction costs. In short, it isn't axiomatically true that intellectual property results in static inefficiency, as the dogma of non-rivalry has it. This shouldn't come as a surprise. The law restricts the transmission of information in any number of ways – think of privacy rights or confidentiality agreements – and there is no reason to think that these are inherently wasteful. IP law can and does perform similar functions, but the non-rivalry story can make it hard to see this. Copyright laws are used to advance interests in privacy and artistic integrity, for instance, a fact that is difficult to assimilate into the received learning about incentives as the only conceivable function such rights can perform.[39]

At the same time, however, the full potential to use IP rights in this manner is unrealized. I will focus in particular on copyright and patent law, the two forms of IP consciously contemplated by the Constitution. These rights are subject to significant limitations, three of which merit special mention here. First, patents and copyrights are available only to creators of protectable works (and their successors in interest). They aren't simply sold off to the highest bidder. Second, they come with expiration dates, roughly twenty years for patents and one hundred years for copyrights. Finally, both are replete with limitations on the protection of "ideas," or what might be thought of as upstream raw materials. Patent protection is unavailable for natural laws, abstract ideas, and natural phenomena, for example.[40] Copyright protection is unavailable for facts, however difficult it may have been to obtain them, as well as for "ideas," as distinguished from particular "expressions" of them.[41]

It is by no means impossible to offer utilitarian justifications for these limitations but those justifications are hardly airtight.[42] Consider the exclusion of basic research

---

[39] *Cf.* Jeanne C. Fromer, *Expressive Incentives in Intellectual Property*, 98 Virginia Law Review 1745, 1777 (2012) (discussing the incentive possibilities of creative interests).

[40] *See* Alice Corp. v. CLS Bank International, 573 U.S. __, 134 S. Ct. 2347 (2014).

[41] *See* Feist Publications, Inc., v. Rural Telephone Service Co., 499 U.S. 340 (1991).

[42] These include the difficulty defining and communicating the property status of information goods, dangers of monopolization, rent-seeking, costs of administration, potential overinvestment in information relative to other economic goods, and dynamic inefficiencies due to diminished follow-on development. *See* Lemley, *supra* note 37, at 1058–65, Richard A. Posner,

from patent protection and of ideas from copyright protection. It is said that follow-on creators need access to these materials, and that protection will therefore impede further development. This objection ultimately depends on transaction costs, otherwise, someone who developed a useful application of a valuable idea could license the idea from the rights-holder, just as a follow-on developer can obtain a license from the holder of a pioneer patent. In other words, the problem is that it would be too cumbersome to obtain the necessary permissions in cases where rights-holders would otherwise be willing to grant them.

The transaction cost argument is incomplete, however, for it is equally the case that the transaction costs for someone who would be harmed by such development and who would be willing to pay to prevent it might be considerable. Indeed, in many cases, the effect is asymmetric. Someone interested in preventing the use of an information good will often be harmed when it is used by anyone and thus if that information good is placed in the public domain, the person must bargain "in rem" – with the whole world – to ensure it isn't used. The converse paradigm is simpler. If an information good is subject to IP protection but a large number of people want to use it, transaction costs can be mitigated through any number of institutions that capture, aggregate, and channel social demand – manufacturers of finished products that use protected information goods as inputs, businesses that transmit information goods to the public directly such as publishers and broadcasters, licensing organizations like ASCAP and BMI, and non-profit and educational institutions. To a considerable extent, these sorts of entities serve as representatives of the public at large. Private property does not eliminate transaction costs, but it can reduce them.[43] The essential question is whether the default order property rights establish is so systematically wasteful (or the cost of administering the system so great) as to offset whatever gains they offer in facilitating voluntary reconfigurations.

From an efficiency standpoint, it is unclear whether more widespread use of IP rights to mediate conflicts over information goods would be desirable. The advantages of such a regime depend on the magnitude of the external costs of various activities that would be captured by a more robust system of patents and copyrights and any transaction costs that would be saved by instituting such a system. The disadvantages include the value of any foregone activities, the transaction costs necessary to obtain rights to undertake activities, and the not-inconsiderable costs of administering such a system. These variables are hard to assess. From ten thousand feet, it is difficult to rule out the possibility that more widespread use of IP rights to mediate conflicts over the use of information goods would lead to more efficient outcomes, at least in some discrete categories of cases. But if the empirics

---

Do We Have Too Many Intellectual Property Rights?, 9 MARQUETTE INTELLECTUAL PROPERTY LAW REVIEW 173 (2005).

[43] *See* Harold Demsetz, *Toward a Theory of Property Rights*, 57 AMERICAN ECONOMIC REVIEW PAPERS AND PROCEEDINGS 347 (1967).

are uncertain, the verdict of the legal system is not. A more generalized system of private rights in information goods – one available, say, to non-creators – has not emerged. Ultimately, the rejection of such a system offers some evidence that the concept of property is stickier and the foundations of classical liberalism a bit surer than Grey imagined.

* * *

It is interesting that conflicts between use and non-use appear to be more common in the context of expressive works than practical technologies – that is to say, in the domain of copyright rather than patent law. At least some of the difference is probably an artifact of the legal system, rather than a reflection of the underlying realities of social conflict. The relatively short duration of patent protection, as well as the demanding requirements of novelty and non-obviousness that must be satisfied for a patent to issue, make patent law a generally poor mechanism for controlling the use of technologies. An opponent of capital punishment or birth control, for instance, would generally do better to lobby the Food and Drug Administration to restrict the use of the drugs used to carry at these practices than to try to acquire a patent for them. Copyright has its limitations, to be sure, but it nevertheless provides rights-holders a more effective set of legal tools to limit disfavored uses of the information goods whose use it governs.

Even making allowance for these contingent institutional differences, however, it seems to be the case that creators, copyright-holders, and even third parties are more easily troubled or offended by the use of expressive material than is the case in the domain of inventions and technology. The reported cases offer numerous examples of copyright-holders motivated to sue others who copied their works for reasons that are essentially nonpecuniary.[44] Analogous patent infringement cases are much harder to find, and it seems likely this would be so even if the structural contours of patent law were more like those of copyright.

Why might this be? For one thing, it may suggest that a creator's personality is perceived as being implicated in a more significant way for expressive works than for inventions. So-called moral rights protection, for example, has thus far been adopted only for those perceived to be involved in the creation of art.[45] There is also a certain extent to which objections to the use of technologies may be more limited than objections to expressive works. In particular, the most immediate negative effects stemming from the use of technologies may be more spatially or geographically circumscribed than for communicative works. The character of the objection to a practical technology, we might say, is more practical and more a function of physical

---

[44] *See, e.g.,* Bridge Publications v. Vien, 827 F. Supp. 629, 632 (S.D. Cal. 1993); Salinger v. Random House, Inc., 811 F.2d 90 (2d Cir. 1987).

[45] *See* Mark A. Lemley, *The Economics of Improvement in Intellectual Property Law,* 75 Texas Law Review 989, 1031 (1997).

location than an ideological objection.[46] In many cases, someone who dislikes windfarms or subwoofers might not care much or at all about uses taking place outside their immediate environs. By contrast, someone who thinks a particular book is blasphemous might desire its suppression everywhere. Obviously such a distinction isn't at all absolute. It is not hard to imagine instances where someone might object to the use of a technology far away. Nevertheless, it's probably true that harms caused by the use of technologies often will be more localized than harms arising from expressive works. The upshot is that the desire to restrict the use of objectionable technologies may align more neatly with the framework of territorially defined public regulation.

At any rate, if, as appears to be the case, it is more likely individuals will desire to restrict access to expressive works than to practical technologies, it is notable that the law offers a more forceful challenge to attempts to do so. Copyright protection is often thought to be limited by free speech values and even, perhaps, by the hard limitations of the First Amendment. In a post-*Lochner* world, there is no equivalent principle that operates to limit patent protection, or, for that matter, the regulation of technologies generally. This may tell us a bit about freedom of speech, as both a social value and a constitutional limitation on state action.

A central question for advocates of free speech is why speech is "special," why speech must be tolerated when other kinds of behavior are not.[47] For its part, classical liberalism tends to look somewhat dubiously on the post-New Deal tendency to exalt such liberties over so-called economic rights of property and contract. The patterns of intellectual property protection and the enforcement of intellectual property rights point toward what may be a relevant difference – the likelihood that the expression of ideas will inspire regulation, and especially ideologically-motivated regulation, to an extent material or practical goods will not.[48] This explanation only makes sense, however, if such regulation itself is somehow thought to be suspect – if there is some reason to prefer freedom to speak over freedom from speech. In other words, there appears to be a certain libertarian sensibility undergirding the free speech idea. To this extent, the special weight given to free speech concerns in constitutional doctrine may be more consistent with a classical liberal outlook than first appears. And this provides a window into some broader features of intellectual property law.

The general question posed here is why the legal system appears to be reluctant to capitalize on the notion of IP as regulation and to use IP rights as a tool to internalize the costs that various activities involving the use of information goods impose on others. Why not, for instance, establish a general system of private rights

---

[46] I am grateful to Lee Fennell for this suggestion.

[47] *See generally* Frederick Schauer, *Must Speech Be Special?*, 78 NORTHWESTERN UNIVERSITY LAW REVIEW 1284 (1983).

[48] *Cf.* FRED SCHAUER, FREE SPEECH: A PHILOSOPHICAL ENQUIRY 86 (1982) (endorsing "government incompetence" theory of free speech).

to control the use of genetically modified foods or elevator music? These notional "things" bring pleasure to some but distress to others, at least in certain contexts and sometimes across-the-board. A system of tradeable rights to regulate such activities might be thought to bring about a more efficient set of permissions and prohibitions than command-and-control legislation. What, then, has stopped intellectual property law from embracing such a paradigm?

The libertarian undercurrent in freedom of speech commitments suggested above offers a useful place to start. The notion that information goods are non-rivalrous in consumption and that private rights therefore aren't needed to internalize externalities implicitly distinguishes between two kinds of costs that an activity could have on others and ignores one of them. The first arises when someone's consumption of a good diminishes the ability of someone else to consume the good herself. The claim that IP is non-rivalrous and therefore a kind of artificial property considers these costs but assumes they are basically non-existent. The second sort of costs arises where one person's consumption of a good upsets someone else or causes some kind of harm unrelated to a diminishing their ability to use or consume the good. These kinds of external costs are implicitly ignored.

So far as understandings of intellectual property are driven by a commitment to preference-satisfaction, the nonrivalry story entails a certain laundering of preferences.[49] That may not be consistent with the premises of neoclassical economic analysis, but it has significant intuitive appeal. Here the law of real property – that is, ownership of land – is illuminating. In advocating a live-and-let-live principle in nuisance law, the influential nineteenth century jurist Baron Bramwell suggested that relatively small harms arising out of ordinary social behavior should not be actionable because the benefits of being able to engage in such behavior are reciprocally shared. Today's victim, in a sense, is tomorrow's beneficiary.[50] But reciprocity – a stylized version of equality – is itself indifferent between equal rights to restrict and equal freedom from restriction. It might, so to speak, be the case that everyone is happier or better off being King for a day and a subject the remaining three hundred sixty-four than in a state of constant equality.

Richard Epstein, Bramwell's latter-day champion, has made just this point and attempted to shore up Bramwell's position with the further assertion that it simply is true as an empirical matter that the benefits of freedom exceed the value to be had in restricting others. Perhaps this is right but reasonable minds might well differ. To be sure, there are obviously some cases where it holds. An equal right to eat is more desirable than an equal right to demand that others starve. But there are also

---

[49] Cf. Howard F. Chang, A Liberal Theory of Social Welfare: Fairness, Utility, and the Pareto Principle, 110 YALE LAW JOURNAL 173, 183–86 (2000).

[50] See Bamford v. Turnley, 122 Eng. Rep 27, 32–33 (Ex. 1862). At some point, protection against de minimis harms might be more trouble than it's worth, but Bramwell seems to have something else in mind than simple administrative cost, which could be an adequate reason to ignore such injuries even in the absence of any kind of reciprocity.

obviously cases where it does not. An equal right to commit murder is less desirable than an equal right not to be murdered. In between these polar cases, the balance of utilities grows elusive. The utilitarian case against easements for light and view is debatable, as the different attitudes struck by English and American law suggest.

What seems likelier, at least as an explanation of why things are the way they are, is that harms arising personal distaste, offense, contempt, and the like are viewed with disfavor as a basis for recognizing duties that restrict the ability of others to act as they see fit. Such impulses can be expressed, if at all, only through rights instituted on some other basis, such as rights against trespass to property. Curtailment of the freedom to act requires justification, and certain justifications that are anti-social or psychologically malleable are widely seen as inadequate to meet that burden. In short, freedom – and its corollary, toleration – is understood as having value in and of itself, not simply a more convenient or efficient state of affairs. The assertion "It's none of your business" doesn't entirely rest on a conclusion that life would be more cumbersome if "business" were defined broadly but on an idea of what is a matter of legitimate concern to someone else. There may well be an efficiency-based case to be made for stronger rights to control irritating, disfavored, or offensive uses of inventions and creative works. But both the legal system and the supposedly utilitarian theoretical accounts frequently used to analyze it implicitly adopt the view that freedom to act and objections by others to such action stand on unequal footing.

A second point, often made, concerns labor. One need not be a thorough-going Lockean to appreciate the connection between private property and productive labor as a matter of simple social reality. The idea that a person has a claim to the fruits of her labor – to the direct consequences of purposeful, valuable action – has some intuitive force, and the notion that there is something somehow unjust about taking away or destroying what someone else has labored to build seems hard completely to escape. The extent to which intellectual property law is actually necessary to encourage the production of information goods is extraordinarily difficult to establish, but it doesn't really seem to matter. Intellectual property may be misbegotten, but its strength conceptually and politically clearly derives in substantial measure from normative intuitions associated with property rights in physical resources. At the same time, intellectual property rights aren't generally available as an all-purpose tool to regulate the conduct of others in part for the very reason that they are tied to acts of creation.

Finally, viewing property rights as nothing more than a form of regulation seems to miss something important about the position property is seen to occupy within the larger framework of the law. The idea that ownership is a version regulatory authority is in tension with certain deep philosophical commitments. The distinction between public and private was attacked by the Realists and their successors in order to justify greater curtailment and redefinition of recognized forms of private right. But, as noted earlier, the line between public and private also distinguishes public from private interests in ways that limit private power. Thus the New Deal included not only curtailments of private right, but also attempts to confer substantial grants of regulatory authority on industries.[51] This corporatist model never achieved substantial popular appeal, however, and complaints about "crony capitalism" in contemporary politics reflect continuing antipathy to the notion of treating public authority as a private plaything.[52]

Imagine a member of Congress presented with the idea of establishing a system of privately held, tradeable rights to regulate technologies. No member of Congress would dare advance such a proposal, not because it might prove to be inconvenient but because the notion that regulatory power should be privatized offends widely shared notions of the basis for government power. The supposedly moribund public-private distinction operates here as a limitation on the "delegation" of public power.[53] Within our legal tradition, neither property nor intellectual property is seen as a form of regulation equivalent to an exercise of the police power or an administrative rule-making. The view that private rights and public powers are different in kind is almost certainly at least part of the reason that copyright law isn't generally taken to offend the strictures of the First Amendment. But this separation between public and private also limits the justifications available for legal institutions and constrains the forms that they may take.

This isn't in any way to deny that efforts to understand and improve public institutions can be enriched by lessons from the context of private ones, or that private institutions and actors can be employed by public officials to accomplish public ends. It is simply to call attention to the dog that does not bark – the manifest unacceptability within our political culture of selling off public legislative powers as private goods to be exercised in the private interest. Intellectual property law is constrained by the concept of property, as well as by preferences for liberty of action and by notions of creation and dessert, and it cannot comfortably be re-imagined as a mechanism to bring about a more efficient, market-based set of conduct regulations.

CONCLUSION

The purpose of this discussion has been to explore the possibility of using IP rights as a form of regulation to address the problem of spillovers from the use of information goods and to see what light such an investigation might shed on the claims about private property and classical liberalism memorably articulated by Thomas Grey. Grey was surely right that today's law is far from what the classical liberal would

---

[51] *See, e.g.,* DONALD R. BRAND, CORPORATISM AND THE RULE OF LAW: A STUDY OF THE NATIONAL RECOVERY ADMINISTRATION 11 (1988) ("Scholars have unanimously referred to the National Recovery Administration . . . as America's foremost experiment with corporatism.").

[52] *See* Paul H. Rubin, *Crony Capitalism,* 23 SUPREME COURT ECONOMIC REVIEW 105 (2015).

[53] *Cf.* Henry E. Smith, *On the Economy of Concepts in Property,* 160 UNIVERSITY OF PENNSYLVANIA LAW REVIEW 2097, 2115 (2012) (describing property as a delegation of decision-making).

hope for, but just how far is not as easy to assess. The assertion that property is no longer a meaningful part of our legal system is plainly incorrect. The vitality of intellectual property law testifies to that. It isn't simply that patents, copyrights, trademarks and the like are referred to as "property" or that they incorporate property terms like "possession,"[54] "conveyance,"[55] or "in gross."[56] In addition to terminology and rhetoric, they adopt the formal structures and concepts of property law and are shaped by its theoretical foundations. Resistance to using IP rights as a regulatory device to manage the social costs of behavior more efficiently reveals an implicit bias toward liberty of action and an implicit commitment to the idea that private rights do something other than implement public powers acquired through market exchange. And if public powers should not be repackaged as private rights, the conceptual resources remain to argue that private rights should not be repackaged as public benefices, forever subject to reformulation in the name of the public good.

---

[54] *See* Capon v. Eshhar, 418 F.3d 1349, 1357 (Fed. Cir. 2005).
[55] *See* 28 U.S.C. § 201(d).
[56] *See* Green River Bottling Co. v. Green River Corp., 997 F.2d 359, 362 (7th Cir. 1993).

13

Classical Liberalism and the Problem of Technological Change

Justin (Gus) Hurwitz and Geoffrey A. Manne

INTRODUCTION

The relationship between classical liberalism and technology is surprisingly fraught. The common understanding is that technological advance is complementary to the principles of classical liberalism – especially in the case of contemporary, information-age technology.[1] This is most clearly on display in Silicon Valley, with its oft-professed libertarian (classical liberalism's kissing cousin) affinities. The analytical predicate for this complementarity is that classical liberalism values liberty-enhancing private ordering, and technological advance both is generally facially liberty-enhancing and facilitates private ordering.

This analysis, however, is incomplete. Classical liberalism recognizes that certain rules are necessary in a well-functioning polity.[2] The classical liberal, for instance, recognizes the centrality of enforceable property rights, and the concomitant ability to seek recourse from a third party (the state) when those rights are compromised. Thus, contemporary technological advances may facilitate private transactions – but such transactions may not support private ordering if they also weaken either the property rights necessary to that ordering or the enforceability of those rights.

---

[1] This chapter focuses on "contemporary technology." That is, generally, those technologies associated with the information revolution of the past generation: computers, the Internet, and related information communications and processing technologies. A treatment of the relationship between classical liberalism and a more generalized concept of technology is beyond the scope of this chapter. It is, however, the authors' view that the discussion offered here is relevant to such a broader conceptualization.

[2] *See, for example,* JOHN LOCKE, TWO TREATISES ON GOVERNMENT at §57 ("[T]he end of the law is, not to abolish or restrain, but to preserve and enlarge freedom. For . . . where there is no law there is no freedom."); FRIEDRICH A. HAYEK, LAW, LEGISLATION AND LIBERTY, VOLUME 1: RULES AND ORDER (1978) at 33 ("Liberalism . . . restricts deliberate control of the overall order of society to the enforcement of such general rules as are necessary for the formation of a spontaneous order, the details of which we cannot foresee.").

This chapter argues that technological advance can at times create (or, perhaps more accurately, highlight) a tension within principles of classical liberalism: It can simultaneously enhance liberty, while also undermining the legal rules and institutions necessary for the efficient and just private ordering of interactions in a liberal society. This is an important tension for classical liberals to understand – and one that needs to be, but too rarely is, acknowledged or struggled with. Related, the chapter also identifies and evaluates important fracture lines between prevalent branches of modern libertarianism: those that tend to embrace technological anarchism as maximally liberty-enhancing, on the one hand, and those that more cautiously protect the legal institutions (for example, property rights) upon which individual autonomy and private ordering are based, on the other.

This chapter proceeds in four parts. Part I introduces our understanding of classical liberalism's core principles: an emphasis on individual liberty; the recognition of a limit to the exercise of liberty when it conflicts with the autonomy of others; and support for a minimal set of rules necessary to coordinate individuals' exercise of their liberty in autonomy-respecting ways through a system of private ordering. Part II then offers an initial discussion of the relationship between technology and legal institutions and argues that technology is important to classical liberalism insofar as it affects the legal institutions upon which private ordering is based. Part III explores how libertarian philosophies have embraced contemporary technology, focusing on "extreme" and "moderate" views – views that correspond roughly to liberty maximalism and autonomy protectionism. This discussion sets the stage for Part IV, which considers the tensions that technological change – especially the rapid change that characterizes much of recent history – creates within the classical liberal philosophy. The central insight is that classical liberalism posits a set of relatively stable legal institutions as the basis for liberty-enhancing private ordering – institutions that are generally developed through public, not private ordering – but that technology, including otherwise liberty-enhancing technology, can disrupt these institutions in ways that threaten both individual autonomy and the private ordering built upon extant institutions.

I WHAT IS CLASSICAL LIBERALISM? A TECHNOLOGY-RELEVANT ACCOUNT

It may seem unnecessary to provide a background understanding of classical liberalism in a single chapter in an entire book on the subject. But, although the general contours are consistent, there is no universally acknowledged statement of the principles that define classical liberalism and they vary enough from understanding to understanding that it is useful to define how the term is used here. Moreover, the discussion that follows addresses how technology affects what we think of as certain of the *defining* characteristics of classical liberalism. As such, it is particularly useful for us to place these characteristics on the table and explain their importance before considering how technology may affect them.

At the outset, it is worth clearly stating, as a matter of discursive convenience, that we classify classical liberalism and libertarianism as closely related but distinct philosophies, where libertarianism encompasses a more restrictive view on what is properly the purview of the state. This is not intended to be analytically rigorous nor a complete characterization of either. Rather, it is based in the recognition that many technologists, both in academia and in industry, style themselves as libertarian (or "cyberlibertarian"), and that there is a certain complementarity between some of these views and our understanding of classical liberalism. The views of self-styled libertarian technologists therefore present a useful frame through which to consider the broader features of the classical liberal understanding of technology.

Other contributions to this volume discuss the origins and principles of classical liberalism in more detail and with more sophistication than is required here. For our purposes, it is enough to explain classical liberalism as a political philosophy that values reliance on a minimal set of autonomy-respecting rules to facilitate voluntary, welfare-enhancing transactions between individuals.[3] By and large, these "autonomy-respecting rules" are property rights.[4]

Importantly, this sets up an inherent tension in classical liberalism. Property is not the same thing as liberty and, in fact, it is a *constraint* on liberty. The nineteenth century French anarchist, Pierre-Joseph Proudhon, famously declared that "[p]roperty is theft!"[5] and, in a sense, it is: By recognizing or by defining and assigning property rights (and by enforcing them), the government removes something of value from the commons that was formerly accessible by anyone and transfers it to a particular person.

But just as importantly, the benefits of property are enjoyed by everyone. The system is decentralized such that *anyone* may, in principle, claim a property right over whatever she chooses provided she is the first to, say, possesses a piece of land,

---

3   Among many other sources for this general conception of classical liberalism, see, *for example*, Richard A. Epstein, *Let "The Fundamental Things Apply": Necessary and Contingent Truths in Legal Scholarship*, 115 Harvard Law Review 1300, 1302 (2002) ("[A] strong (but not absolute) *institutional* preference for consensual over forced exchanges; the legal system should find the former presumptively acceptable and the latter presumptively unacceptable. From this framework, we can mount a defense of private property and freedom of contract, subject to the usual provisos regarding the role of government in protecting individuals against the use of force and fraud, regulating monopoly, and providing public infrastructure.").

4   In the economic sense, as much as the legal sense, insofar as they establish not only a stable legal order for achieving distributive justice in Nozick's sense, *see, for example*, Robert Nozick, Anarchy, State and Utopia 149–52 (1974), but also enable an efficient economic order by reducing transaction costs, see, *for example*, Armen A. Alchian and Harold Demsetz, *The Property Right Paradigm*, 33 Journal of Economic History 16 (1973).

5   Pierre-Joseph Proudhon, What Is Property? An Inquiry into the Principle of Right and of Government (1840; Benjamin R. Tucker, trans., 1890), *available at* http://bit.ly/2toxPDC.

or otherwise assert her right as the result of voluntary exchange or by operation of law. Moreover, the incentives to invest, hire workers, produce things of value, and trade enabled by a system of property rights result in widespread social benefit. For classical liberals, the justification for the constraint on liberty entailed by property rights arises not from an appeal to natural order, but from the perceived social advantage it confers. As Richard Epstein has written:

> [T]hese rights are defensible because they help advance human happiness in a wide range of circumstances, so that their creation under a set of general prospective rules satisfies the most exacting of social criterion. They tend to leave no one worse off than in a state of nature, and indeed tend to spread their net benefits broadly over the entire population—including both those who gain property rights under the standard rules of acquisition by first possession, and those who participate in the system only through the ownership of their own labor and their ability to enter into voluntary transactions with all individuals for the exchange of labor, property or both.[6]

Such a system has at least two important characteristics.

First, because it is premised on respect for individual autonomy, including rules that provide for the protection and disposition of all individuals' property, classical liberalism is built upon what is commonly accepted to be a sound moral foundation.[7] Second, because such rules channel interactions between individuals into *voluntary* transactions, these transactions tend to be welfare enhancing. At the same time, because respect for autonomy necessitates that an individual cannot use or dispose of her property in a way that interferes with the rights of others, these transactions tend to enhance (or, at minimum, not detract from) *social* welfare, as well.

The mechanism by which these principles operate – and also their ultimate goal – is private ordering: "What really matters is that we develop a system of secure property rights that allows people to transact at low cost and high reliability."[8] Rather than rely on an external, third-party, decision maker to attempt the efficient ordering of individuals' affairs, classical liberalism advances a system that recognizes the limits of knowledge and the risk of abuse of power inherent in that model. Instead, classical liberalism advances a system that depends upon individuals' localized knowledge and their own self-interest to order their conduct. The key virtue of such

---

[6] Richard A. Epstein, *Why Libertarians Shouldn't Be (Too) Skeptical about Intellectual Property*, Progress & Freedom Foundation Progress on Point Paper No. 13.4, at 2 (2006), *available at* https://papers.ssrn.com/sol3/papers.cfm?abstract_id=981779.

[7] We observe that, at least in its basic design, a classical liberal order can satisfy the morality of a broad array of thinkers. For instance, on Rawls' account – someone not typically considered a classical liberal – "justice as fairness" requires something like Pareto-optimality in the distributions within a society. JOHN RAWLS, A THEORY OF JUSTICE 58 (1999).

[8] Richard A. Epstein, *The Property Rights Movement and Intellectual Property*, REGULATION 58, 63 (Winter 2008).

a system is that it does not presuppose the existence of an external decision maker with sufficient knowledge, ability, and incentive to order the affairs of others. And, again, such a system has the virtue of being morally sound: Whereas a system that relies upon an external decision maker must empower that decision maker to use (potentially arbitrary) force to implement its social ordering in the face of intransigent parties, classical liberalism advances a system in which transactions are voluntarily achieved by virtue of mutually beneficial exchange.

In part because of its preference for private ordering, classical liberalism is often characterized as being opposed to government regulation and espousing extreme views of regulatory minimalism. But such characterizations are overly simplistic and fundamentally wrong. Classical liberalism properly understood both requires and respects strong legal institutions – particularly well-defined property rights – in order to facilitate and enforce the private ordering that is its *sine qua non*. Moreover, many classical liberals recognize that the system of private ordering espoused by classical liberalism necessarily advances only allocatively efficient transactions; it does not necessarily promote distributive efficiency, and such distributional adjustments of wealth by government may be necessary on the back end of the system.[9] And classical liberalism may even admit of the possibility of regulatory intervention through public law institutions where private legal institutions are insufficient or relatively inefficient.[10]

In contemporary discussions, the core principles of classical liberalism are not infrequently framed in terms of Coasean and welfare economics. These perspectives focus attention on allocative efficiency.[11] The predicates for classical liberalism, however, were established well before Marshall and Coase, and all of the foundational ideas are contained in contemporaries of the Scottish Enlightenment, most notably in the works of David Hume and Adam Smith.[12]

That said, both welfare economics and Coasean, transaction-cost economics are particularly useful for understanding the classical liberal perspective on technology.

Welfare economics offers a useful lens for understanding classical liberalism's concern with individual autonomy. An important concept in welfare economics is the distinction between Pareto-efficient transactions and Kaldor-Hicks–efficient

---

[9] *See, for example,* Hayek's discussion of the potential need for some form of welfare programs in sufficiently wealthy societies. F. A. HAYEK, THE ROAD TO SERFDOM 133–35 (1994).

[10] *See, for example,* RICHARD EPSTEIN, SIMPLE RULES FOR A COMPLEX WORLD 280–81 (1995) (describing the shift from a civil legal regime toward a public regulatory regime for the management of damages from small amounts of pollution affecting a large number of parties).

[11] *See, for example,* Armen A. Alchian and Harold Demsetz, *The Property Right Paradigm*, 33 JOURNAL OF ECONOMIC HISTORY 16, 21–22 (1973).

[12] *See, for example,* ADAM SMITH, AN INQUIRY INTO THE NATURE AND CAUSES OF THE WEALTH OF NATIONS (1776) (Edwin Cannan, ed., 1904), *available at* http://oll.libertyfund.org/titles/smith-an-inquiry-into-the-nature-and-causes-of-the-wealth-of-nations-cannan-ed-in-2-vols;   David Hume, *On Government*, 5 (1777) (Liberty Fund, ed., 2013), *available at* http://lf-oll.s3.amazo naws.com/titles/2472/Hume_OnGovernment1777.pdf.

transactions. A Pareto-improving transaction is one that makes at least one party better off without making any parties worse off. For instance, Orlando has an apple but prefers oranges; Alice has an orange but prefers apples. If Orlando and Alice exchange fruits, each is better off (and neither is worse off). In a transaction that is Kaldor-Hicks–efficient, however, parties may be made worse off provided that, on net, society is made better off. Thus, Orlando has no fruit and Alice has an orange. Orlando likes oranges more than Alice does. If he simply steals Alice's orange he has gained more than Alice has lost. Under a Kaldor-Hicks standard (assuming no expenditures to prevent the theft), this is an efficient, socially-beneficial transaction.

The justification for Kaldor-Hicks–efficient transactions is that, in principle, Alice could be compensated for Orlando's theft. For instance, the government could tax Orlando in order to compensate Alice; or Alice could sue Orlando and recover compensatory damages. And, the theory goes, it is better to allow Orlando to put Alice's orange to socially-valuable uses than to risk losing out on the benefit of those uses because of Alice's intransigence or difficulties that Orlando may face (i.e., transaction costs) in bringing such a transaction to fruition.

From the classical liberal perspective, however, only Pareto-efficient transactions are presumptively legitimate. Such transactions are inherently beneficial to all parties (or, at least, beneficial to some parties and not harmful to any), and these benefits create incentives for parties to engage in these welfare-enhancing transactions. If they are truly welfare-enhancing, no coercion should be necessary for them to occur. If there are obstacles to these transactions occurring, classical liberalism holds that we should address those obstacles rather than adopt (Kaldor-Hicks-efficient) rules that would allow Orlando to violate Alice's autonomy. Doing so facilitates private ordering and protects individuals such as Alice from undue encroachment by either Orlando or the state. (As we will see, however, extreme cyberlibertarianism would readily countenance Kaldor-Hicks improvements).

The background concern for transaction costs implicitly runs through many, if not all, legal constructs that developed at common law. As Tom Merrill and Henry Smith have observed,[13] the goal of creating and using legal constructs is to manage the transaction costs ("information costs" in their account) inherent in a world of scarce resources. For instance, they describe the difference between applying an *in rem* regime and an *in personam* regime for managing property. The wisdom of applying one or the other in any given context comes down to their relative abilities to manage the information costs associated with settling disputes relating to ownership and use.[14]

---

[13] *See, for example,* Thomas Merrill and Henry Smith, *The Property/Contract Interface,* 101 Columbia Law Review 773, 792–797 (2001).

[14] On Merrill and Smith's account, *in rem* rights provide a way of minimizing the overall information costs associated with these disputes because the locus of ownership is fixed on the property itself. In the end, what matters in a particular dispute is which party gets the right to use a piece of property; but the way you arrive at that conclusion matters a good deal. If rights

Coase similarly offers a useful lens for understanding classical liberalism's focus on the relationship between legal institutions and private ordering. For Coase, the concept of transaction costs is key to understanding the relationship between individual actors' actions, legal institutions, and efficient outcomes.[15] Starting with a counterfactual world in which there are no transaction costs, he explains that legal institutions in such a world do not matter because individual actors will always engage in a series of transactions that result in all resources being put to their highest-value use. But, he goes on, because in the real world there are always transaction costs, well-designed legal institutions play a crucial role in ensuring optimal outcomes by reducing the transaction-cost impediments to efficient transfers. This perspective is very much in line with that of Scottish Enlightenment philosophers, who similarly ascribed great importance to legal institutions.

More to the point, Coase's focus on transaction costs precisely captures why the relationship between classical liberalism and technology is so fascinating and important. As we discuss in Part II, new technology is often developed and adopted precisely because of its effects on transaction costs. But any change in the incidence or level of transaction costs can significantly alter the optimal initial assignment of rights to maximize the likelihood of voluntary exchange. This means that technology may disrupt the structure of the legal institutions necessary to facilitate efficient, welfare-enhancing outcomes. At the same time, the distribution of these effects is often uneven, across both the specific transactions that will be entered into, as well as the individuals who will benefit. This may further exacerbate the effects of technological disruptions upon existing legal institutions, creating the possibility that a technological advance could both dramatically benefit some parties but dramatically disadvantage others in indirect and unpredictable ways. Where this is the case, technology has the potential to undermine both the moral foundations and the welfare justifications for classical liberalism.

II WHY TECHNOLOGY MATTERS TO CLASSICAL LIBERALISM

Technology in its broadest sense is merely the means by which we do things; technological advance is a change in the way we do things that increases benefit and/or lowers cost. The waterwheel allowed us to use a constant linear force

to use were always attached to individuals, the disputes would not just be between A (the putative owner of a piece of property) and B, but between A and all possible B's, a situation that would exponentially grow the social costs associated with settling property disputes. By locating the attributes of ownership within the property itself, however, the costs are linear, as each B who would challenge a use examines her claims against a single record of entitlements attached to the property itself. The goal of establishing this order is to create an efficient system of private ordering that is more likely than not to promote Pareto-optimal transfers (in theory, if not in practice).

[15] *See generally*, Ronald H. Coase, *The Problem of Social Cost*, 3 JOURNAL OF LAW AND ECONOMICS 1 (1960).

(the flow of water) to drive a rotational shaft that, in turn, could be used to drive a range of tools. It was a vast improvement over human- or animal-powered machines. The advent of the steam engine offered even more benefit by allowing us to drive the same rotational shaft almost anywhere, without the need for a source of running water. The advent of the internal combustion engine, in turn, provided yet another improvement, allowing us to drive a rotational shaft on a more reliable and efficient scale. In the same way, the Internet is a technological evolution of the telephone, which is an evolution of the telegraph, which is an evolution of postal carriers, which is an evolution of private couriers – all technologies that allow individuals to communicate with one another at a distance.

Technology, and especially technological advance, is important to the maintenance and advance of classical liberalism. Technology is a key input into liberty, effectively defining what individuals can do: that is, defining the practical boundaries of an individual's liberty. And, as technological advance can expand the scope of these boundaries, it is often liberty-enhancing.

Such gains are realized in multiple ways. For instance, some technology enables new types of conduct. The transition from the waterwheel to the steam engine to the internal combustion engine dramatically expanded where individuals could live and increased their quality of life. Other technology affects how people are able to engage in conduct that they already enjoy, largely by reducing the costs associated with that conduct. Improvements in technology for writing and communications, for instance, reduce the costs of interacting (and transacting) with others: The costs of transactions in a world where communications are recorded on papyrus and transmitted by courier are dramatically different than those in a world where they are recorded as bits on a computer that are transmitted via wires.

As a result, as an initial matter, the classical liberal position entails a distinct skepticism of the development of new rules, or even the application of existing rules, to impede technological advance:

> [T]here is a robust body of literature establishing the contributions of technological innovation to economic growth and social welfare ... [E]ven apparently small innovations can generate large consumer benefits. It is because of these dynamic and often largely unanticipated consequences of novel technological innovation that both the likelihood and social cost of erroneous interventions against innovation are increased.[16]

The story of technology is not necessarily all positive, however. Assessing the net effect of technological advance is particularly complicated by the possibility (or likelihood, even) that its effect on liberty, autonomy, and the institutional environment may simultaneously push in opposing directions.

---

[16] Geoffrey A. Manne and Joshua D. Wright, *Innovation and the Limits of Antitrust*, 6 JOURNAL OF COMPETITION LAW AND ECONOMICS 153, 168 (2010).

For one thing, the benefits of technological advance or the problems that new technology can (or cannot) improve upon will inevitably fall unequally across members of society, thus altering, and often impeding, social, legal, commercial, or other relationships in unexpected ways. The advent of the waterwheel, for instance, endowed those near running water with benefits unavailable to others, and diverted economic resources away from activities that could not benefit from the operation of the waterwheel, all without respect to those activities' relative social value.

For another thing, technologies that benefit private parties and expand their liberties can also benefit government and expand its power (and constrict the populace's liberties). While the advent of the telephone, for example, certainly conferred enormous benefit and substantial liberty upon the populace, it also extended the reach of government and just as certainly facilitated to the rise of a more centralized and invasive state.[17]

Moreover, new technologies that increase the ease of or benefits from transactions between private parties (and thus expand opportunities for private ordering) may impose greater external costs upon third parties, either because the nature of the transactions may entail new externalities or simply because of the increase in the number of transactions that impose externalities.

These concerns are not unique to "technology," although they may appear particularly acute in the context of technological advance. And this critique should not be read as anti-technology Luddism. To the contrary, "problematic" technological advance, where it occurs, often accompanies great social welfare gains from increased productivity and widespread dispersion of wealth. Moreover, such problematic technological advance frequently spurs beneficial advances in response. The classic example is Schumpeterian competition, in which firms leapfrog one another in a series of short-lived monopolies, each achieved through technological advance and maintained only so long as the then-monopolist can maintain its advantage. While this may bear the superficial hallmarks of monopoly, such dynamic competition in technology markets is actually perfectly consistent with strong competition and procompetitive outcomes.[18] Each successive "winning" firm

---

[17] See Henry G. Manne, *Reconciling Different Views about Constitutional Interpretation* in THE CONSTITUTION, THE COURTS, AND THE QUEST FOR JUSTICE 55, 60 (Robert A. Goldwin & William A. Schambra, eds. 1989) ("As a practical matter … [e]ffective application of federal law [at the time of the Constitution's drafting] was severely constrained by the primitive technologies of transportation and communications … But the rapid development of communication and transportation technology through the nineteenth and twentieth centuries made physically possible a degree of federal law enforceability inconceivable in 1787.").

[18] See, for example, Thomas M. Jorde and David J. Teece, *Antitrust Policy and Innovation: Taking Account of Performance Competition and Competitor Cooperation*, 147 JOURNAL OF INSTITUTIONAL AND THEORETICAL ECONOMICS 118 (1991). Note also that "competition for the market" can be as constraining as within-market competition. See Harold Demsetz, *Industry Structure, Market Rivalry and Public Policy*, 16 JOURNAL OF LAW AND ECONOMICS 1 (1973).

must be committed to investing its profits in developing new and better technologies in order to try to preempt or co-opt the next technological wave and maintain its position. The benefits of this "free-market innovation machine," as William Baumol dubbed it,[19] redound not only to the firm, of course, but also to its customers and to society writ large.

Thus, further confounding any evaluation of the benefits of technological advance, such changes must be considered in a dynamic context. The mere fact that a new technology has some deleterious effects today does not necessarily justify corrective intervention through legal institutions; rather, today's apparent techno-logical costs may actually drive Schumpeterian competition, creating incentives for further technological advance to improve upon those effects.

The important insight here is that, as noted, classical liberalism is concerned with protecting and advancing both the liberty of the individual *as well as* the autonomy of other individuals and the ability of the institutional environment to facilitate private ordering. Technologies that are liberty-enhancing may nonetheless be con-cerning from the classical liberal perspective if they risk encroaching upon the autonomy of others or impeding welfare-enhancing transactions.

The effect of technological change on the institutional environment is particu-larly important and underappreciated. Changes that expand liberty for some people may also alter the relative incidence of transaction costs between contracting parties and thus alter or impair the (previously) efficient allocation of property rights. The institutional environment is not – nor should it be – static. Just as libertarianism is concerned with ensuring that laws and regulations not needlessly impair welfare- and liberty-enhancing technological progress, it should be sensitive to the ways that technological advance may alter the desirability of *status quo* institutions.

Because of the reallocation of relative rights and powers inherent in technological change, even an effort to maintain the constancy of institutions – *not* to change them in response, in other words – results in a reordering. Perhaps most troublingly (and in a fashion seemingly woefully underappreciated by most classical liberals), this exogenous technological change even inherently alters the fundamental polit-ical ordering embodied in the Constitution:

> In 1787, [] the idea that the federal government could effectively regulate matters relating, for example, to coal mine safety standards would have seemed absurd, not merely as a legal matter but, much more important, as a practical matter. It was not physically possible for the federal government to serve its writ widely enough to allow it effective authority over every detail of all commercial matters ...

> Then ... enormous systems of roads, telephones, radio, television, airplanes, and computers appeared ... As a result a gross alteration of the federal government's physical power to regulate commerce had occurred. Yet when the courts looked to

---

[19] WILLIAM J. BAUMOL, THE FREE-MARKET INNOVATION MACHINE: ANALYZING THE GROWTH MIRACLE OF CAPITALISM (2003).

the words of the document and to the "original intent . . .," [t]he legal concept of interstate commerce grew *pari passu* with the federal government's ability to administer laws locally. While the words did not change, the Supreme Court allowed the constant expansion of federal regulatory powers in keeping with the changes in markets and market structure occasioned by the new technology . . .

What had actually happened to change our constitutional reality in this drastic fashion? Had there been an amendment or a revolution? No, there had been only the invention or introduction of new technologies by nonelected scientists and entrepreneurs . . . In other words, the accidents of technological development deter-mine the real limits on the restraining influence of the Constitution.[20]

At the same time, classical liberalism must deal with the effect of technology on the perceived distribution of rights and rents through political institutions and the effort to change them accordingly. At minimum, to the extent that technological change alters the social distribution of liberty and autonomy under existing institutions, classical liberals must grapple with the reality that the backlash against such changes may result in demand for – and political acquiescence to – subsequent institutional changes to restore the previous distribution of rights across society in ways that, even net of the gains from technology itself, are socially harmful.

In other words, although technological advance can (and usually does) increase overall social welfare in broad strokes, the political response to the redistribution of rights, power, and rents it may entail can lead to a net reduction in welfare – including through reductions in private ordering.

This problem is particularly acute in the case of implementations of technological innovation where the narrow redistribution of rents may be immediately apparent, but the broad, social benefits of new technology or new business models adapted to it may not be understood for some time. Importantly for a consequentialist approach like that of classical liberalism, this effect may be abetted by non-political actors including economists and legal scholars who tend to underappreciate the limits of their knowledge about novel technology and novel business arrangements.[21]

Consider an important and contentious contemporary example: privacy. Prior to the modern era in which a great number of social interactions are carried out online, it was relatively easy for individuals to keep information about themselves private and difficult for third parties (including the government) to observe and record that information. Today, by contrast, it is comparatively difficult for

---

[20] Manne, *Reconciling Different Views about Constitutional Interpretation, supra* note 17, at 66–67 (emphasis added).

[21] *See, for example,* Ronald Coase, *Industrial Organization: A Proposal for Research,* in POLICY ISSUES AND RESEARCH OPPORTUNITIES IN INDUSTRIAL ORGANIZATION 59, 67 (Victor R. Fuchs ed., 1972) ("[I]f an economist finds something – a business practice of one sort or another – that he does not understand, he looks for a monopoly explanation. And as in this field we are very ignorant, the number of ununderstandable practices tends to be very large, and the reliance on a monopoly explanation, frequent.").

individuals to keep such information private and easy for third parties to observe and record that information. Despite changes in the value people attach to privacy that inevitably accompanied that evolution, changed technology may have shifted not only the efficient delineation of privacy rights (from a regime in which individuals were assumed to have waived control of information absent efforts to retain it to one in which they are instead assumed to retain control absent voluntary waiver of that control), but also the *perception* of the appropriateness of the resulting allocation of rights (such that a "correction" was required to shift from a presumption of waiver to a presumption of prohibition absent affirmative waiver).

Indeed, the modern American political discourse on privacy and its legal and regulatory treatment has its origins in Samuel Warren and Louis Brandeis's seminal 1890 article, *The Right to Privacy*,[22] which was written in significant part in response to the advent of a disruptive new technology: the portable box camera (the Kodak camera), introduced in 1888. It is worth quoting Warren and Brandeis at length, not only because the article addresses so directly the problem of adapting existing institutions to technological change, but also because it is an important progenitor of one branch of the contemporary cyberlibertarian approach to technology and institutions that, perhaps excessively, elevates liberty over private ordering:

> That the individual shall have full protection in person and in property is a principle as old as the common law; but it has been found necessary from time to time to define anew the exact nature and extent of such protection. Political, social, and economic changes entail the recognition of new rights, and the common law, in its eternal youth, grows to meet the new demands of society.
>
> * * *
>
> Recent inventions and business methods call attention to the next step which must be taken for the protection of the person... Instantaneous photographs and newspaper enterprise have invaded the sacred precincts of private and domestic life; and numerous mechanical devices threaten to make good the prediction that "what is whispered in the closet shall be proclaimed from the house-tops ..." [T]he question whether our law will recognize and protect the right to privacy in this and in other respects must soon come before our courts for consideration.
>
> * * *
>
> It should be stated that, in some instances where protection has been afforded against wrongful publication, the jurisdiction has been asserted, not on the ground of property, or at least not wholly on that ground, but upon the ground of an alleged breach of an implied contract or of a trust or confidence.
>
> * * *

---

[22] Samuel D. Warren and Louis D. Brandeis, *The Right to Privacy*, 4 Harvard Law Review 193 (1890).

But the court can hardly stop there. The narrower doctrine may have satisfied the demands of society at a time when the abuse to be guarded against could rarely have arisen without violating a contract or a special confidence; but now that modern devices afford abundant opportunities for the perpetration of such wrongs without any participation by the injured party, the protection granted by the law must be placed upon a broader foundation ... [S]ince the latest advances in photographic art have rendered it possible to take pictures surreptitiously, the doctrines of contract and of trust are inadequate to support the required protection, and the law of tort must be resorted to.[23]

Regularly changing delineations of legal entitlements that may occur during periods of rapid technological change are potentially problematic for the very concept of property, reducing the durability of property rights, injecting uncertainty into the contours of ownership, and ultimately limiting the viability of private ordering. Indeed, even if these changed delineations improve overall efficiency in the allocation of entitlements, the mere fact of the change imposes transaction costs that can, in principle at least, be substantial. This is particularly the case where change is frequent, such that systems built upon long-term expectations of property delineations are kept constantly out of equilibrium.

Scholars have long recognized that legal institutions are shaped by technology and that changing technology may change those institutions. For instance, Roman citizens enjoyed a very different concept of "freedom of contract" than we do today; they were free to enter into any of a finite number of pre-defined contracts, but they were not free to draft contracts with their own bespoke terms. Today, largely any terms that can be rendered into recorded prose can be made contractually binding. The driving differences between these paradigms are the cost and availability of underlying technology: at Roman law, literacy was limited and it was costly and difficult to record terms; today literacy is assumed and recordation is widespread.

Similarly, at early English common law, courts recognized a finite number of forms of legal claims (*trover, covenant, assumpsit, detinue, trespass, and replevin*). These forms were recognized to standardize legal process: The costs of recording and transmitting precedent were high, so courts channeled precedent into standardized forms to reduce the burden upon jurists and counsellors to facilitate the development and uniformity of the law.

But this came at a cost. Courts would often find claims that could not be fit into one of the standard forms nonjusticiable. But as technology improved and the costs of recording and transmitting precedent decreased, common law courts developed a generalized form of action, *trespass on the case*, which plaintiffs could argue in cases where their claims did not fit into a standard form. Over time, this generalized form largely displaced historic practice, to the point that the historic writs have been abolished in favor of generalized rules of civil procedure.

---

[23] *Id.* at 193–211.

The same trend has also been seen in the case of the transition from *in rem* to *in personam* rights. Over time the law has increased the closed number (*numerus clausus*) of forms of *in rem* property that it recognizes, including allowing for an increased range of property-like transactions to be recorded through *in personam* contractual relationships. As with the expansions in the forms of contract and forms of action recognized by the law, the expansion in the forms of property has been driven by advances in technology that reduce the relevant transaction costs and consequentially alter the efficient structure of legal institutions.

These examples demonstrate the ever-evolving relationship between technology and legal institutions. But they are also examples that have not proven problematic for classical liberalism because the rate of technological advance has been slow enough that legal institutions have been able to evolve apace.

But this alignment between the rate of technological and institutional change is not always present – as in the current technological setting (and perhaps that of most future technological changes, given their seemingly inexorable rate of increase). The ICT revolution has seen the transition from mechanical printing presses and analog telephones to palm-sized supercomputers and the Internet over the course of a lifetime, and from individuals who grew up without the Internet to individuals who grew up with omnipresent Internet access over the course of half a generation. Even more starkly, the advent of the (inexpensive) portable camera, along with photographic paper and film rolls that enabled easy and cheap processing of photographic images, led to the extremely rapid and widespread diffusion of the ability to record and disseminate visual images in the late 1800s. As evidenced by the tone (and influence) of *The Right to Privacy* (published a scant two years after the invention of the Kodak) this led to the rapid and distinct disruption of the legal institutions surrounding privacy – a disruption that has continued through the development of modern technology and that we are still working to resolve today. In such a setting, technological change and legal institutions can easily be in tension. This tension is explored in Part III.

III DUELING VIEWS OF CONTEMPORARY TECHNOLOGY AND THE LAW

Elements of classical liberal philosophy have featured prominently, if accidentally, in contemporary discussions of the regulation of technology. Roughly mirroring the advent and growth of the commercial Internet, many technologists – and, in many ways, the tech industry writ large – have embraced various forms of liberty-focused, and generally liberty-maximal, philosophies. By and large, these individuals label themselves as libertarians of one form or another (whether libertarian, cyberlibertarian, cryptolibertarian, technolibertarian, cryptoanarchist, or some other variant). Although they rarely identify as "classical liberals" (indeed, it is likely that few are even familiar with that term), their priors are nonetheless closely related to those of classical liberals. These views, therefore, provide a useful survey of views on the contemporary relationship between technology, liberty, and the law.

The discussion that follows divides these views into two broad categories: "extreme" and "moderate" libertarian views. In both cases the reference is to little-l libertarian, indicating that these are liberty-focused philosophies. The extreme libertarian view generally sees technology as liberty-maximizing, so tends in turn to be strongly permissive of technological change. The moderate view also sees technology as liberty-enhancing, but is more circumspect about technology's ability to undermine the protection of important autonomy values.

A *The Extreme Libertarian Embrace of Technology*

Libertarianism is related to, but (we contend) more restrictive than, classical liberal philosophy. In its more extreme form, it takes the preference for private ordering that classical liberalism rests upon and broadens it to its maximum extent. Under this form – often referred to as a variant of anarchism or anarcho-capitalism – the only morally acceptable order is the purely private order. The state, based as it is on a more-or-less involuntary premise (i.e., that it has a monopoly on the use of force, and an individual cannot opt out of it) is to be avoided as a source for rule making and enforcement.

In the contemporary technological setting, this branch of thought often falls into one of three categories: cyberutopianism, cyberexceptionalism, or cyberanarchism. These are not meant to be precisely defined categories – indeed, there is substantial overlap between each. But this categorization typifies key features of contemporary, extreme libertarian views on technology.

Cyberutopianism, as exemplified by John Perry Barlow's *Declaration of the Independence of Cyberspace*, is the notion that the traditional legal rules developed to handle disputes in the "real" world are wholly inapposite in online environments because the innate, exalted characteristics of the online world render them superfluous (and even deleterious):

> Governments of the Industrial World, you weary giants of flesh and steel, I come from Cyberspace, the new home of Mind. On behalf of the future, I ask you of the past to leave us alone. You are not welcome among us. You have no sovereignty where we gather.

> We have no elected government, nor are we likely to have one, so I address you with no greater authority than that with which liberty itself always speaks. I declare the global social space we are building to be naturally independent of the tyrannies you seek to impose on us. You have no moral right to rule us nor do you possess any methods of enforcement we have true reason to fear.

> * * *

> You claim there are problems among us that you need to solve. You use this claim as an excuse to invade our precincts. Many of these problems don't exist. Where

there are real conflicts, where there are wrongs, we will identify them and address them by our means. We are forming our own Social Contract. This governance will arise according to the conditions of our world, not yours. Our world is different.

* * *

We are creating a world where anyone, anywhere may express his or her beliefs, no matter how singular, without fear of being coerced into silence or conformity.

Your legal concepts of property, expression, identity, movement, and context do not apply to us. They are all based on matter, and there is no matter here.

* * *

We must declare our virtual selves immune to your sovereignty, even as we continue to consent to your rule over our bodies. We will spread ourselves across the Planet so that no one can arrest our thoughts.[24]

Barlow's views captured the zeitgeist of the moment – a sincere belief that "cyberspace" was a new and better place than the physical world. It was a place in which individuals could explore and express their liberty in the purest and most extreme forms possible, and could do so free of the constraints of the physical world or territorial governments – and possibly even without concern for encroaching upon the autonomy interests of others.[25]

Today, the utopianism of Barlow's vision of the cyber has fallen from its once dominant intellectual position, though strands of it remain in the cyberanarchist perspective (discussed below). Rather, as the Internet grew in social, economic, and political importance – and, importantly, as the Internet came to distinguish itself more for its transformative ability to facilitate (and extend) the same sorts of social interactions that occurred offline, rather than as the birthplace of an entirely new kind of social order – the same social, economic, and political institutions important in the offline world naturally came to exert influence in the online world. These efforts occurred largely through the operation of existing legal principles and, where necessary, the establishment of new legal rules designed to extend those principles into the online world. This intrusion of offline institutions into the new online space gave rise to the next – and arguably still dominant – wave of extreme cyberlibertarianism: cyber-exceptionalism. The cyberexceptionalist perspective is to accede that cyberspace *can* be brought to heel by traditional institutions, but that it *should* be exempted from such treatment.

[24] John Perry Barlow, A *Declaration of the Independence of Cyberspace* (1996), *available at* www.eff.org/cyberspace-independence.
[25] Barlow was not alone in his views, although his powerful prose captured the imagination of many. *See also, for example,* Esther Dyson, George Gilder, George Keyworth, and Alvin Toffler, *Cyberspace and the American Dream: A Magna Carta for the Knowledge Age,* Progress & Freedom Foundation Future Insight No. 1.2 (Aug. 1994), *available at* www.pff.org/issues-pubs/futureinsights/fi1.2magnacarta.html.

One of the more influential strains of cyberexceptionalism is so-called permissionless innovation. Permissionless innovation holds that individuals should be able to operate and innovate online (and, in fact, in the realm of information technology more generally) without impediment from any authority. In its most extreme view this includes not only government actors directly, but also private parties whose assertion of property or contractual rights might "impede" others' ability to freely innovate.[26] In its most fully developed form, permissionless innovation holds that the state should, short of compelling circumstances, refrain from interfering with private ordering in the digital context entirely. Adam Thierer has characterized this position as:

> the notion that experimentation with new technologies and business models should generally be permitted by default. Unless a compelling case can be made that a new invention will bring serious harm to society, innovation should be allowed to continue unabated and problems, if any develop, can be addressed later.[27]

This view is focused almost entirely on the positive value of innovation, holding that the gains from innovation will tend to overwhelm any potentially complicating realities, or that potential complications will themselves be addressed by subsequent innovation. Thus, Internet platforms should be permitted to experiment with new services without *ex ante* constraint, even though we understand, for example, that third-parties often use these platforms for illicit purposes. The exceptionalist perspective is that concern about those illicit uses does not justify placing any limits on the development of new technological platforms.

The advent of the automobile, for instance, was overwhelmingly positive for society, even though it upended much of tort law. Likewise, the advent of driverless cars will certainly lead to new ways for people to be injured and hard questions for the law in assessing and apportioning liability for those injuries – but it will likely make automobiles substantially safer than they are today and increase the efficiency (and decrease the costs) of driving so substantially that we should push ahead in the development of the new technology and address such concerns once the technology has arrived.

Similarly, the Internet has unquestionably been one of the most beneficial and important developments in the history of humankind – but it has also facilitated child pornography and other forms of exploitation on a scale never before known. The exceptionalist perspective is that the new technology should be forgiven these

---

[26] *See* Geoffrey Manne, *Permissionless Innovation Does Not Mean "No Contracts Required,"* Truth on the Market (Jun. 26, 2014), http://bit.ly/2tok6fV. This version of permissionless innovation thus implicitly hearkens back to cyberutopianism, shunning even private ordering if it is facilitated by traditional institutions, denying, in effect, that the "harm" of contract or property law violations exist in cyberspace.

[27] Adam Thierer, Permissionless Innovation: The Continuing Case for Comprehensive Technological Freedom 1 (revised and expanded, 2016).

ills in favor of its overwhelming benefits.[28] Particular implementers or users of new technology who use it to harm others should be penalized accordingly, but the technology itself should not be constrained in order to deter such harm – even if the most (or only) practical way to do so is by limiting the technology (and even if users' ability to evade the law is, in fact, a function of the new technology). The exceptionalist perspective holds this view even despite the fact that, in numerous offline situations, just such "intermediary liability" is common.[29]

The rationale for this exceptionalism is that new technologies are less likely to develop if their developers are held accountable for the harms that some will inevitably use them to cause. Such liability would increase the costs of new technologies – especially "generative" technologies (i.e., technologies (like platforms open to user-generated content and peer-to-peer interactions) that can give rise to new, unpredictable, uses). At the same time, once the technology is established, suitable institutions can be put in place to protect against specific, harmful uses of the technology.

This view of permissionless innovation is liberty-maximalist, both in the short run and the long run. It frees innovators to develop new technologies as they see fit, furthering their liberty interests. And successful technologies will tend to be those that benefit others, enhancing their liberty interests as new technologies are developed and permeate the market.

But this view is also autonomy-agnostic. It pays no heed to concerns that a given technology may tend to be used to cause harm to its users or to third parties, and expressly argues that harmed parties be denied recourse against the implementers of the technology for such harms. Importantly, this is the case even where future harms are predictable, and even where the technology is developed in such a way that it makes it particularly easy for parties to be harmed or difficult for them to seek redress. In other words, under dominant cyberexceptionalist views, platforms and intermediaries are under no obligation to design their technologies in ways that prevent harm, allow for recovery when harm occurs, or even facilitate action being taken against the party causing harm.[30]

---

[28] According to many proponents of cyberexceptionalism, in fact, this immunity has been written into US law. *See* 47 USC § 230(c)(1) ("No provider or user of an interactive computer service shall be treated as the publisher or speaker of any information provided by another [provider or user]."). Courts have largely been willing to go along with the exceptionalist interpretation of this language. *See, for example,* David S. Ardia, *Free Speech Savior or Shield for Scoundrels: An Empirical Study of Intermediary Immunity Under Section 230 of the Communications Decency Act,* 43 LOYOLA LAW REVIEW 373, 435 (2010) (finding that Section 230 provided immunity to defendants in over sixty percent of relevant cases).

[29] Courts have long dealt with out-of-reach offenders by enjoining the conduct of intermediaries: *for example,* by prohibiting local stores from selling foreign-manufactured counterfeit goods, or requiring that taverns prevent patrons from driving drunk.

[30] Again, this approach largely harkens back to the cyberutopian view that in a very real sense traditional conceptions of "harm" do not apply online, because cyberspace is not bound by the physical or social constraints of the real world that prevent a harmed party from removing themselves from a harmful situation or engaging in self-help.

The third category of extreme libertarian views on technology is different in kind, although it draws on ideas from both cyberutopianism and cyberexceptionalism. Cyberanarchism views technology as a remedy against the sins of the state. This view is particularly prevalent in contemporary discussions about privacy, surveillance, encryption, and cryptocurrencies. Cyberanarchism views government surveillance in particular – whether through wiretaps and warrants, the intelligence community, collection of public information, or issuance of subpoenas to collect information from private platforms – as an undue encroachment on individual autonomy and an impermissible limit on liberty. Technology can and should be used to frustrate these governmental functions, thereby enhancing liberty.

There is, of course, an obvious trade-off with such an approach. Cryptocurrencies, for instance, were developed at least in part to provide an anonymous and largely untraceable alternative to fiat currency and traditional online payment systems. In many contexts anonymity in financial transactions is valuable, of course, but cryptocurrencies can be and are used to facilitate harmful or criminal conduct. Likewise, TOR and other encryption technologies have enabled individuals to trade illicit goods and services as well as nonillicit goods and services under anonymous conditions. Privacy-enhancing encryption technologies are also broadly seen as tools to circumvent state restrictions on speech (particularly in hostile regimes), and to avoid state surveillance.

Although it is true to some extent for all of the different strains of the extreme libertarian view, for privacy and cryptocurrency advocates, in particular, technology is viewed as a means for resisting any government regulation – and even private ordering abetted by government institutions – completely.

Cyberanarchism hearkens back to the central cyberutopian view of the fundamental illegitimacy of government, especially in the technological age – that those "Governments of the Industrial World, [. . .] weary giants of flesh and steel . . ., are not welcome among us [and] have no sovereignty where we gather."[31] Of course, this assumption of illegitimacy is rejected by the classical libertarian perspective. It is surely the case that some of the government functions that animate these causes are illegitimate excesses. But others are not, and these technologies do not discriminate between interfering with illegitimate and legitimate government functions.[32]

---

[31] Barlow, A *Declaration of the Independence of Cyberspace, supra* note 22.

[32] A prime example of this tension was the court order requiring Apple to render assistance to law enforcement by defeating encryption on one of its iPhones. *See In the Matter of Search of an Apple iPhone Seized During Execution of a Search Warrant on a Black Lexus IS300, California License Plate 35KGD203,* No. ED 15–0451M, 2016 WL 618401 (C.D. Cal. 2016). Although arguably resting on fairly well-established legal footing, the court's order, based on the All Writs Act, 28 U.S.C. § 1651, was met with cries of outrage from certain techno-libertarian quarters. This outrage, again, was premised on the idea that there is something unusual about data and digital devices that warrants a completely different legal treatment. But, as with other instances of such extreme cyberexceptionalism, the explanation about just *why* it is that technology should be in a legal class of its own was never adequately explained.

B *The Moderate Libertarian Embrace of Technology*

It is almost a misnomer to characterize the moderate techno-libertarian position as an "embrace." The moderate libertarian or classical liberal perspective on technology is, at root, nothing special, insofar as classical liberals do not presume that any social construct should receive a *per se* different treatment under the law.

The moderate libertarian view admits room for the state to establish a framework of neutrally administered and enforced rules against which individuals arrange their private ordering. Technology is evaluated by its effects upon the rule-based expectations of individuals, and is not regarded as inherently outside of (but acting upon) the legal order. Fundamental to this approach is the view that technology is not regarded as exceptional in any *a priori* sense; it matters only how it is used or how it affects the optimal institutional ordering. Technological innovations do often offer significant benefits (not only in terms of liberty and autonomy, but general consumer welfare), of course, and any benefits arising from the adaptation and application of existing legal rules should be weighed against the possible costs of deterring the creation or welfare-enhancing deployment technology. But in principle any technology, no matter how revolutionary, can be brought within the ambit of predictable, neutrally administered legal rules.

One key component of the moderate libertarian view is that immunity from established legal principles should not be assumed even if extension of those principles to new technology requires novel applications of common law precedents, or even the adoption of new regulations or legislation. Internet platforms, for example, may entail a *different* liability structure, but there is no reason to believe that they should engender *no* liability.

Unlike the more extreme approaches, the moderate libertarian approach to technology would not inherently object to extraterritorial application of a country's laws, for example, as is often considered to be necessary on the Internet. While cloud-based activity and cross-border data flows can be particularly complicated to untangle, this does not mean that territorial courts should be presumed unable to adjudicate disputes arising out of multi-nation digital trade. Courts are skilled at parsing conflicts of laws, as well as parsing facts in complex or difficult cases. Determining jurisdictional competencies for Internet-based disputes is only a difference of degree, not of kind.

Similarly, under the moderate libertarian view, technologies that are used to secure privacy online or in the cloud will have to yield in some cases to the needs of the state, just as in the offline context. For instance, although the answer may not be to build in purposeful security holes such as back doors, in cases where a firm *could* theoretically help override encryption, as in the Apple-San Bernardino dispute,[33] they can lawfully be required to do so.

---

[33] *See generally* Justin (Gus) Hurwitz, *Encryption*^*Congress* *mod (Apple + CALEA)*, 30 HARVARD JOURNAL OF LAW AND TECHNOLOGY 355 (2017).

Intellectual property ("IP") draws into stark relief the distinction between the hard-core and more-moderate libertarian approaches. IP presents a rather unique circumstance. By defining a property right around a novel technological idea (patent) or original expression, including of technologically sophisticated software code (copyright), IP comes close to treating technological advance itself (as opposed to the use or implementation of technology) as exceptional.[34] In this sense, it could be argued, the mere definition of IP rights represents a problematic extension of the legal order beyond a system necessary for mitigating transaction costs to one that inherently curtails liberty *regardless* of countervailing social gain: Because IP rights are granted before any welfare-improving transaction is undertaken, even essentially valueless technology can receive IP protection, subject only to the (largely arbitrary) cost to an applicant of obtaining it.[35] For moderate libertarians, however, a system of IP rights readily overcomes this apparent defect.

Not surprisingly, however, the hard-core libertarian argument against IP extends from precisely this apparent quirk. Hard-core libertarians generally advance two arguments against IP. First, IP is a creation of government: As suggested above, not only the *ex post* regulation of technology, but its very definition through patent or copyright is an "artificial" function of statute. Moreover, because this government-created property right entails a right to prevent unauthorized use of protected technology and the concomitant right to extract monopoly rents in exchange for authorization (license), it amounts to an unjustifiable (and possibly inefficient) government transfer of rents. Second, unlike real and personal property, another's use of an idea (or copying of an expression) is not inherently rivalrous: it can be accomplished without depleting the idea or expression and without limiting anyone else's ability to implement or copy it. Similarly, absent enforcement of the artificial, government-granted monopoly (or concealment), it is *very* difficult (if not

---

[34] It is important to note, however, that (under US law, at least) both patent and copyright law encompass core elements that mitigate this exceptionalism to some extent. For an idea (invention) to be granted a patent, for example, it needs to be *useful*: It cannot exist merely as an abstract idea, but must be a functional "process, machine, manufacture, or composition of matter." 35 U.S.C. § 101. And for original works to receive a copyright they must be "fixed in any tangible medium of expression ... from which they can be perceived, reproduced, or otherwise communicated." 17 U.S.C. § 102(a). Again, it is clear from this statutory limitation that abstractions *per se* will not receive protection unless they are actually implemented in a useful form. Nevertheless, these eligibility requirements do not *entirely* undermine the idea that "technology," rather than "the use of technology" is protected by IP rights because, once the conditions of eligibility are met, IP protections extend beyond those limitations to restrict others' implementation of the new technology.

[35] Because copyright attaches automatically to any original expression once it is fixed in a tangible medium, even this limitation doesn't exist. Of course, the investment required (including opportunity costs) to create a patentable invention or copyrightable work acts as a limitation, as well, and one that is decidedly more closely related to expected social value. But even ideas discovered accidentally and (nearly) trivial works of authorship are still eligible for protection, so there remains a significant scope for legal constraints to attach even without any indication of their social value.

impossible) to exclude others from the use an idea or of copyright-protected content, particularly digital content. On top of all of which, the system for granting and enforcing IP rights is costly and, inevitably, complex. As a result, so the argument goes, IP rights erect artificial and costly impediments to the liberty of people to do (and say) what they will and should not be enforced.[36]

But this is, yet again, a case of cyberexceptionalism. Property rights, if they have any meaning or utility, are always creatures of the government. In fact, as we have noted, a central feature of libertarianism is the recognition that the definition and enforcement of property rights is inarguably a valuable function of government. Without the implicit imprimatur of the state on one's claim to a particular "thing" (whether tangible or intangible), the value of that claim (and thus the thing itself) is approximately zero.

> No one can defend any system of property rights, whether for tangible or intangible objects, on the naïve view that it produces all gain and no pain. Every system of property rights necessarily creates some winners and some losers. Recognize property rights in land, and the law makes trespassers out of people who were once free to roam. We choose to bear these costs ... because we make the strong empirical judgment that any loss of liberty is more than offset by the gains from manufacturing, agriculture and commerce that exclusive property rights foster. These gains, moreover, are not confined to some lucky few who first get to occupy land. No, the private holdings in various assets create the markets that use voluntary exchange to spread these gains across the entire population ... [T]he inconveniences [IP] generates are fully justified by the greater prosperity and well-being for the population at large.[37]

It is also important to note that the presumed "monopoly" granted by IP rights is not actually a monopoly in any meaningful sense. Because patent rights and copyrights are limited in both time and scope, they do not foreclose the development and implementation of competing ideas or competing expressions any more than the owner of a single house can avoid competition from her neighbors.

IV A CLASSICAL LIBERAL VIEW OF TECHNOLOGY AND THE LAW?

On first blush, it seems that the moderate position on technology (more accurately, technological advance) enjoys the better claim to the mantle of classical liberalism – and in many ways it does. While the extreme position appears to be more acutely protective of liberty from government interference, its myopic focus on freedom

---

[36] See, for example, Tom W. Bell, *Indelicate Imbalancing in Copyright and Patent Law*, in COPY FIGHTS: THE FUTURE OF INTELLECTUAL PROPERTY IN THE INFORMATION AGE 4 (Adam Thierer & Clyde Wayne Crews Jr. eds., 2002).

[37] RICHARD A. EPSTEIN, INTELLECTUAL PROPERTY FOR THE TECHNOLOGICAL AGE 8 (Manufacturing Institute, 2006).

from all constraints leads it to reject even transaction-cost-reducing rules that further autonomy and voluntary exchange and thus overall social welfare.

Consider the concept of permissionless innovation again which, as noted, is important to both the moderate and extreme liberal positions regarding technology. On the one hand, the extreme version of permissionless innovation does not stand for neutral application of generally applicable legal rules and principles to new technology, but for the avoidance of all legal rules that might constrain the ability to develop any particular, new technological advance. This view of permissionless innovation – the extreme libertarian view – treats even *private* constraints arising out of enforceable property rights as inherently outdated. It is, under this approach, a problem not only that innovators might have to seek "permission" from the government to deploy new technology, but that they might have to seek it from private property holders through contract or license – by transacting with them, in other words. On this view, the transaction itself becomes an unjustified cost, and rules that enable rightsholders to limit an innovator's liberty – even if efficiently – are problematic. This seems too solicitous of liberty and too dismissive of autonomy and the broader, systemic benefits of well-defined property rights.

On the other hand, the moderate view runs the risk of naïve deontology, embracing and preserving rules for their own sake. The moderate position is that permissionless innovation denotes the ability to experiment, enter into transactions, and develop and deploy new technology without requiring the adoption of new rules that apply with special force to new technology, that overly constrain it out of excessive fear of its potentially harmful effects, or that protect incumbents from new competition. It would, at the extreme, seem willing to sacrifice even welfare-enhancing innovation for the sake of legal constancy: the continued, neutral application of existing rules and the avoidance of new rules, regardless of whether either would clearly further technological advance.

The problem with this view, of course, is that there is no inherent reason to think that the specific, *status quo* structure of rights is optimal in the face of any given technological change, particularly, as we have noted, when it is relatively rapid, disruptive change. The classical liberal embrace of rules and legal institutions is consequentialist and utilitarian, not deontological: public rules are needed solely because we gain more from their ability to facilitate private ordering and preserve autonomy interests than we lose from the constraints on liberty they entail. But that (emphatically) does not mean that any specific rules *per se* are worth the cost. The challenge is understanding how rules should evolve alongside changing technologies.

We frequently see this on vivid display in regulated industries that undergo technological disruption: as the cost and reliability of air travel improved leading to commoditization; as electricity generation was separated from transmission and became increasingly competitive; as new network technologies enabled the transition from a monopoly telephone network to one of widespread intermodal competition; as ride-sharing platforms like Uber and Lyft have disrupted heavily regulated taxi monopolies. Most classical liberals would cheer the disruption of these legal regimes and celebrate the technological innovation that hastened the transition away from industry-specific regulatory regimes.

In fact, this is the case even as we can recognize the losses faced by the energy company with stranded investments, the telecommunications carrier whose rate of return was dependent on regulated prices, and the driver who paid $1 million for a taxi medallion that is now worth a quarter of that. Recall Richard Epstein's import-ant point that "[e]very system of property rights necessarily creates some winners and some losers ..., [but] the inconveniences ... are fully justified by the greater prosperity and well-being for the population at large."[38]

The "losses" here are largely only distributional; they arise because the rejiggering of property rights enables technology to expand the size of the pie, even as it also redistributes the pieces. But it is the *transition* from one state of affairs to another, frequently brought on by technological advance, that creates the appearance of loss. Behind the metaphorical veil of ignorance, everyone would prefer technological dynamism to stasis, even with the disruption it entails. For the same reason, classical liberalism should countenance some reordering of rights in order to facilitate or respond to new technology.

Thus, an important and underappreciated role of technological change is to highlight these fault lines between appropriate, transaction-cost-reducing back-ground rules and those laws and regulations (or specific enforcement decisions of otherwise-desirable background rules) that may *appear* to facilitate trade, but really impede the creation of wealth and the exercise of liberty.

Not that it requires an Uber to see that taxi medallions are almost certainly examples of the latter, and not the former. They constrain non-medallion holders' liberty without even facilitating value-maximizing transactions for those who hold them. But it does often take an Uber to bring into relief the but-for world that such laws deter. Absent this information, the classical liberal approach is far less likely to succeed in influencing law and policy – in overcoming the politics and rent-seeking that prop up welfare-limiting or -reducing laws or allow them to come into existence in the first place. There is thus a second-order – and ironic – benefit to the more extreme libertarian position, which would, at the margin, enable deployment of more disruptive technologies, some number of which will confer this political economy benefit – improving the reliability of the law – independent of the direct benefits they may also entail.

If the extreme position can be too ... extreme, the moderate position can be too cautious, overweighting present autonomy interests (the protection of existing prop-erty rights and the ability for their holders to demand license) and underweighting future liberty interests (the ability to undermine existing property rights for the sake

[38] Id.

of dynamic efficiency gains). But unless we are able to reduce transaction costs far beyond what is likely, the optimal classical liberal position will still require background rules: So long as transaction costs exist, rules will be required and the challenge will be to implement the rules that yield the most efficient of outcomes.

While there can be little doubt about the inefficacy of maintaining status quo regulatory regimes in the face of technological change, the classical liberal position is not so obstinate. When it comes to the intrusive, industry-specific, regulatory oversight of the administrative state that has come to dominate in the contemporary era, the classical liberal position is invariably skeptical, and technological change is one of the most important reasons for classical liberal efforts to unwind (or prevent) such regimes in the first place: For the classical liberal, most such regimes are ill-advised from the start.

But things are more complicated when it comes to rules of general applicability. It is more difficult to countenance abrupt shifts in overarching regimes governing things like competition, intellectual property, privacy, and consumer protection (among others). Not that even these regimes are likely optimal *ex ante*, of course. But the inherent tension between liberty and autonomy interests is somewhat more complicated to resolve when technological advance disrupts them.

This is particularly true where such regulatory regimes were adopted to address perceived lacunas in the basic realms of operation of the common law, often brought about by previous technological change. In the main, it is important to note, classical liberals favor customary and common law.[39] These evolutionary systems adapt to technological (and other) changes over time, maintaining relative constancy, minimizing the frustration of expectations, and eschewing preemptive constraints that may turn out to be inefficient or otherwise undesirable. But statutory rules of general applicability also evolve through iterated judicial enforcement (in part in response to technological changes), and also effect an allocation of property rights and set expectations.[40] While the slow, deliberate evolution of the common law is certainly preferable, where they exist, the relative constancy of these long-standing statutory schemes is similarly important in maintaining the background rules against which transactions take place.

The central tension here is that classical liberalism posits the need for legal institutions to promote private ordering, but these institutions themselves are often established, maintained, enforced, and updated through a process of public

---

[39] *See generally* FRIEDRICH A. HAYEK, THE CONSTITUTION OF LIBERTY (1960); FRIEDRICH A. HAYEK, LAW, LEGISLATION AND LIBERTY: A NEW STATEMENT OF THE LIBERAL PRINCIPLES OF JUSTICE AND POLITICAL ECONOMY (1973).

[40] The operative language of Section 1 of the Sherman Act, for example, comprises the following: "Every contract, combination in the form of trust or otherwise, or conspiracy, in restraint of trade or commerce among the several States, or with foreign nations, is declared to be illegal." 15 U.S.C. § 1. The courts have, for the 125 or so years of the law's existence, been responsible for interpreting the law and giving it its real content (subject, of course, to the strong influence of enforcement agencies' exercise of their prosecutorial discretion).

ordering. Indeed, even institutions that evolve through private ordering quickly take on a public character in any society beyond a trivial level of complexity.[41] And such rules can easily fall victim to the perils of public choice, erring on the side of excessive constraint due to limited knowledge, an excess of caution (the so-called precautionary principle), and the lure of rent extraction. The very rules that classical liberalism depends upon in order to ensure private ordering and autonomy can be captured through public means to *limit* private ordering and undermine autonomy. The extreme libertarian position has the undeniable virtue that it is a purely private mechanism, one that can disrupt legal institutions that have lost their way – even if that disruption has great costs. So too does the classical liberal's common affinity for the common law – an institution in which changes to the law are predicated on private disputes, which serves to check the problematic characteristics of public ordering.[42]

CONCLUSION

Classical liberalism is often conflated with libertarianism, and, on issues relating to technology, libertarianism writ large is often conflated with particular strains of anarcho-capitalism and techno- and crypto-libertarianism. These strains embrace extreme views of the liberty-enhancing potential of technology. But they are also in tension with the classical liberal acceptance of a minimal set of legal institutions as necessary to protect individual autonomy and promote stable private ordering. Indeed, the hallmark of much of the techno-libertarian ideal is disruption – including disruption of the very institutions that classical liberalism identifies as necessary in order to promote individual liberty and social welfare.

This suggests tensions between the classical liberal and the ascendant libertarian impulses that drive many in the modern technology sphere. These tensions are real. But the greater tensions are within classical liberalism itself. Classical liberalism accepts – even posits – the need for legal institutions, but does not provide an endogenous explanation for the origins, extent, or nature of those institutions. Contemporary thinkers in the classical liberal tradition are likely to ground these institutions in welfare and transaction cost economics. But technological changes can lead to meaningful changes in transaction costs and shifts in the allocation of social welfare (that is, the efficient ordering of private resources). In other words, technology is exogenous to the principles of classical liberalism, such that the

---

[41] *See generally* ELINOR OSTROM, GOVERNING THE COMMONS: THE EVOLUTION OF INSTITUTIONS FOR COLLECTIVE ACTION (1990); ROBERT ELLICKSON, ORDER WITHOUT LAW: HOW NEIGHBORS SETTLE DISPUTES (1991).

[42] See, for example, Justin (Gus) Hurwitz, *Data Security and the FTC's UnCommon Law*, 101 IOWA LAW REVIEW 955, 981 (2016) (discussing that, while common law judges do make law, "they do not embrace this function warmly," and the various obstacles that exist to limit the scope of judicial rule making).

fundamental institutions of classical liberalism are themselves defined (at least in part) exogenously. This leads to the peculiar result that, lacking internal principles to guide the private ordering of its institutions, classical liberalism must rely in part on a public ordering of the institutions that govern the private ordering that it seeks to facilitate.

The modern era of disruptive technology has magnified this tension. There is little question that much of modern technological advance ends up enhancing liberty and promoting private ordering. But disruption almost by definition implies winners and losers, and the spoils of disruption do not necessarily fall efficiently, either to the winners or the losers. The classical liberal prefers Pareto efficient transactions, and is relatively averse to transactions that are merely Kaldor-Hicks efficient. But technological advance – and especially disruptive advance – places us squarely in the uncomfortable realm of Kaldor-Hicks efficiency: Either we allow disruption, allowing harm to those disrupted; or we deny disruption, denying benefits to would-be disruptors. Without both a sense of the magnitude of harm and an efficient means by which to compensate for it, we are no longer operating in the realm of voluntary private ordering – that is, in the realm of classical liberalism.

The safest response to this conundrum for the committed classical liberal is likely to recommit to the basic principle of simple rules developed through the common-law mechanism. These are least likely to be disrupted and most likely to transfer relatively unscathed between technological regimes. Too often legal institutions have embraced complexity, either on their own or in response to specific technologies. Such complexity runs counter to classical liberalism and compounds the confounding conundrum that technology poses to principle. Instead, when confronted with technological change, classical liberalism's future more likely lies in its past. As usual, Richard Epstein got things right: "The proper response to more complex societies should be ever greater reliance on simple legal rules, including older rules too often and too easily dismissed as curious relics of some bygone horse-and-buggy age."[43]

---

[43] Richard A. Epstein, Simple Rules for a Complex World 21 (1995).

14

Classical Liberalism, Race, and Mass Incarceration

Aziz Z. Huq

PART I

Perhaps classical liberals cannot be faulted for wholly failing to engage with the question of race in the contemporary American legal context, however much one is tempted to resist the manner or results of their efforts. But still, their attention has been relatively blinkered in terms of the ways in which racial identity, and responses to racial identity, inflect the availability of economic, political, and social opportunities. The classical liberal study of race is to date narrowly channeled into an unstinting effort to demonstrate, with the unstinting vigor of a crusader marching under the banner of St. Bernard of Clairvaux, that regulatory intervention into private markets inevitably harms racial minorities.[1] Labor markets, however, are not the only (or even any longer the most important) domain of American life in which racial disparities persist and reproduce in troubling ways. At least since Reconstruction, the problem of race has been inextricably woven with the problem of criminality and social order., particular in the context of northern cities. Race too is entangled with the most important material expansion of the American state into the daily lives of its citizens. Today, roughly one in three black men and one in five Latino men will be incarcerated during their lifetime.[2] Yet the question of mass

---

[1] *See, for example,* RICHARD A. EPSTEIN, FORBIDDEN GROUNDS: THE CASE AGAINST EMPLOY-MENT DISCRIMINATION LAWS 31–47 (1992) (arguing that competitive markets with free entry protect against discrimination better than antidiscrimination law); David E. Bernstein, *Roots of the "Underclass": The Decline of Laissez-Faire Jurisprudence and the Rise of Racist Labor Legislation,* 43 AMERICAN UNIVERSITY LAW REVIEW 85, 87 (1993) ("Lochnerian judicial intervention to protect free labor markets could have saved hundreds of thousands, perhaps millions of blacks from being permanently deprived of their livelihoods.").

[2] BRUCE WESTERN, PUNISHMENT AND INEQUALITY IN AMERICA 31–39 (2006) (describing the growth of the incarcerated population over time, and describing racial inequalities); Cassia Spohn, *Race, Crime, and Punishment in the Twentieth and Twenty-First Centuries,* 44 CRIME & JUSTICE 49, 55 (2015) (noting that in 2001 "the chances of ever going to prison were highest among black males (32.2 percent) and Hispanic males (17.2 percent)").

incarceration, while an occasional consideration on the agenda of antiregulatory political forces,[3] does not impinge on the writings of leading classical liberals of the legal academy.[4] It would seem sometimes that one can be 'against government' while blinking the most fiscally and materially important extrusion of the state into the physical liberty of its citizens.

My modest task in this chapter is to sketch out why classical liberals should not only take a position on the growth of the carceral state, but should make its reform a centrepiece of their agenda. It is not just that those who profess a philosophical commitment to liberty from state coercion really ought to have something to say about a system that reliably generates some of the highest per capita of incarceration (and liberty deprivations) in the world, and this notwithstanding a decade plus of falling crime rates.[5] It is that mass incarceration is underwritten by precisely the sort of political failures that classical liberal pride themselves on exposing and deflating. It is that mass incarceration operates in ways that predictably preclude large slices of the population from the labor market in ways that diminish the scope and effectual operation of free markets. And it is that mass incarceration propagates racially disparate patterns of economic exclusion and isolation across generational lines in ways that entrench racial and economic stratification – phenomena that thoughtful and principled classical libertarians have properly recognized as moral anathemas in other contexts. I will make, in short, a case for thought and action by classical liberals against mass incarceration as it obtains today.

A caveat: I do so as an outsider the classical liberal tradition. I am not a fellow traveler to the roughly right-of-center, antiregulatory camp of policy scholars and think tanks that might reasonably be ranked under that rubric in the United States. Nor, by making this appeal to classical liberals, to I seek admission to their ranks. Indeed, I should be candid at the opening that I sharply disagree with classical liberals about the empirical frequency of market failures, the historical and moral case for redistribution (as opposed to the maximization of net welfare), and the moral value of economic equality. I am unpersuaded by their ranking of economic liberties and property rights as against other normative margins, including dignity, antisubordination, and the freedom from invidious discrimination based on race, creed, or sexual orientation. I am further unpersuaded by their predictive claims about the inevitability of a slippery slope of state intrusion into salutary private ordering that begins with the quotidian regulatory state. My aim here, though, is

---

[3] The Coalition for Public Safety, *Press Release: Fair Sentencing and Fair Chances Campaign*, June 2015, available at http://2s7urjgj9be4a0k0x1ye6t6i.wpengine.netdna-cdn.com/wp-content/uploads/2015/06/CPSFairSentencing.pdf.

[4] For instance, I ran a search in Westlaw's Law Review database for work by Richard Epstein, and "mass incarceration" or "prisons." To my surprise, the nation's leading legal scholar of classical liberalism – a self-professed philosophy of liberty, if nothing else – has literally no articles on that database that mention mass incarceration; six mention "prisons," but none do so in the context of an analysis of the carceral state.

[5] WESTERN, *supra* note 2, at 31–39.

not to air those disagreements (even if I should be candid that they exist), but to offer something that might provoke useful reflection among this book's intended audience.

Why should classical liberals care about the American penal state? Some basic empirics provide a threshold justification for paying attention to the changing use of the criminal law, incarceration, and other forms of state supervision if one priorities the liberties to engage in market transactions and to own property without respect to race, creed, or class. I set out these empirics first (albeit briefly given that the basic facts have been well aired by many in the past). With some rather elemental facts in hand, I then flesh out three distinct reasons for classical liberals to pay close attention to mass incarnation, and in particular its racial aspect.

Since the late twentieth century, the American deployment of incarceration as a tool of social control has been historically and geographically unprecedented in its scale. President Barak Obama succinctly summarized matters as follows in his 2017 *Harvard Law Review* commentary:

> In 1980, there were less than half a million inmates in U.S. state and federal prisons and jails. Today, that figure stands at an estimated 2.2 million, more than any other country on Earth. Many people who commit crimes deserve punishment, and many belong behind bars. But too many, especially nonviolent drug offenders, serve unnecessarily long sentences. With just 5 percent of the world's population, the United States incarcerates nearly 25 percent of the world's prisoners. We keep more people behind bars than the top thirty-five European countries combined, and our rate of incarceration dwarfs not only other Western allies but also countries like Russia and Iran.[6]

Incarceration is also not evenly spread across the population. Since the 1970s, the United States has experienced explosive growth in the size of its prisons. The resulting mass incarceration, as is well known, unequally effects different racial groups. Black men lacking a high school diploma are more than five times more likely to be incarcerated, for example, than similarly situated white men. One in eight black men in their twenties is in prison or jail on any given day. Some 69 percent of black high school dropouts are imprisoned over their lifetime, compared with just 15 percent for white high school dropouts.[7] For young black men, prison has therefore become a regular, predictable part of the life course. It is for these reasons that astute and careful analysts of American criminal justice

---

[6] Barack Obama, *The President's Role in Advancing Criminal Justice Reform*, 130 HARVARD. LAW REVIEW 811, 817 (2017).

[7] This paragraph draws on the following: Bruce Western and Christopher Wildeman, The Black Family and Mass Incarceration, 621 ANNALS OF THE AMERICAN ACADEMY OF POLITICAL & SOCIAL SCIENCE 221 (2009); Bruce Western and Christopher Muller, *Mass Incarceration, Macrosociology, and the Poor.* 647, ANNALS OF THE AMERICAN ACADEMY OF POLITICAL & SOCIAL SCIENCE 166 (2013).

perceive therein "a systematic and institutional phenomenon that reproduces racial inequality and the presumption of black and brown criminality."[8]

Indeed, the term "mass incarceration" has been coined precisely to capture this quite distinct confection of institutional attributes. In the sociology literature, it is properly used to connote the use of imprisonment that is both "markedly above the historical and comparative norm for societies of this type," and that is also disparately allocated among social groups such that "it ceases to be the incarceration of individual offenders and becomes the systemic imprisonment of whole groups of the population."[9] This accurately captures the existing form of the state and federal American criminal justice systems in net, where the "groups" in question are functionally defined in terms of the intersection of racial and class characteristics.

A couple of misapprehensions about this distinctly American phenomenon of mass incarceration are worth clarifying at the threshold. These are worth bearing in mind in relation to the potential classical liberal justifications for mass incarceration, which I will develop at some length below. *First*, it is often assumed that mass incarceration is driven by the war on drugs. This is not so. As of December 31, 2013, more than half (53.2 percent) of prisoners in state incarceration had been sentenced on the basis of violent offenses.[10] Although much of this violence may be related to the narcotics trade, it remains the case that these inmates are not being punished for their possession or distribution of drugs. *Second*, there is nothing particularly deeply rooted about the scale of American mass incarceration as a historical matter. To the contrary, mass incarceration has emerged as a distinctly novel phenomenon from roughly the 1970s onward. Consider, as evidence for this, how the per day incarceration rate has jumped from 133 per 100,000 (in 1980) to 387 per 100,000 (in 1994), and then to 762 per 100,000 (in 2008).[11] *Finally*, there is one element of mass incarceration that does have a longer historical pedigree: its racial disparity. As a historical matter, large racial disparities in incarceration emerged first with the movement of African-Americans to northern industrial centers during the Great Migration, and have persisted even as the sheer scale of the carceral state has expanded.[12]

---

[8] Naomi Murakawa and Katherine Beckett, *The Penology of Racial Innocence: The Erasure of Racism in the Study and Practice of Punishment*, 44 LAW AND SOCIETY REVIEW 695, 701 (2010).

[9] David Garland, Introduction: The Meaning of Mass Imprisonment, in MASS IMPRISONMENT: SOCIAL CAUSES AND CONSEQUENCES 1, 1–2 (David Garland ed., 2001).

[10] E. Ann Carson, Bureau of Justice Statistics, *Prisoners in 2014*, at 15 (Sept. 2015), available at www.bjs.gov/content/pub/pdf/p14.pdf.

[11] Anne R. Traum, *Mass Incarceration at Sentencing*, 64 HASTINGS LAW JOURNAL 423, 428–29 (2013).

[12] Christopher Muller, *Northward Migration and the Rise of Racial Disparity in American Incarceration, 1880–1950*, 118 AMERICAN JOURNAL OF SOCIOLOGY 281 (2012).

PART II

The classical liberal case against mass incarceration might begin and end with the brute fact of these numbers. What else might better repudiate the ideal of freedom than the persistence of an extensive and intrusive state apparatus of detection and detention? Why worry about a slippery slope to authoritarianism whose opening salve is the federal the healthcare mandate, when there is, in fact, a functionally totalitarian state that grinds into action in the urban schoolyard and thereafter relentless shapes a predictable set of American communities?[13] The resulting disincentives to invest in human capital, the wholesale withdrawals from the labor market, and the sheer deadweight cost of the resulting economic waste are impressive and perhaps decisive on their own.

I want to work through three further reasons for classical liberal concern about mass incarceration as I have depicted it, and in so doing respond to what seems to me the most straightforward justification that the classical liberal might give for accepting, and even embracing, the American carceral state. Both the origins and persistence of mass incarceration, I will suggest, are entangled in the repudiation of classical liberal ideals of maximally private ordering and a minimal, Nozeckian state. Classical liberalism, moreover, may have a distinctive own critique of mass incarceration notwithstanding its own potential culpability in the latter's creations.

To begin with, it is implicit in what I have already said that the modern phenomenon of mass incarceration is not an obvious or necessary correlate of the free market. It is, rather, a recent and geographically idiosyncratic phenomenon (except insofar as it has large, racially disparate effects that has predictable local coordinates). Even the United Kingdom – a nation that is perhaps closest to the United States in terms of social welfare and regulatory provision than any other comparable democracy – does not have anything like the extent of incarceration that America does.[14] Mass incarceration is not a necessary or an appropriate correlate of the free market state. The night watchman state, in other words, need not be engorged with coercive power to be effectual. And to the extent it is possible to maintain economic freedoms without the extensive apparatus of investigation and punishment, then the latter should be rejected as incompatible with the maximal definition of liberty across the population. This conclusion is not without

---

[13] SARAH E. REDFIELD AND JASON P. NANCE, AM. BAR ASS'N, SCHOOL-TO-PRISON PIPELINE: PRELIMINARY REPORT (2016), www.americanbar.org/content/dam/aba/administrative/diversity_pipeline/stp_preliminary_report_final.authcheckdam.pdf [https://perma.cc/2TWQ-LGW2].

[14] For a comparison of the United States and the United Kingdom, see NICOLA LACEY, THE PRISONERS' DILEMMA: POLITICAL ECONOMY AND PUNISHMENT IN CONTEMPORARY DEMOCRACIES 27–28 (2008).

its problems, especially once considered in a comparative political economy perspective,[15] but it has sufficient force for our purposes today.

Yet recall now the large role that violent crime has played in the growth of mass incarceration. That fact points to a potential riposte to the argument from mass incarceration's sheer scale, which would go as follows. The United States has experienced an unprecedented wave of crime in the second half of the twentieth century, one that has no analog in our European or North American neighbors. Reported street crime quadrupled in the twelve years from 1959 to 1971, and homicide rates doubled between 1963 and 1974.[16] Public punitiveness increased markedly in that period as a result of this crime wave (and continued to rise steadily even as crime rates started to recede in the 1990s).[17] The emergence of mass incarceration simply reflects and responds to these underlying realities: If American criminal policy-making in the late twentieth century is distinctive, that is, this is because of changes in the social reality of crime. This argument is best developed by John Pfaff in a series of empirical and doctrinal contributions.[18] One classical liberal inference from these empirical facts is that neither the scale nor the racial disparity of mass incarceration should be all that morally troubling. For it is just a product of our time, our troubles, and the inevitable public reaction to them.

While is there much to learn from Pfaff's scholarship in particular, I do not think it is possible to neutralize the moral concerns raised by mass incarceration in the way that I have just described. There are a number of reasons for this. To begin with, the best studies of the effect of crime on incarceration rates suggest that at best only about half of the rise in the latter can be explained by the rise in crime.[19] Still, given

[15]   There is an argument, though, that mass incarceration develops in the absence of thick social welfare provision for less wealthy segments of society. For empirical evidence, see Katherine Beckett and Bruce Western, *Governing Social Marginality: Welfare, Incarceration, and the Transformation of State Policy*, 2 PUNISHMENT & SOCIETY 43, 46 (2001). If a robustly redistributive welfare state and a robustly punitive carceral state are indeed functionally necessary substitutes, there is a question for classical liberals of which alternative they prefer. Moreover, it may well be that US economic growth is in decline, and that a bifurcated labor market with few avenues of income mobility will be unavoidable in the near term. *See* Robert J. Gordon, *Is U.S. Economic Growth Over? Faltering Innovation Confronts Six Headwinds*, NBER Working Paper No. 18315, Aug, 2015. Under these conditions, it may well be impossible to maintain social control without a robust social safety net or a robust punitive state. And since the United States is likely incapable of the former, it is stuck with the latter.

[16]   GARY LaFREE, LOSING LEGITIMACY: STREET CRIME AND THE DECLINE OF SOCIAL INSTITUTIONS IN AMERICA 20–22 (1998).

[17]   Peter K. Enns, *The Public's Increasing Punitiveness and Its Impact on Mass Incarceration in the United States*, 58 AMERICAN JOURNAL OF POLITICAL SCIENCE 857, 862 fig. 1 (2014).

[18]   *See, for example*, John F. Pfaff, *The Durability of Prison Populations*, 2010 UNIVERSITY OF CHICAGO LEGAL FORUM 73 (2010); John F. Pfaff, *The Myths and Realities of Correctional Severity: Evidence from the National Corrections Reporting Program*, 13 AMERICAN LAW AND ECONOMICS REVIEW 491 (2011); John F. Pfaff, *The Empirics of Prison Growth: A Critical Review and Path Forward*, 98 JOURNAL OF CRIMINAL LAW & CRIMINOLOGY 547 (2008).

[19]   Yair Listokin, *Does More Crime Mean More Prisoners? An Instrumental Variable Approach*, 46 JOURNAL OF LAW & ECONOMICS 181 (2003).

the scale of American mass incarceration, this leaves much to be explained. Just as the comparison between Britain and American isolated a substantial fraction of carceral growth this side of the Atlantic that remains unexplained, so the empirical evidence suggests the rising crime rate can only do so much justificatory work.

Moreover, the causal connection between changes in the crime rate and shifts in legislative policy is a complex and contingent one. Public attitudes to crime have never mechanically responded to changes in criminality levels. Rather, they have lagged considerably behind.[20] Partisan mobilization among political elites aimed at rendering crime salient as an object of policy-making instead played a necessary mediating role between observed crime rates and perceptions of crime as an object of public policy.[21] The classical liberal scepticism of the democratic process here might be put to an effectual use here: For it cannot be assumed that crime drives public policy in some simple way, or that the only way to respond to increasing crime is through increasingly punitive measures. The punitive turn of US political rhetoric at a moment of relatively low crime outside a cluster of northern cities is a timely reminder of that. Finally, the evidence that increases in incarceration lead to decreases in crime is surprisingly weak.[22] The marginal deterrence effect of each new prison year accrued as mass incarceration has swelled, experts argue, has dropped precipitously as the number of years imposed on the modal prisoner has spiralled upward.[23] A functional argument that seeks to reason from the fact of rising crime to the moral legitimacy of mass incarceration in classical liberal terms, in short, lacks many of the necessary empirical predicates to be persuasive.

The second reason for classical liberal engagement concerns the political economy of mass incarceration. On my read, classical liberals are commonly deeply suspicious of the political demands of organized labor and of factions within the government (i.e.., public-sector unions) as anti-market forces.[24] Separately, they are also deeply skeptical of administrative discretion, which they view as fundamentally

---

[20] Vesla M. Weaver, *Frontlash: Race and the Development of Punitive Crime Policy*, 21 STUDIES IN AMERICAN POLITICAL DEVELOPMENT 230, 245 fig. 4 (2007); *see also* Joachim J. Savelsberg, *Knowledge, Domination, and Criminal Punishment*, 99 AMERICAN JOURNAL OF SOCIOLOGY 911, 920 (1995).

[21] KATHERINE BECKETT, MAKING CRIME PAY: LAW AND ORDER IN CONTEMPORARY AMERICAN POLITICS (2000).

[22] STEVEN RAPHAEL AND MICHAEL A. STOLL, DO PRISONS MAKE US SAFER? THE BENEFITS AND COSTS OF THE PRISON BOOM (2009); Timothy Head and Grover Norquist, *The High Costs of Over-Incarceration*, NATIONAL REVIEW (Aug. 13, 2015, 4:00 AM), http://www.nationalreview .com/article/422476/over-incarceration-not-making-america-safer [https://perma.cc/3S2U-ZHB2]

[23] For an excellent summary of the relevant research, see Daniel S. Nagin, *Deterrence in the Twenty-First Century*, 42 CRIME & JUSTICE 199 (2013).

[24] On public sector unions, see Richard A. Epstein, *Labor Unions: Saviors or Scourges?*, 41 CAPITAL UNIVERSITY LAW REVIEW 1 (2013). On unions more generally, see Richard A. Epstein, *A Common Law for Labor Relations: A Critique of the New Deal Labor Legislation*, 92 YALE LAW JOURNAL 1357 (1983).

in tension with the rule of law.[25] Examination of the causal foundations of mass incarceration yields examples of why both these criticisms can have some force, if given the right facts with which to work. Public sector unions now provide necessary political support for the maintenance of mass incarceration as a growing concern. This political support matters in particular because of imprisonment's exorbitant fiscal cost which might otherwise force reform upon cost-conscious state legislators. Prison costs now account for one out of every fifteen state general fund discretionary dollars. Criminal justice is the second-fastest-growing category of state budgets, lagging behind only Medicaid: 90 percent of that spending goes to prisons, rather than on preventive measures such as increased police presences. Compounding the normative objection from classical liberal principles, the discretionary authority exercised by officials such as police, prosecutors, and prison guards (who are often if not inevitably members of those public sector unions) is also a likely cause of a substantial tranche of the observed racial disparities in the criminal justice system.

The role of prison unions, on the one hand, and investigative and prosecutorial discretion, on the other, is especially important here. Joshua Page's work on the California Correctional Peace Officers Association (or CCPOA) demonstrates how that union has successfully thwarted even inframarginal efforts to bend the carceral curve in that state.[26] Page explains that the CCPOA did not exist at the beginning of the 1980. But by the late 1990s, the union was consistently the largest donor to state senate and assembly candidates in California. In a perverse example of what Paul Pierson calls the "policies making politics" dynamic, the CCPOA's political influence grew roughly in lockstep with the state's prison expansion, making it a powerful force in California politics that was able to repeatedly defeat reform attempts to deal with overcriminalization and overcrowding. Statal growth thus begat the conditions under which institutional metastasis was impossible to cure. Prison unions are not the only element of organized labor to play an instrumental role in maintaining mass incarceration. Police unions have also played a role in defeating both legislative and referendum-based reform efforts, thereby locking in revenue flows associated with a large carceral state.[27] Police unions have also been responsible for installing bespoke procedural protections for officers charged with unlawful violence, protections that have the effect of making the investigation and punishment of such illegal acts practically impossible.[28]

---

[25] *See, for example,* Richard A. Epstein, *The Perilous Position of the Rule of Law and the Administrative State,* 36 HARVARD JOURNAL OF LAW AND PUBLIC POLICY 5 (2013).

[26] JOSHUA PAGE, THE TOUGHEST BEAT: POLITICS, PUNISHMENT, AND THE PRISON OFFICERS UNION IN CALIFORNIA (2011).

[27] Michael C. Campbell, Politics, Prisons, and Law Enforcement: An Examination of the Emergence of "Law and Order" Politics in Texas, 45 LAW & SOCIETY REVIEW 631, 661–62 (2011).

[28] For a documentation and legal analysis of these provisions, see Aziz Z. Huq and Richard McAdams, *Litigating the Blue Wall of Silence,* 2016 University of Chicago Legal Forum 213 (2016).

The effects of these lobbying efforts by police and prison unions are not racially neutral. Rather, the size of a local jurisdiction's police force is in practice tightly correlated to the racial and ethnic composition of that jurisdiction, even after controlling for crime rates.[29] This suggests that law enforcement is able to leverage perceptions of racial threat to obtain larger rents for their agencies. But it is also important to flag that even as spending on police tends to rise along with ethnic heterogeneity, spending on other public goods, such as roads and sanitation, tends to fall.[30] Hence, it may be that in some jurisdictions, there is no net spending change with an increase in public union power.

In addition, administrative discretion of a species that classical liberalism decries has played a necessary role in the production of racial disparities across mass incarceration. This occurs at a number of different levels. Consider here the case of the war on drugs. Narcotics enforcement is distinct from the regulation of index crimes such as murder, assault or rape. Because it is a consensual activity, participants in the narcotics trade rarely make calls for police aid; self-help likely dominates. On the contrary, it is up to police to develop who and where to police. This discretion is consistently exercised, according to a number of studies, in ways that are better predicted by race than by geographic patterns of criminality. For example, Jeffrey Fagan's study of the allocation of street stops in New York city demonstrated that race, above and beyond local crime rates, predicted the density of stops in a given neighborhood.[31] Katherine Beckett and colleagues' study of drug markets in Seattle shows that enforcement there is channeled to black neighborhoods even when there is open-air dealing in white neighborhoods; and within drug markets, Beckett et al. hence, enforcement is predicted by race, not criminal activity.[32] In the Capitol Hill neighborhood of Seattle, they found for example, three percent of those purchasing narcotics were African-American, while 20.5 percent of those arrested were African-American. They further demonstrated that predominantly white outdoor drugs markets received far less attention from police than racially diverse ones. Nor is the problematic exercise if discretion confined to the investigatory stage of the

---

[29] Brian J. Stultz and Eric P. Baumer, *Racial Context and Police Force Size: Evaluating the Empirical Validity of the Minority Threat Perspective*, 113 AMERICAN JOURNAL OF SOCIOLOGY 507, 535–37 (2007); Olugbenga Ajilore and John Smith, *Ethnic Fragmentation and Police Spending*, 18 APPLIED ECONOMIC LETTERS 329, 331 (2011).

[30] Soomi Lee et al., *Ethnic Diversity and Public Good Provision: Evidence from U.S. Municipalities and School Districts*, 51 URBAN AFFAIRS REVIEW 1, 21 (2015).

[31] Expert Report of Dr. Jeffrey Fagan at 40, *Floyd v. City of New York*, 813 F. Supp. 2d 417 (S.D.N.Y. 2011), https://ccrjustice.org/sites/default/files/assets/files/Expert_Report_JeffreyFagan .pdf; Andrew Gelman, Jeffrey Fagan, and Alex Kiss, *An Analysis of the New York City Police Department's "Stop and Frisk" Policy in the Context of Claims of Racial Bias*, 102 JOURNAL OF THE AMERICAN STATISTICAL ASSOCIATION 813 (2007).

[32] Katherine Beckett, Kris Nyrop, and Lori Pfingst, *Race, Drugs, and Policing: Understanding Disparities in Drug Delivery Arrests*, 44 CRIMINOLOGY 105 (2006); Katherine Beckett et al., *Drug Use, Drug Possession Arrests, and the Question of Race: Lessons from Seattle*, 52 SOCIAL PROBLEMS 419 (2005).

criminal process. The racially disparate exercise of police discretion is not confined to the narcotics context, and can be identified in many other police policy decisions, such as decisions about how and where to deploy beat-level officers across different geographic areas, and whether to require those officers to aggressively stop and interrogate members of the public. [33] At the adjudicative level, similarly, Sonja Starr and Marit Rehavi find, even holding all else equal, prosecutors are twice as likely to invoke mandatory minimums against blacks as against whites.[34]

To the extent that classical liberalism, in short, is concerned either with labor-side cartelization and its perverse effects on the political process, or with the abuse of administrative discretion, mass incarceration ought to be in its advocates' sights. Even if one were to set aside the deleterious effects on economic and physical liberty at issue here, these should provide independent bases for classical liberal concern.

The final reason for concern about mass incarceration relates to its intergenerational dynamics. Mass incarceration has predictable collateral effects on the private ordering of families and communities subjected to intensive policing. These conduce to the reproduction over time and within families of asymmetrical patterns of economic opportunity and exposure to the criminal justice system across generational lines.[35] As a consequence, constraints on economic opportunity and the operation of free markets are not only engendered but also transmitted across generational lines.

The careful empirical work of Sarah Wakefield and Chris Wildeman is especially illuminating on this point.[36] Most strikingly to me, they show that recent parental incarceration is associated with a 49 percent increase in infant mortality in rigorous specifications, an effect that is substantially greater than the increase linked to maternal smoking. In addition, paternal incarceration doubles the risk of child homelessness, but this risk is allocated differently between racial groups: Parental incarceration has no effect on homelessness in white and Latino families. Its effect is solely concentrated on African-American children. More generally, the adverse effects of parental incarceration are concentrated among children whose parents were arrested for non-violent crimes. One does not need classical liberal lens to see this as a tragedy of grave proportions; still, the classical liberal perspective picks out distinct elements of the resulting opportunity costs that are worth mourning.

Wakefield and Wildeman estimate large black-white gaps in incarceration's effect on children, in particular respecting the risk of homelessness. Because black-white disparities in incarceration have increased since the beginning of mass incarceration

---

[33] Aziz Z. Huq, *The Consequences of Disparate Policing*, 101 Minnesota Law Review 2397 (2017).

[34] Sonja B. Starr and M. Marit Rehavi, *Mandatory Sentencing and Racial Disparity: Assessing the Role of Prosecutors and the Effects of* Booker, 132 YALE LAW JOURNAL 2 (2013).

[35] For an early study, see Dorothy E. Roberts, *The Social and Moral Cost of Mass Incarceration in African American Communities*, 56 STANFORD LAW REVIEW 1271, 1304 (2004).

[36] The following draws from SARAH WAKEFIELD AND CHRISTOPHER WILDEMAN, CHILDREN OF THE PRISON BOOM: MASS INCARCERATION AND THE FUTURE OF AMERICAN INEQUALITY (2014).

in the 1970s, the inequality-related effect on children varies by age cohort. The intergenerational transmission of inequality has grown larger with each cohort from the 1970s onward. Their careful empirical work finds that recent parental incarceration is now associated with an astonishing 49 percent increase in infant mortality in African-American families. Based on this and other findings, Wakefield and Wildeman persuasively argue that mass incarceration has a causal role in the intergenerational reproduction of racial disparities in health, educational and socioeconomic outcomes. That role, to emphasize, is only growing stronger with time, creating ever increasing ripple effects.

The net effect of their findings is that mass incarceration has a self-perpetuating dynamic. It ensures that a predictable class of persons will be consistently denied adequate familial support, and as a result shut out of educational opportunities, labor markets, and otherwise socially marginalized from one generation to the next. Analysed at the level of neighbourhood units, moreover, the policing predicate of mass incarceration turns out to lead to higher rather than lower levels of crime because of incarceration's effect on felons' opportunities in the formal job market.[37] The classical liberal assumption of a baseline in which all participate in the market on roughly equal terms without a thumb on the scale by the state is thus thoroughly compromised by mass incarceration, especially in light of the latter's deep intergenerational consequences.

PART III

I have suggested in this chapter that classical liberalism *should* be concerned with mass incarceration. I want to close by asking a necessarily tentative and exploratory question: But then what explains the glaring absence of mass incarceration in classical liberal scholarship? And notwithstanding the force of the arguments (if any) developed earlier, is there any reason to expect the classical liberal focus to change? I have no firm answers to these questions, and offer here what is concededly a set of tentative speculations.

One possibility is that an academic division of labor is in effect. Classical liberals perceive themselves as focusing on economic liberties in the context of the regulatory state in part because left liberal scholars have occupied the field (or have the ground covered) when it comes to the criminal law and the criminal-justice state. But this would be passing odd insofar as the critiques that classical liberals (which, as I have suggested, might sound in the register of public choice mechanisms and efficiency effects) are distinct and different from those that tend to come from the left. Moreover, I see little reason to believe that individual scholars working in the classical liberal tradition shy away from an area because there are other scholars

---

[37] Jeffrey Fagan, Valerie West, and Jan Holland, *Reciprocal Effects of Crime and Incarceration in New York City Neighborhoods*, 30 FORDHAM URBAN LAW JOURNAL 1551 (2003).

tilling the same ground. Quite the contrary. The argument from the division of labor, in short, seems quite weak.

Another, perhaps more troubling scenario, ought then to be considered: The deregulatory agenda that classical liberal scholars in the legal academy have most aggressively pressed is aligned with one rather than the other political party, although the extent to which deregulation is in fact a Republican domain is in practice more complicated than some believe. The same political party that has embraced deregulation, however, has also embraced a "Southern Strategy" in which anti-crime rhetoric became a way of way of covertly appealing to race-based preferences.[38] If the Republican party welded together racial populists and classical liberals (among others) into an effectual political alliance, the silence of classical liberals on questions of race and criminal justice might be understood to be a predictable response to the dynamics of coalitional politics. It might be understood, that is, as the necessary sacrifice of the pragmatic political actor in the face of inconsistent and warring functional allegiances.

This hypothesis is hard, if not impossible, to prove (although the 2016 election cycle did nothing to abate concerns along these lines). I don't offer it here as anything more than a stimulus for reflection on the relationship between legal scholarship and the felt political necessities of the day.

But it does lead to a broader question. Imagine that the Republican party had consolidated national political power under a leader with strong deregulatory impulses, but also with many other less savory traits – ranging from a tendency to lie and shade on ethical norms; a tendency to disparage others based on race, creed, or gender, and to encourage his supporters to verbally and physically assault those minorities; and a willingness to play fast and loose with the necessary conventions of competitive democracy in ways that place the latter's institutional predicates in peril. What then should the classical liberal do? Her commitments would then be put to the test: At what point, after what indignities against government under the rule of law, or repudiations of elementary human decency, should they dissociate themselves from the political alliance that could further their deregulatory goals? How should they focus their limited political capital when the same actor might be pursuing deregulation and racial or religious exclusion and discrimination? We are not often put to the test of our core commitments. But for classical liberals, and for classical liberalism as a creed, the moral reckoning may come sooner than later, and perhaps sooner than many are prepared to recognize.

---

[38] Tali Mendelberg, The Race Card: Campaign Strategy, Implicit Messages, and the Norm of Equality 135–65 (2001); Kathleen Hall Jamieson, Dirty Politics: Deception, Distraction, and Democracy (1992).

15

Seven Problems for Classical Liberals

Louis Michael Seidman

In this chapter, I specify seven problems for classical liberals. I make no claim that I am the first to notice these problems, that I have explored them in anything like the depth that they deserve, or that classical liberals have not developed responses to each of them. Nor do I claim that every problem I discuss below is implicated in every version of classical liberalism. The label "classical liberalism" applies to a variety of doctrines, predispositions, and ideological stances including Hayekian libertarianism, neoclassical economics, and Lockean political theory, that are not fully consistent with each other. (I return to this point at the end of this comment.)

The claim I do make is that taken as a whole, the problems I identify, presented here as snapshots rather than worked out argument, pose an important challenge for all forms of classical liberalism.

THE PROBLEM OF EXTERNALITIES

Classical liberals have a preference for private markets, but they are virtually unanimous in supporting government regulation when markets fail to function. An important occasion on which they fail is when external costs, not borne by the parties to private transactions, produce inefficient outcomes. In theory, third parties could bargain to eliminate inefficient externalities that harm them, but as a practical matter, high transaction costs (produced, for example, by strategic behavior and difficulties in coordination as well as the literal cost of negotiation) often prevent bargaining, especially when the externalities are diffuse.

If this problem arose only occasionally, it might be domesticated by adopting a rebuttable presumption in favor of free markets and a Pigouvian tax when they fail.[1] Unfortunately for libertarians, domestication is impossible because the externalities

---

[1] *See* Arthur C. Pigou, *The Economics of Welfare* (1920).

problem arises in every case.[2] Every transaction produces externalities, if only because some outsiders simply do not want the transaction to occur.

Consider, for example, the problem of same sex marriage. Same sex marriages make the couples who agree to marry happier, but they make religious conservatives who believe that the marriages violate the will of God less happy. If we are to disqualify the external costs imposed on religious conservatives, we need to develop an official theory of legitimate and illegitimate claims to injury. But such a theory would involve the very sort of public resolution of the legitimacy of private preferences that many classical liberals oppose.

Of course, even if the harm to religious conservatives counted, it might not outweigh the benefit to same sex couples. But that fact produces a new problem. In the absence of a functioning market, there is no way to avoid a public valuation of these costs and benefits. Government would, in effect, establish prices for the "commodity" being transferred, thereby again violating a core tenet of classical liberalism. It bears emphasis that this is not an occasional bug in a well working system. The problem arises in every case.

THE PROBLEM OF CONTEXTUAL CHOICE

Libertarians ask us to respect the choices individuals make in a private sphere, but this is not the only context in which people make decisions. The problem is not just that preferences are formed at least in part by an existing culture and existing distributions of entitlements and power and that the preferences would change if these contingent states of affairs changed. That problem is serious enough, especially if one believes that existing distributions of entitlements and power are unjust. Nor is the problem just that choices are sometimes based on misinformation or are irrational. That problem, too, disrupts the simple equation of choice with autonomy. These problems are compounded by the fact that choices can vary when people think of themselves as private consumers or as public citizens.

I regularly vote for candidates who promise to raise my taxes, but when I sit down with my accountant at the beginning of April, I strive to avoid making voluntary contributions to the Internal Revenue Service. As a public citizen, I worry about the welfare of desperate refugees around the world, but that doesn't stop me from spending money on food for my dog when I could use the money to contribute to agencies that assist migrants.

These contradictions are not special to me. All of us have different and contradictory public and private preferences. Classical liberals need to explain why private preferences should prevail over public preferences. The economist's insistence that preferences be "revealed" by willingness to pay begs rather than answers the

---

[2]   The argument I make here restates the point made in Duncan Kennedy, "Cost-Benefit Analysis of Entitlements: A Critique," 33 STAN. L. REV. 387, 394–402 (1981).

question. Insisting on preferences elicited under market conditions is simply another way of insisting that private preferences should prevail. Why not force people to reveal their preferences by willingness to vote for a candidate?

Of course, there is also no reason to systematically favor public choices. More-over, elections are an imperfect way to measure those choices. Votes may not measure intensity of preference and when we aggregate them, they are subject to well-known Arrovian and public choice problems.[3] But markets are not perfect proxies for private choices either. They are subject to a parallel set of similarly well-known difficulties produced by wealth and endowment effects and market imperfections. And even if markets functioned perfectly, we still have no reason for conclusively preferring the choices that they elicit. Put more globally, classical liberals need a theory for why the problems of democratic choice are more serious than those of free markets.

THE PROBLEM OF PRIVATE POWER

Classical liberals fear government coercion. I make no claim that this fear is baseless. Still, one must balance the danger of private coercion against this risk. As Robert Hale demonstrated almost a century ago,[4] every private transaction is infected by coercion. In Hale's example, a baker who agreed to work more than ten hours per day was not doing so because of the deep, sensual pleasure derived from making bread. He accepted these conditions because he was threatened with starvation if he refused them. Similarly, in our own time, individuals do not "freely" accept sexual harassment on the job, live in substandard housing, or give up their privacy when they go on line. They do these things because they are threatened with a worse alternative if they do not comply.

At the simplest level, Hale's critique suggests that sometimes, authentic freedom is produced by government intervention that curbs private power. But the critique cuts deeper than this. As Hale explicitly acknowledged, a world where workers had greater bargaining power would not produce perfect freedom. If workers had more bargaining power, they would coerce employers. Whatever the distribution of power, all decisions are embedded in a context that makes one outcome seem better than the other. That context can always be characterized as a "threat" that is coercive.

Robert Nozick, among many others, has shown that the difference between offers that expand freedom and threats that contract freedom depends on the baseline from

---

3   *See, for example,* KENNETH J. ARROW, SOCIAL CHOICE AND INDIVIDUAL VALUES (1963); JAMES
    M. BUCHANAN AND GORDON R. TULLOCK, THE CALCULUS OF CONSENT (1962).
4   *See* Robert L. Hale, "Coercion and Distribution in a Supposedly Non-Coercive State," 38 POL.
    SCI. Q. 470 (1923).

which one starts.[5] One "threatens" to take away an existing entitlement, but one "offers" to transfer a new one. A well-known hypothetical illustrates the point. If A is drowning and B comes by with a rope, B can say "I'd like to offer you the rope for $100," or "if you don't give me $100, you are going to drown." Without a specification of entitlements, the only difference between the proposed transactions is B's choice of words and tone of voice. Once one specifies whether there is a duty to rescue, however, then B is either extorting money to maintain an existing entitlement or offering a free exchange to create a new entitlement. Of course, the problem for libertarians is that if "freedom" is dependent on the distribution of entitlements, then it cannot also be true, as libertarians suppose, that entitlements should be distributed so as to maximize freedom.

There are two ways out of this circle, neither of which is friendly to classical liberalism. First, we might decide on some other grounds – efficiency, perhaps, or justice, or simply taste – how to distribute entitlements. The problem here is that the initial distribution will inevitably be a collective decision made by government, and there cannot be a libertarian world of private freedom if the very categories of freedom and coercion are defined by government choice.

The second escape is to treat freedom and coercion as phenomenological rather than analytic categories. On this view, people have the experience of acting freely or being coerced, but the experience is not reducible to a theoretical construct. The problem with this resolution for libertarians is that for many people, the most immediate and powerful experiences of coercion come from other private actors – from their supervisor at work, their spouse, the aggressive driver who cuts them off on the highway, or simply the larger private market that limits their opportunities. In these circumstances, government intervention can alleviate, rather than aggravate the lived experience of coercion. Worse yet, perceptions of public and private coercion might themselves be rooted in libertarian or statist ideology. To the extent that is true, we have not escaped the circle at all.

THE PROBLEM OF FEASANCE AND NONFEASANCE

Liberal theory makes no sense unless an autonomous private sphere is possible, but that possibility, in turn, rests on a strong distinction between feasance and nonfeasance. The problem arises on two different levels. First, in order for the private sphere to function, government must protect the rights of individuals acting within it. But the distinction between a rights invasion, on the one hand, and the exercise of freedom, on the other, usually depends on the distinction between doing and letting

---

[5] *See* Robert Nozick, "Coercion," *in* SIDNEY MORGENBESSER, PATRICK SUPPES, AND MORTON WHITE, EDS., PHILOSOPHY, SCIENCE, AND METHOD: ESSAYS IN HONOR OF ERNEST NAGEL 440, 447 (1969).

happen. As Ronald Coase among many others saw,[6] without such a distinction, there are merely two incompatible activities with neither having a presumptive advantage and an unavoidably collective choice between them.

Second, classical liberals must distinguish between government action that threatens freedom and government inaction that permits it. For obvious reasons, that distinction also rests on a strong differentiation between feasance and nonfeasance.

The first level distinction is illustrated by the drowning hypothetical discussed above. At common law, A had no right to be rescued because B, simply by letting A drown, did not invade A's rights. If B had pushed A into the water – if she had acted rather than failed to act – then she would have invaded B's rights and, so, been legally responsible.

The second level distinction is embodied in the "state action" doctrine that is central to American constitutional law. When the government "acts," it is subject to a variety of limits that are thought to protect us from tyranny. When it merely fails to act, it is not constitutionally responsible for evils it might easily avoid. For example, if the government fails to regulate private media, it is not responsible when the media limits the "freedom of speech" of unpopular groups that are denied access.[7] But if the government acts to guarantee fair access, it may well violate the media's first amendment's free speech guarantee.[8]

The problems posed by both of these distinctions are well known, and intuitions about them are easy to destabilize. Has the doctor who fails to change the battery on the heart-lung machine merely failed to act? Is it unconstitutional for the government to enforce restrictive covenants preventing African Americans from purchasing homes in a neighborhood?

The problem is not just with unstable intuitions, however. We have already explored the logical circle at the heart of the first distinction. In fact, the common law regularly punished people who merely failed to act. Individuals under contractual obligation to act could be held to their contracts. Parents could be punished for failing to feed their children, and voluntary rescuers could be held liable when they failed to complete the rescue. More broadly, the "no duty to act" rule was qualified by an exception that provided for liability when there was a "legal duty to act." The circle here is too obvious to require further explication. The upshot is again the bounding of a supposedly private sphere by the publicly determined allocation of entitlements.

A similar problem lies at the heart of the second distinction. As many commentators have pointed out, all supposedly private decisions are made against the backdrop of government action that allows them to occur. The Supreme Court

---

[6] *See* Ronald Coase, "The Problem of Social Cost," 3 J. Law & Econ 1 (1960).

[7] *See, for example,* Columbia Broadcasting System v. Democratic National Committee, 412 U.S. 94 (1973).

[8] *See, for example,* Miami Herald Publishing Co. v. Tornillo, 418 U.S. 241 (1974).

has recognized that the government "acts" when courts grant injunctions enforcing restrictive covenants.[9] Had the justices so chosen, they also could have recognized that the government "acts" when it enforces laws that prevent dissident groups from propagating their messages by hacking into the networks controlled by media companies.

The omnipresence of background state action has led many commentators to argue that we should stop talking about a "state action doctrine" and focus instead on the substantive constitutional question: Is the state action that is always in the background constitutionally permissible?[10] Unfortunately, however, this move entraps us in more circular reasoning. Background state action violates the Constitution's substantive commands if it impermissibly interferes with a private sphere, but the boundaries of the private sphere are defined by the background state action.

These analytic problems with the feasance/nonfeasance distinction are serious, but the more serious problem is moral. Is there an attractive moral theory that draws a clear line between imposing injury and permitting easily preventable injury to occur? Is the person who cannot be bothered to help really morally superior to the person who actively inflicts injury? Standard, usually farfetched, hypotheticals involving out of control trolleys,[11] Indian rebels,[12] and redistributed kidneys[13] can test the strength of our intuitions, but I do not pretend that they can resolve the controversy. Nor do I mean to claim that no lines can be drawn or that moral responsibility for feasance and nonfeasance is always identical. I do mean to claim that, for me at least, the bright and impregnable line between feasance and nonfeasance that classical liberals insist on reflects a kind of moral prissiness that is unattractive. Passive aggression can be a very bad thing. An insistence on keeping one's own hands clean in the face of human suffering that could be avoided by getting them dirty requires a defense, and question-begging references to rights, liberty, and natural states of affairs do not provide it.

THE PROBLEM OF FUNDAMENTAL DISAGREEMENT

Suppose that classical liberals are right. Even if some form of perfectionist liberalism is an attractive comprehensive doctrine, classical liberals must still respond to John Rawls' famous challenge grounded in political liberalism.[14] Whether or not

---

[9] Shelley v. Kramer, 334 U.S. 1 (1948).

[10] *See, for example,* Larry Alexander, "The Public/Private Distinction and Constitutional Limits on Private Power," 10 CONST. COMM. 361 (1993); Robert J. Glennon Jr. and John E. Nowak, "A Functional Analysis of the Fourteenth Amendment 'State Action' Requirement," 1976 SUP. CT. REV. 221.

[11] *See* Judith Jarvis Thompson, "The Trolley Problem," 94 YALE. L. J. 1395 (1985).

[12] *See* Bernard Williams, "A Critique of Utilitarianism," *in* J.J.C. SMART AND BERNARD WILLIAMS, UTILITARIANISM: FOR AND AGAINST 75, 98 (1973).

[13] *See* Leo Katz, "Form and Substance in Law and Morality," 66 U. CHI. L. REV. 566, 588 (1999).

[14] *See* JOHN RAWLS, POLITICAL LIBERALISM (1996).

classical liberals are ultimately right, their views are contested, and the contest is unlikely to be resolved any time soon. How should classical liberals respond to reasonable dissenters from their views who cannot reasonably be expected to accept those views?

Unfortunately for liberals, the effort to respond again entraps them in contradiction. Classical liberals believe that disagreements should be resolved on the individual level by people making choices in a private sphere. But what about the disagreement respecting how disagreement should be resolved? The status of liberalism itself cannot be determined privately. If we are to have a liberal society, there must be some sort of collective choice that establishes and nourishes it.

The first contradiction, then, is that classical liberalism depends for its existence and survival on decision procedures inconsistent with its core premises. If government decision making suffers from all the pathologies that liberals claim for it, a government decision to establish a classically liberal regime should be distrusted and might, for the very reasons that liberals advance, be illegitimate.

The problems become still more serious when one tries to determine the form of collective decision making that would determine the fate of classical liberalism. Clearly, liberal principles cannot be held hostage to majority approval. The core commitment of many classical liberals is to the prepolitical status of natural rights. The whole point of the doctrine is to protect those rights from transient majorities.

But if liberalism is not subject to democratic contestation, then its status must be guaranteed by force against putative popular majorities who disapprove of it. That unfortunate fact puts the much praised liberal defense of civil liberties in a different and much less attractive light. Yes, in a classically liberal society, individuals have religious and speech freedoms, but to what end? As individuals, they can think and say what they want in splendid isolation, but should they organize together to act on their beliefs, the iron fist of liberalism denies them collective autonomy. And all of this in the name of human freedom.

THE PROBLEM OF DISTRIBUTION

Perhaps none of this would be a problem if classical liberalism promised us a just society. But it does not. Free markets allocate goods based upon wealth, but wealth is not the same thing as utility. The declining marginal utility of money results in the rich accumulating more goods than the poor even if the poor would benefit more from the asset. This problem might be corrected by redistributive taxation, but for many classical liberals, taxation is just another form of government regulation, which they oppose.

If the rich were more deserving than the poor, this allocation might be justified on deontological grounds, but there is no reason to think that they are. Inherited wealth, family and cultural backgrounds, genetic traits, and luck are not things that people earn or deserve. They provide no justification for the huge disparities in well-being that classical liberalism produces.

Here and elsewhere, classical liberals are likely to respond with the "compared to what" challenge. That is fair enough. Government regulation and redistribution can impair the incentives to create wealth and can aggravate rather than alleviate inequality. It is a sad fact that wealth disparities produced by private markets seep into political decision making which, in turn, reinforces the most inequitable features of private markets.

But what follows from these observations? Not that private markets are always just and that government intervention is always unjust, as classical liberals suppose. What follows is that the choice between private and public decision making is always contextual and political. When progressives manage to seize the instruments of government power, intervention will be a good thing. When plutocrats control government, deregulation is a good thing. Liberal theory's effort to decontextualize and depoliticize these choices is bound to fail.

THE PROBLEM OF HISTORICAL LOCATION

These observations lead to the deepest problem for classical liberals. The topic of this book presupposes that there is a canonical definition of classical liberalism and that its tenets as so understood produce unambiguous policy recommendations. Each of the problems I have outlined above is rooted in this presupposition.

In fact, though, classical liberalism is not like the Catholic Church. It is not a formal organization with core commitments that define membership or an accepted hierarchy that rigidly controls unchangeable doctrine. (In fact, even the Catholic Church is not like the "Catholic Church" in this respect.) At its inception, classical liberalism responded to a particular set of economic and political difficulties. As those problems have changed, positions taken by people who call themselves classical liberals have changed as well.

As is true of all ideologies, the tenets of classical liberalism are subject to different interpretations, and the boundaries of the ideology are a subject of contestation. Moreover, even to the extent that interpretations and boundaries have been fixed, they intersect with the background social and political situation in different ways at different times. In some circumstances, classical liberalism can be a force for reform and for justice; in others, it can stand for reaction and oppression.

The right question to ask, then, is how classical liberalism intersects with our own circumstances. It is possible to imagine a modern, reformist version of classical liberalism that would emphasize certain strands of the tradition well suited to remedying our present difficulties. We could benefit from clear-eyed critiques of left orthodoxy and creative alternatives to reflexive statism. Market-based proposals to deal with poverty, environmental degradation, health care, and racism might make important contributions. Nor need we merely imagine modern classical liberals who are pursing these goals. There are currently people working within this tradition who have things to say that those of us on the left should spend more time listening to.

The most serious problem, though, is that the tradition is also being put to other uses. It is the preferred ideology of the smug and satisfied who want to entrench huge disparities in power, wealth, and life chances. It provides intellectual ammunition for the forces obstructing collective efforts to control catastrophic outcomes produced by private markets, of which global warming is only the most serious. It is the home for those who reject government regulation designed to end discrimination based on race, gender, and sexual orientation. In short, it is an ideology that some people use to prevent urgently needed measures to make our country morally and materially sustainable.

Reformist classical liberals need to wrest their tradition from the hands of those who would use it for these destructive purposes. Even if they had no other problem, solving this one would be more than enough to keep them busy.

16

Meeting the Fundamental Objections to Classical Liberalism

Richard A. Epstein

There is little doubt that populist movements have gained great strength in recent years. The standard explanation for the British decision to leave the European Union in June 2016 and for the United States to elect Donald Trump as its president in November of that same year both converge on one point: the massive dissatisfaction that many ordinary people have had with the progressive elites that have governed both Great Britain and the United States. The key sources of that unrest have been the sluggish performance of the economy stretching back for many years; the ever-growing size of their government bureaucracies; and the annoying sense that progressive and socialist elites act as if they are morally superior to the rest of the population, which they treat in both words and deeds, with ill-concealed disrespect, or in Hillary Clinton's two most important words uttered in the 2016 election campaign, as "the deplorables."

The out-groups that have gained power and influence in these two transformations are a diverse lot. One fraction can be regarded as nativists and protectionists who are trying to impose isolationism on both Great Britain and the United States. On their behalf, I have nothing to say. But the significant, and probably the dominant, fraction of the protestors can loosely be described as people who show greater respect for private decisions than did the progressive elites whom they have dislodged. In this tumultuous political environment, scholars and commentators should show a greater willingness to reexamine the first principles of government. The results, I believe, will prove congenial to the basic tenets of classical liberalism, which I have championed for my entire academic career of nearly fifty years. That theory, of course, was very much out of favor when Harold Wilson was the prime minister of England and Lyndon Johnson was the president of the United States. The theory had something of a revival with the near parallel rise to power of Margaret Thatcher, prime minister of Great Britain from 1979 to 1990 and Ronald Reagan, president of the United States from 1981 to 1989. Those theories then went into partial eclipse thereafter, most notably during the presidency of Barack Obama from 2009 to 2017, just concluded.

The current turn in political sentiments makes this an opportune time to determine whether the principles of classical liberalism are able to meet various theoretical challenges. In order to answer, it is first necessary to set the table and state precisely the principles of classical liberalism. The easiest approach is to contrast it with hard-core libertarian beliefs in the anarcho-libertarian tradition that are far more restrictive of government power than those held by classical liberals.[1] The two theories start from a common premise of accepting four key rules. The first is a respect for individual autonomy. Normally, every person is entitled to the exclusive control of his or her own body, and thus is able to devote his or her labor to whatever he or she sees fit, with whatever associates that he or she wants. The strongest argument behind this position is consequentialist. Under a legal regime that respects individual autonomy, a person is better off because he can choose the labor and company that he values most. As a first approximation this assumption ought to hold against the claims of other individuals to control or direct any person's personal decisions. Self-ownership is a social conception because it extends to all persons equally, and thus does not introduce any selection bias by race, creed, sex, color, or any other line which private individuals may consider relevant for at least some aspects of their personal lives. Second, initial rights entitle people to own property in the external world, of which land, chattels and animals are the obvious categories. The classic way to acquire property is to possess it first. It is therefore worth noting that no traditional legal system has ever allowed initial occupation to establish private ownership of air, water, and the beach. Those forms of property are, to use the Roman phrase, *res commune*, or open to all, and not *res nullius*, or owned by none until taken by one. I shall explain the reason for this distinction later on.[2]

Now once the rules of self-ownership and property ownership are established, two further rules kick in. The first is the simple proposition that individuals can enter into voluntary transactions for their mutual benefit. In general, their agreements create positive externalities by increasing the transactional opportunities of parties outside the immediate transaction, thereby augmenting the total amount of wealth in society available for further exchange as well as for further investment. The last of the four basic rules is that the entire system of autonomy, property and exchange is protected by a system of tort law that is directed to the use of force and/or fraud against any of these three interests. The law of assault and battery protects the

---

[1]   For a detailed statement of the differences, see Richard A. Epstein, "The Libertarian Quartet, Review of Randy Barnett, The Structure of Liberty: Justice and the Rule of Law," REASON, Jan. 1999, at 61.

[2]   For the initial statement, see Justinian's Institute, Book II, title I. For my defense of that distinction see Richard A. Epstein, "Property Rights in Water, Spectrum, and Minerals," 86 U. COLO. L. REV. 389 (2015); and Richard A. Epstein, "On the Optimal Mix of Private and Common Property," SOC. PHIL. & POL., July 1994, at 17.

integrity of the person; the law of trespass and nuisance protects interests in property, including various indirect harms, like the setting of traps and administrating of poisons; and the law of defamation and interference with advantageous relationships prevents one person from using either force or fraud, both called unfair competition, against other individuals. In effect, the purpose of these rules, as becomes clearer later on, is to stop negative sum games and to advance positive sum games.

These four rules make up a huge start to a sensible society. Even so, this sketch is fatally incomplete. Although it takes into account the risks of aggression in all its protean forms, it pays no attention to the risks of coordination breakdown from various hold-out conditions, including those needed to form the state. Hence the major opposition between the libertarian position and the classical liberal position attaches to the role of forced exchanges. Hard-line libertarians regard them as a core violation of individual autonomy. Classical liberals take the opposite view on such key issues as privilege (as with private necessity) and in the public arena with taxation and exercises of the eminent domain power. Both of these are essentially forced exchanges that are justified on the ground that they overcome holdout problems while leaving, to the extent possible, each individual better off than he or she was in the earlier state of affairs. Under the classical liberal approach, just compensation can take explicit or implicit forms to minimize the distortions that are always inherent in large-number settings. So, taxation is permissible, but to minimize political games, it should be confined to a single base – preferably consumption over income – to minimize the risk that individuals or groups will lobby to increase their share of benefits or reduce their share of costs. Takings of property, both for outright takings and for fractional interests such as liens, leases, air rights or mineral rights, should also be compensated. The compensation could come in the form of in-kind benefits generated by the regulatory scheme itself – that is, by parallel restrictions imposed on all for the benefit of all, thereby creating a Pareto improvement, with some real chances of getting proportionate returns for all investors.

The model for these arrangements is the planned unit development, as created by voluntary agreements in ways that bind all present and future members vis-à-vis each other.[3] But these organizations always have governance structures which allow for collective deliberation over goods that cannot be supplied separately to different individuals, *for example*, the governance of common areas and the operation of the delegated management functions. These organizations often get antecedent consent to resolve difficult choices through a solution that a political system cannot precisely imitate.

---

[3] *See, for example*, for the early implementation, Neponsit Property Owners' Ass'n v. Emigrant Indus. Sa. Bank, 15 N.E.2d 793 (1938). For the instantiation, see Restatement (Third) of Prop.: Servitudes §6 (2000). For my defense of the overall system, see Richard A. Epstein, "Notice and Freedom of Contract in the Law of Servitudes," 55 So. Cal. L. Rev. 1353 (1982).

Just compensation is not perfect – no system can be, given the usual frictions that infect all social arrangements. But even after these limitations are taken into account, the basic classical liberal scheme goes a long way to minimizing the difficulties in building a system that reconciles individual liberty with the common good – more so than any alternative that could be put into its place. Accordingly, I shall defend this system against outsiders' objections, which Michael Seidman presented as disjointed queries in his short but provocative paper that purports to summarize the criticisms of classical liberalism.[4] It is noteworthy that Seidman studiously avoids directing these same questions at any alternative systems, including his own progressive world view. Nonetheless, these alternative approaches should be judged by the same test: whether the system tends to overall improvement in the real, not the best possible, world. Subject to this caveat, I think that these objections are important enough that every theory, including variations of modern progressive theories, must respond. So, in this paper I shall give the answers that flow from classical liberal theory, taking into account whenever necessary other writings, including those prepared by other contributors to this conference volume.

Seidman raises seven major questions. The first of these is the problem of externalities. The second is the problem of contextual choice, covering both the mechanics of preference formation and the role of political theory in sorting out past injustices. The latter involves placing private preferences in their larger social and historical context. The third question is the so-called problem of private power. The fourth is the justification and scope of affirmative duties in both the private and the public spheres. The fifth is the question of how classical liberals can resolve, outside the marketplace, the fundamental disagreements that arise in governance. The sixth is the problem of redistribution. The seventh is the problem of historical location, which is whether there is a uniform classical liberal theory that crosses generations, and, if so, whether it has evolved into a tool to oppress and disadvantage the poor. It is notable that Seidman declined to ground a single one of his seven objections in supporting references or critically apply these objections to actual classical liberal literature. Nor does he provide answers to the objections from his own progressive perspective that get beyond the usual bromides to trust big government to fix all the problems that big government creates. But for the moment, I shall give in basic form the classical liberal response to his seven objections.

EXTERNALITIES EVERYWHERE?

The first objection to classical liberal theory is that it cannot contain the ubiquitous presence of externalities. Classical liberals defend competitive markets for yielding the highest output of goods and services because they exhaust all possible gains from trade in any setting. Seidman notes that their defense falters in those cases where the

---

[4] Louis Michael Seidman, "Seven Problems for Classical Liberals" (Chapter 15).

markets "fail to function," but he draws the mistaken inference that markets always fail to function because every voluntary transaction necessarily imposes negative externalities on other individuals. These externalities are so pervasive that they cannot be corrected by multitudinous market transactions, which would be prohibitively expensive to execute. Seidman calls the theory broken because "the externalities problem arises in every case."

His proposition is literally true, but it is of no consequence in its broadest form. Externalities must be evaluated by distinct type, each understood in its own specific context. The point is shown most clearly by the simple contrast between pure competition on the one hand and the use of force against strangers on the other. Both produce a raft of positive and negative externalities. There is a reason why both the common and the Roman law forbid the use of force and similar activities. Empirically, gains to the winner are just about always smaller than the losses to the loser. That is manifestly true in cases of harm to life and limb, but it is also true in cases of theft, even if the damages are less. Accordingly, no legal system starts with a diffuse Millian "harm principle" writ large.[5] Instead, each starts on the ground that force, when directed to innocent parties, creates negative sum games. The relevant losses include the harms to family, friends and business associates of individuals whose lives are destroyed or whose property is taken by others. It is precisely this set of concerns that authorizes the use of force in self-defense, because everyone knows that a legal remedy after death or bodily injury cannot restore a life or a limb. The legal prohibitions against force deal with those externalities that, if magnified, are destructive to social life. The individual losses therefore correlate perfectly with social losses, which is why private remedies against aggressors complement the enforcement of the criminal law.

Market transactions generate a very different set of consequences. Whenever anyone sells goods, the benefit not only goes to the buyer and the seller but to all parties that deal with them. At the same time, the disappointed competitors and their supporters are left worse off. At this point, it looks as though the ubiquity of these externalities requires a hopeless burst of legal activities, whose administrative expenses could smother all productive activity. It is precisely to avoid this horror story that every working legal system draws a distinction between actionable externalities and nonactionable externalities. The basic point is that society will be better off if it does not seek to provide redress for every person who claims that he or she is left worse off by the actions of others. Instead, the question of externalities is reverse engineered. The most important theorem of economics is that competitive markets

---

[5] *See* JOHN STUART MILL, ON LIBERTY (1859): "The only purpose for which power can be rightfully exercised over any member of a civilized community, against his will, is to prevent harm to others. His own good, either physical or moral, is not a sufficient warrant." For my critique, see Richard A. Epstein, "The Harm Principle – and How It Grew," 45 U. TORONTO L. J. 369 (1995). Note all the cases in the middle that are excluded, including all holdout problems.

produce the optimal division of goods and services precisely because the law offers no protection to the expectations of disappointed competitors. From a social point of view, the disappointments have to be set off against the gains that consumers receive from the greater choices that a competitive market generates. Moreover, the losers in the particular struggle are of course free to reinvest their resources elsewhere, and should do so, lest inefficient producers displace efficient ones, backed by the barrel of a gun. Unlike the case of force, there is no divergence between private and social welfare when negative competitive externalities are ignored. That result was achieved under Roman law under the banner of *damnum absque iniura*, and within standard economic theory by the notion that pecuniary externalities are not to be counted in the social welfare function. Both those positions point to the same conclusion – one huge class of externalities is now removed from legal contemplation.

That conclusion, moreover, generates huge social benefits, for it is the only powerful position that stands between the endless calls from disappointed competitors for various systems of entry restrictions and price controls, all of which lead to monopolies, which *do* create genuine social losses because they reduce total output, increase legal uncertainty about the choice of trade regimes, and add immeasurable administrative costs. The classical liberal has no regrets for its strong procompetitive position. In the monopoly or cartel case, it is wrong to treat consumer losses as noncognizable because these losses *do* correlate with social losses. The monopolist prices its products above marginal cost and thus produces welfare losses that are not found under competition. It is therefore appropriate to engage in legal actions to curb monopolies through the antitrust (or European competition) laws, which are intended to preserve competition against the risk of monopoly. To be sure, these rules have to be cost-effective, and they can go astray when, as with the case of predatory pricing, procompetitive behavior is confused for anticompetitive behavior. But by the same token, it is equally clear that various price-fixing and territory divisions are in general negative sum games, and therefore should be proscribed. Mergers mix efficiency and restrictive trade and therefore tend to be evaluated on a case-by-case basis. Finally, in those cases of legal and natural monopoly, some degree of rate regulation is in principle admissible to bring monopoly prices down to competitive levels. But here too caution must be exercised, because various forms of rate and entry restrictions could – when considered dynamically – perpetuate monopoly power by blocking new entrants with superior goods and services.[6]

The classical liberal theory does not address externalities solely in the context of various economic harms. It also extends to other kinds of social interactions. First, in land use disputes, the theory discourages common law nuisances which, roughly

---

[6]   See generally Harold Demsetz, "Why Regulate Utilities?," 11 *J. Law & Econ.* 55 (1968).

defined, are nontrespassory invasions of noise, odors, and filth of various sorts[7]. But by the same token, it refuses to recognize either competitive losses from nearby businesses or any losses from blocking the views from one plot of land by building on another. The explanation on this last point again relates to the simple question of whether the private right of action is positively or negatively correlated with social welfare. Cases of nuisances are negative-sum, which is why they are prohibited in any planned-unit development, whether condominium association or gated community. But blocking of views goes the other way. If X cannot build to block Y's views from his own dwelling, then he can justly claim that Y cannot build in the first place because her actions will prevent him from building in the second period. The choice therefore is between both parties building or neither, and the overall output is surely greater with free development than without any development at all. The modern practice of incumbents imposing zoning restrictions on their late rivals is a classic abuse of the police power, unless these are accompanied by payments for the loss of development rights, routinely denied today at high social costs.[8]

The same logic applies to speech, where it is commonly and correctly held that the mere offense, no matter how intense, that someone takes to the actions or statements of another is not an actionable form of harm.[9] The logic here is the same as in other cases: allowing any private right of action against such speech, or subjecting it to government regulation, correlates negatively with overall social welfare. Once personal offense at the actions of others becomes a potential justification for the use of state power, each person has an incentive to magnify his or her indignation in order to increase the probability of obtaining state assistance. The classical liberal position, which affords no private return to these activities, has the opposite effect of dampening conflict by reducing the private return to asocial actions. This approach does not, of course, require that one abandon the ancient law of defamation, which applies precisely because these false statements violate the classical liberal prohibition against the use of misrepresentation in social interactions.[10] By making false statements about others, the party who engages in either slander or libel undercuts the ability of any targeted individuals or groups to make sensible transactions with the defamed party. The third-party listener's losses from doing business with a defamed party may be sufficiently small ≈that they can find

---

[7] Restatement (Second) of Torts §821D.defines nuisance as "a nontrespassory invasion of another's interest in the private use and enjoyment of land."

[8] For the broad assertion of zoning authority, see Euclid v. Ambler Realty Corp., 272 U.S. 365 (1926).

[9] *See* Texas v. Johnson, 491 U.S. 397 (1989) (holding flag burning protected by the First Amendment).

[10] For the standard definition of defamation, which stresses consequences to voluntary social interactions, see RESTATEMENT (SECOND) TORTS, § 559 (1977): Defamatory Communication Defined: "A communication is defamatory if it tends so to harm the reputation of another as to lower him in the estimation of the community or to deter third persons from associating or dealing with him."

transactions elsewhere. But the defamed party could lose out on potential business transactions, prospective social advantages, including marriage and membership in various social organizations, or face ostracism and abuse by third persons. These harms are worlds apart from the simple case of one person voicing his resentment to one party about another.

To see how this works, recall that Seidman challenges the classical liberal with the case of same-sex marriage. It is hard to see why. If the sole reason to ban these relationships is that they cause offense to other people, the claim is always insufficient. Indeed, the same can be said about the so-called moral objections to polygamy, which remains criminalized today even after same-sex marriage has been legalized by judicial decision.[11] That decision to allow a wide range of marital freedom is in line with classical liberal norms. This is not to say that the decision was correct even under the Equal Protection Clause of the US Constitution invoked in *Obergefell* but not discussed in *Bowers*, which has historically been read as subject to an extensive "morals" head of the police power, which has given states vast control over sexual relations, gambling and similar activities.[12] Ironically, this police power justification is the one that is most in tension with classical liberal ideals, precisely because it proposes a very broad definition of social harm that is inconsistent with the underlying social welfare base of classical liberal theory, which is what equips the theory to resolve externality problems.

PREFERENCES IN CONTEXT

The next argument made against classical liberalism is that it attaches too much weight to the preferences that individuals reveal in various settings. It is surely the case that these preferences are socially influenced. But many of those social preferences are themselves derivative of the full set of biological necessities to which all individuals, and all groups, must respond. It is therefore noteworthy that all traditional political theories pay much attention to the imperative of individual self-preservation, without which it is not possible to have or enjoy any other right,[13] and

---

[11] *Compare* Obergefell v. Hodges, 135 S. Ct. 2584 (2015) (offering constitutional protection to same-sex marriage), *with* Reynolds v. United States, 98 U.S. 145 (1878). (defending criminal prosecution of polygamy, including forfeiture of property against a First Amendment Challenge based on the Free Exercise Clause).

[12] *See, for example,* Bowers v. Hardwick, 478 U.S. 186, 192–96 (1986) (discussing the state's power to regulate moral behavior because of federal constitutional limitations), overturned in Lawrence v. Texas, 539 U.S. 558 (2003).

[13] *See, for example,* Marcus Tullius Cicero, De Officiis, Book {11} IV, *available at* http://www.constitution.org/rom/de_officiis.htm: "First of all, Nature has endowed every species of living creature with the instinct of self-preservation, of avoiding what seems likely to cause injury to life or limb, and of procuring and providing everything needful for life – food, shelter, and the like." Note the unabashed reliance on Nature, capital N. The passage talks about motivations, not about the legal relations that allow for multiple individuals to live in harmony, which is critical.

continue, without missing a beat, to speak about the necessity of reproduction for the preservation of the human race.[14] In dealing with these simple but inexorable imperatives, any social group chooses between two approaches. The first commands individuals to provide sustenance and support for others. The second commands each individual to refrain from the use of force that threatens the bodily integrity, and by extension, the property and possessions of others. In fact, every legal system adopts a mixed solution. The principle of active protection applies to parents who must supply the wherewithal for their children until they reach an age of self-sufficiency. This obligation fits well with human behavior because it reinforces the ties of natural love and affection that link families by virtue of their shared genetic inheritance. On the other side, with respect to strangers, the theory does impose a uniform prohibition on aggression, which the state is then organized to support under, of course, the traditional Lockean theory.

We do know that the social contract so enforced does not come from actual consent binding across territory or time. Rather, it is imposed socially, within some defined territory, on the ground that all individuals who are subject to this rule are left better off insofar as the taxes that support government institutions are intended to leave them all better off than they are in the state of nature. Putting that program into place requires complex social institutions that are strong enough to compel support but not so strong as to threaten the lives, heath, safety and property of the individuals who are part of the society. It is also the case, as Daniel Hemel notes in his contribution to the conference, that this system creates high variance in the fortunes of various individuals as they move from the state of nature into civil society. But it does not follow that the state need provide, in addition to the standard forms of protection, some positive bounty raised by taxing the more fortunate to pay the less fortunate. The first reason is that the less fortunate are still better off without the bounty in society than they would be in the state of nature. A second reason is that a more efficient way to address wealth disparities does not depend on how or why they arise, but instead relies on a system of "imperfect obligations" under which persons are required by conscience and social convention, but not state force, to render assistance to those less fortunate than themselves.[15] States can contribute by providing matching grants, for example, charitable deductions, for those who perform these obligations, on the grounds that the increased social stability justifies that extra benefit. Also, any state or local government can set up public facilities to help persons in extreme want, without making some general payment across the board. But throughout it all, none of these key issues depend on any special views of

---

[14] *Id.*
[15] For an early but still accurate account, see JOSEPH STORY AND MORRIS L. COHEN, JOSEPH STORY AND THE ENCYCLOPEDIA AMERICANA 123 (1844): "We call those rights *perfect*, which are determinate and which may be asserted by force, or in civil society by the operation of law; and *imperfect*, those which are indeterminate and vague, and which may not be asserted by force or by law, but are obligatory only upon the consciences of parties."

preference formation. All of these responses follow from the simple view that people with wealth understand in their own ways the principle of the diminishing marginal utility of wealth. They do not need the command of the sovereign to back it up.

There are of course additional problems that arise when people are ill-informed. But one has to be careful about the process of correction. Coercion is highly dangerous because any inbred errors may also be in found in the same people entrusted with the coercive power of the state to enforce corrections on their fellow citizens. It therefore is the case that persuasion, when the putative persuader could be himself persuaded, is institutionally a far safer way to go about shaping the preferences of both targeted individuals and public opinion writ large.

On this score, the question of gay rights again shows the dangers of coercion. It is one thing for the state to allow two (or more) people to marry. It is quite another for the state's law to force businesses to close if they do not serve all customers, even when to do so would contradict the owners' religious beliefs.[16] Yet it is all too common today for intemperate and intolerant civil rights authorities to hurl insults at others who do not do their bidding on this issue. In this context, coercion is the most dangerous of all alternatives. The key point here is that obligations of universal service should only be imposed on individuals that enjoy a monopoly position, typically associated with common carriers and public utilities, that offer standardized services for which there is no close substitute.[17] In the midst of the hubbub over whether photographers, bakers, and florists should have to serve same-sex couples, recall that there is not a single reported instance of any same-sex couple who has not been able to get those services from equally capable vendors. The business of preference formation can quickly transform itself into the suppression of discrete and insular groups that have little power to stand up for themselves in the political process, and they are thus worthy of strong protection.[18]

Nor is there any reason to think that there is some magic gulf between public and private preferences. Thus, many people who support programs of public redistribution are not narrow egoists in their own lives. Many contribute to charitable operations. The question is whether public or private assistance is more effective. People must always make choices at the margin, and many people with substantial means both live high on the hog *and* make generous contributions to charitable organizations. It is not correct to assert that their preferences as consumers deviate

---

[16] For the dangers, see U.S. Commission on Civil Rights: PEACEFUL COEXISTENCE: RECONCIL-ING NONDISCRIMINATION PRINCIPLES WITH CIVIL LIBERTIES 160 (2016), whose chairman Martin Castro takes the view "These laws" – which seek exceptions to the antidiscrimination laws – "represent an orchestrated, nationwide effort by extremists to promote bigotry, cloaked in the mantle of 'religious freedom.'"

[17] For my defense of this position, see Richard A. Epstein, "Public Accommodations under the Civil Rights Act of 1964: Why Freedom of Association Counts as a Human Right," 66 STAN. L. REV. 1241 (2014).

[18] The phrase "discrete and insular minorities" originates in United States v. Carolene Products Co, 304 U.S. 144, 153, n 4 (1938).

from their views as public citizens. They bring the same basic set of preferences to both settings, and may well oppose some kinds of public benevolence because they think that is wasteful or misguided. It is too easy and fashionable for people to proclaim that individuals are irrational based on their superficially conflicting behavior. Indeed, the constant difficulty with behavioral economics is that it identifies so many different shortfalls that it cannot offer a sensible overall account of human behavior that incorporates them all. Of course, people make mistakes, even when they try hard to avoid them. To verify that conclusion we do not have to run experiments, whose results everyone would disregard in light of the constant evidence to the contrary. It takes a peculiar genius to insist first that people overweight the immediate event, and thus are influenced by some availability heuristic, only to discover that they gave undue weight to past priors under the anchoring heuristic. Doubtless we all do some of both at different times. But these are just perturbations on the basic rational choice model, under which educated people will learn to correct against either or both biases to the extent that they cause them personal harm.

Finally, in dealing with preference formation, every legal system must cope with a genuine problem of rectification to deal with past injustices, like slavery, apartheid and segregation, that have infected many societies. The first point to note here is that these forms of wrongful conduct are categorically condemned by classical liberal theory, which grants presumptive protection to individual autonomy and freedom of association. But understanding the wrong does not reveal a simple cure.[19] One temptation that should be emphatically avoided is the insistence that big government is necessary to right the wrongs of the previous generation's government. Instead, the first order of business is to free up markets for all, so that people who were oppressed can now participate in the full range of social activities. In and of itself, that action will not supply compensation for past losses. But reparations are more difficult to achieve because often the wrongdoers in question have died long before they can be required to make redress. In many cases, moreover, they have dissipated the gains so that tracing the benefits to descendants is a fruitless endeavor. Probably the best path is granting special benefits or lump sum transfer payments to the wronged parties, or, in practice to their descendants, a group which it becomes ever more difficult to identify with each passing generation. And so it is that the the mechanics necessarily ever more difficult to work out given that any program of transfer payments is likely to be subject to major pitfalls in its design and implementation. But these difficulties of designing a system to rectify past wrongs are also faced any and all political theories.

---

[19] The leading argument for reparations is Boris I. Bittker, The Case for Black Reparations (1973). For my more cautious views, see Richard A. Epstein, "The Case against Black Reparations," 84 Boston U. L. Rev. 1177 (2004).

THE PROBLEM OF PRIVATE POWER

Perhaps the most hackneyed objection to classical liberal theory arises from the work of Robert L. Hale, who in a famous, if misconceived essay, defined coercion so broadly that it is no longer a rare event but an inescapable feature of human life.[20] His key argument was that any refusal to deal leaves at least one person worse off than before, which thus makes it coercive and hence subject to the same condemnation as other forms of coercion. That definition is a billion times as broad as the standard definition that coercion involves the use or threat of force. By Hale's standard, any form of give-and-take in ordinary business negotiations is simultaneous coercion by both sides. Yet the only reason markets work is that people on both sides of any potential deal have the absolute right to walk away. Otherwise, every person is under a duty to deal with everyone else, even when he expects to gain nothing from the exchange. Civilized life could not go on if a simple refusal to deal were tantamount to murder or theft.

It does not follow that refusals to deal may always be done with impunity. As noted in the discussion on externalities, a refusal to deal could be the source of liability in common carrier or public utility cases, in which the side with the monopoly power is under a duty to deal with all comers on fair, reasonable and nondiscriminatory terms. At this point, we know why we impose the duty, which is the incredible inconvenience from shutting out people from basic services when they have nowhere else to go. In practice, improved technology should reduce the number of situations to which the common carrier rules apply.

Indeed, this broad definition of coercion is doubly unfortunate, for forbidding refusals to deal tends to convert competitive markets into monopolistic ones, with major adverse consequences. Here are two leading examples of this form of coercion. One is the duty to bargain under the National Labor Relations Act, which gives a union monopoly control over what would otherwise be a competitive labor market. The second is the duty to renew leases under the standard rent control or rent stabilization system, which creates a huge disparity in the positions of those renters currently in possession and the outsiders who have to scramble for decent housing with the units that remain outside the government's rent stabilization program. It makes no sense whatsoever to treat landlords in competitive industries as though they were public utilities, for the reduced revenues and the higher expenses are sure to reduce their net return below competitive levels. Yet under Hale's definition of coercion, landlords outside of rent control systems are coercing tenants to either pay up or be homeless. Forcing landlords to enter into a deal is the proper form of coercion, notwithstanding the massive resource misallocations that

---

[20] Robert Hale, "Coercion and Distribution in a Supposedly Non-Coercive State," 38 POLITICAL SCIENCE QUARTERLY 470 (1923). For a more detailed account of coercion, see Richard A. Epstein, "Hayek's Constitution of Liberty – A Guarded Retrospective," REVIEW OF AUSTRIAN ECONOMICS 1 (2016).

follow from the perpetuation of state-created monopolies. The classical liberal tradition rejects these innovations, wisely and categorically.

MISFEASANCE AND NONFEASANCE

There is little doubt that a distinction between misfeasance and nonfeasance is critical to the development of both private and constitutional law. But it is absolutely vital to identify the limited, if crucial, role that this distinction plays. Starting with the private law, the key distinction is between those harms that arise between strangers and those harms that arise out of a consensual arrangement. The consensual arrangements are large and varied. They include such traditional relations as buyer and seller, bailor and bailee, physician and patient, occupier and licensee, parent and child, and guardian and ward. Some of these are set by contract, and others are set by status or statute.

In the stranger setting, the operative behaviors that generate prima facie liability are the use and threat of force, or the creation of dangerous conditions like traps that catch people unaware. In my view, the correct rule in the stranger case is one of strict liability, in which the defendant cannot escape liability by showing that he had acted with due care or intended no harm to the plaintiff.[21] The rival position that allows for these defenses has similar allocative effects, but differs insofar as it places the risk of losses not worth avoiding on the plaintiff instead of the defendant, requiring that someone be able to work a standard cost-benefit analysis. Those differences are small enough in the grand scheme of things that both approaches will work in practice, even if the strict liability system gives a cleaner and simpler set of outcomes. The risk, moreover, of excessive liability is offset because strict liability is not absolute liability, but is subject to affirmative defenses from such matters as plaintiff's misconduct and assumption of risk. The system can be expanded to cover intentional harms, for which it is possible to build in defenses based on self-defense, necessity and the like.

Under this system, as a first approximation, there are no affirmative duties to rescue for the simple reason that the defendant did not engage in any action that put the plaintiff in the perilous position that she found herself, and hence as a legal matter has to fend for herself. This situation gives rise to obvious uneasiness whenever it can be said that a defendant could at little or no cost or risk to himself effectuate the rescue. And many people have argued that the overall system would be more efficient in the strong Paretian sense if everyone were subject to that form of duty. Yet while oft proposed, the rule has never been adopted for several reasons. Most obvious, it is difficult to identify which of many persons should be subject to rescue, and just how to draw the line between easy and not-so-easy rescue cases. To require someone to pay for the death of another whom he did not rescue is pretty

---

[21]   See Richard A. Epstein, "A Theory of Strict Liability," 2 J. LEGAL STUD. 151 (1973).

tough when the obligation comes out of the blue. But more important, perhaps, there is simply no need to convert a moral obligation into a legal rule because ordinary people will intuitively engage in the easy rescues without being asked. The current law provides for a restitution action for the rescuer that does not intend his actions to be a gift, but as far as one can tell, no one has ever brought suit on this section.[22] Sometimes the rescued provides informal compensation, from a dozen roses to tickets to a Broadway show. Compensating rescuers risks excessive efforts to rescue, which often results in needless deaths and confusion undertaken by people who do not rescue themselves.[23] Imposing a legal duty could only exacerbate the situation further, which is why the good Samaritan rule, that no person is under a legal obligation to rescue a stranger remains firmly in place today.

On the other hand, it is equally clear that all sorts of affirmative duties can be imposed on individuals who have voluntarily entered into special relations with others. All the cases that Seidman cites for duties to act arise out of special relationships. At this point, there is no risk of imposing liability on some random person who is in the wrong place at the wrong time, and it is possible to define the duties in such a way that they will not deter responsible people from taking care of the persons and property of others. At this point, the correct locution is taking care of other people, always by engaging in affirmative actions when necessary, which is a far cry from having to take care to avoid contact with a total stranger. Thus, medical malpractice can be defined in terms of customary care, but never in terms of strict liability for bad outcomes, which would require a premium so large as to shut down the market. It follows that the appropriate standard of care covers both omissions and actions, so that the doctor who does not change the battery on the heart-lung machine when required is manifestly liable for this inexcusable omission. Similar duties can be imposed on everyone from babysitters to lifeguards, where the effort is to give some boost to the caregiver who is, after all, chosen precisely because of the willingness to assume these duties. There is no reason here to go into all the variations between objective and subjective standards of care, or to ask whether liability should be restricted, as in cases of discipline, to malicious efforts.[24] For these purposes, it is enough to recognize that these lines have been drawn since Roman times, and that the situation only gets out of control when judges think that their function is to social engineer these relationships instead of figuring out the default rule that best measures the joint intentions of the parties.

The situation with respect to government is of course more complex because states engage in many different forms of activities, all of which need not be subject to

---

[22] Restatement (First) of Restitution §116 (1937) (Preservation of Another's Life or Health); *id.* at §117 (Preservation of Another's Things or Credit).

[23] David Hyman, "Rescue Without Law: An Empirical Perspective on the Duty to Rescue," 84 U. Tex. L. Rev. 653 (2006).

[24] Richard A. Epstein, "The Many Faces of Fault in Contract Law: Or How to Do Economics Right, Without Really Trying," 107 Mich. L. Rev. 1461 (2009).

the same rule. On this score, it is well established that in general no private right of action lies against the government because of the negligence of any public law enforcement official discharging the government's duty to protect the lives and property of its citizens.[25] That exemption from liability is explicitly incorporated in most municipal codes dealing with liability.[26] There is, to be sure, a general notion that a government that engages in actions that harm strangers should be responsible under tort law, notwithstanding the doctrine of sovereign immunity, which is why the Federal Tort Claims Act[27] offers a large waiver of sovereign immunity. I think that this liability should also extend to ordinary malpractice cases where the private analogies are close, but the case law tends to exempt these cases under a statutory provision that denies the state immunity when it exercises its regulatory authority in connection with some "discretionary function," when the immunity is carefully preserved. In many cases, this immunity has gone too far, but what is clear is that all federal and state statutes that deal with immunities have many complex rules that carefully exempt some but not all activities from liability.

The most striking cases, however, arise in connection with the duty to rescue and assist, or as in *DeShaney v. Winnebago Cty. DSS*,[28] in which the Supreme Court refused to impose liability on the state for what amounted to reckless indifference when its social workers did nothing to protect a small child when they knew that his father was beating him mercilessly. Interestingly, the educational establishment rose in unified protest against this form of liability, thinking that the potential losses from such suits dislocate their operations.[29] Better for some children to be hurt because of neglect than the state shut down its social services division for want of funds. The problem of affirmative duties is thus a real one subject to powerful budgetary constraints, and it is not easy to come up with a set of rules that both create the liability and limit it sensibly, which is why elaborate codes have sought to arbitrage the difference. And note that this problem again is one that has to be faced by every legal theory, including progressive ones.

---

[25] Riss v. City of New York, 240 N.E.2d 860 (N.Y. 1968).

[26] *See, for example,* ILLINOIS COMPILED STATUTES, Section 2–103: "A local public entity is not liable for an injury caused by adopting or failing to adopt an enactment or by failing to enforce any law."

[27] 28 U.S.C. §2674.

[28] 489 U.S. 189 (1989).

[29] *See, for example,* Amicus Curiae of the National School Boards Association in Support of Respondents, DeShaney v. Winnebago Cty. DSS, 489 U.S. 189 (1989), relying heavily on the misfeasance/nonfeasance distinction. But the concerns were substantive: "If the principle sought in this case were to be established by this Court, federal courts would be opened for lawsuits claiming constitutional violations for 'gross negligence' in failing to protect students from accidents on the playground, school bus accidents, injuries caused by defective athletic equipment and a myriad of other negligence actions which are more appropriately handled in state court under general principles of tort law." *Id.* at 7–8.

THE PROBLEM OF FUNDAMENTAL DISAGREEMENT

One of the central problems of government arises from the ambiguous definition of a public good. In the simplest of situations, it refers to those indivisible, nonrivalrous goods that must be supplied collectively if they are to be supplied at all. The logic on behalf of this conclusion, dating back at the latest to Mancur Olson, is unassailable.[30] Each self-interested person makes a private calculation of his or her own benefits and costs. If one such person knows, or even thinks, that he will get the same benefit whether or not he pays for it, he will not pay for it because he is better off securing the benefit without having to pay the cost. That logic can be extended to cover situations where his or her failure to contribute results in some decline in the value of the public good, but by an amount that is below the private cost of securing the good. The problem here is the refusal to support is the dominant strategy for all persons, so that the needed good is not supplied even if the case where the private costs of each person are, say, less than half their private benefits. A system of taxation for the provision of that public good is thus worth imposing, unless the cost of running that system exceeds the gains from its application. For basic governmental services, that calculation is in favor of state intervention, especially for the services supplied in a classical liberal state – protection, infrastructure and control of monopoly behaviors.

The collective action problem is a serious one for hard-core libertarians who do not accept the legitimacy of the taxing power. But Seidman is flatly wrong when he writes: "Classical liberals believe that disagreements should be resolved on the individual level by people making choices in a private sphere." To be sure, that belief does hold in dealing with divisible goods that can be supplied in a competitive marketplace, for there is no reason not to respect the different preference functions of different persons. After all, rarely do any two people choose the same basket of goods at the supermarket. But in dealing with homogenous goods that can be supplied only collectively, the classical liberal finds this as the *ideal* case in which to invoke collective action that, on the assumption given, secures a Pareto improvement – indeed a Pareto improvement with an equal division of the surplus. There is no deep contradiction here. There is only a serious concern that one or another group of individuals will try to hijack the entire process by laying off some fraction of the costs on others, or by hogging a disproportionate share of the gain. At this point, there is a serious problem for any and all theories of collective action. Someone has to determine whether at the margin it is worthwhile to invest public resources in order to prevent the implicit transfer of wealth between interests, which is desirable when the costs of prevention are below the anticipated benefits, and undesirable when they far exceed it. It is for this reason that a disproportionate impact in

---

[30] MANCUR OLSON, THE LOGIC OF COLLECTIVE ACTION: PUBLIC GOODS AND THE THEORY OF GROUPS (1965).

particular cases signifies that something is deeply wrong, which accounts for the powerful influence of this one sentence from Justice Black in *Armstrong v. United States*[31]: "The Fifth Amendment's guarantee that private property shall not be taken for a public use without just compensation was designed to bar Government from forcing some people alone to bear public burdens which, in all fairness and justice, should be borne by the public as a whole."[32] It was for that reason that the Court held that the United States could not stiff a subcontractor who had attached a valid materialman's lien to a U.S. boat by sailing it out of Maine waters. The benefit of the boat was public, not private. From this simple point follows the general rule that flat, that is, proportionate taxation, is preferred to progressive taxation, and that compensation should be provided to individuals whose property is taken for public use. There are obviously many close cases in between, and resolving these is, if anything, a greater difficulty for progressive theories that refuse to acknowledge the force of this proposition and insist that only "ad hoc" rules can determine whether, and if so why, government compensation is required for something as straightforward as the condemnation of air rights – where it is denied.[33] They often understate the problem and hence rely on the putative advantages of expertise and good faith to deal with these systems, often with disastrous consequences in areas dealing with such issues as rent control and environmental protection.

The overall situation becomes more difficult when the needed decision is necessarily collective, but the problem is one for which there is a strong difference in the preferences of the electorate. Decisions about how to deal with wars, climate change, judicial appointments, and constitutional amendments can all raise these problems in situations where the decision that pleases the majority must bind the minority as well. Indeed, for these decisions, it is not feasible to think of any ex post transfer payment from winners to losers. In this case, all theories of political organization, classical liberal theories included, have to switch from a model of property rights to a model of public discourse and deliberative decision, sometimes by supermajority and sometimes not. Corporations of course face similar problems, but there at least the option to sell shares makes it easier to avoid any major impasse. Under these circumstances, the right of minority groups to speak their mind before a decision is made becomes critical, which is why protecting free speech under the First Amendment becomes an indispensable part of any holistic solution.

There is no clear path here, but by the same token the classical liberal position strongly endorses the articulation of fair procedures under which all sides are given a fair chance to express their views before the decision is made. *Audi alteram partem* ("always hear the other side") and *nemo iudex cause sua* ("no one should be a judge in his own cause") have been part of the natural law legal tradition since Roman

---

[31] 364 U.S. 40, 49 (1960).
[32] *Id.* at 49.
[33] *See* Penn Central Trans. Co. v. City of New York, 438 U.S. 104, 124 (1978).

times. Indeed, these two principles are both subsumed under "natural law" in the British system, then morphed in Due Process under the American system.[34] The key lesson to learn from these problems is that the smaller the public domain, the less the pressure on collective decisions.[35] Hence, the progressive tendency to convert competitive markets into public utilities, be it through zoning laws, rent control laws, agriculture adjustment programs and the like should be strongly discouraged precisely because separable decisions on goods and services should be preferred to collective ones on these same topics. Indeed, this preference in favor of separation should get *stronger* as societies become more diverse, given that the intensity of differences is likely to grow exponentially. Thus, if two sides are at +1 and − 1, the gulf may be two. But if they are at +2 and -2, that gulf could be eight-fold ($2^2 + 2^2$), if the intensity of the difference is the sum of the squares of the distances of the two positions from the origin. It is just this relationship that dominates the organization of private structures from corporations to clubs to planned unit developments. The pressure on governance is reduced if the right to exclude is exercised in ways that narrow the differences among members. It is for that reason that some condominiums exclude children, and some corporations only take shareholders whose wealth is above some stated levels. But this method of freedom of association does not work in the public sector, where membership is highly inclusive and exit rights are costly to implement. Hence the need to limit the functions to reduce the variance, precisely because there is no clean solution to the problem of variance in any social system.

THE PROBLEM OF DISTRIBUTION

It is a well-known axiom that a classical liberal system that gives strong weight to freedom of contract can produce vast disparities in wealth, a point that has been recognized, for example, in judicial decisions that have defended those principles in opposition to mandatory regimes of collective bargaining. As Justice Pitney wrote in *Coppage v. Kansas*[36]:

> [S]ince it is self-evident that, unless all things are held in common, some persons must have more property than others, it is from the nature of things impossible to uphold freedom of contract and the right of private property without at the same time recognizing as legitimate those inequalities of fortune that are the necessary result of the exercise of those rights.[37]

---

[34] For discussion, see JAMES R. STONER, JR. COMMON LAW AND LIBERAL THEORY: COKE, HOBBES, AND THE ORIGINS OF AMERICAN CONSTITUTIONALISM 49–51 (1992).

[35] For discussion, see Richard A. Epstein, "Redistribution within Collective Organizations: What Corporations, Condominiums and Unions Tell Us about the Proper Use of Government Power," 8 NEW YORK UNIVERSITY JOURNAL OF LAW & LIBERTY 280 (2014).

[36] *See* Coppage v. Kansas, 236 U.S. 1 (1915).

[37] *See id.* at 17.

It is equally clear that most people, including most classical liberals, believe in the diminishing marginal utility of wealth, such that the extra dollar in the hands of a poorer person will generate some greater level of utility than the same dollar in the hands of a rich person. The question then arises: what should be done, either privately or collectively, to handle this problem?

Within the classical liberal system part of the answer turns on the recognition of imperfect duties of benevolence toward those who are less fortunate than one's self, which I noted earlier. There is little dispute that theories of this sort influenced private behavior in the period of laissez-faire and continue to do so today, but in more muted form given the development of an oversized transfer system that covers not only transfers from rich to poor, but also all sorts of other transfers, including from young to old through a combination of social security and Medicare payments.

Within the classical liberal theory, the first line of defense is to figure out how to reduce the scope of the problem under the principle that I call "redistribution last."[38] The point here is simple enough. Start with systems of market liberalization that break down barriers to trade across the entire income spectrum. That should produce an overall increase in wealth, some fraction of which will redound to the benefit of people at the lower end of the income spectrum. As they move up, the case for redistribution weakens even if the top moves up more. It is one thing to stand indifferent when people are below the subsistence level. It is quite another if the poorest group enjoys many of the creature comforts of life. No one thinks of redistribution as a moral imperative for moving income by coercion from people who earn a $1,000,000 per year to those who earn $100,000. It is a lot more salient to do it from people who earn $100,000 to those who earn $10,000, and it becomes imperative to implement some such system to ensure transfers from people who earn $10,000 to those who have $1,000, where subsistence is at $2,000 per year. Greater wealth thus eases the burden. Yet even here, there is always this qualification. The program is one of redistribution if in the ex ante position we knew with certainty who is rich and who poor. But in many situations in life, there is massive uncertainty as to whose crops will be harvested or whose house will be burnt, or whose business will be rendered obsolete. In these cases, various pooling mechanisms to protect those who fare badly looks more like an insurance system than a system of straight transfer, although it is highly likely that there is some mixture of both components in many such schemes. And it is surely the case that many of these voluntary programs do seek to implement redistribution at some levels. There is nothing in the theory of classical liberalism that puts a sharp prohibition on these activities. But there is a great concern that pushing them too far can lead to economic stagnation and political conflict.

---

[38] Richard A. Epstein, *Decentralized Responses to Good Fortune and Bad Luck*, 9 THEORETICAL INQUIRIES IN LAW 309 (2008), available at www.law.uchicago.edu/files/files/383.pdf.

Given these limitations, the hard question is how best to engage in redistribution when such is needed. Voluntary contributions are preferable in principle because they do not generate perverse incentives against production in both groups. But if taxation is needed, it hardly follows, as Seidman suggests, that it must come from progressive taxation. Flat taxes will produce in fact high levels of redistribution in at least several ways. The first is that some fraction of these revenues goes to the creation of traditional public goods, like sewers, from which the poor benefit enormously, even if their contributions to the collective project are constrained by their limited wealth. The second is that flat taxes can generate enough wealth to provide some redistribution to the poor. In dealing with this issue, flat taxes are a constraint but not a panacea, because one problem here is whether the extent of redistribution is too great, which is more likely to happen under a progressive tax system.

In making all these contributions, the question of individual dessert always enters into the equation. People struck by acts of God or senseless acts of random violence are more appealing targets for assistance than those who are not, because there is far less likelihood that they have engaged in, or will lapse back into, some self-destructive behavior when the immediate crisis is over. So, the problem of redistribution always asks, which conditions, if any, should be attached to transfer payments? That point in turn is hard to resolve because there is always an uneasy sense of paternalism that accompanies various form of assistance. In some cases, many groups give benefits in-kind and under close supervision, so that the resources devoted to assistance are spent in ways consistent with the preferences of the donors and not the recipients. Give the needy a meal, and not the money to buy one, which could be spent elsewhere. Give assistance, but only to those who perform some useful work at the same time. There are huge variations on these programs, and it is hard in the abstract to figure out the best execution. But what is clear is that the entire enterprise is fraught with risking too much redistribution, as well as too little.

THE PROBLEM OF HISTORICAL LOCATION

The last problem that Seidman poses to classical liberals is said to be its deepest: the question of its historical location. This problem is said to come in two forms. The first is definitional and the other is substantive.

On the definitional issue, Seidman claims that there is no "there" there, for classical liberalism is not a coherent theory, but a set of responses that varies with the political and social conditions of the time. But the point shows utter confusion of what is at stake. The writers in the classical liberal tradition all differ from each other on point of detail, but the main lines of their position are surely evident. It is a system that starts with the assumption of individual autonomy and believes in the central role of private property and freedom of contract under a system of limited government. It is not a pure libertarian theory because it also accepts the necessity for taxation, but it also seeks to limit both the objects on which those taxes can be spent to classical public goods and the means by which it can be raised, usually to proportionate taxes. It accepts the need for some redistribution but has some genuine uneasiness as how to carry this out.

The application of the theory will obviously vary with time and conditions. One did not have to worry about intellectual property before the printing press, and the regulation of the internet was not something to which Roman lawyers devoted undue attention. But what is clear is that anyone who cares to study the history and evolution of legal doctrine will be struck by the tremendous durability of early legal conceptions even into modern times. As a long-time teacher of Roman law and a sometime teacher of medieval legal history, I am struck at the persistence of the doctrine on all major, not its vagaries. The basic principles of contract, property and tort that come down from Roman times show only minor variation, whether we deal with Roman or common law rules. In dealing with just this issue of natural law, Gaius in the opening paragraphs of his Institutes notes that the basic relations of marriage, contract, partnership, hire, sale, barter, bailments and many others are constants across time and across cultures, even if the formalities by which these principles are implemented will vary necessarily from culture to culture. That observation is as true today as it was then, for the similarities across legal cultures are much more important for social survival than their differences. And these principles that derive from the natural law are all strongly in the classical liberal tradition that remains true to itself to this day. The flimsy charges of social relativism ring false to anyone who has bothered to study closely the historical and modern sources.

Seidman's second criticism of classical liberalism goes over the top when he writes: "[T]he most serious problem is that their doctrine is being used by the smug and satisfied who want to entrench huge disparities in power, wealth, and life chances." Really? The classical liberal tradition is at its strongest when it opposes the state creation and protection of monopolies by any group. It holds that all rich people are subject to the same competitive pressures as everyone else, and stoutly resists the tariffs and special privileges that all sorts of groups use to entrench themselves. Of course, there are capitalists who favor subsidies for their businesses, and farmers who want nothing more than ethanol mandates for their crops. But there are also unions that viciously fight any form of school choice in order to protect entrenched interests by denying decent educational opportunities to poor children of color. The defenders of these children are hedge-fund managers and other entrepreneurs who understand the power of markets that can lift the position of the underprivileged. There is no classical liberal who wants to "obstruct collective efforts to control catastrophic outcomes produced by private markets, of which global warming is only the most serious." On the first point, no classical liberal is opposed to legislation that limits the risk of runs on the bank, which is not to say that it is sensible to support every single provision of Dodd-Frank, many of which are likely to create systematic forms of financial failure that could be stopped more easily by stressing the capital requirements for various financial institutions. And there is every reason today to think that the science put in favor of global warming is itself subject to serious doubt, and is used by the champions of progressive politics to wage a war against fossil fuels in ways that, if surely successful, would create untold suffering for millions of people.[39]

In this chapter, I have sought to give in capsule form answers to the challenges posed to classical liberalism. I have offered far more detailed answers to these questions in multiple publications, only some of which I have cited here. But the key point here is simply this: the same questions should be asked of any legal tradition. The progressive tradition's basket of monopoly practices has long led to disastrous social consequences, which progressives try to attribute to a classical liberal system that they neither understand nor respect.[40] Seidman's questions are as salient to the progressive tradition as the classical liberal tradition, yet only the classical liberal tradition can answer then satisfactorily.

---

[39] For reasoned arguments to the contrary on global warming, see Matt Ridley, "Global Warming v. Global Greening, The 2016 Global Warming Policy Forum Lecture," The Royal Society London (October 17, 2016), available at https://perma.cc/44JU-6E9J.

[40] *See* Richard A. Epstein, "The Progressives' Deadly Embrace of Cartels: A Close Look at Labor and Agricultural Markets 1890–1940," *in* THE PROGRESSIVES' CENTURY: POLITICAL REFORM, CONSTITUTIONAL GOVERNMENT, AND THE MODERN AMERICAN STATE 339 (Stephen Skowronek, Stephen M. Engle, and Bruce Ackerman, eds., 2016).

Index

Acemoglu, Daron, 25–26
Acton (Lord), 15
adjudicative authority, 141–48
  ALJs, 141–43
    independence of, 141–43
    removal of, 142–43
    under separation of powers, 142
  fact-finding and, 146–47
    adjudicative facts, 146–47
    judgmental facts, 147
    legislative facts, 147
  interpretation of, 143–44
    Auer deference, 144
    Chevron deference, 144
    Skidmore deference, 144
  through policymaking, 145–46
    by congressional approval, 145–46
    cost-benefit standards in, 146
    default rules, 146
    limitations of, 145
    restrictions on, 146
    scope of decisions, 145
adjudicative facts, 135, 146–47
administrative courts. *See also* appellate
    administrative courts
  judicial review of, 147–48
administrative law. *See also* adjudicative authority;
    rule-making authority; separation of powers
  classical liberalism and, 105–6
  fact-finding in, 146–47
    adjudicative, 135, 146–47
    in deference, 135–37
    judgmental, 136–37, 147
    legislative, 135–37, 147
  guidance documents, 149–51
    private parties and, penalties against, 151

independent court systems and
  deferences in, 108–9
  establishment of, 107–8
informal adjudication of, 151–52
judicial review, 150
legislative rules, review of, 108–9
REINS Act proposals, 108
substantial-impact test, 150
administrative law judges (ALJs), 141–43
  independence of, 141–43
  removal of, 142–43
  under separation of powers, 142
Administrative Procedure Act, U.S., 137
Aesop's Principle, 208
Affordable Care Act, U.S., 119
African Americans. *See also* anti-discrimination
    laws; mass incarceration; race; racism
  Jim Crow laws against, 49–51
Against Democracy (Brennan), 168
ALJs. *See* administrative law judges
anarcho-capitalism, 256
Anderson, Terry, 69
anti-discrimination laws
  freedom of conscience under, 53–54
  function and purpose of, 48
  against hate speech, 48
  Jim Crow laws and, 49–52
    Civil Rights Act and, 51–52
    federal takeover of local governments
      and, 51
    non-violent protests against, 51
  libertarian skepticism of, 47–48, 53
  religion under, 53–54
  scope of, 48–49
  sexual orientation under, 54
  societal effects of, 52